POLITICAL USES OF UTOPIA

NEW DIRECTIONS IN CRITICAL THEORY

Amy Allen, General Editor

New Directions in Critical Theory presents outstanding classic and contemporary texts in the tradition of critical social theory, broadly construed. The series aims to renew and advance the program of critical social theory, with a particular focus on theorizing contemporary struggles around gender, race, sexuality, class, and globalization and their complex interconnections.

POLITICAL USES OF UTOPIA

NEW MARXIST, ANARCHIST, AND RADICAL DEMOCRATIC PERSPECTIVES

EDITED BY
S. D. CHROSTOWSKA
AND JAMES D. INGRAM

Columbia University Press
New York

Columbia University Press
Publishers Since 1893
New York Chichester, West Sussex
cup.columbia.edu
Copyright © 2016 Columbia University Press
All rights reserved

Library of Congress Cataloging-in-Publication Data
Names: Chrostowska, S. D. (Sylwia Dominika), 1975- editor. |
Ingram, James D., 1972- editor.
Title: Political uses of Utopia / edited by S.D. Chrostowska and James D. Ingram.
Description: New York : Columbia University Press, [2016] | Series: New directions in critical theory | Includes bibliographical references and index.
Identifiers: LCCN 2016041212| ISBN 9780231179584 (cloth : acid-free paper) | ISBN 9780231179591 (pbk. : acid-free paper) | ISBN 9780231544313 (e-book)
Subjects: LCSH: Utopias—Political aspects. | Political science—Philosophy.
Classification: LCC HX806 .P64 2016 | DDC 321/.07—dc23
LC record available at https://lccn.loc.gov/2016041212

Columbia University Press books are printed on permanent
and durable acid-free paper.

Printed in the United States of America

Cover design: Rebecca Lown

CONTENTS

Introduction: Utopia and Politics
James D. Ingram ix

I. REVIVING UTOPIA

1. THE HISTORY OF UTOPIA AND THE DESTINY OF ITS CRITIQUE

MIGUEL ABENSOUR

3

2. IS THE CLASSIC CONCEPT OF UTOPIA READY FOR THE FUTURE?

RICHARD SAAGE

57

3. UTOPIA AND NATURAL ILLUSIONS

FRANCISCO FERNÁNDEZ BUEY

80

II. QUESTIONING UTOPIA

4. MARX AND UTOPIA

FRANCK FISCHBACH

117

5. GENERAL WISH OR GENERAL WILL? POLITICAL POSSIBILITY AND COLLECTIVE CAPACITY FROM ROUSSEAU THROUGH MARX

PETER HALLWARD

126

6. AFTER UTOPIA, IMAGINATION?

ÉTIENNE BALIBAR

161

7. A STRANGE FATE FOR POLITICS: JAMESON'S DIALECTIC OF UTOPIAN THOUGHT

JOHN GRANT

165

III. UTOPIA AND RADICAL POLITICS

8. THE REALITY OF UTOPIA

MICHÈLE RIOT-SARCEY

179

9. NEGATIVITY AND UTOPIA IN THE GLOBAL JUSTICE MOVEMENT

MICHAËL LÖWY

190

10. UTOPIANISM AND PREFIGURATION

RUTH KINNA

198

IV. PERMANENCE OF UTOPIA

11. THE SENSES AND USES OF UTOPIA

JACQUES RANCIÈRE

219

12. REALISM, WISHFUL THINKING, UTOPIA

RAYMOND GEUSS

233

13. DESIRE AND SHIPWRECK: POWERS OF THE *VIS UTOPICA*

ÉTIENNE TASSIN

248

CODA

UTOPIA, ALIBI

S. D. CHROSTOWSKA

269

Contributors 311
Index 315

INTRODUCTION

Utopia and Politics

JAMES D. INGRAM

Utopia, we might think, is nothing if not political. Its best-known examples, from Plato via More, Campanella, and Bacon to Owen, Morris, and Bellamy, present cities, the political form of life par excellence, organized to remedy the defects their authors perceived in their own. To this extent they offer up political solutions to political problems. At the same time, however, utopias are forever being criticized for seeking to escape or eliminate politics, and not without reason. For if utopias present solutions to political problems, by building the common good into the design of the worlds they depict, they do away with the need to contest it. Such contestation of the common good—along with its less high-minded correlates, like fighting for power, advantage, recognition, and resources—is precisely what makes up what is ordinarily regarded as politics. Ergo, utopias are inherently antipolitical. We may want to object that the fact that the cities described in utopias tend to do away with politics is not to say that the genre or activity of inventing or reflecting on them does. As interventions into public life, as literary or theoretical acts, utopias are political through and through, written to raise political questions and even to advance political causes, even if the worlds they depict belie this by presenting imagined answers to these very questions.[1]

In view of this tangled intimacy, it may seem odd that the question of utopia's relationship to politics and political thought should have been mostly absent from the revival of utopian studies in recent decades. As no less an authority than Lyman Tower Sargent—a pioneer in the field, one of its leading figures for over half a century, and a political theorist by training and profession—put it in a short introduction to utopianism in 2010: "At the time of writing, there is no general study of the role utopianism plays in political theory."[2] In a seminal article published forty-six years earlier Sargent had argued that utopia has three "faces": literary (utopia as an artistic genre), communitarian (utopia as an "intentional community"), and social-theoretical (utopia as a means for reflecting on society, its problems, and its possibilities).[3] What is striking about this earlier list in light of the author's much later diagnosis is what it omits: politics itself, be it in the mode of action or reflection, practice or theory. Whether we understand it as an activity or a domain, in terms of unity or plurality, solidarity or conflict, harmony or strife, politics per se does not make it in—hidden, as it were, behind three faces that approach it without ever coinciding with it. The province of politics, it seems, is somehow absent from the map of utopia.

The same missed encounter can be observed from the other side in the sense that, just as utopianism has kept a distance from politics and political theory, political theory has had little time for utopia over most of the last three generations. To be sure, Sir Thomas More's classic remained on reading lists and references to the general idea of utopia continued to figure in historical as well as normative political theory. Yet, in ways and for reasons I discuss below, in the postwar period the standing of utopia and utopianism within Anglophone political theory fell to its modern nadir. Where utopia was not attacked, it was dismissed; where it was not dismissed, it was ignored; where it was not ignored, it was taken up in forms so impoverished as to suggest not only that nothing had been learned from the long history of utopian reflection, but that much had been forgotten. For most political theory in English, the problem has been less an absolute ignorance of utopianism than a failure to think seriously about how it might inform politics and political thought. A burning question in the nineteenth, eighteenth, and even sixteenth centuries, utopia, along with the sophisticated strategies developed for negotiating it, became a label signifying that something did not bear serious consideration, and was thus lost to political reflection.

How might we understand this disjuncture between utopia and politics, or between utopianism and political theory? In part, utopia's estrangement from politics and political thinking can be understood as an effect of the critical and imaginative distance utopias always take from the status quo, not infrequently cited as one of utopia's raisons d'être; it is only possible to find or construct a utopia, in words or in bricks and mortar, at a remove from the world we live in. But the gap between politics and utopia is also a product of recent political-intellectual history, of the trajectory of politics and political theory, especially in English-speaking countries, over the last five or six decades. Nothing shows the contingency of this trajectory more clearly than the fact that things evolved quite differently elsewhere. Indeed, the idea of utopia denotes and connotes different things not only in different fields but also in different national and linguistic contexts.[4] Even more significant than the cultural-geographical peculiarity of the factors that drove utopia and politics apart in English-language political theory, moreover, is their boundedness in time, which ties them to a moment that combined the recent experience of totalitarianism with a world organized by the Cold War.

The intuition behind the present book is that times have changed, and that, as I will argue in this introduction, circumstances that recommended wariness concerning utopia have given way to those that favor giving it a new look. These new circumstances are both political and theoretical. On the political side, in recent years, partly in response to various crises (financial and economic, but also political, ecological, and the like) and the manifest inadequacy of political responses to them, activists and ordinary citizens have increasingly expressed a desire for fundamental changes to society beyond what existing political institutions and even imaginations seem to be capable of. Conditions that formerly allowed antiutopians to insist that dreams of a perfect world are inherently dangerous have given way to ones in which a leading activist mantra is that "another world is possible"—a utopian claim, no doubt, but a strikingly modest one. At the same time, developments internal to utopian social and political thought have largely addressed the features of utopianism that led earlier political thinkers to reject it. Some of these innovations are relatively recent; others arise from new approaches to the history of utopianism, which have uncovered new perspectives on older sources. Both present political circumstances and theoretical developments within utopian studies, then, present an opportunity to rethink the politics of utopia on new bases.

This collection seeks to begin this rethinking by mapping the new political-intellectual terrain and providing resources (some new, some not so new but hitherto unavailable in English) for a wider debate on the politics of utopianism. What is the political specificity of utopia and utopianism? What can utopian thinking contribute to politics? If little or nothing, what are its specifically political limitations? In order to start asking these questions, we have brought together authors from different languages, national contexts, intellectual and political traditions, and generations, who take up utopianism from a political perspective—both pro and contra—beyond the terms that have tended to hamper debate in English-language political theory. Before introducing them and our common project, I will take the balance of this introduction to indicate the need for a fresh look at utopianism in political thought by tracing its exile from political theory in the postwar period, the partial and limited nature of its subsequent return, and the deficits of contemporary discussions.

UTOPIA AFTER 1945: ECLIPSE AND REVIVAL

By general consensus, the decades after World War II marked the nadir of utopian thought in the West. Utopianism was all but universally felt to have been fatally compromised by its association with totalitarian political projects—first and perhaps most plausibly Communism, but also nationalism, fascism, and even Nazism. To call a political ideology or project "utopian" in this context was not only to signal that it was unrealistic or unrealizable, an association that has accompanied utopia ever since its appearance in various European vernaculars in the fifteenth century. In the wake of the disastrous experiments of the first half of the twentieth century, utopianism came to be perceived as irresponsibly and actively dangerous, an effort to exert political control over whole societies, freeze history, deny social complexity, and treat human beings as so much raw material for the fulfillment of grand philosophical visions. The intellectuals who had indulged in utopian dreams had both incited and justified the worst atrocities in human history.[5]

Unlike earlier currents of militant antiutopianism, such as those that grew up in response to the French Revolution or 1848, the postwar antiutopians were not by and large reactionaries or even conservatives. For the most part they were liberal meliorists, thinkers who did not object to progress per se, only to attempts to force it by political means.[6] Antiutopianism in this guise dominated the center of intellectual opinion during the immediate postwar period, and included many of the luminaries of the age: not just famous anti-Communists like Arthur Koestler, Jacob Talmon, Karl Popper, Friedrich Hayek, and Sidney Hook, but also liberals and even republicans from Hannah Arendt and Judith Shklar to Ralf Dahrendorf, Isaiah Berlin, and Raymond Aron. Generally speaking, this current was united less by shared principles (though historians increasingly note a common mood and even content running through "Cold War liberalism")[7] than by what it rejected. Miguel Abensour has written of this period as a "trial of the master dreamers," suggesting that the latter had been convicted, often on the flimsiest of evidence and without any proper defense, of inspiring extremism and ultimately the worst political evils.[8]

Even at the height of the Cold War there were, to be sure, countercurrents. Some thinkers defended utopia as a vehicle of social criticism, a means of taking a critical distance from existing social arrangements, even if they insisted that there should be no attempt to realize these visions.[9] While Marx and Engels themselves had been famously critical of utopianism, calling instead for a scientific approach to society and politics, certain heterodox Marxists, most notably Ernst Bloch, recast it as a permanent tendency of human beings to dream of and strive for a better world.[10] Some non-Marxist philosophers and social theorists, following Karl Mannheim's *Ideology and Utopia* (published in 1929), likewise saw utopianism as a necessary aspect of how we understand the social world and our place in it, an ineliminable counterweight to ideology.[11] And if the Cold War liberals avoided utopia in the classic style, later efforts to develop a more normatively ambitious liberalism, above all those of John Rawls (to whom I return presently), showed that reflection on an ideal society could be philosophically respectable and politically unthreatening. These usages remained relatively marginal, however, especially in contrast to the prominence utopia had enjoyed in the nineteenth century, when utopian novels were bestsellers and "intentional communities" found numerous recruits.

The tide began to turn for utopia only when a new generation appeared on the historical stage. While it has since become common to speak of the "utopian energies" of the 1960s,[12] and certain famous slogans ("*l'imagination au pouvoir*," "*sous les pavés, la plage*") contributed to this impression, the utopianism of the 1960s is for the most part a retrospective construction. In the moment, utopia was either too close (even if it could not be realized within the present order), as Marcuse had it,[13] or quite irrelevant to the struggles of the day. The great movements and general upheaval of the period inspired a new interest in utopian discourse and ideas, but utopia itself emerged as an explicit theme only in subsequent literary and scholarly developments. On the one hand, the passing of the most immediately revolutionary energies of the 1960s was marked by a wave of explicitly utopian texts exploring the concerns of the day, from Le Guin's *The Left Hand of Darkness* (1969) to Callenbach's *Ecotopia* (1975) and Piercy's *Woman on the Edge of Time* (1976).[14] On the other hand, the New Left had catalyzed an interest in anticapitalist possibilities beyond and against Marxism, an interest that took different academic forms in different national and disciplinary contexts. British radicals' turn to cultural and intellectual history, for instance, exemplified by Raymond Williams and E. P. Thompson, sparked a return to neglected indigenous varieties of "utopian socialism," from Winstanley to Morris. They were inspired in part by scholars in France who had begun to reconstruct the revolutionary utopian ferment of the mid-nineteenth century in a search for theoretical and political alternatives to Marxism. If in the United States, in contrast, there tended to be more interest in present-day cultural and countercultural trends, this ended up feeding into a utopian revival of a quite different kind, with contemporary culture rather than history taking center stage.

In retrospect we can see in these developments the lineaments of a renaissance of utopian studies that would only fully flower over the subsequent decades. I would suggest that two main tendencies distinguish this new, post-'68 utopianism from its predecessors. First, while utopianism had always been a mode of political-philosophical reflection, its main historical form was of course literary. Not the treatise but the imaginative discourse, dialogue, or narrative—and more recently the novel—was the utopian genre par excellence. The study of utopia accordingly started to take off in the North American academy when scholars began to treat it not as a kind of political theory, but, partly in response to a wave of literary, filmic, and televisual production, as an artistic and cultural phenomenon.[15] This new interest in utopian literature and film was supported by parallel developments within literary studies in the 1970s, including a new inclination to submit forms of writing outside the narrow confines of belles lettres to literary analysis, buttressed by a language of "theory" that borrowed heavily from continental philosophy. This merging of literary studies with what was developing separately in the United Kingdom as "cultural studies" probably achieved its highest articulation stateside in the work of Fredric Jameson. Through Jameson's efforts along with those of his collaborators and students beginning in the late 1960s, utopia, often via contemporary pop-cultural texts, became a vital object of cultural investigation.[16]

If utopianism came back onto the academic agenda first as a literary genre, it appeared soon after in social-theoretical guise. While the embers of utopianism had been kept alive through the labors of a handful of historians, mostly notably Frank and Fritzie Manuel, when surveys of utopianism finally began to reappear in the 1980s, it was typically from sociologists.[17] Here the project was not the Jamesonian one of using utopias to diagnose the cultural contradictions of the present, but a combination of the historian's work of documenting the variety and continuity of past utopias with the social theorist's task of abstracting or deducing from this variety a "utopian function" (Bloch). The 1980s and 1990s thus saw a flourishing of utopian studies, above all in the British Isles, with a steady accumulation not only of histories of social and political utopianism, but also of defenses of its desirability and even necessity. These (admittedly stylized) American and British cultural-literary and social-theoretical trajectories can be said to have met not only literally in the Utopian Studies conferences starting in North America in 1975 and in Europe in 1988,[18] but also substantively in the convergence of Ruth Levitas's foundational social-theoretical work with that of Jameson on a Blochian conception of utopia as necessary and even ubiquitous, but defined by nothing more specific than a desire that the world somehow be otherwise.

At the dawn of the post–Cold War age, then, utopia was back—at least as an academic pursuit, if not in any immediately political sense. David Armitage went so far as to suggest that the two phenomena might be related: only with the extinction of really existing Communism as a practical alternative could the mainstream safely return to the genre of political thought once reproached for inspiring it.[19] Now that it was completely disarmed, utopia, like Communism, could be comfortably studied—from the rubbish heap to the dissecting table. The relation between intellectual interest and practical import naturally works the other way around as well, with utopia standing in as a compensatory refuge for a radical Left that saw itself hopelessly outmatched, with dwindling and finally no prospects of escape from a relentlessly instrumentalized, desolidarized world. This tendency developed a certain poignancy in the 1980s, with thinkers like Jameson and Levitas fastening onto ever thinner, weaker, and vaguer "utopian moments" against the Reagan–Thatcher onslaught. It is not surprising, then, that one of the most common uses of "utopia" outside utopian studies was by historians to describe the kinds of programs, dreams, or desires for revolutionary transformation that once shook the world and whose echoes could now only faintly and intermittently be heard over the empty din of globalized neoliberal capitalism. Utopia now existed primarily in the past, as a lost possibility and object of nostalgia.[20] If utopia had finally cast off the shadow of being dangerous, it seemed, it had managed it only at the price of becoming irrelevant.

UTOPIA AND POLITICAL THEORY

While utopia has flourished most in literary and historical studies rather than in the domain of political thought, it was revived by the last generation of political theorists in a few notable versions—even if, as I will explain, these uses remained at some distance from the classical utopian tradition from More or even Plato to the late nineteenth century. The first and most important such revival was by most accounts also the most important venture in Anglo-American political theory in the later twentieth century: the work of John Rawls. While much else changed from *A Theory of Justice* (1971) to *Political Liberalism* (1993) to *The Law of Peoples* (1999), Rawls's central project always remained the construction of a "realistic utopia," which he took to mean an ideal vision of society subject only to the constraint that it not be incompatible with (adopting Rousseau's formula from the *Social Contract*) "men as they are and laws as they might be." Even if this foundational reference to utopia tended to be underplayed and was seldom explicitly linked to the utopian tradition, the pursuit of what Rawls and his followers called "ideal theory" could be said to have returned a form of utopianism to the very heart of political philosophy.

A second, related version of neoutopianism that achieved prominence in recent English-language political theory is what the American sociologist Erik Olin Wright has termed "real utopias."[21] These refer to institutions and practices that are by no means impossible but have not yet been brought into being, at least not in the polity the authors share with their imagined readers. Indeed, in some cases itemized by Wright in a recent book—participatory budgeting, Wikipedia, worker cooperatives, and basic income allowance—they in fact exist somewhere, but appear farfetched in the author's own (national) social and political circumstances (this being their "utopian" aspect). This kind of utopianism has a close cousin in the Rawlsian enterprise of "applied theory," which tries to work out how the normative vision articulated by the ideal theorist could best be approximated under real-world conditions. And such political-theoretical operations are by no means the exclusive province of normative social theory or political philosophy. We can observe a similar venture on the historical-materialist Left in what Immanuel Wallerstein has termed "utopistics," the development of "realistic" futures that avoids what Wallerstein regards as the unhelpful unreality of "utopian" theory.[22] In all these cases, the effort either to complement or to avoid the impracticality of utopianism entails giving up its more radical ambitions.

If "ideal theory" on one side and "realistic" or "applied theory" on the other represent the main contemporary legacies of utopianism in recent English-language political theory, we could say that it finds itself entangled once again in the double bind already diagnosed by utopia's nineteenth-century critics. Either utopia/ideal theory asks too much, consigning itself to irrelevance, or it asks too little, ratifying the status quo, falling into reformism, and foreclosing future creativity. The most prominent recent variant of this dilemma can be readily discerned among Anglophone theorists in the debate over the relative merits of "ideal" and "realistic" theory. Critics of the former denounce the otherworldliness and impracticability of pure normative theory, whose defenders in turn argue against the grubby pragmatism of the realists' "utopophobia" and "practicalism" on the basis that theory need aim only at truth, not at real-world effects.[23] While this debate has produced numerous refinements and a sprawling literature, what has been lost from view is the fact that *neither* ideal *nor* applied theory resembles most, and certainly not the best or most interesting, of what has been written under the heading of utopia. If we feel a certain unease in, as Rawls seems to suggest, reading Rousseau's *Social Contract* as a "utopia," that would certainly be more plausible than reading it—or More's *Utopia*, Plato's *Republic*, or any of the other classic utopias—as "ideal theory" in the Rawlsian style.[24]

Indeed, a short glance back at the utopian tradition—the common object, in different respects, of the literary, intellectual-historical, and social-theoretical revivals discussed above—allows us to see the limits of its more recent philosophical incarnations. If there is one thing to which students of utopia following in Jameson's footsteps have been attentive, it is *form*, especially the ironic, self-reflexive devices that make so many utopias, whether literary or philosophical, irreducible to the programs, models, and arguments of their analytical epigones. Whatever else might be said about recent Anglophone political theory's reduction of the "utopian" to the "ideal," the "unrealistic," or the "unusually normatively demanding," it clearly leaves no place for the debates that have always gone on around the classical utopian texts concerning their authors' designs. Did Plato (or Plato's Socrates) or More (or More's Hythloday) or Rousseau (in the *Social Contract*) imagine their ideas could be simply translated into social-institutional reality? If so, why did they leave so much textual evidence that they meant their (or their speakers') visions to appear far-fetched, contradictory, or even impossible? What lessons can we take from the political insights these works of genius nevertheless convey? If answers to this last question vary enormously, one hermeneutic possibility can be excluded at the outset: that these works set out solutions to social-political problems determined by simple ratiocination, to be administratively imposed onto social reality after adjusting for local conditions—in other words, ideal theory.

Intellectual historians have likewise called attention to the many ways in which utopian authors have learned to guard against simple attempts to impose ideal visions on social reality. Abensour notes a shift from "systematic" to "heuristic" utopias after 1850, while Russell Jacoby distinguishes "blueprint" from "iconoclastic" ones.[25] As early as 1965, in response to the original postwar antiutopians, George Kateb noted that "any serious utopian thinker will be made uncomfortable by the very idea of a blueprint."²⁶ Whatever the great utopians were up to—and this, of course, remains richly and permanently disputed—it was something more and *other* than either pure regulative ideals or defeasible proposals for social improvement. In their admirable pursuit of transparency and rigor, it would seem, many leading figures in English-language political philosophy and social theory have lost track of the ways in which earlier utopians escaped their critics' charges. And by the same token they have unlearned much of the subtlety, provisionality, conditionality, reflexivity, and self-criticism that the genre of utopia was developed to cultivate.

While these first two types of neoutopianism—"ideal" and "real" or "applied" normative theory—seem only to reproduce the old oscillation between totalitarian perversion and otherworldly dreaming that led to the exile of utopianism from political reflection in the first place, a third recent strand of political theory avoids these dangers only to fall into another. This can be seen, for example, in Seyla Benhabib's reconstruction of the Frankfurt School tradition, *Critique, Norm, and Utopia*, published in 1986, which argued that critical social theory needs a "utopian moment" if it is to amount to more than generic social or moral criticism. To go beyond critique to utopia in her view is to go beyond justice and aspire to happiness, to go beyond fulfilling the universal normative promise of modernity and anticipate a more radical social transformation.²⁷ While defending a more substantive notion of utopia than Jürgen Habermas's, however, Benhabib, like him, avoids utopia's totalitarian propensities by rendering it almost completely indeterminate. In this, she expresses a Blochian inspiration, where utopia stands for a more or less vague sense of ideal or radically other possibilities. Indeed, even when critical theorists in the Frankfurt style seek to revive utopia in more emphatic terms than Benhabib, as does, for instance, Maeve Cooke in her recent work, they tend to devote more attention to ensuring its nondogmatic, epistemically provisional status than its social content, let alone its politics.²⁸

If critical theory has learned to avoid the cruder versions of utopianism as social engineering, it has tended to fall into the opposite danger: identifying utopia so broadly with normativity, idealization, or the desire for another world as to deprive it not only of social and political content, but of any features that distinguish it from ideality in general. Ruth Levitas has voiced similar doubts about the general shift in utopian studies in which she played a leading role, namely, the Blochian turn she shares with

Jameson, the later Frankfurt School, and many others: a turn from content to form, from prescription to self-criticism, reflexivity, provisionality, and pluralism. "Utopia survives," she writes, "but at a cost, and that cost is the retreat of the utopian function from transformation to critique."[29] Thus, the generalization of the utopian spirit effected in different ways by Mannheim, Bloch, Abensour, Levitas, and Jameson has revived utopianism by showing that utopia persists even where it may seem to be absent and without the pernicious consequences its critics allege, but at the price of being watered down to the point that it can be found both nowhere and everywhere.

While the defense of the bare possibility of thinking otherwise is certainly central to the utopian enterprise, in posing as our question in this collection the *uses* of utopia *for politics*, we mean to suggest that utopianism must have something more, and something *more specific*, to offer politics and political reflection. On one level, a too-inclusive conception of utopia concedes too much to its radical critics, from Marx down to the present, by allowing that utopia amounts to nothing more than a vague desire that things be otherwise, with little to say on *how* they should be or how they might get that way. On another level, construing utopia in so abstract a way abandons the disciplining exercise that the great utopian texts performed through their elaborate textual games of self-correction and self-reflexivity, and that utopian advocates and activists faced in their own way in the test of practice. In both cases (the literary as well as the practical), the details of utopia are an essential part of the exercise, and addressing them is one of the most important ways that utopias can contribute to, in the phrase Levitas adapts from Abensour, "the education of desire." Letting utopianism dwindle to desire alone robs it of what gives it its specific character and distinguishes it from other forms of social, political, or moral speculation or idealization.

In sum, utopianism has returned at least to the edges of political theory, but only in forms that lose many of the advantages of the classical models. If normative political theory, whether in its "ideal" or its more modest, "applied" version, has in its way taken up certain utopian elements, it has interpreted them too literally, either by drawing up the kinds of blueprints subtler utopians abandoned long ago or by losing themselves in generality and abstraction. Lost in this translation of utopia into the dialects of modern political philosophy are the irony, reflexivity, playfulness, and attention to detail that make utopias something more than a series of more or less desirable or plausible models or normative ideals—something closer, perhaps, to a series of reflections on the possibility and challenges of social-political transformation. As the contributors to this collection debate and illustrate in various ways, this kind of reflection, richer, more expansive, and more internally differentiated than simple idealization or normative thinking, has been fundamental to the political education utopias have historically provided. To this extent, political theorists of all stripes can learn both from the work done under the umbrella of utopian studies and from canonical authors in the utopian tradition, whose counsel and subtlety have been lost. It is clear, in any case, that any argument for the uses of utopia for politics today will have to move beyond the alternatives considered so far. But it will have to be mindful not just of these theoretical lessons, but also of a new political constellation.

A NEW LANDSCAPE AND NEW CHALLENGES

The exile of utopia from postwar political theory, I have suggested, grew out of a particular historical conjuncture, on one side shaped by a fear of transformative politics in the wake of Communism and fascism, and on the other comforted by the prospect of gradual progress under consensual, relatively depoliticized, liberal or social-democratic governance. If the lesson of the first half of the twentieth century was the danger of too much political experimentation and change—in short, too much utopia—the steady rise of living standards and social inclusion through the immediate postwar decades showed what could be achieved when expectations were managed and tried-and-true methods and institutions relied upon. The international outburst of '68 may have temporarily upset this view, but by 1989 it had become clear that the revolt's main significance had been cultural, a youthful rebellion against a social conservatism and authoritarianism that advanced societies had already largely outgrown. Politically, in contrast, it appeared in hindsight as a last spasm of the revolutionary illusions that had disfigured the last two centuries and could finally be abandoned. From the dominant midcentury perspective, the recipe for future progress—in essence, prudentially managed liberal-democratic consumer capitalism—lay not in pursuing but precisely in abandoning utopia.[30]

The situation today is in many respects the opposite. In place of the postwar fear of political power, of its being used recklessly or for evil ends, there is now a widespread indifference to it in light of what appears to be its repeatedly demonstrated impotence. Everywhere, but perhaps especially in the mature capitalist liberal democracies, people resign themselves to the idea that very little, certainly nothing fundamental, can be changed by political means, be it for good or for ill. In place of the postwar faith that progress will gradually unfold on its own, there is now generalized anxiety that economic, technological, and environmental trends are working themselves out independently of human control, leading only to ever-greater disasters. We take our Promethean powers for granted but have little faith in our ability to consciously harness them; the notion that we live in an "anthropocene" age, in which we produce our own environment, is seen not as an emancipation from the realm of necessity to that of freedom, as our recent ancestors might have dreamed, but as the forecourt of apocalypse. On an ideological level, the ideas that hold sway over our societies today seldom receive any better defense than a gesture toward the lack of practicable alternatives. Movements that spring up in response to economic crises or failures of governance find broad popular resonance, but as a rule do not have anything in particular to propose. We live in a dystopian age, one that does not have reason to be afraid of, but cynical about and disenchanted with, politics.

Such a situation, where a sense of political impotence and impending disaster meets consensus on the level of ruling ideas and unfocused dissatisfaction among the ruled, changes the terms on which utopia is debated. The old liberal worry about utopianism's authoritarian tendencies—that it will try to take over politics, impose itself on the whole of society, and program the future—sounds empty and possibly in bad faith when the status quo persists mostly by virtue of inertia. Indeed, the ambitions of present-day radicals and theoretical utopians seldom stretch further than some hazily imagined possibility—hardly the sort of threat that preoccupied Popper, Shklar, et al. At the same time, the symmetrical Marxist worry that a utopian desire for social transformation without an eye on underlying trends and opportunities amounts to empty dreaming or even an inadvertent defense of the existing order seems no less off target. The aspiration to an understanding of history and politics that is at once scientific and strategic, which underlay Marxism for more than a century, has been universally, perhaps definitively, abandoned.[31] Indeed, within radical political thinking today there is a general consensus that the challenge is not to grasp but precisely to burst the conditions of historical necessity. By the same token, social and value pluralism are now so widely accepted within radical and progressive political circles that, as with historical contingency, to argue for them is to push against an open door. The principal threat to plurality is less any attempt to impose a particular ideology than the very absence of any such vision that is the background ideology of globalizing capitalism.

Just as the perversions into which earlier utopias once fell have been more or less purged and their dangers defused, the felt need for utopia, understood minimally as, but not limited to, the possibility of some positive alternative future, has perhaps never been greater. In this context, where what is needed above all is the possibility of overcoming the limits on social and political thought and action, utopian thinking offers a singularly promising resource for sustained reflection on the desirability, character, and possibilities of—as well as problems with—radical transformation.[32] The time, in short, is ripe to reopen utopia as a political question. But for this discussion to be fruitful, it must be conducted on new bases, beyond the impasses and static oppositions outlined above.

As the postwar antiutopians recognized, a recipe-book conception of the relation between theory and practice, between the ideal and the real, is as unrealistic as it is dangerous. It ignores the fact that politics is perhaps uniquely subject to the law of unintended consequences—that, as Hannah Arendt noted, since it always and only deals with people in the plural, it can never imagine them being subjected to a single dream or vision. The common starting point of the contributions to this volume is dissatisfaction with how the relationship between utopia and politics has for generations been framed—namely, by the assumption that utopia must be viewed either as a political ideal that is impossible to realize by definition, and therefore a mere thought experiment, or as something achievable, a model or blueprint. All our authors agree that neither of these models will do and that the political uses of utopia lie, if anywhere, between—or, better, are something other than—these alternatives. Moreover, although they reflect in different ways on the grand tradition of Western utopianism, they are interested less in the tradition per se than in its relevance and specific valences within the current situation.

Utopia as discussed here is always utopia that presupposes plurality and contingency. This observation extends, moreover, beyond textual utopias to their really existing, practical-experimental counterparts (Sargent's second, "communitarian" face of utopia). Unlike the classic "intentional communities" from Fourier's *phalanstères* to Owen's New Lanark to the communes built to preserve the spirit of '68, the prefigurative utopianism associated with contemporary anarchism and the recent Occupy movement, mentioned here by Michaël Löwy and explored by Ruth Kinna, is acutely aware of the danger of reifying rationalistic, unlivable designs. If anything, the utopias tentatively opened up by today's radical activists are provisional and ephemeral to a fault—utopias of practice, not planning.[33] Like the theoretical utopianism represented here, they never seek to "freeze" society or to override democratic decision-making processes. To the contrary, they seem, if anything, to favor perpetual dynamism and democratism.

But if the utopias discussed in the following pages are not simply designs to be implemented or solutions to social-theoretical problems, neither are they reducible to simple figures of "social otherness." To the contrary, at every moment they pose the question of politics, albeit in different ways and on different registers. One thing the essays gathered here have in common is a concern with establishing a link between utopian indeterminacy in theory and democratic indeterminacy in practice *without* dwindling into empty abstraction or the contentless affirmation of the possibility of something different. Whereas the utopias condemned by Cold War liberalism tended to submit society to their ideal visions, the types of utopia discussed here are highly sensitive to the need to resist the totalization that comes with shovel-ready blueprints. Moreover, as Miguel Abensour realized very early on, even among less ironic utopian writers, this sort of self-critical reflection was part of what he terms the "new utopian spirit" at least as far back as 1848. This is not to say, however, that the old objections against utopianism can be simply laid to rest; to the contrary, they return with renewed force, drawing on the classical lines of criticism, above all Marx's. But these critiques can no longer be directed against the easy targets of the past.

OVERVIEW

The aim of this book is to bring together work from different political currents with a deep connection to utopianism, to take a full measure of nineteenth- and twentieth-century views on utopia and politics, and to relate them to the specific challenges for radical political thinking of the present. To this end we have constructed this volume not simply as a defense of utopia, but as a debate in which some of the strongest, most self-reflexive versions of utopia and their most articulate and nonreductive critics are represented. Partly in order to correct for the limitations of discussions of utopianism within English-language political theory, we present previously untranslated material by important continental European authors alongside original contributions by Anglophone scholars.[34] The result, we believe, demonstrates at once the depth and nuance of utopian thought, its complication of narrower political commitments, and its possible lessons for transformative politics at large. The perceptive reader may observe that the resulting political-ideological constellation recalls in certain respects that which prevailed at the time of the last great flourishing of utopian ideas, the nineteenth century: an open contest within radical political thought between (1) a nondogmatic Marxism or revolutionary socialism, (2) various forms of anarchism, and (3) a more diffuse set of left-wing commitments that can be called, taking up Marx and Engels's pejorative label, utopian socialism. But in other respects, if only owing to the theoretical and political developments of the intervening century, we are off to a fresh start.

We begin with reconsiderations of the history of utopianism by three pioneers in the field, all of whom have made enormous contributions in their own languages but whose writings on utopianism remain mostly unknown in English: Miguel Abensour, Richard Saage, and Francisco Fernández Buey.[35] While Abensour's work in radical democratic theory is finally becoming known in English,[36] his career began with a major study of utopia in relation to the radical political thought of the nineteenth century. This work exerted an outsized but almost entirely unrecognized influence on English-language utopian studies via Raymond Williams and E. P. Thompson. The essay translated here originally appeared in two installments in the short-lived French journal *Textures* in 1973 and 1974. It takes up two of the most important themes of Abensour's lengthy dissertation. In the first half of the essay Abensour shows that Marx and Engels remained in much closer dialogue with the utopian tradition than had been generally appreciated, and that standard interpretations (including that of the later Engels) that oppose Marxism to utopian socialism tend to misconstrue what was at stake between them. In the second half Abensour shows that in its great efflorescence after 1848 utopian socialism gained a self-critical lucidity that makes it a permanent counterweight to the dogmatic tendencies of other, historically more successful ideologies, including the main currents of Marxism.

Richard Saage came to utopia later in his career. Having already written on a variety of other themes, from Kant to property to fascism, Saage published a major study of early-modern utopias just in time for the fall of the Berlin Wall.[37] This turned out to be only the beginning of more than two decades of intensive engagement with the subject, marked by two complementary traits: on the one hand, a comprehensive historical scope reaching from Herodotus and Plato to the latest science fiction; on the other hand, constant interrogation of utopianism's political significance—historically, to be sure, but especially in the present, when the collapse of state socialism was often, in Germany as elsewhere, taken to have brought the age of utopias to an end. Saage's comparative historical research ultimately yielded a four-volume study of utopian writings in the Western tradition since More that is one of the major recent accomplishments of utopology.[38] Throughout this period he published essays on the continuing relevance of utopianism in view of changing cultural-political circumstances. In the essay translated for this volume Saage reflects on the ongoing political significance of this tradition, showing how the classical forms of utopianism contain political insights that more modern constructions of utopia have lost. Far from being apolitical, he argues, the classical utopias show how the political effects of utopian thinking may in fact be deeper and more lasting when they are indirect.

The philosopher and political theorist Francisco Fernández Buey was celebrated in Marxist and emancipatory-ecological intellectual circles throughout the Spanish-speaking world and was also a noted public intellectual in his native Catalonia, but again he is almost completely unknown in English.[39] His writings cover a wide range of philosophical, historical, and literary topics, but it was only in what turned out to be his last major book, *Utopías e ilusiones naturales* (Utopias and natural illusions, 2007), that utopia became central to his vision. This sweeping work takes up the literary, philosophical, and political history of utopia since the sixteenth century in order to make sense of the revival of radical political energies he was cheered to witness in the early years of the twenty-first century. In the chapters excerpted here, Fernández Buey revisits the origins of utopia from a Hispanic and postcolonial perspective typically neglected within utopian studies, beginning with Thomas More's often forgotten New World inspirations and echoes, in order to draw lessons for the present, when a new political-historical moment obliges us to revise Herbert Marcuse's famous proclamation in 1967 of the end of utopia.

Part 2 turns to what is historically the most important political dialogue in the modern history of utopian thinking, that with Marxism. As recent scholars have stressed and all our authors are acutely aware, despite its self-definition in relation to utopianism from the *Communist Manifesto* to Engels's *Socialism: Utopian and Scientific*, Marx did not simply reject utopianism and its leading thinkers without at the same time drawing heavily on them. All of the authors in this section stand in some kind of critical intimacy with the Marxist tradition. We begin with a concise and lucid account of Marx's own criticisms of political utopianism by Franck Fischbach, a leading younger French Marxist. Fischbach, who has written extensively on German Idealism, stresses the Hegelian roots of Marx's suspicion of utopianism, but also how Marx went beyond Hegel in admitting certain utopian elements into his thought. Peter Hallward, a representative of a younger generation of Marxists working in the United Kingdom, turns to Marx but even more to Rousseau and the theorists and practitioners of revolutionary politics to criticize utopianism. The revolutionary tradition, he argues, from Robespierre to Che Guevara, has always understood that transformative politics cannot consist only of a utopian *wish*—"desire," as it has been recuperated by recent utopian studies—but requires a revolutionary *will*, the necessary condition for a political project with any hope of success.

One of the most important Marxian philosophers and political theorists tout court of his generation, Étienne Balibar lodges a parallel complaint against utopianism with reference not to the past but to the present, and not to the will but to *imagination*. Utopianism, argues Balibar, has been rendered obsolete by recent social, economic, and cultural changes. Utopia, the pure "elsewhere" or "otherwise" that was imagined in earlier ages as the site of political alterity, located far away at an imaginary point insulated from us by time or space, has been rendered inoperative by our overwhelmingly interconnected present. Since there is no longer any place for a utopian elsewhere, we must now learn instead to transform the world we occupy from within. The political theorist John Grant, finally, takes on the most important attempt to bridge Marxism and utopianism in recent English-language letters, that of Fredric Jameson. Reading some of Jameson's more recent essays, Grant shows that Jameson's practice of identifying utopianism with affirmative cultural moments even in profoundly regressive contexts forecloses the political possibilities that could arise from a properly negative dialectic. To this extent, Grant argues, Jameson's Marxist reconstruction and defense of utopianism are (of all things) insufficiently dialectical, and for this very reason insufficiently political.

If many in the Marxist tradition still find reason to doubt the political efficacy of even the most sophisticated utopianisms, in part 3 we collect authors from a range of radical positions who insist, in different ways and with reference to different cases, on the direct relation between utopia and political movements. Michèle Riot-Sarcey, a leading French historian of nineteenth-century women's and workers' movements, maintains that these movements were often both utopian and practical. The essay presented here, "The Reality of Utopia," taken from her book of the same title, published in 1998, argues that utopias are "real" in a double sense: not only are they historically specific critiques of a particular society, they are interventions into society that have real effects through the individuals and movements they enlighten and inspire. In the nineteenth century, Riot-Sarcey argues, they had these effects by politicizing issues that had hitherto been exiled from the political to the social realm. Michaël Löwy, best known in the English-speaking world for a series of essays and books on Marxism's utopian and messianic offshoots, looks here to the contemporary global justice movement, showing how its utopian impulse has consistently gone beyond mere rejection to attempts to envision another world. Ruth Kinna, finally, a leading authority on utopianism in the anarchist tradition, considers its place in the theory and practice of the recent Occupy movement, arguably the most important popular antisystemic mobilization in the centers of global power in many years. In deliberately putting the political values they enacted in practice ahead of any strategic ends or simply advancing their cause, Kinna argues, Occupy developed an original form of "prefigurative utopianism" that may shape radical politics for years to come.

Part 4 of the book takes another approach to the political uses of utopia, analyzing distinctly political elements that run through the long history of utopian thinking. Jacques Rancière, whose insistence on the irreducibly conflictual, dissensual character of politics has become highly influential in recent years, shows how utopia, always reproached for seeking to escape politics, can in fact serve to reopen it. Taking two nineteenth-century examples, one from the Saint-Simonians and another from Balzac, Rancière shows how the utopian desire to eliminate the imperfections and the "gaps" of social reality in fact opens up gaps in which the politics of emancipation can play out. Raymond Geuss, who has achieved considerable notoriety as a critic of ideal theory and defender of "realism" in political theory, seeks to rescue utopia from its liberal advocates. In the essay presented here, written in German as a clarification of his book *Philosophy and Real Politics* (2008), Geuss distinguishes between utopianism and wishful thinking. Whereas the latter distorts reality, rendering us less able to confront it and act within it politically, utopia can project a desired horizon toward which we can strive. The realist critique of ideal theory, according to one of its leading practitioners, leaves utopia intact. And Étienne Tassin, a leading representative of the French tradition of radical democracy that includes Abensour, Claude Lefort, and Cornelius Castoriadis, shows how utopian fictions play an important political role in educating us on the necessary distance between the *idea* of justice or utopia and the *illusion* of being able to realize it. Critical and radically democratic politics can—indeed must—have a utopian moment, but must do so in a way that does not confuse its desires with reality.

The coda by S. D. Chrostowska, finally, suggests new horizons opened up by and beyond the present discussion. Chrostowska addresses the progressive disembodiment or spiritualization of utopia in twentieth-century theory, which she argues gives up the very ground—the body—on which so many radical movements, political as well as intellectual, have staked their claim in decades past. Chrostowska suggests that a reconsideration of the body may help bring utopianism closer to political practice and recent political theory, connecting it to vital present-day developments. As befits a book meant to stage and advance a dialogue rather than put forward a line or position, Chrostowska offers no conclusion as such, only a challenge to bring utopia into meaningful proximity to the real world, to give it some purchase on politics, without collapsing the distance that is its raison d'être and the basis of its critical and political efficacy.

This collection grew out of a series of conversations about the current theoretical-political landscape, and in particular, to use a Blochian phrase, what seemed to be "missing." It struck us as regrettable that the desires of those who seek radically new political and social futures (activists and thinkers working to invent new, freer, and more democratic political prospects, typically on the margins of contemporary social life) could find so little resonance in the scholarly field arguably responsible for theorizing their struggles, namely, utopian studies. We felt that at least in English, political theorists had largely shut themselves off from one of the richest resources for thinking about how such futures can be conceived and imagined politically, the long utopian tradition. We saw in this state of affairs an opportunity to put utopia back on the agenda, in the first place by infusing it with insights from other disciplinary, ideological-political, national, and linguistic contexts.

In order to give structure to our conversations and to broaden their participation, we held a workshop at York University in Toronto in the spring of 2013. Some of the texts that follow were circulated in advance to stimulate discussion, others were presented in some version at the meeting, others were written in response to it. The editors would like to thank our coorganizer, Martin Breaugh, of York University Political Science;

our graduate assistants Nika Jabarova and Hugo Bonin; Peter W. Nesselroth, Manuel S. Almeida, and Devin Zane Shaw for their translations; as well as our generous sponsors: the Faculty of Liberal Arts & Professional Studies, the Canadian Centre for German and European Studies, Founders College, the Faculty of Graduate Studies, the departments of Political Science and Humanities, the Program in Social & Political Thought (all at York University), and the Social Sciences and Humanities Research Council of Canada. We want, finally, to thank those workshop participants whose words may not appear in the volume but whose contributions enlivened it.

NOTES

1 To say that utopias are antipolitical, in other words, is to confuse an imaginary creation with what that creation depicts, the saying with the said. Of course utopias "don't exist"; that is their mode of existence. To object that they are *really* antipolitical is often simply to misunderstand this, akin to complaining about the fire hazard posed by dragons or fairies' tendency to get underfoot.

2 Sargent, *Utopianism: A Very Short Introduction* (New York: Oxford University Press, 2010), 142.

3 Sargent, "The Three Faces of Utopianism," *Minnesota Review* 4, no. 3 (Spring 1964).

4 France in particular has been a utopia for utopia, a fact we have eagerly exploited in assembling the present volume.

5 For a classic statement, see Popper, "Utopia and Violence" (1948), in *Conjectures and Refutations: The Growth of Scientific Knowledge* (New York: Basic, 1962).

6 Indeed, this antiutopianism went along with a different, passive sort of utopianism on another level. Many of those during the postwar decades who rejected utopia as necessarily entangled with reckless social experimentation tended to assume both indefinite technical progress and gradual ideological convergence. In this way, the "end of utopia" went along, in a certain midcentury imaginary represented by Daniel Bell or Raymond Aron, with the "end of ideology."

7 See Jan-Werner Müller, "Fear and Freedom: on 'Cold War Liberalism,'" *European Journal of Political Theory* 7, no. 1 (2008); Amanda Anderson, "Character and Ideology: The Case of Cold War Liberalism," *New Literary History* 42, no. 2 (2011): 209–229.

8 Abensour, *Le Procès des maîtres rêveurs* (Paris: Sullivan, 2001).

9 For example, Mulford Q. Sibley, "Apology for Utopia I: an Examination of Professor Sait's Excogitated Ideas" and "Apology for Utopia II: Utopia and Politics," *Journal of Politics* 2, nos. 1–2 (1940); George Kateb, "Utopia and the Good Life," *Daedalus* 94, no. 2 (1965).

10 Bloch, *The Spirit of Utopia*, trans. Anthony A. Nassar (Stanford: Stanford University Press, 2000); Bloch, *The Principle of Hope*, trans. Neville Plaice, Stephen Plaice, and Paul Knight (Oxford: Basil Blackwell, 1986).

11 Mannheim, *Ideology and Utopia: An Introduction to the Sociology of Knowledge*, trans. Louis Wirth and Edward Shils (New York: Harcourt, 1954); Paul Ricœur, *Lectures on Ideology and Utopia*, ed. George H. Taylor (New York: Cambridge University Press, 1981).

12 See, for example, Paul Berman, *A Tale of Two Utopias: The Political Journey of the Generation of 1968* (New York: Norton, 1996); Luisa Passerini, "Utopia and Desire," *Thesis Eleven* 68, no. 1 (2002).

13 On the idea that late capitalism had practically exceeded utopianism by making every possibility actually available, though practically denied, see Herbert Marcuse, "The End of Utopia and the Problem of Violence," in *Five Lectures* (Boston: Beacon, 1970).

14 The timing of this wave of utopian literature is central to Fredric Jameson's case for utopianism as an outlet for and displacement of the energies of frustrated radical politics.

15 Sargent, "The Three Faces of Utopianism Revisited," *Utopian Studies* 5, no. 1 (1994).

16 Many of Jameson's major essays on the theme are collected in *Archaeologies of the Future: The Desire Called Utopia and Other Science Fictions* (London: Verso, 2005), but they are practically coextensive with his work on contemporary culture. See also Darko Suvin, *Defined by a Hollow: Essays on Utopia, Science Fiction and Political Epistemology* (Oxford: Peter Lang, 2010); Tom Moylan, *Scraps of the Untainted Sky: Science Fiction, Utopia, Dystopia* (Boulder, Colo.: Westview, 2000); Phillip Wegner, *Imaginary Communities* (Berkeley: University of California Press, 2002).

17 For example, Krishan Kumar, *Utopia and Anti-Utopia in Modern Times* (Oxford: Basil Blackwell, 1987); Ruth Levitas, *The Concept of Utopia* (Syracuse: Syracuse University Press, 1990).

18 Peter Fitting, "A Short History of Utopian Studies," *Science Fiction Studies* 36, no. 1 (2009): 121–131.

19 David Armitage, "Out of this World," *London Review of Books* 17, no. 22 (November 16, 1995): 15–16.

20 For example, Susan Buck-Morss, *Dreamworld and Catastrophe: The Passing of Mass Utopia in East and West* (Cambridge, Mass.: MIT Press, 2000); Jay Winter, *Dreams of Peace and Freedom: Utopian Moments in the Twentieth Century* (New Haven: Yale University Press, 2006); Samuel Moyn, *The Last Utopia: Human Rights in History* (New York: Columbia University Press, 2010).

21 Erik Olin Wright, *Envisioning Real Utopias* (London: Verso, 2009). See also Archon Fung and Erik Olin Wright, "Deepening Democracy: Innovations in Empowered Participatory Governance," *Politics and Society* 29, no. 4 (2001): 5–41, for a related project.

22 Immanuel Wallerstein, *Utopistics: Or, Historical Choices of the Twenty-First Century* (New York: New Press, 1998).

23 These terms come from David Estlund, "Utopophobia," *Philosophy and Public Affairs* 42, no. 1 (2014). The controversy was launched by Bernard Williams's posthumously published essay "Realism and Moralism in Political Theory," in *In the Beginning Was the Deed: Realism and Moralism in Political Argument*, ed. Geoffrey Hawthorn (Princeton: Princeton University Press, 2005).

INTRODUCTION XXXIII

24 Not even Rawls reads the *Social Contract* as a social model that could be simply approximated, though he devotes little time to the paradoxes in Rousseau's thought that consume deeper readers. After praising Rousseau as a stylist, Rawls observes that a powerful style may "add to or detract from the clarity of thought a writer hopes to convey." Rawls, *Lectures on the History of Political Philosophy*, ed. Samuel Freeman (Cambridge, Mass.: Belknap Press of Harvard University Press, 2007), "Lectures on Rousseau," 191.
25 Abensour in this volume, chapter 1; Jacoby, *Picture Imperfect: Utopian Thought for an Anti-Utopian Age* (New York: Columbia University Press, 2005).
26 Kateb, "Utopia and the Good Life," 454.
27 Seyla Benhabib, *Critique, Norm, and Utopia: A Study of the Foundations of Critical Theory* (New York: Columbia University Press, 1986). For a more recent, explicitly Blochian return to this theme, see Benhabib, *Dignity in Adversity: Human Rights in Troubled Times* (Cambridge, Mass.: Polity, 2011), chap. 10.
28 For example, Maeve Cooke, "Redeeming Redemption: the Utopian Dimension of Critical Social Theory," *Philosophy and Social Criticism* 30, no. 4 (2004): 413–429.
29 Ruth Levitas, "For Utopia: The (Limits of the) Utopian Function in Late Capitalist Society," *Critical Review of International Social and Political Philosophy* 3, no. 2 (2000): 25.
30 With this depiction, I mean to suggest that essentially the same antiutopianism that runs through liberal political thinking in the 1950s and 1960s, which I associated with Daniel Bell and Raymond Aron above, extends to such more recent figures as Tony Judt, François Furet, and their inheritors.
31 To be sure, this crude version of Marxism's relation to utopianism had already been problematized by the more serious students of their point of intersection, not only in French (as by Miguel Abensour in the essay translated as chapter 1 in this volume), but also in English. See especially Vincent Geoghegan, *Utopianism and Marxism* (London: Methuen, 1987; republished by Peter Lang in 2008).
32 Recent years have seen a marked uptick in politically radical books signaling their longing for the possibility of meaningful social-political alternatives with the term "utopia": for example, Benjamin Kunkel, *Utopia or Bust: A Guide to the Present Crisis* (London: Verso, 2014).
33 Benjamin Arditi, "Insurgencies Don't Have a Plan—They Are the Plan: Political Performatives and Vanishing Mediators in 2011," *JOMEC Journal: Journalism, Media and Cultural Studies* (June 2012).
34 The Eurocentrism of this selection is the result of painful choice rather than inadvertence or a dearth of material. Another book at least as long and as rich as this one could be composed out of recent meditations on utopia and utopianism from the postcolonial world, with a special emphasis on Latin America, South Asia, and Africa. The work of Bill Ashcroft and Ralph Pordzik provides valuable starting places here.
35 Abensour's and Saage's voluminous work on utopia is known in English through just a few translated essays: see Abensour, "To Think Utopia Otherwise," *Graduate Faculty Philosophy Journal* 21, no. 2 (1998): 251–279; Abensour, "Persistent Utopia," *Constellations* 15, no. 3 (2008): 406–421; Saage, "Utopia, Contractualism, and Human Rights,"

in *Thinking Utopia: Steps Into Other Worlds*, ed. Jörn Rüsen, Michael Fehr, and Thomas W. Rieger (New York: Berghahn, 2005), 53–66; Saage, "Socio-Political Utopianism and the Demands of the 21st Century," *Spaces of Utopia: An Electronic Journal* 2 (2006). Fernández Buey's has entirely escaped translation into English. The publication of Abensour's *Utopia from Thomas More to Water Benjamin*, trans. Raymond N. MacKenzie (Minneapolis: Univocal Publishing, 2017), written decades after the essay translated here and bookending its focus on the nineteenth century, taken together with the first chapter of this volume, now allows readers of English a kind of overview of Abensour's thinking on utopia.

36 See Miguel Abensour, *Democracy Against the State: Marx and the Machiavellian Moment*, trans. M. Blechman and M. Breaugh (Cambridge, Mass.: Polity, 2011).

37 Saage, *Vertragsdenken und Utopie: Studien zur politischen Theorie und zur Sozialphilosophie der frühen Neuzeit* (Frankfurt: Suhrkamp, 1989).

38 Saage, *Utopische Profile*, 4 vols. (Münster: LIT, 2001–2004).

39 There is reason to hope that this is about to change with the new translation of a collection of Fernández Buey's essays on Antonio Gramsci from 2001 for the "Historical Materialism" book series: Fernández Buey, *Reading Gramsci*, trans. Nicholas Gray (Leiden: Brill, 2015).

POLITICAL USES OF UTOPIA

I

REVIVING UTOPIA

1

THE HISTORY OF UTOPIA AND THE DESTINY OF ITS CRITIQUE

MIGUEL ABENSOUR

It will then become evident that the world has long dreamed of possessing something of which it has only to be conscious in order to possess it in reality. It will become evident that it is not a question of drawing a great mental dividing line between past and future, but of realizing *the thoughts of the past. Lastly, it will become evident that mankind is not beginning a* new *work, but is consciously carrying into effect its old work.*

KARL MARX, LETTER TO ARNOLD RUGE, SEPTEMBER 1843[1]

This text, written in late 1971 and early 1972, is only the first part of a larger whole. Its ambition is to propose another model of interpretation than that of the classical problematic, or that of Marx and Engels's critical operation with respect to utopias, which appears as a double salvage by transplant: rescuing the utopian orientation toward the future, and rescuing the inclination toward alterity. Marx's theory is not the place utopian energy comes to die in order to make way for science; it is where socialist-communist utopia grows and is transformed into critical communism. Marx is not the gravedigger of utopia; he recovered and took its energy to another level by projecting it into the real movement of communism, the ontological foundations of Marx's communism, which requires, moreover, avoiding the pitfall of a new orthodoxy in statu nascendi. To show that Marx effectively salvaged utopias by transplantation—Is *this not to attempt to save Marx once again? Is it not to affirm the uncriticized idea that Marx's theory necessarily comprehends "lower forms of socialism"? Yet Marx does not sum up the socialist tradition; the socialist tradition encompasses Marx. If we grant the hypothesis of "salvage by transplant," we must still examine to what extent this salvage is accompanied by a loss of utopian energy, by a repression, in the name of a new form of rationality, of creative possibilities for a utopian movement, a true decentering of classical reason. At this point in our reasoning, we can assume that the very desire to pose the question of the connections between critical communism and utopia is no stranger to the desire to then examine the critical work carried out by Marx and Engels with regard to utopias.*

There are statements that function as genuine institutions. Speaking about the Leninist break, Félix Guattari signaled the existence of such formations, which are frozen and definitively cut off from their enunciative situations. "Once they had been put in the position of dominant discourse, their subsequent function was to master any disruptive enunciation."[2]

The opposition of "scientific socialism" to "utopian socialism" is one of these fundamental signifiers marking a break and offering a master key. Even if there are certain harbingers that this myth of their radical separation is tending to be undermined, it still constitutes an effective mechanism of dismissal that weighs heavily on our historical period—all the more so because all conservative forces, beyond their political differences, are taking up little by little the same antiphony as the bourgeois writers of the 1840s: war on utopia! And these are not calls of an incantatory kind that will turn out to be right. For that which is often nothing more than a "brew and stew of the heart" [Hegel] cannot but consolidate the wall between the two camps and reinforce the division.

One very clearly finds in this opposition the characters developed by Guattari:

- The place of birth. The principled rupture with which the somewhat theatrical clash between Marx and Wilhelm Weitling in Brussels in

March 1846 was consumed. And Marx's closing cry: "Ignorance has never yet helped anyone!"

- The repetition ad infinitum within the different groups claiming to follow Marx. A "scientific" style was born and the label "utopian socialism" or "regression to utopianism," a terribly effective weapon, served to condemn the most diverse oppositional tendencies. But such is the irony of history that this condemnation of utopia was turned against Marx, notably by Eduard Bernstein and Georges Sorel.³
- The creation of a field of inertia whose effect was to suppress attempts to leave the field of the classical opposition.
- The institutionalization of the break. As evidence we need no more than the recent publication of a selection of Lenin's articles and speeches (Editions du Progrès, Moscow, 1960), under the title *Socialisme Utopique et Socialisme Scientifique* (Utopian socialism and scientific socialism).

It is only certain revolutionary interpretations that have attempted to reexamine the debate and question this fundamental signifier. It is necessary to reckon here with all the practical and theoretical forays of the new utopian spirit. But these forays, coming out of marginal currents, and for this reason silenced or deformed and moreover dispersed, affirmative rather than demonstrative in form, did not overcome the myth of radical separation. It is also necessary to reckon with the antiutopian tendency of our "one-dimensional" time. It is not homages to utopia, the majority of which are so many attempts to invest it with radicality, that diminish its intensity. It therefore appears necessary to reopen the debate. To do this, we will content ourselves here with taking into consideration three series of facts that tend to deconstruct the classical problematic:

- The misrecognition of the exact place and meaning of the critique of utopia in Marx and Engels. Also, after an initial examination, we should replace the *science/utopia* doublet with the distinction that establishes the critical matrix, namely, the opposition *radical revolution/partial revolution*.
- The implicit attribution to Marx and Engels of a monopoly over the critique of utopia, the effect of which is to obscure the gap between their discourse and the critical bourgeois discourses contemporary with it.

- An evolutionist and antidialectical conception of the history of utopia, whose movement ceases with the failure of the Revolution of 1848.

Our program will be to return to the Marxian critique of utopia its specific meaning and historical entry-point, that is, to give it back its revolutionary edge and, ultimately, to restore to utopia itself its true historical dimension.

MARX, ENGELS, AND THE QUESTION OF UTOPIA

Traditionally, judging the critique of utopia in Marx and Engels required only two major texts: section 3 of the third part of the *Communist Manifesto*—"Critico-Utopian Socialism and Communism"—and Engels's pamphlet *Socialism: Utopian and Scientific* (1880). Yet there are in the oeuvre of Marx and Engels a number of fragments, scattered remarks, and even whole texts pertaining to the critique of utopia. What relation can be established between these two types of texts?

Written in sufficiently distant periods, the *Communist Manifesto* and *Socialism: Utopian and Scientific* do not fail to arouse a temptation in the interpreter: the temptation to compare. The interpreter is, in effect, seduced and lulled into taking from the comparison of these two texts an invariant critique of utopias. The method then consists of appreciating how the theses, so removed from each other, are announced or begun in the works predating the earlier text, resumed or confirmed in intervening works, and definitively enshrined in the later text. Many have given in to it. The method—close to exegesis, producing repetitive, sterile commentary—represents, like all enterprises that aim more to affirm or confirm orthodoxy than to pursue theoretical work, the inconveniences of a Procrustean bed: in the first instance, the location and choice of texts considered pure and essential; in the second instance, the selection, reduction, and overwriting of other texts, on the basis of such casual norms, by necessarily eliminating the possibilities these texts carry and, in a more general fashion, eliminating every element, every lateral meaning that does not agree with these arbitrarily established norms.

This method, obviously, cheapens every dialectical point of view. It blithely abstracts from the theory's development, its progress as well as regression, and does not allow itself to consider the theses it examines as conditioned by the totality of the historical and social process of which they are the expression. Furthermore, we should ask ourselves about the nature of these texts. They are, in the nonpejorative sense of the term, works of propaganda. They convey the conclusions of a long theoretical voyage without retracing the itinerary, or giving away its complexity.[4] This consideration is important above all for the *Communist Manifesto*, which is situated at the culmination of the period 1843–1848, a privileged time when it comes to the relations between critical communism and utopia.

Rather than extracting a set of theses from the *Manifesto*, it seems more fruitful to re-create the theoretical path that led Marx and Engels to the *Manifesto*. A condensation and crystallization of extremely complex theoretical and political work, the *Communist Manifesto* cannot be the object of a naïve reading. It is not so much a matter of finding in it theses concerning socialist and communist literature as of "deploying" or unfolding them, and thereby unveiling their presuppositions and repercussions. Marx himself recommended recourse to this method in *Herr Vogt* (London, 1860)—a foundational text indeed. In it Marx recognizes, first of all, the complexity of the critique of utopia and, consequently that the chapter of the *Communist Manifesto* devoted to it can only deliver the conclusions of a long and difficult theoretical labor. He also indicates what detours to make, which path to take through his theoretical works, in particular *Poverty of Philosophy*, and what principles to rely on when reading them—in this case, taking into consideration problems that at first glance appear to be unrelated to the critique of utopias. Finally, Marx insists on the twofold movement of this critique: a refusal to impose a new utopian system, but also an intervention into the knowledge of causes in the process of historical change at work in society:

> Techow thus "imagines" that I have written a "Proletarian Catechism." He means a *Manifesto* which criticizes and, if he likes, "ridicules" socialist and critical utopianism of every kind. Only, this "ridiculing" was not such a simple matter as Techow "imagines," but required a fair amount of work, as he could see from my book against Proudhon, *Misère de la*

philosophie [1847]. Techow further "imagines" that I have "tailored" a "*system*," whereas, on the contrary, even in the *Manifesto*, which was intended directly for workers, I rejected systems of *every* kind and in their place I insisted on "a critical insight into the conditions, the line of march and the ultimate general results of the real movement of society." Such an "insight" cannot be blindly repeated, nor can it be "tailored" like a cartridge pouch.[5]

One should, therefore, submit the *Communist Manifesto* and Engels's short work to a twofold reading. This twofold reading consists of two distinct approaches: on the one hand, reinserting these two texts, political writings in popular form, into the constellation of texts that deal explicitly with the critique of utopia; on the other hand, systematically relating the Marxian critique of utopia to the whole of Marx's theory and its underlying point of view, that of communism. What remains of the classical opposition between "utopian socialism" and "scientific socialism" after this superimposition of these different types of texts?

Remaining within the principal period for the problem that concerns us, we can and should make a detour through texts other than *Poverty of Philosophy*. To cite the main ones:

- "Critique of Hegel's Philosophy of Right," "On The Jewish Question," "A Contribution to the Critique of Hegel's Philosophy of Right: Introduction," the program-letter to Ruge (September 1843), and Engels's very important article from the Owenist periodical *The New Moral World*, "Progress of Social Reform on the Continent" (October–November 1843);
- in the *1844 Manuscripts*, the third manuscript: "Private Property and Communism," "Various Stages of Development of Communist Views," "Crude, Equalitarian Communism and Communism as Socialism Coinciding with Humaneness";
- "Reading Notes" (1844);
- "Critical Marginal Notes on 'The King of Prussia and Social Reform. By a Prussian'" (1844);
- *The Holy Family*, above all chapter 8 (1845);
- *The German Ideology* (1845–1846);
- "Circular Against Kriege" (1846);

- Engels's article "The True Socialists" (1847);
- "Moralizing Criticism and Critical Morality" (1847);
- *The Principles of Communism* by Engels (1847);
- numerous articles in the *Neue Rheinische Zeitung* (1848–1849).

Reading this collection of texts, it becomes apparent that, contrary to what Techow and many interpreters after him (epigones or not) had imagined, the critical problematic of utopias is not simple from any point of view—neither in its genesis, nor in its presuppositions, nor in its effects.

The work required for this critique is nothing other than the production, in the course and on the occasion of various theoretical and political struggles, of a new theory of social revolution. The critique of utopias cannot be dissociated from the constitution of critical communism. The latter was born from, among other things, the critical "treatment" to which Marx and Engels submitted socialist-communist utopias. We must not let ourselves be dominated by the dramatic Marx–Weitling confrontation. Too often, interpreters represent Marx, critic of utopia, as a kind of Jupiter hurling thunderbolts in the name of "science" upon the cohort of utopian dreamers—beautiful souls, a little frail, making sentimental and vague pronouncements about humanity and the communion of beings. We should break with the naïve image of mighty Marx contra the almost feminine utopian Weitling. This break is all the more imperative if the critical definition of utopia in the form it took from 1842 onward is not seen as the fruit of sudden illumination, flashed one night by Marx's "demon" in his "frying pan." The product of a long theoretical and political march and, among other things, of the discovery of French and English socialist writings, contemporary with the progressive sharpening of a new revolutionary praxis, the critique of utopia is situated at the culmination of a real theoretical revolution—the production of a theory of history. Also, far from being the critique of a thinker completely external to the object of his reflection, it appears more as the critique of a certain number of projects that Marx subscribed to with his whole being, or that, at a given moment, had exerted over him a real seductive power. In 1846 Marx had broken with Weitling, but shortly before, Weitling's "massive" communism, this "*titanic* and brilliant literary debut of the German workers," contributed to the elaboration of critical communism.[6] It is a matter, then, of a critique that is the same time internal and external, whose meaning can only be constituted in relation to the overall development of the one presenting it. The critique of utopias, real critique, is neither an auxiliary nor a peripheral problem. True "*Bildung*," it is at the heart of Marx's theory. To take its exact measure necessarily implies a general interpretation of the theory.

For whoever agrees to retrace with Marx and Engels the path toward truth—and the path toward truth is as much a part of the truth as is its result—the result appears in a new light, as living truth, as it were. Stripped of its cold generality, enriched by multiple detours and new determinations, the result then takes up the totality of the theory, no longer allowing itself to be manipulated by political opportunity. It offers much stronger resistance to any attempt to turn science into a new hypostasis against the real movement's development.

The disappearance of the original philosophical research that helped the development of the critique of utopias makes retracing this path all the more important. There remains only the science/utopia signifying machine. The referent and even the categories of the critique have undergone a transformation, followed by a modification of content. The most extreme form of this was the reduction of a theoretical critique to an organizational viewpoint.

Let us add that the critique assumed an extensive knowledge of the great utopians. Now, the degradation of this real theoretical critique to a ritualistic statement, in a language of exclusion in the hands of political machines, had the effect of making this knowledge practically impossible. The critique of utopias, therefore, quickly became incomprehensible. Even beyond deliberate political manipulation, classical Marxists were content, under the high patronage of science, to parrot this critique without inquiring into its real range and about what could constitute a critique that is "up to" the object criticized. Marx's critique of Hegel long suffered the same fate. In 1870, the German social-democratic leader Wilhelm Liebknecht received from Marx and Engels a reprimand for having dared to treat Hegel like "a dead dog." The contemporary critique of utopias is to the great utopias roughly what W. Liebknecht was to Hegel: a pug at the foot of a mountain. We can hope that the renewal of utopian studies can lead to a new examination of the connections between Marx and socialist-communist utopia, just as the renewal of Hegelian studies since the beginning of the [twentieth] century has brought about a new reconsideration of Marx's relations to Hegel's system.

One of the first questions raised by this reading is no more and no less than the doubt cast upon the very existence of the fundamental signifier: the utopia/science antinomy. In the course of the theory's development, the opposition is never stated as such. In *The Holy Family*, Marx uses the qualification "scientific" on two occasions.

The first time, he applies it to Proudhon's *What Is Property?*: "Not only does Proudhon write in the interest of the proletarians, he is himself a proletarian, an *ouvrier*. His work is a scientific manifesto of the French proletariat and therefore has quite a different historical significance from that of the literary botch-work of any Critical Critic."[7]

This laudatory qualification does not seem determined by an exclusively epistemological point of view. In this area, Marx's judgment is much more nuanced, already aware of the limits of Proudhonian critique. As Marx demonstrates, Proudhon's work, the first critique of a science, is necessarily imprisoned in certain presuppositions about the science it combats. Proudhon criticizes political economy from the point of view of political economy and law from the point of view of law. In submitting the hypothesis about the basis of political economy—private property—to a critical examination, Proudhon revolutionized political economy, made a "great scientific advance," and made possible "a real science of political economy." But one cannot avoid the fact that Proudhon's critique, by not considering wages, commerce, value, and so on as different forms of private property, remains inferior to Engels's *Outlines of a Critique of National Economy* (1844). "Proudhon's treatise will therefore be scientifically superseded by a criticism of *political economy*, including Proudhon's conception."[8]

"Scientific," then, seems certainly to refer to the critical examination to which Proudhon submitted the hypothesis of the basis of political economy, but even more so to the adequacy of his point of view to that of the proletariat. *What Is Property?* is the scientific manifesto of the French proletariat as much as it is an expression of a real historical interest—the interest of the masses pushing toward a crisis, as opposed to an abstract and fabricated interest like that of critique. And in 1846, in the letter to Annenkov concerning Proudhon, Marx has recourse to the same use of the qualifier "scientific." The term again designates the adequacy of theoretical production to the viewpoint of a class destined to play an important role in the self-critical movement of modern society. "Mr. Proudhon has the merit of being the scientific exponent of the French petty bourgeoisie, which is a real merit since the petty bourgeoisie will be an integral part of all the impending social revolutions."[9]

The second time, Marx applies the qualification to French materialist communists. These latter have the merit, in Marx's eyes, of taking up materialist theory on a higher level of evolution and of establishing links between French materialism and communism. "The more scientific French Communists, Dézamy, Gay and others, developed [like Owen–M. A.] the teaching of materialism as the teaching of real humanism and the logical basis of communism."[10] Cabet, on the contrary, despite attacks by Fourier against the traditional moral systems of the passions, persisted in building Icaria on the basis of self-sacrifice. Dézamy had spiritedly attacked this persistence.[11] Founding his communist system on a theory of needs, he wrote an "anti-Cabet" to expose the contradictions and weaknesses of Cabet the theorist.

One encounters, it is true, the expression "scientific socialism" in Engels's hand, in a chapter of *The German Ideology*. But it is not set in opposition to either utopia or utopian socialism. The formulation is all the more ambiguous for having been borrowed from his adversary Grün.[12]

If we limit ourselves, then, to the statements of Marx and Engels, the opposition moves to another terrain. The critical matrix of utopia is both uncovered and formulated as early as 1843, in a foundational text. The critical point of view is defined in the very gesture of rejecting democratic utopia, *political* utopia—the bourgeois form of emancipation. Marx is through with the utopia of the bourgeoisie as a revolutionary class—in short, with the project of the modern state. At the same time, he articulates the cardinal distinction between partial and total revolution. Utopia is on the side of partial revolution, human emancipation on the side of radical revolution: "It is not the *radical* revolution, not the *general human* emancipation which is a utopian dream for Germany, but rather the partial, the *merely* political revolution, the revolution which leaves the pillars of the house standing."[13]

The axis drawn here is fundamental to the critique of utopias. The above distinction will be applied to different objects and enriched by multiple contents. It constitutes one of the invariants of radical theory. Here, not in the utopia/science couple, is the site of the original break. Science can also be on the side of partial revolution—first and foremost, the science of the utopians, says Marx. Social science ruins, kills utopia. Rather than painting utopia as a countertype of science, Marx denounces scientificity as utopia's congenital defect. Hence the opposition between two types of science, doctrinaire science and revolutionary science. Two passages are crucial in this respect. From *Poverty of Philosophy*:

> Just as the *economists* are the scientific representatives of the bourgeois class, so the *Socialists* and *Communists* are the theoreticians of the proletarian class. So long as the proletariat is not yet sufficiently developed to constitute itself as a class, and consequently so long as the struggle itself of the proletariat with the bourgeoisie has not yet assumed a political character, and the productive forces are not yet sufficiently developed in the bosom of the bourgeoisie itself to enable us to catch a glimpse of the material conditions necessary for the emancipation of the proletariat and for the formation of a new society, these theoreticians are merely utopians who, to meet the wants of the oppressed classes, improvise systems and go in search of a regenerating science. But in the measure that history moves forward, and with it the struggle of the proletariat assumes clearer outlines, they no longer need to seek science in their minds; they have only to take note of what is happening before their eyes and to become its mouthpiece. So long as they look for science and merely make systems, so long as they are at the beginning of the struggle, they see in poverty nothing but poverty, without seeing in it the revolutionary, subversive side, which will overthrow the old society. From this moment, science, which is a product of the historical movement, has associated itself consciously with it, has ceased to be doctrinaire and has become revolutionary.[14]

And, again à propos of Proudhon, from an article in the *New Rhenish Gazette* dated August 5, 1848:

> Mr. Proudhon then enters upon the specification of his tax system and he becomes once again "scientific." This "science" which has always been Proudhon's weakness becomes his strength in this narrow-minded

> Chamber by giving him the boldness to combat with his pure, genuine "science" the defiled financial science of M. Thiers. . . . What we were attacking in Mr. Proudhon's theory was the "utopian science" by which he wanted to settle the antagonism between capital and labour, between proletariat and bourgeoisie. We shall come back to this point. His whole system of banking and his entire exchange of products is nothing but a petty-bourgeois illusion.[15]

It is therefore not the failing of a scientific model but the lack of a theory of history—a lack that it will be necessary to nuance—that makes for the "weakness" of other forms of socialism or communism. We only know one science: the science of history, affirm the authors of *The German Ideology*. It is, then, with good reason that Guy Debord emphasizes the scientificity of utopian currents of socialism in order to criticize their refusal of history.[16]

The theory of history is the bridge thrown by Marx and Engels between critico-utopian communism and critical communism.[17] One is not, for all that, authorized to deduce from it that critical communism is the most accurate name for their theory, since they burned the bridge after crossing it. It is, then, a matter of returning to the exact distinction made by Marx and Engels on different occasions ("The True Socialists," "Moralizing Criticism and Critical Morality," the *Communist Manifesto*, "Revelations Concerning the Communist Trial in Cologne," "History of the Communist League"), namely, the distinction between critico-utopian communism and critical communism. The term "critical communism" is, to be sure, obscure and ill suited for discourse in the public forum. But we know only too well that if we begin by giving up words we will end by giving up things. Let us abandon to understanding and to the servants of tradition the *science/utopia* signifying machine. It suits perfectly those who are not afraid of solidified thoughts. Because our time lacks the cult of critique, "critical communism," by virtue of its very esotericism, is all the more resistant to processes of petrifaction and institutionalization. We have known since Hegel what is necessary: never, ever make peace with dogma.

One text, it is true, clearly articulates the opposition between utopia and science. The author is not Marx but Auguste Comte, at the time of a symptomatic break with the Saint-Simonians in 1832: "Instead of long and difficult preliminary studies of all the fundamental branches of natural philosophy which determines absolutely my manner of proceeding in social science; instead of toilsome meditations and profound searches of the laws of political phenomena it requires, it is much simpler and quicker to give oneself up to vague utopias in which no scientific condition intervenes to halt the growth of an unchained imagination."[18] Nothing similar to this declaration from the founder of positivism will be found in Marx. Suffice it to say here that, as far science is concerned, still more than other things, original philosophical research productive of the critique of utopias has disappeared. For anyone wanting to take it up again, it will seem that the fundamental signifier *utopian socialism/scientific socialism* rests on a historical and theoretical confusion that, at its limits, verges on mystification.

BOURGEOIS CRITIQUE AND ITS INVERSION BY RADICAL CRITIQUE

Between the critique of utopia from the viewpoint of the dominant class, or the Right critique, and the Left critique, founded upon knowledge, there is a complete break. A banality, some will say. Perhaps, but banality in whose eyes? For Marx, Engels, Blanqui, or any other nineteenth-century revolutionary, no doubt, but does the same go for our contemporaries? Also, at the risk of seeming trivial, it would be well worth insisting on this basic banality.

This reminder is all the more pressing because, reading the partisans of the classical thesis, it would seem that Marx and Engels had in their day a monopoly on the critique of utopia. From a historical point of view, such an affirmation is completely inaccurate: they had neither a monopoly nor—and this is a still more important point—the initiative. In the history of social utopias, the nineteenth century is distinguished by a true utopian explosion, but also by the production of a plural, complex discourse on utopia, issuing as much from the defenders of the existing order as from their adversaries—an often dull discourse where, behind the platitudes of common sense and reminders of eternal truths, one can read bourgeois fears, but a discourse nonetheless at times sparkling, which knows and speaks the power of "allegorical arms" to rally the oppressed to fight for the city of the future. This discourse is ignored by interpreters. The fame of Marx and Engels's critique should not obscure its existence. This discourse does not cease to pose a fundamental question: What is the position of Marx's critique in the ideological field of its time? What are the orientation and specific connotation of the concept of utopia in Marx and Engels's text? What are its positional properties, its type of participation or nonparticipation in the contemporary cultural field? In brief, does Marx participate in the cultural unconscious of his age—or, better still, does his critique break with what is explicit and, even more, with the unthought of this discourse?

An initial general answer is possible. Historically, the concept of utopia underwent, in effect, a radical inversion. The concept originally came from reactionary critique—and Blanqui responds to all the public prosecutors of the world who denounce the "knights of the impossible" and "their guilty utopias": "There are no utopians, in the extreme sense of the word."[19] The concept was then taken up and diverted from its original usage by Left critique. The same Blanqui repeatedly admits his reticence with regard to utopias. What happened between the two assertions? This is the fundamental problem.

Now, either one denies, or ignores, or pretends to ignore this inversion completely or else—even when warned of its existence—one prevents it from being brought out in all its scope and playing out all its effects. In this latter, more frequent case, the ideological imprecision of the concept of utopia that we are speaking of leads one to enter the debate on a highly equivocal footing, even to contaminate it and introduce, at the heart of a critique that calls itself "leftist," arguments that at their extreme would not be disavowed by a conservative critique.

At this level, we have a very impure mixture, a real knot of ambiguities—not fortuitous but resulting from a certain history and a certain political practice—that needs to be cut.

What is at issue here is the concept of utopia. To determine its content, we should always pose a double question: Who is speaking, and to whom? But this preliminary precaution will not suffice; to resolve the concept's ambiguities, it is important to describe its genesis in the course of the nineteenth century, to trace its principal orientations, and to carefully measure the stakes and field of the debate. To this end, let us look back to

Karl Mannheim, even if the criterion he proposes for distinguishing between ideology and utopia leaves a lot to be desired. According to this interpreter, social classes that represent the social and cultural order will experience as reality the structure of relations of which they are the bearers, whereas groups that want to reverse the present order will orient themselves toward the first tremors of the new social order to which they aspire. It follows that the representatives of a given order designate as utopian all the conceptions of existence that, from their point of view, are in principle unrealizable. And, as Mannheim insists: "The very way in which a concept is defined and the nuance in which it is employed already embody to a certain degree a prejudgment concerning the outcome of the chain of ideas built upon it."[20] The defenders of the existing order will thus have a natural propensity to blur the frontiers between absolute and relative impossibility, or more precisely, between utopias that aim, for example, to negate intangible physical laws and those whose project is the transformation of a given historical formation. Are not effacing the distinction between nature and history and moving the historical over to the side of nature precisely what distinguish conservative thought? There is no better procedure for creating a map of human impossibilities. It can thus be claimed that it is as utopian to desire perpetual spring as it is to want to abolish private property. Conversely, an opponent of the existing order will propose a concept all the narrower and more precise to ensure that the two types of impossibility are not confused. Mannheim chose to draw a narrow concept. Herbert Marcuse, for example, takes care to give a very restrictive definition of utopia: "The project of a social transformation, however, can also be considered unfeasible because it contradicts certain scientifically established laws, biological laws, physical laws; for example, such projects as the age-old idea of eternal youth or the idea of a return to an alleged Golden Age. I believe that we can now speak of utopia only in this latter sense, namely when a project for social change contradicts real laws of nature. Only such a project is utopian in the strict sense, that is, beyond history—but even this 'ahistoricity' has a historical limit."[21]

It is, thus, between these two uses or senses, the broad and the narrow, that the concept developed and took shape in the nineteenth century. It should be noted, moreover, that the liberal critique at the origin of the concept, to the extent to which it attempts to sketch a "sociology of utopia" and searches for the phenomenon's historical origins, started with a relatively precise concept, even if for reasons of ideological struggle and in view of the urgency of some problems it rapidly ended up with a diffuse notion that could not possibly be confused with that of communism, considered as the real enemy, or lend itself to the equation *utopia is communism, communism is utopia*. If, however, we retained only the narrowness or laxity of the definition, we would fail to discern the abyss that separates the liberal-conservative critique from radical critique. At this level, should we not enter into the balance sheet the oppositional pairs and the entirety of the notional field? In relation to what other notion is utopia defined? What type of relation is involved: a relation of contradiction, even of exclusion, or, rather, of differentiation or transcendence? In short, the knot of ambiguities will only be cut if one succeeds in bringing out and reformulating as neatly as possible the implicit problematic, or the systems of questions of the different discourses about utopia.

In the years 1830 to 1848, one can observe in France the constitution of what Michel Foucault called a history of limits precisely in the form of a critique of utopia written very often from a "pathological" perspective and from the point of view of the existing order. From the elder Blanqui (Adolphe) to Adolphe Thiers, there is a transition from a liberal critique to an openly counterrevolutionary one. The bourgeoisie and its publicists, after having admitted, for the first time, dialogue or confrontation—in the salons of the 1830s it was still good form to speak of utopia and one could support it without renouncing the liberal credo that was so often detrimental to it; a little utopia, provided that it was concrete or realistic, could be useful—soon after threw utopia out on the street among the barbarians and even into psychiatric asylums, and showed those who would be tempted to take utopias seriously that the bourgeoisie also had a solution to the social question, namely, grapeshot. In the course of the Revolution of 1848, the division is taken to a point of no return and produces the totally reified opposition between reality and utopia. Its consequence is utopia's expulsion from bourgeois society. Utopia, in all its forms, becomes that over which the dominant class exercises its censorship. It will not be surprising that this often obscure discourse had been forgotten. Characteristic of this kind of history is the necessary forgetting, the deepest possible burial of the memory of one class. It is also necessary to write the history of this division, which cuts through others, and through which the bourgeoisie gains its positivity, its homogeneity, and designates in the same move the establishment and the rejection of what is heterogeneous. It is equally a period of elaboration for positivist philosophy and the official rule of eclecticism.

It will appear, then, that, in bringing together under the same category the elder Blanqui, Reybaud, or Sudre and the classical utopian triad (Saint-Simon, Fourier, Owen), Marx and Engels endowed the concept of utopia with a radically different content and function. Here the concept in question is not only narrow, restrictive; it is different by virtue of the very place of its formulation. One can now submit as the first preliminary and as the condition of a rigorous reading, free of all ambiguity, that the critiques of Auguste Comte or Marx and Engels articulate not the point of view of reality, or that of adaptation to the real, but the point of view of the subversion of existing reality, of the revolution that is to disrupt all social spheres.

It follows that the distinction marked by revolutionary theory between itself and utopia is not rooted in the same terrain as the break established by bourgeois society between its own positivity and any social theory or practice it designates as utopian. In the latter case, we are dealing with a censorship of the heterogeneous, a history of limits, while in the hypothesis of revolutionary critique, it is a matter of a history of differential relations, a history of the movement's phases and the forms of the social movement into which utopia can enter as a moment and where even it can play a role as a distinct, but not fundamentally antagonistic, social or political practice. Confusing these two types of criticism would be as aberrant as confusing Marx and Engels's critique of philosophy with the positivist critique of philosophy, without seeing that, in the case of Auguste Comte, it was a matter of abdicating the critical pretensions of philosophy in view of consolidating the existing order, whereas conversely, for Marx and Engels, surpassing philosophy signified something wholly different from casting it aside and implied the emergence of a revolutionary theory whose mission was to surpass philosophy by realizing it, that is, effecting the transcendence and transformation of the whole of existing social reality.

When it comes to the critique of utopia, then, revolutionary theory, in relation to an earlier discourse of the dominant class, brought about the recovery of a concept that it thereby transformed and whose effects it brought into play within a problematic to which, when this critique first appeared, it was radically heterogeneous. It remains to develop a theory of this recovery and its consequences. The terrain and terms of the debate are different: we no longer confront, as, for example, in the later Blanqui, bourgeois society, political economy, and utopia. Indeed, for him the mission of utopia was to humanize political economy, to correct its unilaterality, and thus to assure the progressive evolution of bourgeois society toward the conciliation of contradictions. History would advance by a process of making the utopias of yesterday banal. Stressing this recovery and this inversion of the concept lays bare a new field of questions. One faces the problem of the relationship between the critique of political economy and the positive intentionality peculiar to socialist-communist utopia, between radical revolution and utopia. One tries to define the specificity of utopia as experimental group practice, or else as the imaginary projection of a future society and what distinguishes it in this respect from foresight, in short, the relations between critical communism and utopia. From such a perspective, utopia no longer appears as the outside of revolutionary theory, and it is no longer possible to maintain that critical communism signifies the end of utopia pure and simple.

If there was a great division between bourgeois society and utopias between 1845 and 1848, defining the difference between critical communism and utopia correctly requires us to posit at the outset that Marx and Engels's theory is situated on the same side of the barrier as utopia, outside bourgeois positivity, and that it was only from this side that their confrontation could originate. If Marx and Engels's critique exposed the "weaknesses" of utopias, it implicitly took their strengths as given.[22] But, the whole of Marxist critique, not alert to this division, had in reality failed to specify the camp in which Marx's critique was situated. As for the social-democratic theoreticians who bear a major responsibility for deforming or concealing the problem, not having observed this reversal, this division, or determined from which side of the barrier, or rather in which camp, the confrontation arose, they took from it only the "weaknesses" of the utopians, incapable of perceiving their strengths. Unless they have simply changed sides.

For Marx and Engels, it was a matter not of sorting through utopias with a view to recuperating valid socialist contents, but of articulating differently the "positive formulas about the future society" with a view to anticipating the morphology of communism.

When Marx and Engels criticize utopia, they perform a virtual inversion of conservative critique. We should specify the mechanism of the Marxian critique of utopias and the original movement of its refutation. There is an indissoluble link between the critique of utopias and the anticipation of communism—or, in other words, communism is that which operates the critique of utopias. A great many texts by Marx and Engels are built on the rhythm of this link. To those who refuse to violate Marx's theory, it appears as a complex movement in two closely articulated steps: the critique of a given utopia and the positive affirmation of communism. The general orientation of the utopia critique is determined by the point of view of its author. It is from the perspective of communism, in which he perceives the real shift in the ground of modern society, that Marx criticizes utopias. The morphological anticipation of communism is what gives substance to the critical matrix defined in 1843 in the introduction to the "Contribution to a Critique of Hegel's Philosophy of Right." From the start, Marx criticizes utopia from a revolutionary point of view: in his eyes, every partial project that attacks only the secondary determinations of a phenomenon and thereby leaves be its essence merits the qualification *utopian*. What for Marx distinguishes utopia is not the "too much," the excess, the extremism, but much more the "not enough"—or, to escape the dangers of this quantitative formulation, what is proper to utopia is not its heterogeneity relative to the existing order but, on the contrary, its homogeneity. Marx designates as utopian every politico-social project whose sin is its lack of radicality and that remains "*volens nolens*" inside the limits of the existing order even as it claims to transform it. The utopian project, far from aiming for a total upheaval of society, "leaves the pillars of the house standing": it achieves only a partial revolution and does not attack the foundations of bourgeois society. More precisely, according to Marx, one can consider as utopian the will to transform or do away with only the phenomenal forms of capitalism by leaving intact the essence of capital. Whether it is a speculative hypothesis or an experiment whose outcome is predictable, the essence of capital, through the play of its internal determinations, continues to produce the same effects and reproduce under the noses of armchair reformers or druggists of the social question the very phenomena they had claimed to eliminate. This form of critique, which unmasks the false starting points, is a constant in Marx. From there, the cardinal distinction, apparently and scandalously ignored by most interpreters, is between utopias that are inventive, creative, in many respects revolutionary, and those that are repetitive, reproductive of bourgeois society. This dividing line indicates that the critique's very structure, its significance, and the relation of revolutionary theory to utopia vary radically, according to whether one considers a utopia that is only the shadow cast by existing society or, conversely, a utopia that offers the imaginative expression of a new world.

ON THE HISTORY OF UTOPIA

Furthermore, the myth of the radical separation [of scientific from utopian socialism] is closely dependent on a set of theses on the history of utopia in the nineteenth century. Its main argument is that the failure of the Revolution of 1848 marks the end of utopia.

Thus, after having undergone a mutation in the second half of the eighteenth century that would allow it to rejoin history at the beginning of the nineteenth, utopia again detached itself from history, this time forever. Utopia relayed by science would once more become a fantasy of compensation; in short, it would lose itself in the byways of literature and derision. It would no longer manifest itself except as a charming and fanciful traveling companion of the henceforth mature workers' movement.[23]

The case seems settled. But in reality this thesis poses more problems than it claims to solve; or rather, it masks and dissimulates the true problems. Without submitting it to exhaustive criticism, we have the right to interrogate it:

- How to explain this ephemeral reign of utopia, this encounter so brief it appears fortuitous, and then this irremediable divorce? Was this reign as ephemeral, and this divorce as irremediable, as they are described?
- How can one seriously claim to retrace a history of utopia in the nineteenth century while abstracting from the Paris Commune and without attempting to elucidate the very complex links between the latter and utopia, and utopia's role in the formation of the communalist movement?

Reductive historians would be quite happy if utopia, the old mole, continued digging its tunnels. From 1848 to 1871, the work of utopia was no less real for being underground. One saw it clearly at the reopening of public gatherings in 1868: "The social question finds itself posed all over again," said Lefrançais. Work of utopia and on utopia, just like the work of revolution and work on the revolution. Many groups and isolated thinkers meditated on the failure of 1848 and, among other things, on the responsibility with which utopia was saddled. They reexamined the corpus of socialist-communist utopias and the whole of the practical movement since 1789. They submitted the one and then the other to the work of criticism and transformation. The fruits of this were not negligible: the rehabilitation of Hebertism, the confrontation between socialism and communism, and revolutionary Fourierism, whose resurgence could be seen in the Commune minority. From various sides Fourier was torn away from his orthodox disciples and phalansterist utopia raised to a higher level. Born in part of certain critiques carried out by Proudhon, revolutionary Fourierism helped combat Proudhonian reformism. From this extraordinary ferment emerged two remarkable developments: Joseph Déjacque arrived at an insurrectional conception of utopia, Blanqui at a utopian conception of insurrection. The field of combat was the city as the theater of class struggle. The Paris Commune was the extraordinary encounter of the historical movement with the separatist tendencies of utopia. Over seventy-two days, the arcades of the capital of the nineteenth century merged with the galleries of the phalanstery,[24] a conjunction of the island complex with that of the sacred city. If utopia has always been the search for an insular utopia, for a parenthetical place, tentatively cut off from the rest of the world, where it can take root here and now before its metamorphosis into an exemplary terminal, can one dream of a more beautiful place for it? The streets, squares, and hills of Paris—place of revolutionary revelation, the human Jerusalem (Victor Hugo, *Paris, 1867*)—could finally exert their passional attraction. In *The Fatherland in Danger*, Blanqui's cold irony took note of this utopian situation.[25]

The Paris Commune constitutes a turntable in the history of the utopian movement. Played backward, it casts vivid light on the slow work of doctrinal germination that, in secrecy or in exile, paved the way for the spring of 1871. Déjacque's *The Revolutionary Question* (1854) appeared as the surprising premonition of the Communards' insurrectional practice.

Played forward, the Commune, a "romantic revolutionary" activity, stands out as a beacon for anyone who saw in it, instead of the signs of revolutionary primitivism, the announcement of a positive experiment harboring infinite and still unsuspected possibilities for the future. Critical of utopia, the Commune realized and raised to a higher level the great utopians' positive intentionality. In its will to shatter historical continuity, it inaugurated a new utopian practice. Its utopian charge was not yet completely spent: it went on to haunt all subsequent revolutions.

How can such a historical pattern account for the resurgence of utopia at the end of the nineteenth century—a resurgence, it is true, that was most often emancipatory in inspiration, but no stranger to the social movement as a whole? This classical presentation of the history of utopia should be abandoned, all the less regretfully since it could only have been elaborated under the influence of hidden, unexamined presuppositions. Prima facie, this pattern is ripe for criticism because it leaves out a number of utopian phenomena that suffice to show, contrary to the pronounced verdict, that utopia did not die in 1848, but continued to exist in other forms. And, by the same token, the classical thesis did not allow those who accepted it to ask the fundamental question about the mutation of social utopia after 1848, trace the moment or moments where this mutation and the changes of function took place, and analyze the new form or forms that arose. What is more, this presentation of the story, appearances notwithstanding, is profoundly antihistorical; it rests, contrary to the history it claims to recount, on the distinction between the true and the false.

This thesis is founded on two presuppositions.

In the first place, such an interpretation of the history of utopia is the product of an opposition between *precocity* and *maturity*, which itself depends on a theory of progress that is hardly dialectical. Utopia corresponds to a social movement that is still uncertain, premature, and its progressive disappearance corresponds to the growing maturity of this movement. But is the too-often received concept of maturity a pure one? And does not its application in social history result in a singular blindness to the revolutionary character of social explosions considered premature, in the name of a historical practice authorized only by having come later? The present rehabilitation of Luddism should put us on guard and remind us of the dialectic of history. How did so-called primitive rebels sketch out radically new forms of combat destined to be understood and reactivated by later generations?[26] Between them and us come the victors. "The only historian capable of fanning the spark of hope in the past is the one who is firmly convinced that *even the dead will not be safe from the enemy if he is victorious. And this enemy has never ceased to be victorious.*"[27] Having rejected this inversely proportional relation between utopia and maturity, perhaps we can admit that the utopian thought of Robert Owen, despite its precocity, is more explosive by far than that of the theoretician of "scientific socialism," Karl Kautsky?

The second presupposition is theoretical. It takes as self-evident truth—since it is perilous to put it into question and since it engages and contains correlative interpretations—that Marxism signifies the end of utopia. This almost universally accepted proposition cannot take for granted quasi-general approval to impose its validity. And this, even less than the parallel dogma, likewise unanimously accepted, that Marxism signifies the end of philosophy, has rightly been denounced—a liberating denunciation whose effect was the resurgence of problems buried for too long.

Yet, those who reject the thesis that the failure of the Revolution of 1848 marked the end of utopia, and who discern its continuation and enrichment beyond 1848, can make out three major forms, considered not as the elements of a formal sociological classification, but as "moments" of a conceptual genesis—as dialectical forms whose very texture bears their relation to the Revolution qua statement and practical movement, their relation, in short, to social struggles that rend the social totality wherever they emerge.[28] It is essentially a matter of the interpreter restoring to utopia as such its true historical dimension, of disturbing things by blurring "ossified" and rigid frontiers. It is a matter of helping raise from oblivion the "infancy" of socialism and what its mature (too-mature) theoreticians have called the "infantile maladies of communism." These are three great moments, or three great utopian machineries, to borrow Walter Benjamin's expression, if one considers the link that each of them makes with the desire of the masses:

- utopian socialism;
- neoutopianism;
- the new utopian spirit.

WHAT IS UTOPIAN SOCIALISM?

Utopian socialism, "in many regards revolutionary," as even Marx and Engels acknowledged, corresponds to what Pierre Leroux, a reliable guide in this matter, calls the "Dawn of Socialism" and is incarnated by the three great emancipators: Saint-Simon, Fourier, and Owen.[29] The three great utopians, starting from an absolute break, tried to enfranchise humanity by presenting it with utopian images of a new world and by imparting to it the utopian instinct to create radically different social relations, destined to open a new path for the human species. The appearance of the great utopians produced a complete shift in utopian orientation, a new impetus.

We know only too well the "weaknesses" of this "dawn," shaped more or less into the school of "scientific socialism" as it was understood by their epigones. Let us interrogate, rather, what makes for its specificity and its force. Against those who might try to pull utopia over to the side of revolt—those who posit a break between revolt and revolution and in whose eyes utopia is invested above all in private relationships, friendship, and sexuality in short aim more at transforming human relations in the direction of transparency than at reorganizing society as a whole— let us remember the unitary and totalizing intention of utopia's extraordinary flourishing at the start of the nineteenth century. On the side of the utopians, Constantin Pecqueur insisted on this totalizing vocation of "social economy" issuing from the great stream of utopian renewal in the 1830s.[30] In the name of the liberal critique of utopia, Reybaud discerned in this tendency toward generalization the "particular stamp" of this novel category of social doctrine:

> [Never was synthesis made more comprehensive, generalization more vast. Often it even leaves] our spheres to launch itself into endless expanses and ascend via cosmogony to divination. Therein lies the distinctive character of these bold conceptions: they pretend to universal science, and do not accept any received ideas, neither in life, nor outside of it.... Nothing could escape contact with them. They wanted to regulate every fiber of humanity, every atom of matter. From this derives their particular rank, their distinctness.... The originality of these revolts lies above all in their being without limits, infinite and universal.[31]

We can also affirm that the trio of great utopians marked a spiritual renaissance leading to the discovery of a new subject matter. Saint-Simon's disdain for Owen's "petty politics" and "peculiarities," which contemporaries opposed with accusations of ignorance, mania, even madness, the Académie Française's condemnation of Fourier's neologisms, the two-pronged method of doubt and of an absolute break—such were the most obvious signs of this renaissance, at once a rupture, a change of scene, and a discovery. Saint-Simon, Fourier, and Owen presented the problems in grand terms. That is reason enough to refrain from analyzing this renaissance, this discovery, in a purely reactive manner, under the pressure of democratic idiosyncrasy that, according to Nietzsche, brought adaptation to the fore. It is, however, a temptation that the majority of sociologists give in to in the presence of the socialist-communist utopia. They are equally good at sidestepping the fundamental concept of activity and at evading that of the autonomous activity of the proletariat.

For Sombart, Durkheim, or Polanyi, utopias are valuable as a solution to the problem of indigence or as a refusal of proletarianization. Theirs are reactive and, moreover, miserabilist interpretations. But the phalanstery, for example, goes far beyond reactionary utopian projections; it represents something wholly different from a simple response to the slums of great industrial cities. Its utility, its aim of refusing proletarianization, is only a symptom of a much more powerful and broader movement.

Contrary to the sociologists, the socialist thinkers within the social movement who refuse to make socialism into an object do not ignore this initial energy deployed and crystallized in the original constellation of utopian socialism. They are right to retrieve a reading of this "moment" instead of offering a positivist sociology in the form of categories.

Social utopia at the beginning of the nineteenth century is first of all a will to happiness not in a flatly utilitarian sense, in terms of gains and losses, but as "conatus," a will to expansion, to the free and joyous deployment of being, at a distance from *ressentiment* and dour passions. It is the product of an energy, a will to fundamental affirmation, an expression of this energy. All reactive symptoms, of which the utopias of the nineteenth century certainly bear traces, should only be considered as taken up and circumscribed by a movement of primary affirmation, as subjugated by this will to happiness. In this sense, one can speak of a new utopian creation that corresponds to new historical needs and desires, a new relation of desire to things that escapes the trap of representation—a contemporary reversal of Sade, according to Foucault. It is the emergence, on the side of the people, of a new desire.

On the threshold of the nineteenth century, we find humanity in the midst of an extremely complex experiment. For many contemporaries, Ballanche, Victor Considerant, Reynaud, Leroux, and others still, it is a matter of a new epoch of social palingenesis, that is to say, an epoch of transition that paves the way for a new era in human history.

Contrary to the miserabilist and reactive interpretation, it is not true that the first objective of socialist-communist utopia was to answer workers' poverty with a refusal of proletarianization. This refusal was first of all a collective enthusiasm for a new form of civilization, as if the secular dreams of the plebeians could finally take concrete form. Nineteenth-century socialist utopia poses the questions in terms of civilization, or rather poses the question of a unitary mutation of civilization. In short, it is the proactive affirmation of a new philosophy of life.

Revolutionary action opened a gap: it elicited "sympathy that borders closely on enthusiasm" (Kant). Jacques Roux, Marat, and many others did not die in vain. Despite all the retreats, the "betrayal" of the revolution, they demonstrated to the future that it was possible to bring centuries of oppression to an end. It was Fourier, though contemptuous of revolutionary politics, who saw the Convention as the fuse of a generalized subversion of civilization: "It seems that the great body of the people was ridding itself of all the ulcers that were desiccating it."[32]

Unfortunately, the Convention weakened before ingrained prejudice—a failure that, for Fourier, was the occasion for a new departure. He launches into the following admirable appeal, which carries the weight of a charter of socialist utopia in relation to politics: "If your wisdom has given us sciences that have done nothing but perpetuate calamity and destruction, give us rather laws dictated by madness, provided that they calm these frenzies and relieve the miseries of the people."[33]

Let us add to this a new knowledge and domination of nature, the appearance of a new class, the proletariat endowed with its own activity and a tendency to appropriate the globe by means of a new social force, capital. Humanity poses, and poses for itself, new problems. Industry, the vertiginous surge, in the eyes of contemporaries, of the productive forces, revealed to man infinite faculties and abysses. The "hubris" of the capitalist system, its incessant movement of expansion (imperialism is the essence of capital) engenders at the same time a grandiose will to reappropriation—the will to reappropriate productive forces extending across the globe, to the planetary system, to interplanetary relations, and, with Fourier, to the infinity of passional combinations. In this way, accumulated energy, renewed and wild, takes hold of a new field of possibility. Certain pages in Marx resonate like a paean to capital. At the limit of all study of the socialist-communist movement in the nineteenth century, these astonishing pages from the *Grundrisse* should figure more prominently than Engelsian theses. Even if they betray a will to inherit, they offer, among other things, a radically new perspective on the utopians, far from the myopic vision of the sociologists. Marx, like Leroux when writing on utopia, sends us in a new direction: no longer utopia and pauperism, or utopia and misery, but utopia and pleasure.

In the history of the human species—and it is toward all of human destiny that the socialist thinkers orient themselves—capital represents the world's greatest force of socialization. From this point of view, the creation of a world market is decisive: it reveals the universal tendency of capital, its own movement that aims at exploding limits, all the limits of the traditional world.

In the *1844 Manuscripts*, Marx posits a relation between the transformation of sensory organs and the development of humanity: "The forming of the five senses is a labour of the entire history of the world down to the present."[34] Capital also upsets and definitively ruins the fixity of desires: through the socialization it effects and the ensuing transformation of sensibility, it opens the way to a new capacity for life and joy. This is one of Marx's fundamental theses:

> The cultivation of all the qualities of the social human being, production of the same in a form as rich as possible in needs, because rich in qualities and relations—production of this being as the most total and universal possible social product, for, in order to take gratification in a many-sided way, he must be capable of many pleasures [*genussfähig*], hence cultured to a high degree—is likewise a condition of production founded on capital.[35]

The movement of capital, essentially fated for excess and immoderation, is made fact through a general investment that, step by step, engulfs the universe—a universal investment that, in and against the historical fetters of capital, tends toward a new victory of the principle of sensualism. According to Marx, the "fixity of desires" is shaken especially deeply, to the point of no return, as capital destroys spiritual barriers and traditional illusions, the relics of past ages. In the grip of constant revolution, capital shatters all harmonious images of possible fulfillment that, however, bearing within them the memory of or nostalgia for anterior social formations, remain, despite their achievement and relative perfection, narrow and unilateral. The expression of a static state of desires, they bear witness only to the search for limited satisfaction that capital had precisely surpassed and rendered null and void.

But capital is, in essence, a contradictory mode of development and production, containing at once a universal tendency and a specific narrowness: "But from the fact that capital posits every such limit as a barrier and hence gets *ideally* beyond it, it does not by any means follow that it has *really* overcome it, and, since every such barrier contradicts its character, its production moves in contradictions which are constantly overcome but just as constantly posited."[36] Capital bears within itself communism as a superior mode of production and as a social movement whose specific trajectory, starting from the "constant revolution of capital" and the resulting socialization, consists in migrating beyond these historical limits.

From the point of view of "passional movement," the essential character of the dialectic of capital is to solicit a new expansion of being and, in the same movement, to leave it totally unfulfilled, the universal objectification leading, within the framework of capital, to a complete destitution of human interiority. In this sense, the socialist-communist movement adopts capital's movement toward universality, but—and it is a weighty difference—rejects its limits. Not only does it want to eliminate the "bad sides" of capital to preserve the "good" ones, it also, and more importantly, tends along the arrow of history toward a real unfettered universality, toward a total objectification that would not be generalized alienation. The socialist-communist movement, whose condition of possibility is capital, is understood first of all as a social movement toward a positive reappropriation and transformation of all the riches of humanity.

The more man augments the level of culture, the more he is capable of enjoyment, the more he is capable of resenting as unbearable the fetters on his pleasure. Hence, at the beginning of the nineteenth century, at the moment when capital appeared with extreme sharpness without yet having acquired the appearance of a "natural" framework—a moment of specific historical tension between the tendency toward universal development and the simultaneous necessity for capital to constantly reproduce its own limits—there was an explosion of dreams outside the frame.

Whence the interpretive possibility of sketching, across the constellation of these dreams, a thematics of socialist-communist utopia that necessarily exceeds the limits of the constellation. In effect, "utopian socialism" brought to light a unique impetus: one could say that a muffled and polymorphous force overflowing the dawn of socialism finally found an outlet that it then worked unceasingly to enlarge, so as to engender something like a utopian "circulus" (Leroux, also Déjacque) pervading all aspects of the century, accumulating a set of ideas and embarking for a new community, a new world. It is this impetus, this tendency born under the sign of the "new," that distinguishes the age of utopian socialism from all others. It was a current that neoutopianism undertook to channel and return to the bed of politics or cooperation, and that the new utopian spirit, alerted by the levees raised to check it, tried with all its might to reactivate and make flow anew so as to restore all its original fecundity and energy—a kind of "vital source" that, once open, tends toward uninterrupted development in the original form of "utopian socialism." Its bearings included: the experiments of the first Saint-Simonians; the new moral world of Robert Owen, without obligations or sanctions; the passionate attraction and the new amorous world of Fourier; the circulus of Pierre Leroux; the eternal return of Blanqui; the Humanisphere of Déjacque; and also the communism of Marx. These are so many signs. Over several decades, all the domesticated secular forces seem to have united to mount an assault on the old world and to explore a plurality of new possible worlds. There is a jungle of utopian thought that we have barely begun to penetrate. The themes frequently overlap, become tangled, but key elements emerge that all point to the definition of a new principle of reality. These elements are: the humanization of nature (the theme of channels serving to marry East and West, the organic body of the new city); the naturalization of man (his reinsertion into the cosmos, new relations with other species); the liberation of nature's potential; the end of the old curse "You will earn your bread by the sweat of your brow"; the transformation of work or indeed the reversal of work into play; the creation of a beautiful humanity, physically and intellectually superior, beyond good and evil (Owen); the end of alienation and the rule of pleasure; the liberation of the infinity of desires; the appropriation and transparency of the human community; the rehabilitation of the flesh (Fourier, Enfantin); the perpetuation of individuals in space (Leroux); the joint reign of beauty and freedom (the nature garden); the disappearance of the dominant masculine principle; the values of childhood; the images of woman as mediator or bearer of a new relation to the world. The plebeian philosophers, the utopians, glimpsed the possibility of reconciliation between a philosophy of reason and hedonism, the possibility of a new social organization in which freedom and beauty coincide. With the new discovery of wealth increase the capacities for pleasure and the desire for new relations to things and humans. A new "being in the world" is sought and unveiled through the enthusiasm of the nineteenth-century socialist-communist utopias.[37]

Utopia, the will to happiness in Benjamin's and Marcuse's sense, is a break with the idealist philosophy of reason forever based on the sacrifice of individuality to universal and superior interests.[38] Fourier haughtily dismisses twenty-five centuries of political and moral speculation, preoccupied solely with administrative or religious innovation, and, with sovereign insolence, gives political genius a new object: industrial or domestic measures. This in no way signifies, contrary to the interpretation of Roland Barthes, who appears to me to fall short of Fourier's problematic, that Fourier sided with the domestic (the order of desire) against the political (the order of need).[39] The displacement of the political accomplished by Fourier in parallel with Saint-Simon (the administration of things) and Owen (the theory of the influence of circumstances and the science of production) is not a choice of the domestic against the political so much as an opening up of a new field of action to political genius: all the needs and desires of the real human being, the sensory satisfactions of prosaic man, in short the totality of everyday life. In so doing, Fourier succeeded in surmounting the pre-Fourierist opposition of politics and desire, underscored and reinforced by Barthes. Better yet, he succeeded in linking them. Fourier does not separate, does not reproduce the classical compartmentalizations; he blurs the frontiers, he associates, no longer to channel the movement of the passions toward the political (utopia's habitual falling back on the state), but to take the political out of its traditional orbit, to open it to desire, to connect it to other types of sociability. In this sense, he subverts the political. One error of civilized politics is to count desire for nothing, Fourier declares, pleading for a complex politics. Humanity must become used to valuing itself as well as the universe that surrounds it. Beyond the desire for politics, the greatness of Fourier is to have proposed, on the basis of this decentering of the political, a politics of desire, to have created a new utopian object where "great politics" takes charge of the infinity of the passions and is able to project the image of new social relations founded no longer on the classical compression of the passions, of the "moral education of humanity," but on the possibility of a harmonious combination of the multiplicity of desires, on Passionate Attraction. Fourier likewise proposes the image of universal sociability, a sociability between man and cosmic forces. From politics subjugated to morality toward politics associated with sensual pleasure, this is the meaning of Fourier's great theme, "politics applied to appetite," and the source of Considerant's observation that history "eroded even desire." Thanks to Fourier, utopia made a leap from need (lack) to desire (the expansion of being). What surprises and scandalizes Fourier is not the desires of men but their lack of desires, their appetitive weakness. Whence in Fourier a utopian strategy close to what Nietzsche called "a reconversion of politics," founded on the positive expression of the passions—a reconversion that, for Fourier, is aligned with revolutionary religions and that participates entirely in the protean will of the nineteenth century to found a new religion. Fourier wrote a crucial text on this: *De la Franc-Maçonnerie et de ses propriétés encore inconnues*. One should remember that politics applied to appetite, associated with sensual pleasure, is what should necessarily create new modes of exposition and action, and what aims at the end of politics. It is a matter of, at the same time, breaking with the pedagogical perspective typical of classical political thought, which consists in the containment of the passions and the satisfaction, against all external universals, of what philosophy excludes by seeing in it only the "lower" tendencies of individuals: "The demand that free individuals attain satisfaction militated against the entire set-up of traditional culture.... The idea of the free and universal realization of individual happiness, *per contra*, denoted an *affirmative* materialism, that is to say, an affirmation of the material satisfaction of man."[40]

There is in this utopian explosion a return to the primitive. It can be said that, in relation to the dominant culture, the great utopians are barbarians. But barbarity is one of the signs by which one recognizes renaissances of the spirit.

Barbarians indeed, in a number of ways. None of the three was a public or official thinker. Private thinkers all, the three great utopians, to differing degrees, were excluded by scientific authorities charged with defining the new contours of homogeneity. But utopia, for the same reasons as violence, excess, delirium, and madness (the association has frequently been made by conservative critics), belongs to what Georges Bataille calls the heterogeneous thing supposedly charged with an unknown and dangerous force: "*Heterogeneous* reality is that of a force or shock. It presents itself as a charge, as a value, passing from one object to another in a more or less arbitrary fashion, almost as if the change took place not in the world of objects, but solely in the subject's judgments."[41] Hence the oft-encountered slippage between utopia and madness or crime. It was not enough for the utopians to disrupt the relations between speculative and practical thinking; like the great navigators—and Fourier, the prince of utopians, always invoked Christopher Columbus—they did not cease exploring unknown lands and pushing through perilous passages. Those who do not share the passion for exploration can laugh and accuse them of delirium. Those, conversely, who have no vocation for inventories or classification will recognize in the utopian fantastic the force and freshness of the dawning socialist project. One can glimpse this force from another angle. If the unthought of political thought is the fear of barbarians, one can say again of the great utopians—since all three have broken with *political* utopia, the utopia of the modern state as the incarnation of reason that runs from More to Hegel—that they are on the side of the barbarians. Thence their common contempt for the law and jurists. Thence their critique of the political that their indifference to political matters should not obscure. A positive and untimely expression of what Max Horkheimer called the revolt of nature, the great utopians took up the cry of the new, secular aspirations of the eternally deceived masses. They outlined the utopian face of what could be the liberation of the drives, the passions, the instinctual life bridled by civilization. Utopia tends toward the rule of active forces.

This representation has little in common with the classical image of the utopian pedagogue. Mannheim reminded us, following Marx and Engels, that Saint-Simon, Fourier, and Owen dreamed their utopias in the old intellectualist style. With an eye to the relation between utopian machinery and the desire of the masses, Bakhtin saw in utopian socialism and its faith in the omnipotence of conviction the expression of a philosophical monologism that accords no value to the interaction between consciousnesses: "In essence idealism knows only a single mode of cognitive interaction among consciousnesses: someone who knows and possesses the truth instructs someone who is ignorant of it and in error; that is, it is the interaction of a teacher and a pupil, which, it follows, can be only a pedagogical dialogue."[42] It is not at all that utopia needs to negate the reality of this pedagogical form. The great nineteenth-century utopians still have a foot in the eminently pedagogical eighteenth century. But is this not a partial characterization? Has not something else appeared beneath the pedagogical dialogue? The socialist utopias did not escape the law that compels new forces to appear in the guise of preexisting forces. At least in part, Saint-Simon, Fourier, and Owen disguised themselves as pedagogues. *Larvatus prodeo* was Saint-Simon's motto. Owen loved to be mistaken for Thomas Spence. To resolve the delicate problem of moving from esotericism to communication, they likewise disguised themselves as messiahs. Owen made use of millenarian language to be understood by the English working class, which was then attuned to this kind of rhetoric. But let us lift the masks. Evoking Saint-Simon's appeals to passion, reformulating the first Saint-Simonians' theory of sympathetic foresight or Fourier's of the relations between history and desire, one can confidently say that they paved the way for reflection on affective social reactions traversing the superstructure. The group experience of the first Saint-Simonians combated violently by the existing order was proof that at least some utopians sought a different mode of relating than that of the teacher to the taught. What remains of the pedagogical relation proper to intellectualist rationalism in the school of passionate attraction?[43]

NEOUTOPIANISM

In its most general definition, neoutopianism represents the fruit of a reconciliation between utopian socialism (the dawn of socialism) and the dominant ideas, or even a reconciliation between the communist movement and the ideas of the dominant class. One effect of neoutopianism is to give a name to the change involved in the cooling off of utopian energy in its anterior or domesticated forms.

By *neoutopianism* I mean one of two things:

- The formation, on the basis of a mother-utopia, of a doctrinaire corpus that, under the cover of orthodoxy, ends up emasculating or domesticating the original project. Moreover, the elaboration of the corpus, the doctrinal systematization of "positive formulas for the society of the future," produces the inevitable effect of closure. In reality, the diffusion of the mother-utopia in the form of a closed and realized system aims to cover over the absolute gap that it has produced, no longer offering the project of a new world but proposing adjustments to the existing order.
- The recovery of utopian contents of various and integrated origin, or else in the form of traditional thinking, or even in a new utopian projection that, contrary to those of the three great utopians, tends not toward the transformation but to a rationalization of the existing order.

Neoutopianism corresponds, then, to the epigones of the three great emancipators, or rather to the diverse utopian attempts and expressions developed since the middle of the nineteenth century and often conceived as a war machine against the communist movement or Marxism. It is the true adversary of radical theory.

Marx and Engels attacked neoutopianism in three of its manifestations.

1. The orthodox Fourierists, or the transformation of utopia into a system. In *The German Ideology*, Marx and Engels declare:

> Fourier's orthodox disciples of the *Démocratie pacifique* show most clearly how little the real content of these systems lies in their systematic form; they are, for all their orthodoxy, doctrinaire bourgeois, the very antipodes of Fourier. All epoch-making systems have as their real content the needs of the time in which they arose. Each one of them is based on the whole of the antecedent development of a nation, on the historical growth of its class relations with their political, moral, philosophical and other consequences.[44]

2. True socialism, or the integration of utopia into a form of traditional thought, philosophy. We know that radical theory is built on a critique of philosophy and, more precisely, of German philosophy that, in its very form, bears the stigmata of German reality, which is not on the level of the modern present. What distinguishes philosophy, as a form of thought, besides the belief that the world of thought constitutes an autonomous sphere, is its inability to leave the world of thought and descend to the real world, its inability to make its way from language to life.

Whether we interpret the Marxian negation of philosophy as philosophy's leap into the "a theory of social revolution, comprehended and practised as a living totality" (Korsch) or as a transition from philosophy to critical social theory (Marcuse), it appears that Marx and Engels's entire effort consisted in breaking, to the shock of the French and English communist movement, with the very form of German philosophy. If communist utopia was anticulture, true socialism proceeded in a way opposite to that of Marx and Engels: it tried to integrate this new form of thought-action, which proposed, among other things, to remake human understanding at the heart of the culture, in the classical form of philosophy. For Marx and Engels, all of the philosophical efforts of the German nation from Kant to Hegel reached their completion in communism, whereas for true socialism, the communist movement had to await its realization in a new German philosophy. "Murdering" French and English communism was, for the true socialists, a matter of rejuvenating the bloodless body of philosophy through an infusion of new blood and, at the same time, of transforming communism into a doctrine, a theoretical nucleus, in short into a philosophical category. It worked to raise real life to the level of thought, abolishing the formal change that the communist movement worked tirelessly toward. Hence Marx and Engels's violent theoretical combat against this resurgence of German philosophy—equally a social one, since to transform socialist-communist utopia into philosophical "sublimation" in this way was to again subject communism to the spiritual domination of the dominant class.[45]

3. The solutions to the "social question" that appeared in Europe after 1850 and that tried to occupy an intermediary position between the worker's movement and the bourgeoisie (Henry George, pulpit socialism, and the like).

When it comes to form, too, the various manifestations of neoutopianism can be boiled down to a regression of "utopian socialism, still in many respects revolutionary," to the phenomena that Marx and Engels, in the *Communist Manifesto*, called "conservative" or "bourgeois socialism," whose essence they defined as follows:

> A part of the bourgeoisie is desirous of redressing social grievances, in order to secure the continued existence of bourgeois society.... This form of socialism has, moreover, been worked out into complete systems.... The socialistic bourgeois want all the advantages of modern social conditions without the struggles and dangers necessarily resulting therefrom. They desire the existing state of society minus its revolutionary and disintegrating elements. They wish for a bourgeoisie without a proletariat.[46]

This neoutopian regression is still more manifest when it turns into juridical socialism. The great utopians contemporary with the beginning of the constitutionalist movement had already denounced law as aping utopia.

Utopia's transition to exotericism and its joining with politics take place only at the price of a loss of original content. This loss stands in direct relation to its chosen communication: utopia gains in social extension what it loses in utopian intensity. What is still more serious, the very structure of utopia is violated. The specific form of utopia disappears, fades in its abandonment to exteriority. The phalansterian utopia becomes the Fourierist program, a necessary effect of the formation of neoutopian thought. The systematization that covers the contradictions and movement of a thought in motion with a veneer of coherence, that practices, that removes the unrealized in order to extract the result, the systematization, the weeding and sorting, according to Considerant ("orthodox" Fourierism marks the end of neologisms and the beginning of translation into the dominant language, the disciples reject the fantastic clothes and censor inwardly)—all this in the name of reducing novelty to current cultural norms. Working as heirs charged with managing an inheritance, the epigones do not seek to pursue a movement but to grow their capital. It is a matter above all of concealing the fundamental decentering that brought to light the unthought of traditional thought. It is a matter of making a force that is naturally heterogeneous homogeneous with the culture. From start to finish, neoutopianism is a return to civilization. Thus, the original utopia settles into a domesticated form. Godin, founder of the Guise Familistère, urges the renunciation of Fourier's utopian exaggerations and reduces the new industrial and sociable world that presupposes a transformation of the mode of production to a doctrine and practice of cooperation. To the extent that the enterprises of the neoutopians, that is, the epigones or those aiming at a utopian syncretism—like Bellamy with *Looking Backward*—want to add one more truth to the culture, they reinforce it by rejuvenating it, and in so doing give up on subverting it. In this case, their relation to the masses is purely pedagogical and elitist. Even worse, it can take the form of a misappropriation of the masses' desire for the purpose of modernizing the existing social system and reinforcing domination. The recent appeals of David Riesman and Daniel Bell in favor of utopia suffice to prove that neoutopianism is not dead.

THE NEW UTOPIAN SPIRIT

A third, more complex mechanism appears after 1848: the new utopian spirit.[47] This constellation is a phenomenon, if not ignored, then at least poorly identified, since it is never named as such. In the "Letter to Doctor Deville," Leroux distinguished the movement and defined the principle of its constitution: critical recovery as well as heresy against its inheritance and the formation of an orthodoxy. In short, it is a dynamic conception of utopia as an uninterrupted movement, the intensification of decentering, the combination with other heterogeneous forces, be they barbaric (Ernest Cœurderoy, *Hurrah!!! ou la Révolution par les Cosaques*) or proletarian (Déjacque, William Morris).[48]

In general, one can discern two major tendencies. The first is the new utopian spirit of autonomous development (Déjacque, Cœurderoy), born of utopia's spontaneous critical work upon itself, coupled with critical reflection on the revolutionary practice of 1848. To perpetuate itself and not give in to the positivist temptation or to being degraded into a political program, the utopian movement engaged in self-criticism, confessing its faults and producing a new form. It was above all a break with the belief in autarchy and in the supremacy of a single consciousness. The utopian renounces the position of inventor of a social science along with the superiority that comes with it and that constitutes, according to Marx, the principal weakness of utopianism. For Déjacque, inventions are the result of collective observations. Cœurderoy affirms the same: "Science is no longer the purview of a few, but of all."[49] By "all" he essentially understands the proletariat, whose conservative instinct begot a "science of revolt."

In liberating utopia from its pretensions to scientificity, the authors of the new utopian spirit effect a transition from doctrinaire science to revolutionary science. They posit the principle of the proletariat's self-emancipation and consequently reject the form of the utopian sect as an authoritarian structure of communication and revolutionary action. There is a parallel rejection of the revolution's denunciation from on high by democratic currents. The Lycurgus and Icarus complexes are equally condemned. Cœurderoy declares:

> What, finally, is your system?—I have neither system nor conclusions to present, I cannot have any, nor do I want to: I want nothing. And if I could establish a government such as Lycurgus's or Icaria or some organization of work—which is very easy—I would not. Consider, rather, what has become of Owen's, Cabet's, and Louis Blanc's magnificent plans for reedification: nothing remains of Fourier but his just criticisms, his universal analogies and grand predictions. There is only one commandment for those occupied with social science: to red-pencil all the edifices that ought to disappear. Man is too narrow-minded to grasp the entire constellation of objects and centuries competing for the reconstruction of society. Humanity as a whole—eternal that it is and mistress of its actions in all milieus—can be reconstructed.[50]

And Déjacque:

> Liberty does not enlist men under the authority of a sectarian leader: it initiates them into a movement of ideas and inculcates in them the feeling of active independence. Authority is unity in uniformity! Liberty is unity in diversity. . . . For me, it is much less a matter of producing disciples than of producing human beings, and one is only a human being on condition of being oneself.[51]

Even if the partisan of the new utopian spirit does not renounce positive intentionality—"A negation, to be absolute, needs to be completed with an affirmation" (Déjacque)—it denounces the form of this intentionality among the great utopians. It is no longer a matter of imposing on the proletariat a system from the outside or from on high, but of communicating the decomposition of modern society and participating in the upheavals of the struggle. For the new utopian spirit, radically opposed to utopian substitutionism (an individual consciousness that substitutes itself for the entire movement), the same applies to the construction of the future society and the elaboration of science: it is valid only as a collective work.[52]

The ambiguity of utopian socialism has been overcome. The utopian rejects the mask of the pedagogue as much as that of the millenarian prophet. A new relation of the masses to desire is established. To invoke Bakhtin's opposition, utopia passes from a monologic to a dialogic form: "The dialogic means of seeking truth is counterposed to official monologism, which pretends to *possess a ready-made truth*.... Truth is not born nor is it to be found inside the head of an individual person, it is born *between people* collectively searching for truth, in the process of their dialogic interaction."[53] Considerant, however neoutopian, evoking the effects of secular domination, found the pole of this mutation: "Evil has penetrated to the marrow, eroded even desire."[54] That is to say, utopia no longer functions to convince or to make comprehensible the value of a model or a solution to the social question; its task is to incite desire, to set in motion the desire of the masses. Utopia becomes a passional maieutics. To be sure, the new utopian spirit draws its élan from the solid ground of the passions. There, the utopian finds a guarantee at once against any exteriority of the masses' desire and against any transubstantiation of these desires into a new ideal that represses drives and disparages life. Déjacque defines with extreme clarity this new status of the true, mediating, passional utopia. Utopia is no longer a discourse emanating from knowledge to clear up ignorance, but an appeal that multiple passionality makes to the multiplicity of the passions:

> I am, I believe, despite my ignorance, in one of the milieus most favorable to taking stock of the needs of humanity. I have all the passions, even if I cannot satisfy them.... It is because of my multiple passionality that I can with any luck hope to handle the success of human society, given

that dealing with it well depends as much on one's knowledge of one's own passions as on the knowledge of the passions of others.⁵⁵

Also modified is the relation between parts: the utopian who has abandoned his position as master, as the possessor of truth as such, appears henceforth as the initiator of a mode of communication and dialogical action.⁵⁶ Practiced in this way, utopia opens wide the door to the unknown, to a true future, that is to say, to the new, irreducible to the present or to idealized images of the past. Moreover, through dissatisfaction and the passional awakening it engenders in its audience, utopia, that untimely provocation, pushes them beyond imaginary projection to effect a *passage à l'acte* in the form of experimental group practice or revolutionary praxis. This is a fundamental tension for the new utopian spirit. Déjacque, on guard against the ambivalence of utopian writing—at the same time countercommunicative and inviting a breach of this closure—transforms it, to escape this ambivalence, into a moment of revolutionary practice. It is a matter of realizing utopia outside a book, in another time than that of writing and reading. It is as if the producer of utopia, at the very moment he is writing his utopia, perceives the insignificance and limits of this writing, the paradox of coercive writing in favor of a left-libertarian utopia, as if writing a utopia necessarily pushes it to inscribe itself elsewhere so as to escape the closure and coercion of a written utopia. This rupture is both founding and double: a rupture with the sect, the esoteric society of closed-circuit communication, and a rupture with the closure of writing. The new utopian spirit gives utopia the freedom Roland Barthes attributes to speech. Linking utopia to revolution, Déjacque reached an insurrectional conception of utopia: for the proletarian, the utopian object merges with the insurrectional object—the barricade, the symbol of popular insurrection. The new utopian spirit does not, for all that, sacrifice the specificity of utopia. It is not so much a matter of putting utopia in the service of revolution as it is of ensuring that utopia is the place where the insurrection of desire links up to the insurrection of the masses. Déjacque affirms:

> This book is not written in ink; its pages are not paper sheets. This book is steel, turned in octavo, and charged with a fulminate of ideas. . . . There is not a worker who, in the hidden reaches of his brain, does not clan-

destinely fashion some thoughts of destruction. You, you have the bayonet and the penal code, the catechism and the guillotine; we have the barricade and utopia, sarcasm and the bomb. You, you are pressure; we are the mine: one spark can blow you up! . . . This book is not a document, it is an act. . . . It is a cry of insurrection, a strike of the tocsin rung with the hammer of the idea in the hearing of the popular passions.[57]

And Cœurderoy as well: "To hell with this book! It is not writing, it is a will, an act, it is a whole channel that opens before the public."[58] The utopian object, the "hammer of the idea" (Déjacque), calls for setting the "material hammers" in motion.

The second figure of the new utopian spirit emerged from within Marxism or, more exactly, within its oppositional or marginal currents. It is this form that clarifies a constellation of utopian phenomena related to Marx's theory, which, having appeared toward the end of the nineteenth century, extended into the 1930s. Neither a repetition of utopian socialism, nor an avatar of neoutopianism, the new utopian spirit was a critical reactivation. Its founding principle: it is not through inheritance that one sustains a movement but through critique. Its manifestations are either theoretico-practical (Morris, certain tendencies within surrealism) or purely theoretical (Bloch, Benjamin).

Like the new utopian spirit of autonomous development, this constellation had as its basis a critique of the utopian movement from the beginning of the nineteenth century. The difference is that the essence of this critique is borrowed from Marx and Engels. But it no less rejects what has been made of them by vulgar Marxism. For the partisans of the new utopian spirit, Marx's critique does not signify the end of utopia but another type of relation that remains to be defined. Better yet, acutely aware of the revolutionary significance of Marx's critique (utopia sins by its lack of radicalism, not by radical extremism), they have made the voice of revolutionary critique heard again and, at the same time, denounced the transformation of this critique into a conservative weapon at the hands of epigones.[59]

Contrary to neoutopianism, whose effect was to make the utopian corpus homogeneous with existing society, the new utopian spirit struggles to preserve the heterogeneity of radical theory and save it from integration into the dominant culture. In effect, the new utopian spirit starts with an observation. Marx's unitary theory of social revolution did not escape the fate of the great utopias. It too has been, for epigones, the object of domestication and bowdlerization. They have inherited it, but as *disjecta membra*. What has been said of neoutopianism holds for neo-Marxism. From the various descriptions of this bowdlerization of the original theory, which historically corresponds to the Second International (1889–1916), one draws the conclusion that neo-Marxism is thoroughly homogeneous with bourgeois society. The apologia for work, for the technical domination of nature, the faith in humanity's unlimited continual progress, taking place in homogeneous and empty time, the respect for culture, which need only be inherited and made profitable for the masses—this is what constitutes neo-Marxist or social-democratic conformism.[60] We also see appear, against the transformation of the original theory into what Arthur Rosenberg calls a professional ideology of organized workers, attempts that situate themselves at the same time in the line descending from Marx and Engels and from Saint-Simon, Fourier, and Owen. This is particularly so with what the same Arthur Rosenberg qualifies as "Marxist theory of the future," which, in a struggle on two fronts—against social democracy on the one hand and Bolshevism on the other—endeavored to maintain a living link to communism qua coming future. To this Marxist theory of the future belong, for example, Rosa Luxemburg, Karl Korsch, and Anton Pannekoek.

Their project was to recover from an absolute break with the original theory. The new utopian spirit, while registering the practical and theoretical critiques to which the great utopias have been subjected, established an active relation with anterior utopian expressions. This second tendency is represented above all in reactions to the fragmentation and disintegration of radical theory and its presentation as positivist evolutionism. They aim neither to repeat nor to restart utopia (or, what would amount to the same, to complete Marx with utopia), but to rediscover the communist program that is at the heart of radical theory via a return to the energy of the great utopians and to their positive intentionality. Reading Marx opposite the communist writings of Théodore Dézamy or Moses Hess from 1845–1846 inevitably yields other results than reading him "in light of" Lenin or the Third International (1919–1943).

This movement from within Marxist theory toward the primitive and the utopian is more a detour than a true return. In reality, it is a matter of returning to Marx by way of a detour through the great utopias. The partisans of the new utopian spirit wanted neither to regress behind Marx's theory nor to go beyond it, but to take up a position in its very center.[61] Implicitly or explicitly, the new utopian spirit takes inspiration from the idea that the real revolutionary critique of utopias formulated by Marx and Engels and deformed or, worse, inverted by the epigones had obscured a fundamental dimension of the theory that forms its center: its straining toward the communist future.

First, we cannot, in effect (in the name of which new orthodoxy?), limit the new utopian spirit to a return to Marx by a detour through the great utopias. In certain of its manifestations, the new utopian spirit was not only commanded by a will to recover, against social democratization, radical theory in its original purity. There was more. Among these more complex, more audacious attempts were ones whose orientation can be schematically presented as follows:

- Rescuing from oblivion the programmatic dimension of Marx's communism.
- Then grafting onto this restored programmatic dimension a new utopia that reactivates the shock-value of pre-Marxian utopias while distinguishing itself from them. This new utopia, taking flight from the solid ground of the projection of communism, explores this something that forms the extreme frontier, or perhaps even the closure of Marxian communism, namely, the reign of freedom. A break with systems, with all solutions to the "social question," with all models, this original utopian practice tests out, in a mode that is neither scientific nor didactic, hypotheses that are deliberately heuristic and that escape the alternative of this or that side of Marxism. These hypotheses are simply other, giving birth to a new relation between utopian subversion and Marxist revolution. So it is that in *News from Nowhere* an epoch of rest succeeds a communist revolution, according to William Morris.
- Or, better still, with the communist program set out, the partisan of the new utopian spirit subjects Marxian theory to a half-jesting, half-theoretical treatment, to what one might term "utopianization." It is as though the interpreter took up certain latent themes, or ones left fallow or even effaced when the theory was founded, and made them work at their maximum intensity. Finally, the partisan of the new utopian spirit can choose to deliberately force Marx's thought in order to wrest it from the continuum of projection and situate it outside history,

elsewhere, in the *nowhere*, that specifically utopian space. To this method corresponds the theme of the "resurrection of nature," present as much in Bloch as in Benjamin.

Alert to "Endangered Socialism," in Domela Nieuwenhuis's warning from 1897, alert also to the first signs of economism and fearing, moreover, the appearance of a new Leviathan in the form of a confusion between the transitional phase and communist society (this was Morris's angle of attack), the authors of the new utopian spirit had specifically developed what Antonie Pannekoek, citing none other than Morris, called the "active side" of the new life, that is, the transformation of work itself, all the programmatic ideas on the upheaval of everyday life. The insistence on the active side of the new life signifies only that the new utopian spirit had the task of giving a utopian garb to the key elements of the Marxian projection, or worse, producing this "monstrous" thing that, according to some, received the name of "scientific utopia." On the basis of the morphological projection of communism, they erected utopian and dialectical images of the future, in Benjamin's sense. "Each epoch not only dreams the next, but also, in dreaming, strives toward the moment of waking."[62] Against those who immobilize the movement in the name of comprehending the reign of necessity, they poured all their poetic-utopian energy into resolutely setting off for the reign of freedom. Not only is the practice of utopia not sacrificed, it is launched on new paths.

The new utopian spirit has often been linked to a revolutionary romanticism that, far from eluding revolution by a program of spiritual or aesthetic renewal, endeavored, on the contrary, to avoid failure by transporting the struggle to a terrain traditionally considered neutral or inessential. Close to or even members of the artistic "avant-garde" (a notion they incidentally rejected), the partisans of the new utopian spirit were highly conscious of the crisis of modern culture and of the decline of art in bourgeois society. Morris has gone from Pre-Raphaelitism to Marx and from Marx along a line leading to Bauhaus. That is why it was not enough for these utopians to feed the apparatus of existing production. These are not routine utopians content to produce a utopia with more socialist content. Their utopian practice, responding also to the will to replace traditional art with a new type of activity, is a constitutive moment of global revolutionary practice, just as the simulation of revolution constitutes an essential moment of their utopian projection. Whence the rupture with the closed model of utopia in the style of Cabet's *Voyage to Icaria*. Like the new utopian spirit of autonomous development, in their search for a form of communication and dialogic action they turned to a new type of image, a new form of utopia, an open work. In the service of passional maieutic utopia, they constructed a new utopian object that had the value of a simulacrum:[63]

- The simulacrum produces an effect of resemblance by different means than the model: it is built upon a disparity and this enables it to liberate difference from all subordination to the similar and the identical. This is why a simulacrum utopia is located elsewhere than in a relation to the not-yet-possible.
- The simulacrum is a work of great proportions.
- The simulacrum is distinguished by a very mysterious mode of apprehension, which looks neither like knowledge nor like correct opinion, but belongs to affectivity. The simulacrum is a rupture with the world of essences, forms, or norms: it opens a new career to becoming and makes possible the invention of the new. Moreover, escaping the constraint of imitation, it affirms the diverse, the multiple—in short, pluralism.

Pierre Klossowski adds other specifications: the simulacrum may be a tableau vivant that suspends conventional gestures and produces a shock effect. It is tied to the presence of a real group, the place where fantasies are exchanged. Reviewing Fourier's utopian prophecy, Klossowski writes: "Thus it is necessary to create a sphere where one or many simulacra may be able to mediate an exchange of complementary phantasms at the level of individuals, and thus permit a co-operation between these different groups." And again: "Once a phantasm comes into existence, it must be reproduced as a simulacrum: the simulacrum in this sense is not, however, a catharsis—that would only be a misuse of forces—but rather reconstitutes and reproduces the reality of the phantasm on the level of play. Fourier gambles not so much on liberty as on liberating creation."[64] Utopia stops being a vision and becomes a seduction, a stimulus to present action. Without further exploring the possibilities of utopia as simulacrum, this change of form, an absolutely fundamental effect must be preserved: it allows utopia to escape the statist temptation that forever hovers over it. The history of utopia proves that the force of utopia has continually been overwhelmed by the desire for the state, has fallen back on the state form.

It is as if with every upsurge of anonymous utopian energy—energy that in its infinite movement is the generalized investment of the social body, of the universe, of the elements, of the whole cosmos—utopia as model functions to "statize" it, to exchange it for the political and the harmonious organization of the polity. In affirming the multiple (the pluralism of Fourier), in marking a rupture with the model, with what is before it and what it should imitate, in simulating the unknown, the inimitable unknown, the simulacrum offers a greater resistance—still, nothing has definitively been won—against the utopian force falling back on the state. The great utopians' critique of politics is not the "blind spot" of their theory, but perhaps something for us to think about.

Utopia entered an era of suspicion. Those who took up the tool bequeathed by tradition, to think the critique of utopia, learned to use in a new way, as a feint. Against the postulate of the one truth of the utopian imagination, freed by a state of grace from the stigmata of present oppression, the new utopian spirit put into play the "power of the false" to free the imagination. The utopia-simulacrum, close to the game, to the waking dream, to myths, to "secular dreams of a young humanity," to everything that is the creation of unsatisfied passions, opened a new space where the desire of the masses could give free rein to the work of fantasy and where, through the mediation of renewed affective forces, it could invent a new future: a new industrial and societal world, a new moral world, a new amorous world. Morris, who nourished his utopia through multiple detours, and Benjamin, who according to Pierre Klossowski inspired the vision of a society radiant in the free play of the passions (Marx with Fourier), tend in this direction.

With regard to this history of utopia, the evolutionist simplicity of the classical thesis, the binary opposition upon which it is based, is blown to smithereens. It will become apparent that there is no one answer to the question of the relations between critical communism and utopia. There can only be multiple answers, in keeping with a differential analysis of forms of socialist-communist utopia.

But is it enough to open up a new space of contention, and to multiply the poles of contention? Is not one effect of the new utopian spirit, in its two tendencies, to transform the very structure of the space of contention by questioning critical communism on what is latent in it, on what it leaves fallow, and even on what it has effaced in the course of its founding? Among some partisans of the new utopian spirit—and here the question remains open—one can perhaps perceive, beyond the struggle against the fragmentation and mutilation of radical theory, a more audacious, more adventurous, action against the much more global historical phenomenon of a socialist dialectic, as though, in the course of its development, between its "infancy" and its "maturity," socialism—Marx included—did not manage to escape the ruses of instrumental reason.

This analysis has a critical bearing on the imperialism of the fundamental signifier, namely, the science/utopia break. It aims to disturb, to turn around the question of utopia. It takes us only halfway. There still remains the question of the relationship between critical communism and utopia, which we must try to think in positive terms, breaking with the thesis that the communism of Marx marked the end of utopia pure and simple. Did he not rather aim to rescue it?

NOTES

Originally published in two parts as "L'Histoire de l'utopie et le destin de sa critique," *Textures* 6–7 (1973): 3–27 and *Textures* 8–9 (1974): 55–81; republished with minor alterations (which we have followed here) in *Utopiques IV: L'Histoire de l'utopie et le destin de sa critique* (Paris: Sens et Tonka, 2016).

1. Karl Marx, Letter to Arnold Ruge, September 1843, "Letters from the Deutsch-Französische Jahrbücher," in *Marx/Engels Collected Works* (Moscow: Progress Publishers, 1975–2005), 3:144. Hereafter the collected works will be referred to as *MECW*.
2. Félix Guattari, "La Coupure léniniste," *Critique*, June 1971, 569–570.
3. Georges Sorel, "Y a-t-il de l'utopie dans le marxisme?," *Revue de Métaphysique et de Morale* 7, no. 2 (1899): 152–175.
4. Here a distinction should be made between the text of the *Communist Manifesto* and Engels's pamphlet. In the former, one finds the expression of a truth won very recently, whereas the object of *Socialism: Utopian and Scientific* is the rehearsal and popularization of a truth already won long ago. What is more, the *Manifesto* corresponds to the primitive form of the theory, which is distinguished from later forms by its "audacity of language" and enormous theoretical daring. Karl Korsch, *Marxism and Philosophy* (1923), trans. Fred Halliday (London: New Left Books, 1970), 58. Besides, why forbid ourselves a priori from examining whether a positivist regression had not

perhaps begun to insinuate itself from the very being of the theory's founders, specifically into Engels's essay? And assessing and decentering the text mean nothing other than comparing it with an article by the young Engels, "Progress of Social Reform on the Continent" (October–November 1843). This comparison will produce a decentering all the more nuanced because in the article from 1843 Engels judges the utopian movement relative to the communist movement, whereas in the brochure from 1880 [*Socialism: Utopian and Scientific*] he judges it relative to science in a sense closer to Darwin's than Hegel's.

5   Karl Marx, "Herr Vogt," in *MECW* 17:22.
6   In 1846, Marx could not forgive Weitling his regression from "massive" communism to "true socialism," which represented dealings with dominant ideas. That noted, it did not prevent Marx hailing, without reservation, Weitling's genius in 1844. "As for the German workers' level of education or capacity for it, I would point to *Weitling's* brilliant writings which surpass *Proudhon's* from a theoretical point of view, however defective they may be in execution. What single work on the emancipation of the bourgeoisie, that is, political emancipation, can the bourgeoisie—for all their philosophers and scholars—put beside Weitling's *Guarantees of Harmony and Freedom*? If we compare the meek, sober mediocrity of German political literature with this *titanic* and brilliant literary debut of the German workers; if we compare these *gigantic* children's shows of the proletariat with the dwarf-like proportions of the worn-out political shoes of the German bourgeoisie, we must predict a vigorous future for this German Cinderella." Karl Marx, "Critical Marginal Notes on 'The King of Prussia and Social Reform. By a Prussian,'" in *MECW* 3:190. And at the start of the *1844 Manuscripts*, Marx acknowledged having used the works of French and English socialists, the "original German works of substance" by Weitling and Hess, as well as his own contribution and that of Engels to the *Deutsch-Französische Jahrbücher. MECW* 3:231.
7   Marx and Engels, "The Holy Family, or Critique of Critical Criticism," in *MECW* 4:38.
8   Ibid., 4:31.
9   Karl Marx, Letter to Pavel Vasilyevich Annenkov, December 28, 1846, in *MECW* 38:95.
10   Marx and Engels, "The Holy Family," 4:130.
11   Théodore Dézamy, *Calomnies et politique de M. Cabet: Réfutation par des faits et par sa biographie* (Paris: Prévost, 1842).
12   "Just as he makes Saint-Simon the pioneer of political economy, he makes him the pioneer of scientific socialism: 'It' (Saint-Simonism) 'contains . . . scientific socialism, *for* Saint-Simon spent his whole life searching for the new science!'" (*MECW* 5:505). It is for Engels a matter of utmost importance not to reduce the development of scientific socialism, the result of a very complex critical process, to a magical formula. And mechanically coupling the words "socialism" and "science" in no way advances the problem.
13   Karl Marx, "Contribution to the Critique of Hegel's Philosophy of Right," in *MECW* 3:8.
14   Karl Marx, "The Poverty of Philosophy," in *MECW* 6:177.
15   Marx and Engels, "Proudhon's Speech Against Thiers," in *MECW* 7:321. The same formulation can be found in the *Communist Manifesto*: "They [the inventors of socialist and communist systems–M. A.] therefore search after a new social science, after new

social laws, that are to create these conditions." "By degrees, they sink into the category of the reactionary [or] conservative Socialists depicted above, differing from these only by more systematic pedantry, and by their fanatical and superstitious belief in the miraculous effects of their social science." Marx and Engels, *Manifesto of the Communist Party*, in *MECW* 6:517.

16   "The utopian strands in socialism, though they do have their historical roots in the critique of the existing social organization, are properly so called inasmuch as they deny history—inasmuch, that is, as they deny the struggle that exists, along with any movement of the times beyond the immutable perfection of their image of a happy society. Not, however, because they deny science. On the contrary, the utopians were completely in thrall to scientific thinking, in the form in which this had imposed itself in the preceding centuries." Guy Debord, *The Society of the Spectacle*, trans. Donald Nicholson-Smith (New York: Zone, 1994), sec. 83.

17   This link between the critique of the scientificity proper to utopia and the affirmation, against this antihistorical scientificity, of a science of history, as critical knowledge of the real movement of modern society, is constant in Marx: "he [Proudhon] and the utopians are hunting for a so-called '*science*' by means of which a formula for the 'solution of the social question' is to be devised *a priori*, instead of deriving science from a critical knowledge of the historical movement, a movement which itself produces the *material conditions of emancipation*." Karl Marx, Letter to J. B. Schweitzer, "On Proudhon," in *MECW* 20:30. Engels also attributes to the discovery of a new theory of history the transition of critico-utopian communism to critical communism and the specificity of the latter form of communism: "And Communism now no longer meant the concoction, by means of the imagination, of an ideal society as perfect as possible, but insight into the nature, the conditions and the consequent general aims of the struggle waged by the proletariat." Engels, "On the History of the Communist League," in *MECW* 26:320.

Critical communism is, then, the most exact name for Marx and Engels's theory.

18   Auguste Comte to Chevalier, January 5, 1832, in *Le Globe*, January 13, 1832, cited by Henry-René d'Allemagne, *Les Saints-Simoniens* (Paris: Gründ, 1930), 210.

19   Auguste Blanqui, "Defence Speech," in *The Red Republican and the Friend of the People*, vol. 2, ed. George Julian Harney (Merlin Press, 1966), 281.

20   Karl Mannheim, *Ideology and Utopia: An Introduction to the Sociology of Knowledge*, trans. Louis Wirth and Edward Shils (London: Harcourt, Brace, 1954), 177.

21   Herbert Marcuse, "The End of Utopia," trans. Jeremy Shapiro and Shierry M. Weber, in *Five Lectures* (Boston: Beacon, 1970), 63.

22   "While we cannot repudiate these patriarchs of socialism [Fourier, Owen, Saint-Simon—M. A.], just as chemists cannot repudiate their forebears the alchemists, we must at least avoid falling back into their mistakes, which, if we were to commit them, would be inexcusable." Karl Marx, "Political Indifferentism," in *MECW* 23:393. It would be interesting to compare this with a text by Déjacque relating to the new utopian spirit, in which the contrast between chemistry and alchemy also makes an appearance: "Those searching for ideal happiness, like those searching for the philosopher's stone, might never completely realize their utopia, though their utopia will be the cause

of humanitarian progress. Alchemy might not succeed in making gold, but it has drawn from its crucible something a good deal more precious than a vain metal; it has produced a science, chemistry. Social science will be the work of the dreamers of perfect harmony." Joseph Déjacque, *L'Humanisphère* (1857; Paris: Champ Libre, 1971), pt. 2, prelude. Likewise, Engels: "In the same manner as German theoretical Socialism will never forget that it rests on the shoulders of Saint-Simon, Fourier and Owen, the three who, in spite of their fantastic notions and Utopianism, belonged to the most significant heads of all time and whose genius anticipated numerous things the correctness of which can now be proved in a scientific way." Engels, addendum to "The Peasant War in Germany" (1874), in *MECW* 10:399.

23 A.-L. Morton, "Un Demi-Siècle d'Utopie (de Robert Owen et Charles Fourier à William Morris)," *La Pensée* 108 (March–April 1963): 26–27.

24 Walter Benjamin, "Paris, the Capital of the Nineteenth Century," in *Walter Benjamin: Selected Writings*, ed. Howard Eiland and Michael Jennings (Cambridge: Harvard University Press, 2003–2006), vol. 3.

25 On this conjunction of utopia and the Commune, which would demand a special study, we will cite just a few indicators. Keeping just to literary works, there are the writings of Déjacque, *La Question révolutionnaire* (1853–1854) and *L'Humanisphère* (1858–1858); those of Cœurderoy; Pierre Leroux's *La Grève de Samarez* (1857); Blanqui's *Instructions pour une prise d'armes* (1864); Victor Hugo's *Paris* (1867); shortly after the Commune *Paris in the Year 2000* by Dr. Tony Moilin, shot by the Versaillais; shortly after that R. de Mericourt's *La Commune en l'an 2073* (1874) and also Blanqui's *L'Éternité par les astres* (1872). An exhibition at the Stockholm Museum of Modern Art tried to take stock of this real conjunction between utopia and the Commune by taking as its theme "Daily Life During the 72 Days of a Utopia."

26 On the critique of the concept of maturity "in action" and on the valorization of the social movement' autonomous utopian tendencies, see E. P. Thompson, *The Making of the English Working Class* (London: IICA, 1963).

27 Walter Benjamin, "On the Concept of History," in *Selected Writings*, 4:391.

28 "The thesis of the primacy of being over consciousness includes the methodological imperative to express the dynamic tendencies of reality in the formation and movement of concepts instead of forming and verifying concepts in accordance with the demand that they have pragmatic and expedient features." Theodor W. Adorno, *Prisms*, trans. Samuel Weber and Shierry Weber (London: Spearman, 1967), 43.

29 Leroux's importance as both theoretician and historian of socialist-communist utopia cannot be overestimated. In both *La Grève de Samarez* (1857) and the "Lettre au Docteur Deville" (*L'Espérance*, October 1858–January 1859), Leroux sets out the basics of a theory and history of utopia freed from antiutopian prejudice and conscious of the links between social utopianism and the Romantic movement (cf. Leroux's article "Le Style symbolique"). See my article introducing the "Lettre au Docteur Deville": Abensour, "Pierre Leroux et l'utopie socialiste," *Cahiers de l'I.S.E.A.*, *Études de marxologie* series (December 1972): 2201–2247 and 2249–2284; republished in *Le Procès des maîtres rêveurs* (Paris: Sens et Tonka, 2013).

30 Constantin Pecqueur, introduction, *Théorie nouvelle d'économie sociale et politique* (Paris: Capelle, 1842). See also Amédée Paget, *Introduction à l'étude de la science sociale* (Paris: Bureau de la Phalange, 1838). This author sees a unitary perspective as what allows the three creators of social systems (Saint-Simon, Fourier, Owen) to be distinguished from philanthropists and other reformers who, at close range, are incapable of perceiving "a general cause that infects the entirety of the social Body."

31 Louis Reybaud, *Études sur les réformateurs contemporains ou socialistes modernes* (Paris: Guillaumin, 1840), 1:vii–viii.

32 Charles Fourier, *Œuvres complètes*, ed. Simone Debout (Paris: Anthropos, 1967), 10:313.

33 Ibid., 1:316.

34 Marx, "Economic and Philosophic Manuscripts of 1844," in *MECW* 3:302

35 Marx, "Grundrisse, III. Chapter on Capital," in *MECW* 28:345.

36 Ibid., 28:346.

37 It would be worth the trouble to explore these nineteenth-century figures of happiness. The two guidebooks are by Leroux and by Engels ("Progress of Social Reform on the Continent"). Leroux recognizes in Saint-Simon the merit of having proposed a new organization of humanity founded on industry, in Fourier of having articulated a critique of the helotry, and finally in Owen of having announced the reign of machines and thereby the end of social dependency. The same approach informs the analyses of Engels, even if the substance attributed to each utopian is different: Saint-Simon discovered the antagonism of classes, Fourier established for the first time the great axiom of social philosophy concerning the collective power of labor, and, as for Owen, he formulated the critique of religion, marriage, and property. For this exploration, see also Benoît Malon, *Exposé des écoles socialistes françaises* (Paris: Le Chevalier, 1872); Marius-Ary Leblond, *L'Idéal du XIXe siècle* (Paris: Alcan, 1909). See also, more recently, the writings of Henri Desroche.

38 "The order of the profane should be erected on the idea of happiness." Walter Benjamin, "Theologico-Political Fragment," in *Selected Writings*, 3:305; Herbert Marcuse, "On Hedonism," in *Negations*, trans. Jeremy J. Shapiro (New York: Penguin, 1968).

39 Barthes, "Vivre avec Fourier," *Critique* 28 (1970): 789–812.

40 Herbert Marcuse, *Reason and Revolution: Hegel and the Rise of Social Theory*, 2nd ed. (London: Routledge and Kegan Paul, 1955), 294. The same approach underpins Marx's critique of politics, notably in the major texts of 1843–1844. Here Marx refused the transubstantiation or catharsis characteristic of even democratic political thought.

41 Georges Bataille, "The Psychological Structure of Fascism," in *Visions of Excess: Selected Writings, 1927–1939*, trans. Allan Stoekl, Carl R. Lovitt, and Donald M. Leslie (Minneapolis: University of Minnesota Press, 1985), 143.

42 Mikhail Bakhtin, *Problems of Dostoevsky's Poetics*, trans. Caryl Emerson (Minneapolis: University of Minnesota Press, 1984), 81.

43 At the same moment that, within the Contre-Attaque group, Bataille posited precisely the necessity of self-interrogation about affective social formations, of constituting and utilizing a system of knowledge pertaining to the social movements of attraction and repulsion as a weapon, he seemed to have found in utopian socialism only morals and

idealism. Cf. "The Psychological Structure of Fascism." In the same period, André Breton, Pierre Klossowski, and Walter Benjamin were more aware of the appeal already made by the great utopians to renewed affective forces. The theorization, or germs of theorization, of utopia in the utopian movement of the nineteenth century—which critics appear to have ignored, and which I will take up elsewhere—remains to be appreciated.

44 Marx and Engels, "The German Ideology," in *MECW* 5:464.

45 "Alongside the German communists, a number of writers have appeared who have absorbed a few French and English communist ideas and amalgamated them with their own German philosophical premises.... They detach the communist systems, critical and polemical writings from the real movement, of which they are but the expression, and force them into an arbitrary connection with German philosophy. They detach the consciousness of certain historically conditioned spheres of life from these spheres and evaluate it in terms of true, absolute, i.e., German philosophical consciousness.... This 'true socialism' is nothing but the transfiguration of proletarian communism, and of the parties and sects that are more or less akin to it, in France and England within the heaven of the German mind and, as we shall also see, of the German sentiment." Ibid., 455.

46 Marx and Engels, *Manifesto of the Communist Party*, 6:513.

47 Nietzsche in *Human, All Too Human* calls for the construction of just such a machine: "99—*The poet as signpost to the future.*—That poetic power available to men of today which is not used up in the depiction of life ought to be dedicated, not so much to the representation of the contemporary world or to the reanimation and imaginative reconstruction of the past, but to sign posting the future:—not, though, as if the poet could, like a fabulous economist, figuratively anticipate the kind of conditions nations and societies would prosper better under and how they could then be brought about. Many a path to this poetry of the future starts out from *Goethe*: but it requires good pathfinders and above all a much greater power than present-day poets—that is to say the innocuous depicters of the semi-animal and of immaturity and abnormality confused with force and naturalness—possess." Nietzsche, *Human, All Too Human*, trans. R. J. Hollingdale (Cambridge: Cambridge University Press, 1996), 235–236. This text is all the more interesting because Nietzsche subjects to the same contempt the utopian creators of the lie of the ideal, disparaging life, and those ecstatic before the force of history, bordering on the idolatry of facticity. As Karl Löwith showed in his works, Nietzsche, in this sense, belongs to the same constellation that produced the Young Hegelian movement, Bakunin, and Marx. Nietzsche saw in the poetry of the future the effective means of escape from the repetition of the present.

48 To my knowledge, it is Max Nettlau who deserves credit for first bringing together these three great utopians: "As a utopian, he [Cœurderoy] aligns himself with Fourier, Joseph Déjacque and William Morris: beauty, art, diversity, and the most extensive freedom are the essence of his dreams." Nettlau, preface to Cœurderoy, *Œuvres* (Paris: P.-V. Stock, 1910–1911), 3:ix. They should brought together both as theoreticians and as practitioners of the new utopian spirit.

49 Cœurderoy, *Œuvres*, 1:53.
50 Ibid., 1:60.
51 Déjacque, *L'Humanisphère*, 90.
52 "The reconstruction must employ workers of all specializations. . . . Society is greater than Mr. Louis le Blanc, wiser than Mr. Cabet, more progressive than the revolutionaries. I am not with the revolutionaries, I am with the Revolution. I am not with the systematizers, I am with science." Cœurderoy, *Œuvres*, 1:61.
53 Bakhtin, *Problems of Dostoevsky's Poetics*, 110.
54 Victor Considerant, *Destinée sociale* (Paris: Bureau de la Phalange, 1837), 1:505.
55 Déjacque, *L'Humanisphère*, 88–89.
56 "I inhabit the depths of society; I have drawn from them some revolutionary thoughts, and I pour them forth, rending the darkness. . . . I sigh after happiness and I conjure up its ideal. If that ideal makes you smile, do as I do, and love it. If you find imperfections in it, correct them. If it displeases you, create another. I am not exclusive, and I will willingly abandon mine for yours, if yours seems more perfect to me." Ibid., 91.
57 Ibid., 86–87.
58 Cœurderoy, *Œuvres*, 1:124.
59 "Meantime, I hold that we need not be afraid of scaring our audiences with too brilliant pictures of the future of society, nor think ourselves unpractical and utopian for telling them the bare truth, that in destroying monopoly we shall destroy our present civilization. On the contrary, it is utopian to put forward a scheme of gradual logical reconstruction of society which is liable to be overturned at the first historical hitch it comes to. . . . And certainly the Socialists who are always preaching to the people that Socialism is an economic change pure and simple, are very apt to repel those who want to learn for the sake of those who do not." William Morris, quoted in May Morris and Bernard Shaw, *William Morris, Artist, Writer, Socialist: Morris as a Socialist: William Morris as I Knew Him* (New York: Russell and Russell, 1966), 307.
60 Benjamin, "On the Concept of History," in *Selected Writings*, vol. 4. See also Arthur Rosenberg, *Histoire du Bolchévisme* (Paris: Grasset, 1967).
61 The practice of detour on which the new utopian spirit rests is opposed to the classical approach. Instead of reading Marx on the basis of what succeeded him, in short, through the screen of his disciples, one performs a return to Marx in his contemporaneity or on the basis of thinkers and movements that Marx "surpassed" or critiqued without actually rejecting. It is as though in the gap opened by this critique or this "surpassing" one can grasp Marx's radicality, the rending and decentering produced at a given moment in the dominant culture, the founding act in its very trajectory. It is a matter of placing Marx's oeuvre in a new space, no longer in that of classical Marxism delimited by Kautsky, Plekhanov, Lenin, Trotsky, and so on, but in the socialist-communist space outlined by the great utopians, Flora Tristan, the Communist League, the French materialist communist movement, Blanqui, and the like. This method, it should be made clear, has nothing in common with the history of ideas. Its project is to deconstruct the ideological and institutional formations erected upon

Marx's work, whose act of foundation has been hidden in its double movement of construction and effacement.

62 Benjamin, "Paris, the Capital of the Nineteenth Century," 3:13.

63 Gilles Deleuze, "Renverser le Platonisme," *Revue de Métaphysique et de Morale* 4 (1966): 426–438.

64 Pierre Klossowski, "The Phantasms of Perversion: Sade and Fourier," trans. Paul Foss and Paul Patton, in *Phantasms and Simulacra: The Drawings of Pierre Klossowski*, ed. Paul Patton, Paul Taylor, and Allen S. Weiss, special issue, *Art and Text* 18 (1985): 22–34.

2

IS THE CLASSIC CONCEPT OF UTOPIA READY FOR THE FUTURE?

RICHARD SAAGE

I

Anyone discussing utopia today has to know that there is no consensus on how the concept should be understood. This dilemma can be seen exemplarily in the social sciences, where it is above all the intentional, totalitarian, and classical concept that has become canonical.

The origins of the intentional conception go back to Gustav Landauer. In his study *Revolution* from 1907, Landauer interprets utopia as a decisive explosive charge of the revolutionary upheavals in Europe that have happened since the sixteenth century.[1] He seeks to isolate its mechanism in the fact that social development always swings between two "states of relative stability." Landauer calls this structure, which encompasses all domains of society and reaches into individual lives, *topia*. Of course the solidity of a *topia* is not absolute, since within the field it affects there are potentials it cannot absorb: utopias. What characterizes them is having withdrawn from the sphere of prevailing social norms and institutions. As a "mass of individual strivings and intentions that are always heterogeneous and individually available," they are negatively directed at the *topia*'s structures of domination.

To the extent that the bearers of utopia, above all intellectuals and artists, succeed in corroding a *topia*, it falls into a legitimation crisis. If this reaches a certain level of intensity, the originally individualized utopias start to combine through an "enthusiastic intoxication" into a "unity and a form of collective life." Now utopia goes from destruction to construction by outlining the fictive scenario of an ideal society—which, however, naturally founders on the restrictive conditions of its realization and produces a new structure of domination. This new *topia* as a rule includes elements of older utopias along with components of earlier systems of domination. But Landauer explicitly rejects all historical determinism. From this we must conclude that it is possible to fall back to the level of *topias* that we believe we have already gone beyond. Nonetheless, utopian potential lives on in individuals beneath the layers of sociopolitical domination.

It is clear that Landauer's concept of utopia is a new creation that has little in common with the approach developed by Thomas More in his famous work from 1516. What binds the two can be represented by a relatively small overlap in meaning, restricted to the confrontation of utopian ideals with tendencies in the society of origin that need to be criticized and the demand for the emancipation of social groups and classes that are oppressed in the existing society. In fact, the general thrust of Landauer's concept of utopia is anarchistic. Utopia takes the side of the unhindered development of the individual against power congealed in institutions that reach from the state to the market into private life. But while according to this understanding utopia represents the medium within which institutionalized forms of power are as it were liquefied, the classical tradition valorized precisely the institutional element of designs. It is no wonder that in *Revolution* Landauer overlooked these pages of More's *Utopia*. In order to be able to integrate it into his paradigm at all, he simply emphasized the relatively liberal elements, like achieving peace, promoting science and art, overcoming the order of estates, selecting officials, religious toleration, and a deistic rational religion.

There are other important differences as well. The classic utopia was from the beginning anti-individualistic: the whole always had priority over the part or individual. This premise was reflected in a design for a whole society whose institutions are rendered in detail, from the economy to the relations between the sexes. In contrast, Landauer and his successors remain rather vague about the concrete arrangements of their plans. They do not, like the classical tradition, challenge the process of individualization in the early-modern period, but rather take it as their starting point. For Landauer, utopian potential has an anthropological basis. It is anchored in the individual in more or less pronounced ways before it mutates to a collective scale. But above all the classical tradition is spatial: the fictive social alternative exists at the same time as the criticized social relations under which it was conceived. At the same time there is a break with history as it has been, which appears as corrupt through and through. In contrast to this assumption, Landauer's approach is temporal, since it locates its goal, a society free of domination, in the future, without of course tying the utopian fiction to a consistent model of progress, as Bloch would later do. As distinct from the spatial utopia, the past is valorized, since elements of past utopias are taken up at each stage of a realized utopia.

The intentional understanding of utopia—intentional because it derives from individual motivations for action—was given important further developments by Karl Mannheim and Ernst Bloch. Indeed, Mannheim reproaches Landauer for assuming that in principle every utopia can be realized; he thus tends toward "blindness of being" and voluntarism by failing to conceive of absolute, that is, unrealistic, utopias. But this distancing goes along with far-reaching agreement. Like Landauer, Mannheim not only sees the first form of utopian consciousness in the chiliasm of the Anabaptists, which tied individual utopian intentions to a transindividual unity. Just as important, he adopts his *topia*-utopia model. Mannheim assigns *topia* to ideology, while he characterizes utopia by its function of exploding *topias*. He also takes over Landauer's thesis that every level of being contains the utopian potentials of earlier social formations, by which they were burst in the movement toward a next being. But, unlike Landauer, Mannheim interprets this process within a right-Hegelian evolutionary model.[2]

However consequential Mannheim's conceptualization of "utopia" and "ideology" has been for the social sciences, its success cannot conceal the fact that in the end Mannheim's social-epistemological approach itself undermines his work. Since their perspectives on social reality are context-dependent and therefore selective, contemporaries cannot distinguish between ideology and utopia. Who can tell what is "being-transcendent" in the sense of transforming social realities and what is an apology for the status quo if the "relative utopia" connected to realization has to become ideology the moment it refuses the transformation to the next level of being? One could say that Mannheim dissolves the concept of utopia as an independent category and defines it as a variant of what he understands as ideology: it appears as an advocate of transformation (utopia) but at the same time must defend the social reality it creates (ideology). Only on this premise can Mannheim subsume Anabaptist chiliasm and liberalism under the same concept of utopia as conservatism and socialism/communism. In terms of his social-epistemological approach, it is a matter of context-dependent systems of thought that are progressively found in sociopolitical reality. What falls through this analytical raster, however, is the specificity of utopia itself: it encompasses all intellectual frameworks that have developed since the early-modern period, and precisely through this claim to totality is as good as nothing.

Ernst Bloch's later Marxist turn, in which utopia, mediated through the category of the "objectively" possible, is integrated into the categorial framework of historical materialism, cannot conceal Landauer's influence, though he does not mention him. For Bloch too, utopian thinking begins with the sixteenth-century social-revolutionary strivings of the Peasants' War and the Anabaptists.[3] Accordingly, like Landauer, he sees in utopia essentially a forward-directed motivation that finds expression in individual dreams, wishes, and longings and urges the creation of better possibilities for an indeterminate future. Bloch is moreover likewise convinced that the development of *topias*, even when they take the form of counterrevolutionary regressions, cannot destroy the utopian potential in individuals. But serious deficits oppose this positive assessment. Landauer had no doubt that utopia is not an autonomous phenomenon, but has a derivative character: it is a by-product of revolutionary upheavals. This reductionism has a price: whatever the revolution demands counts as utopian. Relocated to the subjective level, with Bloch utopia can take on an enormous range of possible expressions, from religious eschatologies, ecstatic states, and orgiastic chiliasms to individual daydreams, fairy tales, and annual markets to Beethoven's Ninth Symphony. Extending a concept so far makes it literally limitless. Utopia then ceases to be a clearly defined object of investigation.

If Mannheim still contains this overflow by reference to systems of thought that can be reconstructed, for Bloch in the last instance utopias can really only "happen." Since they are beyond scientific reach, there is only one way to approach utopia: by directly participating in it as a subjective experience. It is said of this concept of utopia that it has broken through the static "finite ideal representation" and at the same time dynamized the utopian. This reemphasis, which effects a turn from mere intellectual endeavor to a mode of thinking that runs throughout history and mediates theory and practice, has brought about a renewal of utopian discourse, especially in the social sciences.

If Landauer, Bloch, and Mannheim start the original model of the utopian with the Anabaptists and the Peasants' War, Karl Popper traces the totalitarian concept of utopia back to Plato's *Republic*.[4] As a closed, systemic utopia, he recommended it to the Attic democracy with its dynamism, its class struggle, its individualism, and the emancipatory strivings of its underclasses. In modernity, according to Popper, a similar constellation arose: utopian ideas of a closed society, as developed by Marx and Hegel, are to be understood as an answer to the individualizing tendencies and conflict potentials of pluralistic Western societies. What is decisive for Popper's concept of utopia is that he does not deduce it from an ontology or anthropology. Instead, he traces Plato's utopian model of estate-based communism back to the aristocratic tribal societies of Sparta and Crete as well as their forerunners. According to Popper, Plato believed he had found in their stability and static absence of conflict a solution to the problem of class conflict and economic interest.

The decisive formal principle of the utopian model according to Popper is holism or entity thinking, which he interprets as the direct consequence of a "return to the tribe, to the primitive horde." On his view the interest of the "whole" always has priority over the wishes of the individual. Popper accordingly interprets the utopian model of society as a by-product of the premodern structures of a tribal extended family, which in its lack of complexity can only be realized in a differentiated industrial society through terror on a grand scale. It thus always comes into effect when it is connected with historicism and a particular variant of social technology. Historicism too is a by-product of the originary egoism of the tribe, which claims a world-historical mission. At the same time, it functions within the utopian model as the decisive link between the holistic design and the sociopolitical reality that is to be transformed: only when a utopia emerges with the claim to execute a law of history or "historical necessity" does it make a claim to the total revision of social reality. As a "grand-scale method of planning," it creates irreversible facts. The use of totalitarian terror is its necessary correlate, since the continuity of long-term utopian goals can only be secured if the pluralism of competing interests is destroyed along with all the other obstacles that arise from social change and stand in the way of realizing the final goal.

Popper's service surely lies in having exposed the totalitarian potential of closed utopias, together with their historicist validity claims, more systematically than had ever been done before. But the strengths of this concept of utopia at the same time suggest its weakness: namely, that Popper's approach destroys the autonomy of the utopian phenomenon, reducing it to a by-product of totalitarianism—indeed, a synonym for it. The consequences are far-reaching. It leads to a crude disfiguration of the utopian that necessarily occurs when a part is taken for the whole. The equation with totalitarianism leads, on one side, to the extension of the utopian to structures of thought that are foreign to it. Popper thus subsumes the social theories of Marx and Engels under the concept of utopia just as he does the system of fascist domination. On the other side, however, Popper's approach leads to a narrowing of the utopian phenomenon that directly affects its substance. Fixed as a static construct, a derivative of totalitarianism, the utopian is not perceived as precisely what it was from the beginning: a discourse within whose framework alternatives could be thought and could be made sensitive to learning processes.

So Popper's charge that political utopia is structurally undercomplex misses the target. To be sure, in modern utopian thinking there have always also been models whose socially regressive character is unmistakable. But it is part of the ethics of scholarly work to criticize a genre on the basis of its strongest rather than its weakest exemplars. Anyone who compares Thomas More's *Utopia* with medieval social formations, for example, cannot help but see that it breaks with their structures of stratification. The fact that the utopian thinkers of the classical tradition succeeded in integrating scientific-technological progress into their constructs is a logical consequence of this circumstance. If utopian thinking not only took into account the complexity of modernity from the beginning but, as many examples would show, worked through them in advance, it then offers the advantage, not to be underestimated, of reducing complexity by, for example, being able to at least imagine it in other, perhaps more humane contexts as a thought experiment.

The dilemma of the intentional and the totalitarian concept of utopia is clear: both approaches argue reductively because their object always only partially coincides with the phenomenon of the utopian. Those who want to take up political utopia without shortcuts cannot get around turning to the sources in which it took shape. A suggestion from Norbert Elias offers one escape from these difficulties: a return to the classic tradition that began with More's *Utopia*.[5] On the basis of this model, political utopias are fictions of this-worldly societies that concretize hopes or fears. What binds utopias and dystopias is that both are concerned with fictional, rationally imaginable social models that go beyond mere subjective wishes or anxieties, depicting a world we want to have or avoid. In both cases, what dominates is the normative motive of optimizing or at least defending human indispensable values like love, integrity, and social solidarity. The goals projected are distinguished by a precise critique of existing institutions and sociopolitical relations that stand in contrast to an alternative articulated in secular categories. Without the antithetical confrontation of utopian ideal with what needs to be criticized, the classical utopias would lose their identity.

It is no accident that they developed at the beginning of the sixteenth century, with the collapse of the feudal order of estates. Two paths emerged for responding to this collapse. The first was that taken by the representatives of subjective or individualistic natural right. They attempted to reach a new social consensus and give it meaning by placing the autonomous individual and his rational power of judgment at the center. Through a contract that the individual bearers of reason conclude with one another in a prepolitical state of nature, political rule and the social system it presupposes are justified in a mostly secular way. Since the appearance of Thomas More's *Utopia* in 1516, the other way was that taken by the utopians. Themselves products of secularization, they sought from the beginning to arrest its consequences, the individualization and fragmentation of lifeworlds by the rising bourgeois society, with a new, unified structure. Their building blocks were also constructs of secularized reason, but in a collective or monistic mode: they created utopias to show us how the world in which we want to live should or should not be.

The analytical advantages of this concept are obvious, since it avoids the deficits of intentional and totalitarian concepts of utopia. I would like to name three virtues:

1. The classical model of utopia offers clear criteria that distinguish it from other phenomena. According to these criteria, metaphysical and otherworldly visions of Paradise or a Golden Age can no more count as political utopias than dream associations, chiliastic hopes of redemption, religious eschatologies, myths, or various versions of individualistic contractualism. As constructs of secularized reason, they are normatively directed toward the future. For this reason, they cannot be equated with technological anticipations like science fiction or with social-scientific prognostication, like those attempted by Marxism or futurology. While methodologically distilled into an ideal type, however, from the perspective of the classical concept of utopia mixed forms can also be identified.

2. This concept holds to the extent that it grasps political utopia as a phenomenon of both reaction and anticipation, doing justice to the continuity and transformation of its object. Its structural elements, which extend from its social critique of an economic and political system to its claim to validity, remain identical. But it fills them with period-specific contents, since the problems it reacts to change. Since they are not defined by a particular genre, utopian contents can be conveyed by different media, such as novels or social-philosophical discourses.

3. The classical concept of utopia does not have to trace utopian ideas back to pregiven quantities like "revolution" or "totalitarianism." It can converge with them, but it is not identical to them. Giving up reductionist schemas makes way for a critical-hermeneutic investigation of the object. Only such an approach makes it possible to speak of utopia in the plural, in its multifarious shapes, and, perhaps more important still, to grasp it as a phenomenon that can learn, that becomes more sensitive through self-critical reflection, and that has had a lasting impact on modern civilization. To this extent, this approach opens up the effective history of utopia thinking, and so a concrete object of historical, sociological, political, philosophical, and literary research.

II

No one would call Max Weber's influential diagnosis of modern society utopian. Those familiar with his analyses of the "iron cage" are likelier to call him an antiutopian fatalist. And yet in the development his ideal-typical approach he is nearer to utopian methods than one would initially expect. As with utopian designs, ideal types involve a construction of social reality that occurs nowhere in historical reality in its pure form.[6]

If we apply this ideal-typical method to the utopian material that comes down to us in various forms, it seems easiest, following Andreas Voigt, to distinguish between archistic and anarchistic models of utopian thinking.[7] Voigt grounds this difference anthropologically. He sees the decisive criterion in people's different attitudes toward serving and ruling, coercion and freedom. The ideal of the *archistic* utopia is generally a state with a strong, encompassing coercive authority that regulates all its members' relations from cradle to grave. The general idea of the *anarchistic* utopia, in contrast, proceeds from the social ideal of absolute freedom. All coercion, rule, government, police, and criminal justice are abolished. As irreconcilable as the holistic and individualistic premises of the two approaches may appear, one thing binds them together under the general heading of classical utopia: they oppose the possessive-individualistic egoism of the society from which they arose, opting instead for a fictive social model oriented along solidary-communitarian lines. While More's *Utopia*, like almost all utopias of its age, belongs to the archistic type, within the same formal pattern in the Renaissance and Reformation the anarchistic type gradually developed from a fictive ideal of solidaristic community drawing on the spirit of social criticism. Already discernable in Antiquity, it has been ascendant since the 1970s.

My use of these categories differs essentially from Voigt's, however. First of all, I regard their connection to basic anthropological attitudes to be reductionist, since archistic utopias can also be interpreted as an answer to the chaotic conditions of their authors' times, just as anarchistic versions can be traced back to high degrees of regimentation. Moreover, the use of the two categories as ideal types—that is, as heuristic instruments with negative evaluative connotations—goes beyond what Voigt ascribes to them. Finally, for my approach the archistic and anarchistic utopias' different relations to nature are central, whereas they play no role for Voigt. Since Antiquity the utopian imagination that underlies the archistic model has been aligned with the regulation of social mechanisms. There can be no field outside society because it would escape reason. Even nature itself is subordinated to the principle of social use. In contrast, for the anarchistic approach in classical pastoral poetry, political and socialeconomic institutions as well as norms of social action and cultural interaction are peripheral.[8] Nonetheless, politics, as the creation of peace, refers back to, and is measured by, prehistorical pastoralism.

With this help of the ideal-typical distinction, both the reception of ancient models of utopia and the specific profile of modern utopia can be mapped. Thus, despite unmistakable lines of continuity, More makes a significant paradigm shift in the archistic tradition when he revalues work, which Ancients regarded negatively, and at the same time prescribes communal property not only, like Plato, for the elite, but for the whole society. This egalitarianism levels what was still out of the question for Euphemerus, namely, the hierarchical, estate-based structure of society with its ranks and privileges. A second dividing line that separates modern archistic utopia from its ancient predecessors arises from modern natural science and technology: it replaces Plato's contemplative concept of science with the active application of natural-scientific knowledge in the form of a technological sphere that includes the economy, something alien to the Ancients. Dynamized by this process and, from the middle of the eighteenth century, projected into the future as a "timeutopia," teleological progress makes the ancient paradigm of the eternal return of the same as obsolete as the ancient ideal city's manageable and stable size. Surveying the wealth produced by the Industrial Revolution, finally, the modern archistic utopia replaced the iron constraint of scarcity with material surplus, which had previously seemed unthinkable outside the world of myth. In contrast, the "modernization" of the anarchistic approach to utopia only managed to replace the ancient myth of self-regulating nature with the "slavery of the machine" (Oscar Wilde).

With the ideal-typical grid of the classical concept of utopia, however, it is also possible to identify differences when it comes to chiliasm or eschatology. An exclusive result of human efforts and not of a transcendent act of mercy, unlike the idea of Paradise, More's *Utopia* appears as the result of the analysis of the society that the author comes from and that it confronts as a superior possibility. The alternative does not consist in giving up worldly burdens and delights and leading a pious life. Rather, the point is to overcome the indicated causes of misery, which are immanent to the world and for which people are themselves responsible. Only then is the foundation of utopia laid. In contrast to the ideas of early-modern chiliastic enthusiasts, utopias of the "new man" were by no means completely a priori. Their basic anthropological configuration approximates a tabula rasa: they can be modeled positively or negatively on external influences. In opposition to the chiliastic self-understanding, in early-modern, archistic space-utopias institutions play a decisive role: they use the state, economy, family, child-rearing, religious community, and school to encourage peoples' constructive facilities while repressing their destructive potential with rational laws. Indeed, as a rule the space-utopias of the early-modern period do away with mine and thine altogether. Unlike chiliasm, however, they retain a hierarchical order that reaches from the political system to the patriarchal family structure. Finally, what social criticism signifies for utopia is apocalypse for the chiliastic paradigm. It follows from this that the motives that undergird the utopian and chiliastic approaches are mutually exclusive. The apocalyptic paradigm does not aim at enlightenment concerning the causes of depraved social relations for which people are themselves responsible, but the mobilization of individual and collective fears of divine punishment.

Above all, the ideal-typical method allows analytically useful criteria for distinguishing between utopia and science fiction.[9] In contrast to classical utopia, which since Antiquity has reacted to sociopolitical crisis-symptoms in its context of origin, science fiction is an outgrowth of the scientific and technological optimism of the nineteenth century. The brave explorer or inventor and the brilliant engineer do not owe their inspiration to social flashpoints. The two genres' attitudes toward technology also differ. To be sure, from the beginning its esteem played a decisive role for the classical utopian tradition, as we see from even before Bacon's *New Atlantis*. Since the nineteenth century and the onset of industrialization, it became a cornerstone of utopian schemes. But for utopian thinking what matters is not so much technology itself as its consequences for society. In contrast, science fiction emphasizes the whether and how of technological innovation. Its authors are interested in how spaceships can be made to fly as realistically as possible. The protagonists' use of technology and the spectacular deeds it allows are decisive, not a total social picture that is presented as an image to be wished for or feared. The relation of both to the future is also fundamentally different. From its beginnings science fiction has lived, assimilating elements of futurology, from the prognosis of technological developments, even if imaginatively enriched, from Karel Čapek's anticipation of the atom bomb to H. G. Wells. In contrast to this prognostic "if-then" principal that binds science fiction to futurology, since its historical-philosophical turn in the middle of the eighteenth century classical utopian thinking itself has gotten by without prognostics. It has been shaped not by the anticipation of the future by extrapolating from present tendencies, but by the normative fiction of a political or stateless society that we want or do not want—regardless of whether the imaginary community is thought of as a regulative principle, as in spatial utopias, or as in principle realizable, as in time-utopias.

An even greater analytical advantage of the ideal-typical method consists in identifying mixed forms of utopian thinking. In the world of ancient myth there are elements from both the archistic and the anarchistic side without which modern utopia would not have developed. The ancient prototype of archistic social blueprints is rightly held to be Plato's *Republic*. But it should not be missed that it had forerunners in ancient conceptions of the ideal city that, like Hippodamus's, anticipated Plato's model and built it in stone. As artifacts of *ratio*, they represent a "secondary system" organized along geometrical lines that is withdrawn from the chaos of nature and subject exclusively to human control. At the same time, along with the sociopolitical constitution they create the architecture for a "good life" in the physical environment. This concentration of all powers in the struggle against the external forces of nature makes domination inescapable. The anarchistic approach argues the other way round: all problems would be solved if we chose a life not against but for nature. Itself part of nature, the human species will be cared for by nature if it only abandons its Promethean defiance and trusts in its wisdom. The Golden Age, evoked not only by Hesiod but again and again in Roman poetry by Virgil, Horace, and others, is nothing but the mythical expression of this credo. After the criticism of the archistic line of utopian thinking by authors like Zamyatin, Huxley, and Orwell, this anarchistic model of ancient utopia still appears to contain unexhausted potentials to which the so-called postmaterial utopias of the 1960s and 1970s could connect under the sign of ecology or antitotalitarianism.

Despite its deep differences from modern utopia, chiliasm too represents a "mixed model" because it contains elements that have become constitutive of it. Here we could name the this-worldly character of paradise and its premise of the absence of competition on the basis of mine and thine as well as sexual desire. Equally important is the postulate of the perfectibility of human beings as well as the concept of the millennium as an intermediate level between the earthly existence of fallen human beings and the heavenly existence of the saved. If in the end chiliastic thinking in the spirit of Joachim of Fiore advanced not the Church hierarchy but the monks as a model for humanity, this indicates the affinity between the medieval cloister and the organization of the classical utopian community. Of course, this point of intersection can be connected to the idea of a "Christian utopia." Did Gabriel des Foigny (1630–1692) not enthuse about a land where "milk and honey" flowed, and did Johann Gottfried Schnabel not call his utopia, the Island of Felsenburg, an "earthly paradise"? Did More not live four years in a cloister? And was Campanella not a lifelong monk? Yet regardless of the fact that with both of these authors the chiliastic metaphors in no way burst the structure of the utopian model, this interpretive option has a significant disadvantage. It must construe the concepts of utopia and chiliasm so broadly as to include all the differences already indicated. Its heuristic utility and capacity for discrimination is thus very limited.

Likewise, mixed models of classical utopia and science fiction started to appear no later than after the Second World War. Thus, Ursula K. Le Guin's *The Left Hand of Darkness* convincingly integrates elements of science fiction, like interstellar travel, space travel, cosmic temporal differences, aliens, and so on, into the classical utopian pattern without giving up the latter. Conversely, in advanced science fiction literature the fictional social scenario becomes more important relative to the actors. The new designs extended from a united humanity to an unprecedented standard of living for all based on scientific-technical progress to the perfection of human beings in the medium of creative labor and social harmony, itself the result of a differentiated system of child-rearing. *Star Trek: The Next Generation*, in which normative aspects of collective life pushed the action into the background, no doubt refined this trend into a positive vision of the future. Indeed, the combination of rational enlightened thinking, romantic sentiment, the creativity of the explorer, and a "space philosophy" oriented to the universe as a whole made artificial devices for heightening tension, like space battles or chases, seem nearly obsolete. Dystopian variants make it clear, of course, that these utopian elements have by no means exploded the science fiction model. With an image of man that did not relativize fundamental values like solidarity, love, and truthfulness, Zamyatin, Huxley, and Orwell sought to mobilize forces to avoid a future we could not wish for. But the impact of this intention on dystopian science fiction is questionable. It is marked by its tendency to fatalism and covert desire for downfall, and we have to ask whether it is able to exercise the function of the classic "dark" utopias—namely, to serve as a warning of current dangers for the future.

III

But the classical model of utopia is not exhausted by its characteristic as a heuristic principle for discovering its own identity and distinguishing it from other intellectual-historical phenomena. Unlike the construct of the ideal type, the classical utopian model itself became part of the historical process in the early-modern period. Not as a static ideal type but as a historical category, however, it owes its dynamism to its distinctive ability to react to negative developments and anticipate alternatives.

The classic modern utopia indeed risks breaking with the traditions of its world of origin in order to be able to identify an alternative to its faulty social evolution. Yet all the same it would be false to equate utopian constructs only with ideal communities or future horror scenarios and to see them exclusively in this way. Just as important as the utopia design itself is the sociopolitical occasion that gave rise to it. The Renaissance and Reformation utopias of More, Campanella, Andreae, and Winstanley react to the extreme polarization of rich and poor and the feudal and early capitalist exploitation of labor, but also to a state and justice system that has been instrumentalized by a possessive-individualist upper class. Utopias of the Age of Absolutism as conceived by Foigny, Denis Vairasse, Fontenelle, Baron de Lahontan, Fénelon, Schnabel, Louis-Sébastien Mercier, Étienne-Gabriel Morelly, Diderot, Resif de la Bretonne, and others attack the institutions of absolute monarchy as well as such supporting powers as the nobles and the Church. They pillory the luxury of the rich as much as the subjection and misery of the poor.

In the nineteenth and early twentieth century, utopians like Saint-Simon, Fourier, Owen, Cabet, Bulwer-Lytton, Bellamy, Morris, H. G. Wells, and

Alexander Bogdanov set the unexampled social wealth produced by industrialization against the equally unprecedented impoverishment of wide strata of the population. Since the beginning of the twentieth century dystopias by Zamyatin, Huxley, and Orwell took as their starting point the destructive power of modern technology in the First World War and the application of totalitarian techniques of domination in their eastern and western forms. And the so-called postmaterial utopias devised by B. F. Skinner, Huxley, Ernest Callenbach, and Le Guin took up the unrestricted consumerism of rich industrial countries and the increasing pauperization of the South, the ongoing inequalities between men and women, and the growing destruction of the natural preconditions for human life by industrialization.

But the sociopolitical context of classical utopian discourse is not only its trigger. It also works its way into the anticipations of the utopian community that confronts the criticized conditions. It forces on them, if you will, a historically specific shape. To the extent, that is, that utopian thinking plumbs the possibilities of the state of the mastery of nature given by the society in which they originate, its fictions remain at least punctually arrested. This is shown by the science and technology-labor-needs triad that had to serve as the motor of the utopian community's system of material reproduction if it was not to be understood as a mere critical correction to the civilizing process, as in the anarchistic, eighteenth-century utopia of the noble savage, but also as a constructive alternative to it. The great utopians of the Renaissance and Reformation thus draw two conclusions from the limited mastery of nature by science and technology, which not even Bacon could push beyond the boundaries of an agrarian society: they valorize physical labor to an extent that was unknown in the Middle Ages and Antiquity, and they argue for its total mobilization in the most efficient possible way, not infrequently along the lines of a military hierarchy.

Just as importantly, the low level of productivity in Antiquity and the early-modern period corresponded to the iron imperative of a ban on luxury: only the satisfaction of so-called natural needs was legitimate. This allowed the whole economy to be arranged exclusively for the production of essential goods. A dramatic accentuation of this triad came first with the Industrial Revolution in the nineteenth century. For the first time in history, science and technology opened up the prospect of an industrial society that no long saw physical labor but machine production as the source of social wealth, seeming to guarantee a future of unlimited material surplus. Utopians draw far-reaching consequences. The dictate of frugality was replaced by hedonistic mass consumption; in the place of physical drudgery appeared the machine, which did not abolish human labor but redefined it as a field of activity. This scenario drew on the belief that technology was neutral per se: whether it would help or harm humankind would depend exclusively on social conditions. Already in the second half of the nineteenth century, but above all after the slaughter of the First World War, however, this premise ran into doubts. In the classical "dark" utopias, they would condense into a horrifying image of the future. Science and technology were now put forth as an immense destructive power that would completely enslave mankind. But the post-material utopias beginning in the 1960s also refer to the society that gave rise to them insofar as the impetus for their fictions comes from the threat of ecological catastrophe. They promote science and technology only insofar as they help secure the conditions for human survival. And with the contemporaneous valorization of aesthetic and sexual needs, they returned to an ethic of renouncing consumption that went along with freeing human labor from the dictate of efficiency in favor of self-determined activity.

The dependence of utopian fictions on their sociopolitical contexts of origin also becomes clear when we turn to their validity claims. It is no accident that they underwent an paradigm shift in the eighteenth century, at the moment a series of important inventions, from iron smelting to Newcomen's atmospheric engine to new methods of fertilization to the threshing machine, announced a new stage in the mastery of nature that seemed to open up new possibilities for social organization. This turning point of civilizational development left deep traces in utopian thinking. In earlier utopias, the narrator usually found the perfect social order already made; he only had to inform the reader about its functioning. Since the eighteenth century, however, the reader has seen how the utopian community arises. Active subjects become the demiurges of an ideal world. The moment of "feasibility" and planning had always been an important part of utopian fiction, but it stayed in the realm of fantasy. Now, in contrast, the utopian construct becomes a concrete task that can actually be solved—a conviction that finds its most pregnant expression in the transition from space- to time-utopias.

In the Renaissance and the Reformation the utopian community, usually in the form of an island, was thought of as simultaneous with the social relations it confronted as a better alternative. The utopian ideal and the society of origin were connected by a spatial continuum. As against this, now the utopian goal is projected into the future—with the expectation, moreover, supported by the philosophy of history, that reality would catch up with it. This assimilation of utopian designs and the teleological idea of progress may have many bases, but it undeniably has to do with growing trust in the ability of human beings to rationally reshape their social relations. Conversely, of course the experience of the destructive power of technology since the First World War has had an opposite effect on the validity claim of time-utopias. Since Zamyatin's *We* progressive philosophies of history have been discredited by systems of domination justified by elites in their name. In more recent utopian discourse we thus can discern a tendency to return to the validity claim of the older space-utopias: it has the status of a regulative principle that can only be realized by approximation and never aims at a total, revolutionary revision of sociopolitical reality.

IV

But classical utopian discourse not only reacts to conditions that are given to it from the outside. While it accepts them as a limit on the one hand, on the other it seeks to expand them by exhausting their potentials. In this context it is too seldom observed that utopian discourse is marked by alternative thinking and the possibility of learning. It is often rightly pointed out that the authoritarian social utopias of the successors of More and Campanella transform the world into a giant monastery, extending its anti-individualistic impetus to all levels of society. Military discipline and rationalistic planning regiment the individuals' daily routine and lifeworlds from cradle to grave. Privacy is totally or mostly done away with, freedom of movement restricted, needs, morals and customs, ceremonies, even clothing, dwellings, and the layout of cities subordinated to the dictates of total homogeneity.

We must not forget, though, that since the sixteenth century fictional countermodels to this utopian Leviathan have always been devised that make individual freedom and the plurality of needs their highest values. In Rabelais's Abbey of Thélème there is, as an answer to More's *Utopia*, just one rule: "Do as you please!" In Foigny's Australian utopia from the end of the seventeenth century, laws and the state are abolished. All decisions are made locally by equals. In the Age of Absolutism de Lahontan and Diderot especially gave the noble savage a utopian character: at peace with himself and his fellows, he lives in a "well-ordered anarchy" that, free from all external determination, regulates itself according to the law of nature. In the nineteenth century Fourier and Morris formulated the scenario of a community largely liberated from institutional coercion so that individuals can develop autonomously without paternalism. And the tendency to individualize human needs can even be spotted in the utopian fictions of Cabet and Bellamy. In the meantime, since the 1960s these examples have almost become hegemonic within utopian discourse. Unlike the statist social utopians of early modernity, the guarantee of individual privacy and self-directed development has become an indispensible structural element of alternative fiction.

But utopian discourse is not only articulated in alternatives. From the beginning we can see a readiness to question its own premises. Such critical self-correction begins with More himself. Hythloday, partisan of the Utopians, has to respond to the probing question of whether the communist community he propagates does not in fact achieve the opposite of what it aims at, namely, death and revolt as well as dismal leveling and a stultifying lack of initiative. Theodor Hertzka and H. G. Wells criticized the classical tradition, arguing that it placed a much higher value on duty than on individual freedom. This tendency to self-critically question the antiindividualistic emphasis of the classical tradition culminates in twentieth-century dystopias. In fact Zamyatin's *We*, Huxley's *Brave New World*, and Orwell's *1984* can be read not only as responses to totalitarian domination, but also as detailed criticisms of the central structural characteristics of the classical tradition. More simply put, their normative demands were turned into their opposites to the extent that their original intention of emancipating humanity turned into exploitation and oppression.

Since utopians in More's wake never thought their ideal communities on the basis of the individual but always starting with the whole, precisely this conclusion is drawn as soon as the "whole" is equated with the claim to power of a totalitarian caste that is as particular as it is absolute. For Zamyatin, Huxley, and Orwell the positive can only be made out indirectly, in the shadow of the horror of 1984. Postmaterialist utopian discourse has as it were passed through the filter of this critique of utopia. In this way in Le Guin's *The Dispossessed* the positive utopian construct is indeed renewed, but it is stripped of the appearance of the highest perfection of human community. Instead, it offers the utopian design along with its own critique. It has become reflexive since it itself depicts the possibility of the failure of utopian ideals. Finally, it allows for Hans Jonas's ecological critique by tying the fiction of solidaristic society to a partnership between scientific-technological society and external nature.[10] But classical utopian discourse also directs its self-critical focus at its own, gender-specific biases. Hitherto more or less determined by patriarchal interests, since the end of the 1970s at the latest it has transitioned to treating women's issues not only as one political field among others, but by putting them at the center of the whole construction. Apart from a few deconstructive exceptions, the classical model has proven to be sturdy enough to withstand this paradigm shift as well.

The postmodern critics' objection that, as a "grand narrative," classical utopia reproduces what disfigured the profile of modern civilization as totalitarianism in the first half of the twentieth century has been refuted by its very capacity for learning. Those who ignore this enormous potential for self-correction lose sight of utopia itself. It is precisely what guarantees that an emphasis on difference does not destroy integration in a solidaristic community but is rather its presupposition.

V

It cannot be claimed that classical utopian discourse has been without effects. It would be mistaken, however, to assume that the effectivity of utopian thinking is to reality as a scientific hypothesis is to an experiment. To approach utopian thinking in this way is to write it off before really registering it, for everyone knows that all experiments, from the Jesuit state in Paraguay to Owen, Fourier, and Cabet's utopian communes in the United States, failed. The effectivity of utopian thinking comes instead through a complex, indirect process of diffusion.

Beyond a logic of one-to-one implementation, it shaped the structure of both Western societies and Soviet-type systems partly by heightening existing trends and partly by developing new potentials. Time-keeping devices and weather vanes play an important role in Campanella's *City of the Sun*. They symbolize the frictionless operation of individuals in the sociotechnical superstructure of Western civilization. The knowledge of utopians in the nineteenth century in particular, made increasingly dependent by an ever more complex division of labor, dividing each from the others in a widening hierarchy, finds its counterpart in the development of "objective pressures" that compel individuals to behave appropriately. Across systems, utopian models also shaped actual socialist countries. There we find the idea of the authoritarian variant of utopian thinking where the ideal community can only be realized if politics has the upper hand over the economy, bureaucracy over individual rights, planning over individual spontaneity and creativity, surveillance and paternalism over personal autonomy, and the principle of national isolation over the individual's right to freedom of movement. The vision of a "new human being" is also to be found in the utopian discourse of the Bolsheviks. Trotsky gave it emphatic expression when he wrote in 1924 that under achieved socialism the ordinary person would be raised to the height of an Aristotle, a Goethe, or a Marx—above which range new peaks would rise.[11]

Utopian discourse not only left traces in social and political structures; it is present in many other spheres of life in modernity. Architecture and painting are often named as examples. The exemplary character of the classical utopian tradition for modernity is insufficiently appreciated. The building and layout of the Renaissance utopian city are completely functional and rationalistic. Geometrically ordered, they express an instrumental relation to nature. Here we have anticipations of ways of building and urban planning shaped by instrumental rationality that now belong to the quotidian of world civilization. But classical utopian discourse, especially in the nineteenth century, also sets out alternatives. Thus, William Morris abandons city and landscape design based on geometrical structures, placing them in the service of a large-scale renaturalization that gave a decisive impulse to the garden-city movement. And anyone now looking for an alternative to the "unsociable city" can find inspiration in the architectural conceptions of utopian socialists like Fourier and Owen, who based their blueprints on the satisfaction of social needs. What holds for important currents of architecture and urban planning can also be said of modern painting. The Constructivism of the Russian avant-garde between 1913 and 1932 especially closes the door on past artistic forms. The medium in which it worked, recalling central features of Renaissance utopias, was the geometric figure, which, in Malevich's "Black Square on White Background," symbolized the most extreme break with tradition. Planning, a classless society, the rejection of the past, building a "new life" on a "tabula rasa," as well as the turn from analysis to synthesis are elements of an aesthetic program whose origins in utopian thinking are undeniable.[12]

With the fall of real-existing socialism in Europe at the latest, however, talk was of the end of utopian thinking. This thesis is correct if one limits it to the authoritarian line of classical utopian discourse. Social orders of the Soviet type fulfilled all the conditions of their own utopia, from the abolition of private productive property to educational dictatorship to the monopolization of power by a self-appointed elite. Yet it collapsed without need of an external shock. The bases for this world-historical development, among many other factors, have something to do with the totalitarian features of the fiction that finds classical expression in Bogdanow's Mars utopia. I would identify three elements that impaired utopian thinking's ability to learn: a small elite's monopoly over truth and sociopolitical action, an anti-individualistic postulate of homogeneity, and a demand for realization based on the history of philosophy, which in the end robs it of its self-critical power and its validity as a regulative principle that can orient action. Those who tended to see communism as utopia realized can no longer tolerate other utopias. While it was inspired by utopian thinking, it was subject to the compulsion to liquidate utopia. If I am not mistaken, this was the central dilemma of the Soviet Union.

Would it be wrong to equate the end of the authoritarian variant of utopia with the end of utopia as such? The answer to this question depends on the perspective from which it is posed. Those who believe society is essentially intact do not need utopia, but they face the continual pressure of problems that have emerged since More. The quality of these problems has changed so much in comparison to the first decades of the last century, however, that the solutions of the classic tradition, especially the blueprints of the nineteenth and early-twentieth centuries, are no longer equal to them. Today the very conditions for humanity's survival have been placed on the political agenda by the destruction of the rainforests and the ozone layer, the greenhouse effect, the population explosion in the underdeveloped regions of the South, and the atomic holocaust that remains possible. These threats can only be met through a new balance between indispensable rights and the irrefutable demands of a solidaristic whole. The real problem that has been at the center of utopian thinking from the beginning has thus not gone away.

Indeed, it could be that, to the contrary, it is posed again in all its sharpness. In this case, utopian thinking after the experience of an almost five-hundred-year history would only be up to the new global challenges if it draws the relevant conclusions from its own learning processes.

NOTES

Originally published as "Wie Zukunftsfähig ist der klassische Utopiebegriff?," *utopie kreativ* 165 (2004): 617–636.

1. Gustav Landauer, *Revolution, and Other Writings*, ed. and trans. Gabriel Kahn (Oakland: PM, 2010).
2. Karl Mannheim, *Ideology and Utopia* (London: Routledge and Kegan Paul, 1936).
3. Ernst Bloch, *The Principle of Hope*, 3 vols., trans. Neville Plaice, Stephen Plaice, and Paul Knight (Cambridge: MIT Press, 1986).
4. Karl R. Popper, *The Open Society and Its Enemies*, 2 vols. (London: Routledge, 1945).
5. Norbert Elias, "Thomas Morus' Staatskritik: Mit Überlegungen zur Bestimmung des Begriffs Utopie," in *Utopieforschung*, vol. 2, ed. Wilhelm Voßkamp (Frankfurt: Suhrkamp, 1985), 101–150.
6. Max Weber, "Die Objektivität sozialwissenschaftlicher und sozialpolitischer Erkenntnis," in *Gesammelte Aufsätze zur Wirtschaftslehre* (Tübingen: J. C. B. Mohr [Paul Siebeck], 1988), 146–214.
7. Andreas Voigt, *Die sozialen Utopien: Fünf Vorträge* (Leipzig: G. J. Göschen, 1906).
8. Klaus Garber, "Arkadien und Gesellschaft: Skizze zur Sozialgeschichte der Schäferdichtung als utopischer Literaturform Europas," in *Utopieforschung*, vol. 2, ed. Wilhelm Voßkamp (Frankfurt: Suhrkamp, 1985), 37–81.
9. Klaus Burmeister and Karlheinz Steinmüller, eds., *Streifzüge ins Übermorgen: Science Fiction und Zukunftsforschung* (Weinheim and Basel: Beltz, 1992).

10 Hans Jonas, *The Imperative of Responsibility: In Search of an Ethics for the Technological Age* (Chicago: University of Chicago Press, 1984).
11 Leo Trotsky, *Literatur und Revolution*, trans. Rose Strunsky (New York: Russell and Russell, 1957).
12 Hubertus Gaßner, Karlheinz Kopanski, and Karin Stengel, eds., *Die Konstruktion der Utopie: Ästhetische Avantgarde und politische Utopie in den 20er Jahren* (Marburg: Jonas, 1992).

3

UTOPIA AND NATURAL ILLUSIONS

FRANCISCO FERNÁNDEZ BUEY

UTOPIA BETWEEN EUROPE AND AMERICA

The first edition of Thomas More's great work appeared in London in 1516 under the title *De optimo republicae statu deque nova insula Utopia* [*Nusquam*], in Latin, based on an inaccurate text. It was also almost simultaneously published as *Libellus vere aureus, nec minus salutaris quam festivus de optimo reipublicae statu deque nova Insula Utopia* (Lovaina, T. Martens, 1516), then as *De optimo republicae statu deque nova Insula Utopia* (Basilea, J. Froben, 1518, new edition revised by Erasmus). It was translated into Italian in 1548, French in 1550, English in 1551, Low German in 1562, and Spanish in 1637 with a prologue by Francisco de Quevedo. In the beginning More had thought of naming the work *Nusquama*, a nominalization of the Latin adjective *nusquam* ("in no place"). Before giving the work to the printer, he also toyed with the Greek neologism *eutopía*.[1]

More began writing what we know as the second part of the text during the summer of 1515 in the Netherlands while on a diplomatic-commercial mission that took him to Flanders, Bruges, Brussels, and Antwerp. At the same time he was also writing an apology for Erasmus's *In Praise of Folly*. More had come to know Erasmus some years prior, at the beginning of the century, when the latter visited England, and they went on to establish a more intimate relationship in 1508, during More's stay at the universities of Paris and Leuven. In Antwerp More also met Erasmus's friend Peter Giles, whom he praises at the beginning of the work and who plays an important part in the dialogue that develops in the first part of the book. *Utopia*'s second part, written before the first one, is a description of the imaginary state of Utopia, a small island located in Atlantis, whose capital city is Amaurot ("phantom," "castle in the air"). The first part, written in England after More's return from the Netherlands in 1516, is, in contrast, an extended dialogue containing a critical portrayal of the English society of the day.

The starting point for the work's composition seems to have been a series of conversations with other humanists in Antwerp and Bruges about the voyages of Amerigo Vespucci, the New World having been recently discovered, and contemporary speculation about its way of life and system of government. This is already reflected in the identity More creates for the protagonist of his dialogue, Rafael Hythloday ("peddler of nonsense," "visionary," "chatterbox"), who is presented as a companion of Vespucci on his journey to the New World. Besides the information extracted from Vespucci, whose account, according to *Utopia*, "is already read everywhere," and perhaps also from Pedro Mártir de Anglería,[2] More took from Saint Augustine the valorization of the family as the basic element of society and the nation, from Plato the idea of erecting the image of a perfect state on an intellectual plane, and from Erasmus the critique of social and cultural ills. The possible influence of Pico della Mirandola has also been traced, as well as that of the *Epigrams* and *Dialogues* of Luciano de Samosata, two authors More had translated around 1505–1506.[3]

THE NEW WORLD INSPIRES THE OLD

It is not difficult to imagine the mixture of surprise at the new and attraction to the mysterious, still barely known, that the Renaissance humanists in general, and the circle close to Erasmus in particular, must have felt at the news coming from that strange world of which nothing was known before in Europe. At the beginning of the 1520s the pace of "discoveries" and conquests by the Spanish and the Portuguese (what is usually called the European expansion), following the Treaty of Tordesillas (1494), was increasing: the Antilles, the Cape of Good Hope, Terranova, South America, India, Venezuela, Santo Domingo, the coasts of Brazil,

Honduras, the Isthmus of Panama, Colombia, the North African coast, the peninsula of Malaca, Goa, the Maluku Islands, Florida, the "south sea" or Pacific Ocean, and so on.

The rhythm of the expeditions, the travelers' accounts, and the importance of the European expansion are reflected in numerous historical documents. But in spite of the broad dissemination of all types of books around those years in Europe, in 1515 documentation regarding the islands and lands that had been discovered was still limited. Christopher Columbus's travel letters and accounts were only known in Spain by a few and the documents that the Columbus family possessed seem to have been used only, years later, by Bartolomé de las Casas. Although there was much discussion of those lands and peoples, the books published in Spain on the New World before 1520 can be counted on the fingers of one hand.

Thus, the only literary medium through which Erasmus and More could in 1515 satisfy their curiosity about the novelties of that mysterious world was the works of Vespucci. Two of these had spread widely through Europe. The first was titled *Mundus Novus* and was the Latin translation of a letter (now lost) from Vespucci to Soderini. It was published in 1503 in Florence and in a few weeks it was republished in Venice, Paris, Augusta, Nuremberg, Antwerp, Cologne, and Strasburg. It was translated into German and Flemish, seeing about fifty editions in the following fifty years. The second work was the *Lettera delle isole nuovamente trovate*, published in Florence in 1505 or 1506; it deals with Vespucci's four voyages (two, in reality) along the American coasts. It was translated into Latin and French immediately, then included as an appendix to the geographical work of the Alsatian scientist Martin Waldseemüller, *Cosmographiae Introductio* (1507), in whose world map the name America is first applied to the new territories. It was Waldseemüller who, in the prologue to Vespucci's letters, argued that the latter had demonstrated that a new continent existed and for that reason those lands should bear his name. Vespucci's book was widely disseminated and Waldseemüller's suggestion was accepted.

THE IDEA OF AMERICA

It is known that the origin of More's *Utopia* lies in his conversations with Erasmus regarding Vespucci's letter. The protagonist of the first part of *Utopia*, Raphael Hythloday, is presented as an educated traveler who knows Latin and is very well versed in Greek. A companion of Vespucci, he comes to represent the intellectual tie that connects the illusions and preoccupations of Savonarolian Florence at the end of the century—the "Machiavellian moment"—and European reflection on, among other things, the recently discovered New World. On the other hand, it is usually said that if Columbus was a sailor with a still-medieval conception of the Earth, the work of Vespucci is inspired by an already "modern" concept of geographical culture. Indeed, Vespucci belonged to a distinguished Florentine family, was dedicated to commerce, and had carried out various diplomatic commissions related to his patrons' economic interests. A typically Florentine character, Vespucci was interested in commerce, diplomacy, and the politics that came out of Florence at a key moment of its history. He arrived at Seville in 1492 to look after the economic interests of the Medici. In Seville he dedicated himself to providing goods, subsidized by the Berardi house of Florence, for the first Atlantic expeditions, but was soon fascinated by the exploration of the new worlds on which he too decided to embark.

A humanist with knowledge of geography and astronomy, Vespucci entered history as one of the first who, traveling west in the sixteenth century, doubted Columbus's belief that he had arrived in India. In his most important expedition, in 1501–1502, Vespucci probably got to the mouth of the River Plate and then continued south until he managed to cross the fifty-second parallel. Vespucci demonstrated that the uninterrupted coastline, from north to south, from the lands discovered by Columbus to the estuary of the Plate, did not have the least similarity with the coasts of India as these had been described by medieval explorers. From the fact that mighty rivers flowed into the sea he deduced that Columbus had been mistaken and that those western territories were not Asia, as Columbus had wished:

> I have already written a detailed report regarding my experiences in the new territories I have discovered.... The name of the New World is very appropriate, since our ancestors were completely ignorant of its existence. My last voyage has demonstrated that a continent has been discovered whose population is more numerous and its fauna richer than in Europe, Asia, or Africa. The climate is also more favorable and, in a certain sense, more agreeable than in any other region of the earth.

With the *mondo nuovo* metaphor, Vespucci designated not only the recently discovered lands, but also indigenous societies similar to the pagan societies of Antiquity ("men that are just exiting earthly paradise") and a new continent that counters the old. Moreover, Vespucci presented the archaic and primitive forms of American societies as the residue of an ancient Golden Age, when men lived in innocence and without malice. Thus, Vespucci introduced a conception of the "new world" that would overflow the geographical plane and that, in the following decades, would be used to refer to an inverted world or a world of illusions.[4] More's *Utopia* begins precisely from this suggestion. It could thus be said that if the basic ideas of modernity regarding the New World (in the sense of a better world for the Old Continent, an inverted image of the known world) were born in Florence in an environment in which Alberti, Leonardo, Filarete, Savonarola, Machiavelli, and Guicciardini flourished, they also returned to their Florentine origins at the turn of the century—though by then Florentine thought had been Europeanized via Seville, Bruges, Antwerp, Saxony, and London.

Through this miscegenated "Europeanization" of Florentine thought, politico-moral reflection adopts the form of explicit utopia, the story of the society and customs of an imaginary island alternatively called *utopia* (*nusquam* = "no place," following More's original idea) and *eutopia* ("good place"). In More's fable, utopia has no precise location, but it does have an approximate one: it is unequivocally an island of the "new world." Moreover, it has a precise location on the ideal map of philosophical literature: Atlantis. Thus, More picked up on a widespread belief and the classical learning of his epoch.[5] The reference to Plato is another characteristic utopian thought shared with the variants of turn-of-the-century Florentine thought. It should be emphasized that in this period Plato's politico-moral opinions in the *Republic* were no longer of interest. Not so the Platonic myths, however, which functioned as indicators of a new reflection on good government (as is already seen in Machiavelli, Erasmus, and More, and still more clearly with Francis Bacon in the *New Atlantis*).

FROM LONDON TO AMAUROT, OR UTOPIA IN IRONY

Nonetheless, there is an even more significant element having to do with an epochal shift in preoccupations, one that points to the radical discrepancy between Florentine politico-moral philosophy and the utopian thought just then being born: it is the new relation More, like Erasmus, establishes between the philosopher and the prince, in order to affirm the autonomy of philosophy. A sign of the importance More gives to this is that what he began as a narration of the life and customs of the island of Utopia, inspired by Vespucci's accounts, really begins, once the material was reorganized, with a discourse reflecting another Platonic theme, namely, the philosopher and the prince. As Hythloday affirms in dialogue with the work's author, there is no place for philosophers at court, and he contrasts the servitude of the king's counselor with the value of the philosopher's detachment, the liberality proper to Christian humanism. The philosopher is of no use for counsel on matters of state because his commitment to public affairs is as a citizen, and kings are generally insensitive when it comes to the eradication of vices, wars, and social inequalities.

When More makes his protagonist say that there is no place for philosophy at court, he means that there may be a place for the "new," non-scholastic philosopher, since it is philosophy really interested in public affairs and knowledgeable about the theater of the world. There follows a discussion about what More calls *casting about* or the *indirect approach*, whereby "if you are not able to make them go well, they may be as little ill as possible." In this dialogue we can see the origin of the differentiation or polarity in European modernity between the analytical-scientific approach to public affairs and the utopian approach. In an Erasmian manner, More makes Raphael say, following the indirect approach, "all that I could be able to do would be to preserve myself from being mad while I endeavored to cure the madness of others," so that in reality that method is far from being able to change anything for the better.[6]

More finishes the first part of *Utopia* with a plea against private property and the discussion that plea sparks. The dialogue on the abolition of private property and its possible effects on community regulations already introduces the properly utopian element of the work: the direct, not oblique, road. But here we should underline that More has taken precautions when advancing an argument to which it can already be said that "men cannot live conveniently where all things are common."[7] This counterargument is later repeated many times: the lack of incentives leads to idleness, and with it authority declines and society becomes anarchic. In order to escape this theoretical impasse on the contrasting effects of the existence of private property, on the one hand, and of hypothetical communal property, on the other, something more than dialogue is needed. We need some example to illustrate the very possibility of an alternative society. And that is what the island of the Utopians represents: perhaps the London of the future.

The ironical-critical character of the first modern utopia is manifest on the last page of More's text when Hythloday finishes speaking and the narrator, that is, the author, to whom some of the customs and principles that reign in Utopia seem absurd, takes the interlocutor by the arm and takes him for a drink, praising the Utopians' institutions and leaving deep reflection on the details of those problems for a better occasion. It is one thing to ironize as a *literary* device (as in the picaresque novel) at the expense of prophets, bishops, clerics, courtesans, or magistrates and another to convert irony into a genre of *public* expression, in texts that are given to the printing press and circulate through all of Europe with philosophico-moral or philosophico-political intent. Erasmus's *In Praise of Folly* and in part More's *Utopia* are characterized by treating sociopolitical or sociocultural matters deemed serious by tradition ironically, at least in the sense that they had previously almost always been objects of ethical, juridical, or philosophico-political reflection. With the conflict between Catholicism and Protestantism generalized and aggravated, such *public* irony as a form of critique in public affairs becomes difficult, if not dangerous (if we consider More's fate). All of this would have repercussions in the formulation of utopias. And it could be said that the two extremes of the utopian spirit of the time, which oscillated between tragedy and satire, were Müntzer and Rabelais.

UTOPIA IN ACTION

Thomas Müntzer came to represent, in the Germany of 1525, a return of the prophetic spirit of Joaquín de Fiore and Savonarola. His utopia was not a book, although he wrote books;[8] it was an action, a revolutionary action that ended in tragedy. A follower of Luther, Müntzer ended his days as a theologian of peasant revolution. He lived in an epoch of antagonistic movements that arose from the disintegration of the ancient equilibrium between the city and the country, particularly in Saxony, where incipient industrial development was tied to commercial exchange with distant countries, producing constant tension between workers, peasants, the nobility, and the clergy. What in More was a denunciation of the appropriation of communal goods was transformed in Müntzer's utopia into revolt.

Müntzer was a preacher of the Gospel in a radical sense. He preached the good news to the disinherited of this world, whom he considered chosen by God to remake his country. This is why it is usually said that he gave life to the "left wing" of the Reformation, that he was the representative of "radical reform" and is positioned beyond the classic reforms (Luther, Zwingli, Calvin) of the sixteenth century that turned into churches competing with Rome. In his Christian preaching he did not limit himself to a defense of the interior liberation of man, a basic idea from Luther. For Müntzer authentic evangelical freedom should also correspond to relations among Christians in this world, and not only with the Church of Rome. That is why Müntzer's political theology clashed with Luther's adhesion to the German territorial princes. He attenuated the radical pessimism of the classic reformists and emphasized the freedom the Holy Spirit gives to the chosen, liberating them from institutional and sacramental mediation, as if the Holy Spirit manifested itself in them immediately and personally through a motivating illumination. In the conditions of the time this idea has revolutionary consequences since Müntzer gives messianic and prophetic awareness an ethico-political turn, justifying the repudiation of the established order: the human being's abandonment to the divinity stops being mere passivity, becoming a disposition to struggle against the wealthy, the powerful, and the princes. The authentic faith follows the same painful road that led Jesus Christ from suffering to happiness. In the course of daily existence, the chosen, touched by the Holy Spirit, are transformed into the mansion of God that is love.

Although there has been much discussion regarding the real motives of the so-called Peasants' War in Germany and its relation to the chiliastic-messianic movement that surged due to Müntzer's ideas, one thing seems clear: in the months of 1525 Müntzer's activist, politico-theological utopia played an important part in political events. In February of that year, peasants and a group of the petite bourgeoisie seized municipal power in Mühlhausen. From there the revolt began to expand. In April the insurrection of Thuringia-Saxony took place and a short time after Prince-Elector Friedrich died without any descendants. The tragic-utopian spirit of the Reformation emerged out of those circumstances: Müntzer confronted Luther, who was counseling Friedrich's brother not to let himself be impressed by the demands of the peasants because God's hand was on the side of the territorial lord. While Luther wrote *Against the Robbing and Murdering Hordes of Peasants*, a pamphlet calling on the princes to undertake direct action against the peasants, Müntzer supported the insurrection.

This situation brings to mind the Savonarolian moment in Florence some decades prior owing to the demands of the downtrodden, the tie between insurrection and prophecy, and the tragic end of the protagonists. It seems that the Peasants' War was not only a class struggle due to socioeconomic differences, however, which there were (the dispute over the right to hunting and fishing and over the use of old communal lands), but also a struggle for the recognition of political rights and control of municipal government. The rebels' first demand was for the freedom of the community and municipal authority against the nobles and ecclesiastics. This demand against the tyranny of the secular and Christian lords, the Church and the nobility, was supported by preaching about Christian freedom by the various reformers. But the rebels found in Müntzer a politico-moral coherence they did not find in the others. On May 15, 1525, the peasants were defeated by the troops sent by Count Phillip of Hessen. Müntzer was captured, tortured, and finally decapitated on May 27, alongside other rebels. From that moment on, princes, both Catholic and Protestant, undertook numerous reprisals against the peasants. It has been estimated that more than one hundred thousand died.

Just a few years after the utopia in action ended in tragedy in Germany, while Juan Luis Vives rightly complained of the somber times in which "one cannot speak or remain silent without danger," a certain master Alcofribas Nasier converted utopia into parody. His real name was François Rabelais, author of *Gargantua and Pantagruel*. The work is replete with memories and homages to the utopia of More and without a doubt plays with the complicity of the reader who also knows of it: at the age of 804, Gargantua conceives his son Pantagruel with his wife, Badebec, who Rabelais says was daughter of the king of the Amaurots of Utopia. Afterward, Pantagruel and his friends go and confront the Dipsodes, who have devastated a large part of Utopia. They later enter the country of the Amaurots. Utopia's conversion into parody in dark times is a strategy we will find again toward the end of modernity. In the first part of his great work, in the last chapters of the book dedicated to Gargantua, Rabelais constructs his mock-utopia. This utopia is the abbey of Thélème, whose name derives from the Greek "calm" or "mild-mannered." The rules of his abbey, the abbey reasonable people would like, be they religious or not, are the negation of those prevailing in the monastic world. Rabelais's satire turns the sock of history inside out.

UTOPIA AND MIGRATION

One of the interesting things about the first modern utopia is that, born out of the vague news More and Erasmus had of America from the accounts of Vespucci, it only took a few decades to become a realizable social project—precisely in Mexico. This is probably one of the most beautiful stories of Renaissance humanism. It is also indicative of the nature and destiny of modern utopias: an author invents a nonplace, where one lives as one would like to live in our societies, and does so out of a combination of imagination and ad hoc treatment of vague news of a world still almost unknown, existing in reality in some place in America, and thus sharpens the sensibility of contemporary Europeans, who begin to feel the malaise of modernity—so much so that twenty years later Vasco de Quiroga, a Spanish partisan of More's utopia, could propose realizing utopia in a real place, Michoacán, which, in a certain sense, could correspond to the nonplace imagined by More.

Only, he does so now with detailed knowledge that More could not have had of the habits and customs of its inhabitants. The paradox is that More's moral story, written for Europeans, imagining how good it could be for them if they chose to live like the imagined Amerindians, ended up being applied to Americans, not imaginary but real ones, in the name of the ideals of another European, also Christian and humanist, who wanted to help them with More's utopia. The destiny of grand utopian ideas of humanity, and of alternatives in general, at least within the context of European culture, seems to almost always be the following: to become a temple, an institution, or a political-social reality in another place, a place in a polemical relation to the one in which they were conceived. Already in Antiquity something similar happened with the utopias of Moses and Jesus of Nazareth: in order to galvanize support they had to traverse the desert or migrate to the center of the Empire. This is what utopia shares with prophecy.

It remains to be studied why modern utopias, like prophets, do not thrive in their native soil. More's utopia migrated to Michoacán in the 1530s while he who had imagined it paid with his life for the audacity of his critical spirit; the enlightened utopia that was born with English parliamentarianism migrated to revolutionary France; the liberal-chartist utopia born in the home of capitalism migrated to Bismarck's Prussia, where for the first time something like social security was established; the revolutionary socialist utopia born in England, Germany, and France migrated to backward Russia and later to Asia, Latin America, and Africa, where industrial workers were almost nonexistent.

VASCO DE QUIROGA: A MOREAN UTOPIAN

Vasco de Quiroga was one of the most interesting people to come out of Spain in the first half of the sixteenth century. Born in Madrigal de las Altas Torres, a judge and bishop in New Spain, known as "Tata Vasco" by the natives, Quiroga founded the mixed college of San Nicolás in Pátzcuaro and concerned himself with knowing and preserving the indigenous tongues. He also fostered an unprecedented sociocultural experiment in the lands of Tacubaya, Michoacán, and Santa Fe de la Laguna. Quiroga studied jurisprudence, probably at Salamanca, in the first decade of the 1500s. He graduated in canon law in 1515 and he practiced at the Audiencia of Valladolid until 1530, when he left to be a judge in New Spain. He played a distinguished role in the so-called Second Audiencia in Mexico. He founded the hospitals of Santa Fe and Michoacán, whose regulations he wrote himself. He was named bishop of Michoacán in 1538 and promoted an educational experiment for indigenous children and adults based on the defense of *mestizaje,* or miscegenation. He died in Uruapan on March 14, 1565.[9] He appears not to have written anything with the intention of publishing it. His two most cited writings are *Información en derecho* and *De debellandis indis.* In his will he left for the College of Saint Nicholas in Michoacán 626 volumes, mostly works on law and theology, which provides an idea of his culture.

To put Quiroga's intervention in America in context, we have to take into account some events of the age. He arrived in Mexico at the time of the so-called Second Audiencia. Named in 1530, one of its instructions was the prohibition of Indian slavery by order of Emperor Charles and his mother Juana. Nonetheless, the order clashed with the interests of the *encomenderos* and conquistadors, who argued that without slaves the Spaniards would not be up to crushing Indian rebellions. Thus, in 1534 Charles V derogated the previous prohibition and reauthorized the capture of Indians as long as it was in a *just war*. Quiroga was among those who protested against this decision. During his stay in Mexico in 1531, Quiroga wrote to the Council of the Indies condemning the war of conquest and the enslavement of the Indians. He proposed organizing the life of the natives by reducing them to populations that would work the land "with a good police order" and "saintly and Catholic ordinances," supervised by friars "who do not raise their hands against them, until they achieve the habit of virtue and make it their nature."[10] In 1535, after the new legislation was passed, Quiroga wrote a letter in Castilian, the *Información en derecho*, concerning some provisions of the Real Council of the Indies. Like Bartolomé de las Casas, he argued for the reestablishment of the prohibition of 1530, although he adopted a more moderate attitude than las Casas concerning the *encomiendas*. As Silvio Zavala states, "Quiroga only criticizes the implementation of the *repartimientos*, not their essence."[11]

Información en derecho is a difficult work to classify, moving between epistle, chronicle, and treatise.[12] In it Quiroga affirms that a war intended to enslave the Indians is unjust because they are not under the dominion of Christian kings (a thesis defended at the same time by Francisco de Vitoria). He justified, however, war against the Indians if they resisted the preaching of the Gospel or endangered the act of preaching. The Gospel has to be fostered pacifically by persuasion, but those who oppose preaching are liable to attack. Such is the case also with Indians because they do not have a just government, but a tyrannical one. Thus, a war to liberate them from their tyrants becomes just: in this way war becomes the pacification of the Indians. Immediately afterward Quiroga proposed a "mixed politics" for the common good of the Indians and the Spaniards, with aboriginal juries, indigenous governors, and Indian mayors, but over them a Spaniard chief magistrate representing the Royal Audiencia.

The proposal was based on a consideration of the different natures of the Indians and the Europeans, since the former are simple and naïve, while the latter are malicious and victims of ambition. Indians should therefore not be given equal laws, but instead simple rules suited to their simple condition, namely, the laws made up by More in *Utopia*. Quiroga does not limit himself to giving these laws the status of an unachievable ideal; he proposes applying them vigorously. For this reason, Quiroga is considered the main follower of More's ideals in America, alongside the Bishop of Mexico Juan de Zumárraga, in whose library an annotated copy of *Utopia* has been preserved.[13] If Quiroga found in *Utopia* the model for organizing the American communities according to the "innocence" he finds in the aboriginals, he had no doubt about putting More's ideas into practice: he sacrificed part of his wages, bought land, and founded a town-hospital called Santa Fe, continuing this work until when he was named Bishop of Michoacán in 1537. Later, in his old age, he wrote his *Ordinances* for the management of the hospitals of Santa Fe and Michoacán. A comparison with More's *Utopia* clearly demonstrates the latter's influence: joint ownership, the integration of families by groups of different married couples, rotations between the urban and rural population, women's labor, a six-hour workday, a liberal distribution of wealth produced by common effort according to the needs of the residents, abandonment of luxury and useless trades, a familial and elective magistrate. *Utopia* seemed to Quiroga a work "inspired by the Holy Spirit," since "without having seen [that world] he posits it, paints it, and describes it in such ways that many times it makes me wonder . . . how the disposition, location, manners, conditions, and secrets of this land and its natives were revealed to him."

A few years ago Paz Serrano revisited this theme, contextualizing and reconstructing the intellectual itinerary that ran from the nonplace invented by the English ambassador in his *Utopia* to the hospital villages constructed for the Amerindians by Quiroga.[14] She then deepened this beautiful story, studying in detail which ideas expressed by More in *Utopia* most interested Quiroga and why. She compared the habits, customs, and institutions imagined by More in his *Utopia* against those of the English and Europeans in order to underline the causes by which, in the hospital villages of Mexico, the reality promoted by Quiroga was distanced from the utopian ideal imagined by the English chancellor. This separation is undertaken in order to gain a better understanding of the needs of the people but also the correlation of the forces between *encomenderos*, evangelists, and the Indians themselves. Through this comparison we see how the ambiguity of More's utopian proposal, expressed through his ironic distance from Hythloday's tale, resonated in the ambiguity the jurist bishop transferred to Mexico, his mind meanwhile focused on debates regarding colonization and the rights that were being developed on the Iberian Peninsula. Quiroga was also, in a certain sense, *nepantla*, between two cultures, his soul divided between the implications of the evangelist's universalism and the economic-political interests of the Crown, on the one hand, and the conviction that the place of utopia is precisely the New World, on the other. This is why the utopian follower of More, at the same time a protagonist of the Spanish colonization of America, becomes a pragmatist.

OTHERNESS, A PROBLEM

Vasco de Quiroga's activity in Spain between 1547 and 1554 is less familiar. After coming to Spain, he supposedly lived first in Valladolid (between 1547 and 1551) and then in Madrid until 1554, when he returned to Mexico. According to the testimony of Bernal Díaz del Castillo, we know he was in Valladolid in 1550.[15] At the time of the Valladolid controversy he seems to have written the philosophical-theological-juridical treatise *De debellandis indis*, which for some time was considered lost.[16] In a letter written from Madrid on April 23, 1553, and addressed to Juan Bernal Díaz de Luco, Bishop of Calahorra, Quiroga complains of not being invited to participate in the Valladolid controversy and says he is sending a copy of *Debellandis indis*, of direct relevance to the Council of the Indies. If we are to believe the letter, the Council's members, and in particular its president, the Marquis of Mondéjar, "had very much taken [that treatise] into consideration." On the other hand, Quiroga feared that las Casas, due to his extreme rigor, must have disagreed with his thesis that "one does not have control of the Indies and *Tierra Firme* by the Catholic Kings of Castile with less saintly and just title within its demarcations than that of the realms of Castile, but in the case of the Indies with more."[17]

Already the title of the treatise (literally: "On the war that has to be waged against the Indians") seems clear evidence of its author's change of heart. The polemical objective of the text is also crystal clear: he proposes criticizing the opinion of "a lot of religious individuals of no small authority" who insist on denouncing the injustices of colonization and "shout publicly and in tandem deduce crazy things." The juridical substance of the treatise is an affirmation of the primacy of the rights of the pope to the empire over those of its peoples: "Even though the new communities of the Indies would have their principalities by effect of the right of peoples, the pope could not be limited by such right, to the extreme of not being able to transfer the principalities of the Indies to the Spanish princes, since that secondary right of peoples did give the Indians just title to acquire those principalities."[18] In a line that recalls Sepúlveda, Quiroga now rejects even the need of the *requerimiento* and explicitly justifies pillage of the Indians with the excuse that they had insisted on their idolatrous rituals while the Spanish were authorized by their superiority.[19]

In recent decades there has been much discussion, especially in Mexico, not only about the philological problems in identifying the anonymous and fragmented Latin treatise with the *De debellandis indis*, but also about the extent of the change in Quiroga's ideas between 1530 and 1550, and the motives behind it.[20] Renee Acuña tends to minimize the change by showing the proximity of the central ideas of *De debellandis indis* to those expressed by Quiroga in *Información en derecho*. Even still, differences of note remain, the most important being the retreat to a justification of conquest and colonization that on the Peninsula already seemed to have been abandoned. If we accept that *De debellandis indis* is the work of Quiroga, we are faced with a problem that complicates the study of the relationship between utopia and otherness in sixteenth century: this would mean that the same author who tried to realize More's utopia in America, thus promoting the happiness of the Indians, on the other hand justified war against them. If we were to accept Quiroga's authorship, we would have need of two hypotheses: first, that beginning in the 1550s there was a regression of politico-moral thought on the Peninsula from the valorization of utopia to what we might call a *cynical pragmatism*; and second, that even More's Iberian sympathizers used that part of his *Utopia* dedicated to war in order to justify colonization.

These hypotheses are not without foundation. In regard to the first, it could be said that in 1552–1553 even las Casas, in his *Tratado comprobatorio*, justifies the empire of the kings of Castile. This position represents a regression similar to that of Quiroga (or the author of the treatise Acuña attributes to him) and to positions close to Vitoria's. We have to remember that already by the 1550s censorship regarding what was written about America had reached significant proportions, and not even las Casas could submit his work to the printer. In regard to the second hypothesis, one could suppose that, as a humanist inspired by More, Quiroga could have accepted *as is* and even elaborated not only More's utopian point of view about the community of goods, but also a realist and pragmatically Eurocentric attitude concerning the clash between cultures and, in particular, the relations between the colonizers and the colonized.

This notwithstanding, there is another consideration that makes it possible to explain the differences in tone, style, and content between Quiroga and las Casas. Quiroga was an organizer with great practical sense who dedicated a good part of his life to the hospitals of Mexico, solving problems that were both concrete and important. Indeed, after his stay in Spain Quiroga returned to Mexico and continued working on an integrated project. Such labors in time form a character that tends to view the practical side of things and, because of this, is open to deals and the conciliation of opposed positions. Las Casas, on the other hand, had spent too much time going from one place to the next to focus on the minutiae of slow changes of behavior that could already at this time be observed in Mexico and in Peru. This is why, when talks emerge again on the perpetuation of the *encomiendas*, he sees in the proposal the repetition of past history, and his position becomes progressively more critical and fundamentalist. It is no surprise, then, that from that moment on he doubled his efforts to convince his friends in Mexico and Peru that there were no important differences between the *encomiendas* of the 1530s and those of the 1550s. [Editors' note: The New World experiment of Quiroga following More's model marked the beginning of utopian projects as practical blueprints. It would not be until several centuries later that utopia in this sense would be declared dead, its place of death the Old Continent.]

UTOPIA AFTER THE "END OF UTOPIA": FROM BERLIN 1967 TO BERLIN 1989

There were in the second half of the twentieth century at least two claims concerning the end of utopia. Both related to the city of Berlin. The first was made by Herbert Marcuse in 1967, speaking to the rebellious university students of the Free University. The second came in 1989, after the fall of the wall that separated the city's inhabitants. In both cases, when speaking of the end of utopia, the reference was to socialism—frequently without attention to the gulf between the end pronounced by Marcuse in 1967 and that assumed by almost all mass media and not a few philosophers between 1990 and 2000. Since 1990, when mass media spoke about the end of utopia, it was commonly with reference to the absence of alternative ideas, reconciliation with existing reality, recognition of the failure of the socialist experiments of the twentieth century, acceptance of the triumph of nihilism, and things of that nature. In contrast, when on July 10, 1967, Marcuse addressed the students of the Free University of Berlin in a speech titled "The End of Utopia" he had something altogether different in mind.

Already with the shift represented by the election of Thatcher and Reagan and the ascendancy of neoliberalism, the message of Marcuse's talk was easily lost. A hurried politicist interpretation of the events that had taken place in Germany, the USSR, and other countries of Eastern Europe since 1989 pushed many authors to proclaim the definitive end of utopia. It then became common to relate the end of utopia to the end of ideologies and even the end of history in Fukuyama's conception.[21] It has been said many times, in mass media as well as in academic circles, that the failure of socialism represented the ratification of the decline of utopia as part of sociopolitical thought. And, from that line of argument, it has been suggested that, in the best case, the only place left now for utopia is in the aesthetic dimension. This interpretation of world events since 1990 helped prolong an observation already made decades earlier concerning the eclipse of positive utopia as a literary genre. According to it, the fear of the negative effects of techno-science, the consciousness of barbarism brought about by two world wars, and the subsequent crisis of the enlightened idea of progress all contributed to elevating dystopia, antiutopia, and counterutopia to the place that utopia formerly occupied as a literary genre with an alternative social intention. From at least the 1940s onward, techno-science had been transforming into a productive-destructive force, and the relationship between wars and the techno-scientific complex was clearly in evidence. Fuse the interpretation of socialism's failure in Eastern Europe with this other one of the end of literary utopia and you get a theme that has circulated through the media with the aura of a historical truth: the era of modern utopias that had its beginnings in the sixteenth century and extended for three centuries has ended. The dissemination of this view also has an ideological function, in effect killing two birds with one stone: it forcefully exaggerates the supposedly antisocialist intention of the literary antiutopias or counterutopias before 1980 while suggesting that today there is no alternative to neoliberal capitalism, not even in the realm of ideas.

In what follows I will try to disassemble the "end of utopia," which in my opinion is a part not only of neoliberal ideology but also of a journalistic conception of history that trivializes the texts it reads, fails to recognize the texts it does not read, and ignores contexts. Against that trivialization we can still subscribe, and more truthfully at that, to what Octavio Paz said in 1990 during his acceptance speech of the Nobel Prize for literature: "Is this the end of all Utopias? It is rather the end of the idea of history as a phenomenon, the outcome of which can be known in advance. Historical determinism has been a costly and bloodstained fantasy. History is unpredictable because its agent, mankind, is the personification of indeterminism."[22] I will first of all argue that it is not true that dystopias or counterutopias of a negative type displaced utopias with a positive social goal prior to 1980. I will then show (a) that the affirmation according to which we have arrived at the end of utopia is one that runs counter to the facts; (b) that it is not true that utopia was reduced to the realm of the aesthetic, abandoning any social dimension; and (c) that since 2000 we have entered into a phase of the revalorization of utopia, whose key has again come to be discussion of the *concept behind the word*.

If antiutopia and counterutopia have indeed been elements of the social thought of the twentieth century, they were not the only ones, or even the main ones, starting from the recognition of that century's catastrophes. The loss of historical optimism, the successive defeats of socialism (in all its forms), the critique of the enlightened notion of progress, the discovery of the worst side of technology, and even the distrust produced by the techno-scientific complex since the 1950s were not sufficient factors for the displacement of positive utopia, which has continued to express itself alongside dystopias. This can be documented by studying that very interesting chapter in the history of twentieth-century ideas in which thinkers such as Horkheimer, Adorno, Bloch, and Günther Anders confronted the consequences of Auschwitz and Hiroshima for arguments for positive or negative utopia. On the other hand, it has been noted that the university and youth movement of the late 1960s (in California, Paris, Milan, Berlin, Prague, and so on) undertook a drastic reconsideration of the idea that actually existing socialism (in the Soviet Union, mostly) had been the realization of the socialist itinerary. Surely it was because of this that one of the characteristic features of the historical stage known, thanks to Marcuse, as the epoch of the Great Refusal and extending through the end of the 1970s when the ideology of neoliberalism began to displace socialist ideologies was the recuperation of various *heterodox* versions of Western Marxism (Benjamin, Bloch, Korsch, Reich, Marcuse, Guevara), libertarianism[23] (collectivist, communist-libertarian, or situationist experiments), and other socialist imaginaries of the nineteenth century (in particular Fourierism and Proudhonism)—currents that for some time had remained in the background.

We can illustrate this by recalling the influence felt in North American and European universities not only of the currents and authors already mentioned, but also of other thinkers and activists who dwelled between the recovery of utopia in a positive light and the "prognostic hermeneutics," to use an expression Anders began to employ at the time. In the large camp attached to the recovery of utopia in a positive sense, the affirmation of the aesthetic dimension of utopia, the defense of *concrete* utopias, as well as prognostic hermeneutics (connected to negative utopia), we have to include what Paul Goodman wrote at the beginning of the 1960s, in *Growing Up Absurd* and *Utopian Essays and Practical Proposals*, as well as what was written and said by the end of that decade by various protagonists of the European student movement, such as Dany Cohn-Bendit and Rudi Dutschke. In that same camp, which was wide and diverse but always connected to the revision of the old utopian spirit, we would have to include authors such as Theodor Adorno and the Jürgen Habermas of "Technology and Science as Ideology" (1967) and, a bit later, others who surely would not want to find themselves on a list of utopians but who argued with much force in favor of another socialism or another communism, and notably influenced critical and alternative social movements up until the 1980s: Murray Bookchin, Cornelius Castoriadis, Guy Debord, Pier Paolo Pasolini, Michel Foucault, Rudolf Bahro, Wolfgang Harich, and Toni Negri—authors whose writings were representative of the historical period that goes from 1969 to 1980, one of whose main debates was precisely whether the rebellion of the late 1960s was to be interpreted as a renaissance of social utopia in a positive sense or, instead, as the swan song of the old socialism as ideology.

MARCUSE ON THE END OF UTOPIA

For Marcuse the "end of utopia" was the beginning of the possibility of realizing what the (socialist) utopia had anticipated.[24] When this discussion is looked at from today, it is no less interesting that, with his Hegelian language, Marcuse identified the end of utopia with the end of history as the possibility of rupture with the historical continuum that had been humanity's evolution up to then. The "end of utopia" was thus, in that context, the admission of the possibility of realizing socialism and of a new definition of utopia emphasizing the role of subjectivity. Marcuse talked to the Berlin students about the need to consider the idea of a road to socialism that goes, paradoxically, *from science to utopia*, and not *from utopia to science*, as Engels had claimed. He took as his point of departure the negative or pejorative concept of utopia as a project of "impossible" social transformation due to one of two reasons: either the absence or immaturity of objective and subjective factors necessary for socialist society, or a contradiction between such a project and certain biological or physical laws. But from that starting point Marcuse introduces a specification that continues to be interesting, namely, that the only projects of social transformation that are, properly speaking, utopian (that is, *extrahistorical*) are those that *contradict proven or demonstrable scientific laws*. On the other hand, those projects of emancipation or liberation for which the objective or subjective conditions are lacking at a determinate historical moment are not utopias; they are only *provisionally* unrealizable ideals. These projects are no longer utopian once the material and spiritual forces for their realization are present, even if other forces momentarily impede them.

Thus, the thesis of the "end of utopia" in 1967 was that society was mature enough to eliminate poverty and misery, abolish alienated labor, and overcome oppression. The "end of utopia" means the real presence of the material and intellectual forces needed to realize a free society of equals living in harmony with nature. Marcuse thus tied the end of utopia to the potential positive effects of the technification of power and the automation of work, that is, to the emergence of a *surplus consciousness* and the development of aesthetic-erotic qualities—in sum, to the idea of a new anthropology as a mode of existence, of the emergence and development of new human needs, needs that he as well as others called "radical." Curiously, this Marcusian end of utopia, understood as the condition of possibility for the realization of socialism, had its echo in another thinker who could not be considered at the time a friend of utopias: Georg Lukács. It was this later Lukács of the *Conversations*,[25] returning from so many negative experiences and arguing that socialism had to start again due to the degradation implied by Stalinism and its derivatives, who suggested that this beginning should reverse the trajectory proposed by Engels, tying socialism back to what once was called utopian socialism.

From the perspective gained since Marcuse's lecture, it is not difficult to see the wisdom behind this expression. Marcuse was right: the 1960s really represented the end of the Marxists' socialist utopia. But, to the extent that in the forty years since it is not surplus consciousness that has triumphed but rather *surplus cynicism*, and that the anthropological mutation actually produced is closer to a combination of new forms of slavery and the arrival of "mechanical man" than to the realization of the new man, free and unalienated, we can conclude the following: the end of utopia, the end of the social-industrialist utopia, as foreseen by Marcuse, was the beginning of other utopias that emerged precisely out of a new dissatisfaction of human beings, out of the consciousness of a progressive worsening of our metabolism with nature, out of the protest against surplus cynicism. In fact, when this situation is looked at properly, almost at the same time that Marcuse proclaimed the end of one utopia another was already in the making, in the United States, the Netherlands, England, and Germany, a new utopia that would take form in the subsequent decades: the ecopacifist utopia.

Already this observation on the recent history of the end of utopia—that it contains within it the beginning of another utopia—compels us, I believe, to be very cautious when hearing today of *ends* or *overcomings*, be it in postmodern or supposedly dialectical language. Utopias do not decline because a philosopher's decrees it. Like his contemporaries Lukács and Bloch, Marcuse died as the new ecopacifist utopia was brewing. And the fact that eventually the later Lukács and the later Bloch ended up, in regard to utopia, more prudent than the later Marcuse, that instead of talking about the end of utopia they turned their gaze toward the utopias prior to 1848 or revalued *concrete* utopia, provides food for thought. Once again, the interesting point relates to a utopian constant that I have already pointed to: utopia's attempts to come into being in a place for which it was not conceived. It seems to me no coincidence that the later Lukács (from Hungary) and the later Bloch (from the German Democratic Republic) revalued the spirit of utopia at almost the same time that Marcuse proclaimed its end. In reality, all three were speaking of the same world and the same thing, and in the context of the same ideological tradition. But they did so from two different perspectives. Lukács and Bloch had personally experienced, in Hungary and the GDR, the supposed realization of the utopia called "real socialism" and had to deal with those who argued that they had definitively overcome utopia through the exaltation of the great science, historical and dialectical materialism. Not so Marcuse, who in the years leading up to 1967 had criticized Soviet ideology from the other side of the world, and with CIA funding.

BLOCH ON CONCRETE UTOPIA AND HOPE

Of all the authors on utopia from the years of the so-called end of utopia, the most relevant, the one who speaks to us best, continues to be Ernst Bloch. I am thinking of the Bloch who proposed a critical reading of the Bible with eyes trained on the *Communist Manifesto*, who inherited from Hegel the conviction that Paradise is a nature preserve in which only animals can remain (not homo sapiens, the species of hubris), and who dared to claim that the alliance between revolution and Christianity made at the beginning of modernity, during the first thirty years of the sixteenth century, in the Peasants' War, was not the last. At the end of the "brief century," of modernity and the millennium, this intuition of Bloch's would return with great force. One can find it in the latest developments of Latin American liberation philosophy, in the libertarian Marxisms of Michael Löwy and John Holloway, and in the writings of Wu Ming on that revolution without a face that keeps on screaming that another world is possible. Bloch refounded the moral appreciation for utopia without despising rational thought. He established a distinction between *abstract* utopia and *concrete* utopia that corresponds to the distinction between the "utopic" and the "utopian," between the gullible and the hopeful, between daydreaming and, while awake, saying that it is necessary to dream. His notion of utopia becomes a historico-critical reading of what the work of Marx might have represented if it had not turned into a temple, beyond the Engelsian pretension of elevating socialism to the status of a science that overcomes every utopia.

For Bloch, utopia is a regulating principle of reality, a methodological organ for the new, and thus a substantial part of human thought. It is that precisely because utopia is based on the natural and cultural attraction toward what is *not yet*, because authentic thinking means overflowing, going beyond the present, spiritually intensifying toward the future. What gives thought the capacity to modify the objective structure of what is through action is the reference to what is still not present. Bloch proposed a type of knowledge that not only is contemplative but wants to be theoretico-practical: an anticipatory knowledge that links up, of course, with the fantasy and desire of human beings. But the knowledge of utopia is such that, when it becomes concrete, when it wants to become a concrete utopia, it is not only fantasy or an imaginative anticipation of the future, *since the future is also not forever new.* Nor is it a simple negation of the present, of what exists, because then it would end up functioning like nihilism, as the annihilating negation. In contrast to *abstract* utopia, which jumps over the moment represented by the objective structures of reality without mediating between its projection and anticipatory science, Bloch's *concrete* utopia remains close to the intentional structure of collective needs. It does not try to reconcile itself with existing reality; it starts from the new human needs already emerging within it. On the one hand, the concrete utopia of social transformation functions as *a transcendental without transcendence*; it is a secular anticipatory belief in a better society. On the other hand, concrete utopia has learned the lesson of modern Galilean science and knows that in order to contemplate the celestial bodies, human senses are not enough. Telescopes are required.

Perhaps Bloch's most compelling idea today is his reworking of the concept of *hope* in dialogue with the real theoretico-practical adversary of the twentieth century, nihilism. Bloch saw lucidly that hope, not any hope but *learned* hope, is nothing less than the condition of possibility of utopia. And that is because reason cannot flourish without hope, nor can hope speak without reason. This is the fundamental point for deciding if we have truly arrived in the historical epoch of the end of utopia, or if we are only at the end of one utopia and the origin of another. The difficulty lies in simultaneously setting aside the notions of hope as *faith* and hope as *confidence* in the results of a project of transformation. We can turn this into a question: How can we maintain hope for social transformation in the midst of the scandal of inequality, imperialist war, injustice, and pillage? And what kind of hope would it be when we have tasted the tree of knowledge twice, when we have had to abandon the historical optimism that was characteristic of progressive, deterministic, scientistic, and mechanistic utopias? Hope by itself, wrote Bloch when he asked himself these questions, is not optimism; optimism is an indirect, mediated consequence of utopia. It lies in its very presence, not in its results. Hope is looking forward without consolatory guarantees. Hope is filtered through utopia as ultraviolet rays, invisible but active. As Walter Benjamin, with whom Bloch coincided on various points, had already written at the end of his study of Goethe's *Elective Affinities*: "It is only for the sake of those without hope that hope is given to us."

In the meantime, what has changed most in utopia is its *form*. In comparison to utopias prior to 1848, this concrete utopianism now reborn puts the emphasis not on the detail of what the future "city" will be like, but on the *criteria of possibility* for reaching it. And in contrast to the socialism that, after 1848, pretended to have passed from utopia to science, the concrete utopia of the present already knows that science, the scientific knowledge available in the present, *does not prove* or demonstrate the need for an alternative society of the future (call it socialist, communist, or libertarian), but that, instead, the best available science suggests *what cannot be*, what must be considered beyond human limits. The difficulty, of course, lies in agreeing intergenerationally on *what cannot be*, what has to be considered beyond human limits. This is why the qualifier "utopian" has been used so often (and will continue to be used) to disqualify—because, even accepting the plasticity of what we call human nature, we have no certainty with regard to the limits of that plasticity.

COUNTERGLOBALIZATION AND UTOPIA: A DEBATE

The sociopolitical spirit of utopia has recently taken off with greater force in what has been called the *movement of movements*, or the counterglobalization movement. It is worth pausing over because it reveals what it is about utopia today, about the concept behind the word, that is still attractive. On January 29, 2005, Porto Alegre saw a debate titled "Quixote Today: Utopia and Politics," organized by the World Social Forum, which brought together Federico Mayor Zaragoza, ex–Director-General of UNESCO, Ignacio Ramonet of *Le Monde diplomatique*, the Uruguayan writer Eduardo Galeano, and José Saramago, Nobel Prize winner for literature in 1998, to debate before thousands of people related to the counterglobalization movement. As was to be expected from the title, utopia and quixotism went hand in hand in all the interventions. Mayor Zaragoza, Ramonet, and Galeano sang the praises of the positive utopia represented by the *movement of movements* against neoliberal globalization. I will not dwell on its objectives, which are familiar to everyone.[26] But Saramago expressed a dissenting view. He said that today the concept of utopia is fundamentally useless, and that maybe it already was when More published his celebrated work. In his opinion, the word "utopia" lacks rigor and does not mean anything.

The debate was open, but the discussion provoked by Saramago on the concept and the word was curiously foreclosed, at least momentarily, by literary citations and examples. Galeano proposed three of them: León Felipe ("the hour in which Aldonza Lorenzo is transformed in Dulcinea"); Bernard Shaw, when he says: "There are those who observe reality such as it is and ask themselves, why?; and there are those who observe it as it has never been and ask themselves, why not?"; and Fernando Birri, the Argentinian filmmaker, who, asked what utopia was good for, responded:

"Utopia is on the horizon and after I take ten steps it is ten steps beyond; I take twenty steps and it is even farther; and even if I kept going I would never be able to reach it. But that is why utopias are useful: for walking." While continuing to defend the value of utopia, I would give another response, from the utopian classic by William Morris: "I pondered all these things, and how men fight and lose the battle, and the thing that they fought for comes about in spite of their defeat, and when it comes turns out not to be what they meant, and other men have to fight for what they meant under another name."[27]

But I propose that we could subscribe to Galeano's perspective and accept Saramago's point when he affirms that in political or politico-social terms the *word* "utopia" no longer means anything, and even when he suggests (perhaps reminded of the other current of modern political thought that begins with Niccolò Machiavelli) that utopia may have already been useless when More published his great work. We should not dismiss such a perspective, especially when we share its social goal, because ultimately there have been important thinkers, mainly since the nineteenth century, who shared the goal of the utopians but precisely criticized the utopian form. And there are those now who propose new words for the old concept or at least qualify the substantive. If one accepts Saramago's challenge, one is compelled to question the basis of utopia, at the end of modernity as well as its beginning. This is not to say that there are no utopias anymore, only to ask whether the form is still relevant for changing the world and improving it, making it more just, more egalitarian, more hospitable. In order to do so, I will refer to three authors who concerned themselves with this question in recent times: Peter Sloterdijk, Fredric Jameson, and Miguel Abensour.

Sloterdijk recently recognized the persistence of utopia, and, recalling Bloch, asked what meaning that persistence had nowadays. For him, utopia continues to play an *autohypnotic* role, whereby individuals rediscover in it a universally motivational force. But since utopia has lost its innocence, the utopian possesses a sort of artificial unconscious that is deeply motivating. Thus, in our societies, utopia appears as the other face of the search or hunt for success: the dream of losers. Once we overcome the angelical element and the schizophrenia produced by the utopias of the Great Refusal, what is won, according to Sloterdijk, is acceptance from now on not to be constituted by reality. What is redeemable, then, from the old utopia is irony, the different modalities of humor.[28]

The vindication of irony, parody, and satire is shared by those who see in utopia's persistence only a hypnotic or autohypnotic function, those who emphasize the aesthetic dimension of contemporary utopia, and those who embark on the search for an ontological or philosophical grounding of utopia. Jameson, however, following in Adorno's footsteps, has added another consideration: the importance of the *via negativa* for capturing the moment of truth that lies in the utopias of asceticism and pleasure. A review of contemporary science fiction precisely shows the importance of the lessons of addiction and sexuality, so that a genuine reckoning with utopia requires integrating these anxieties in order to overcome the sphere of pure mental experience that, in his opinion, is what has made the utopias of the past politically and existentially inoperable.[29]

For his part, Abensour, who today insists most on the ontological grounding of utopia, has called attention to a third characteristic: the *heroism of the spirit*. Abensour, inspired by Levinas, believes that we have to think of utopia in a transhistorical manner, as something that does not depend on the good or bad times we live in, but as something inscribed in the human condition.[30] Utopian thought would be for human beings a kind of learning process through which we acquire a sixth sense. That does not imply that utopia necessarily relies on a positive vision of human beings. The aspiration toward utopia and its persistence do not have a direct relation with either optimism or pessimism, which are moods; rather, they are tied to heroism of the spirit, which compels us to struggle against exhaustion and catastrophe. Thus, utopia would be the projection into the future of the "not yet," a branching out that is the legacy of traces of suffering of previous generations with all its fragility. There is no triumphant utopia.

A WORKING HYPOTHESIS

Already in the 1970s the ideologues of "really existing socialism" opposed the existing state of things in the USSR to utopian thought, the spirit of utopia, which they attributed to critical Marxists from many decades before (Korsch and Pannekoek, Luxemburg and Gramsci, Lukács and

Bloch, Brecht and Otto Rühle, Havemann and Schaff, Castoriadis and Rubel, Berlinguer and Guevara). Symptomatically, the best of what emancipatory thought with Marxist roots had produced in Europe was ignored or demonized in the Soviet Union from the era of Stalin to that of Gorbachev. The undeniable social "reality" represented by the power of that so-called socialism was presented, counter to the opinion of the majority of critical Marxists, as the only possible socialism. But this dominant point of view in the USSR, GDR, and other countries in Eastern Europe was only the continuation of the scientistic, antiutopian tendency of so-called orthodox Marxism. Thus, properly speaking, it now turns out to be not only more modest but also more correct to identify the end of "actually existing socialism" with the *failure of an illusion that was, precisely and conscientiously, the negation of utopia*. It is absurd and pretentious, on the other hand, to identify the end of that illusion with the end of utopia as such. So-called orthodox Marxism presented itself as precisely the overcoming of utopia, as the conversion of utopia into science. From an epistemological standpoint, however, there is no doubt that the idea of definitively converting utopia into science was and is an aberration.

From this perspective, 1989 can be positively considered as *the end of utopia* in the negative or pejorative conception of the term, that is, the utopia of the scientistic Marxism, of the socialism that pretended to be definitively "scientific," that sprung from the (Engelsian) idea of the passage from utopian to scientific socialism. This latter thesis had already been refuted long ago by thinkers who considered themselves socialists (in a wide sense of the word), from Simone Weil to Bloch, from Benjamin to Pasolini, and from Albert Einstein to Alexandr Zinoviev, to mention just a few from very different orientations. What occurred in 1989 was the practical confirmation of what they had been arguing. Because of this, and against neoliberal ideologues, 1989 does not mean the end of utopia in general. On the contrary, what happened then has opened the road for the reappearance of the moral spirit of the old utopia, extending from More to Engels. And it is symptomatic in this respect that the word "utopia" itself has been used again in its positive connotation even in camps (like the neo-Marxist, neosocialist, neocommunist) that decades ago had only used it in its negative sense.

What confuses many people today is that, in the meantime, the old utopia born with More *has changed its form*. Sometimes the continuation of the old utopia is sought in dominant political thought and practice or in academic moral and political philosophy. It is not found there, and so the claim is made about the end of utopia. Later this absence is rationalized: there is no longer utopia because our culture is wary of the association of utopia with totalitarianism. As if totalitarianism were not also latent in the fragmentary social technology that inspires the majority of powers in today's neoliberal fundamentalism. Indeed, it seems natural not to find what one is looking for in academic moral and political philosophy because the spirit of utopia *is never really there*. Nor was it there before. The spirit of utopia was born out of the distance of moral and political thought from the existing powers. Utopia was born, with European modernity, out of the negation of political thought's unconditional service to the prince. That is what is stated most explicitly in More's seminal work, but also in Maldonado, las Casas, and Quiroga—as well as, with the passage of time, Fourier, Cabet, and Owen. Today as yesterday, we will not find the spirit of utopia in the dominant currents of academic political philosophy. One has to search elsewhere or differently, precisely as had been done by the ideologues of contemporary scientism, in the East and the West, *negatively*. Because it was they, the ideologues of a Marxism that came into power and the ideologues of the end of utopia, who named the utopias of the turn of the last century, just as the powerful did at the end of the nineteenth century. It was the established powers that called Fourier, Fernando Garrido, Marx, and Kropotkin *utopians*, just as it was established powers that since the 1970s have called the critical and alternative thinkers of emancipation by the same name.

Already in the decade of the great confrontation that was the 1930s, when liberalism faced a crisis and Soviet Communism and Nazi fascism were winning over the masses of Europe, the flower of utopia was nearly buried but did not disappear entirely. And this is where we now have to look for the *antecedents of the new utopia*. For example, we have the radically utopian thought of Weil, which reemerged in the 1990s, surprising and exciting in its freedom and autonomy. The idealist-critical utopia running through Weil's pages, from "Perspectives" to *The Need for Roots* and *Writings from London*, remained unfinished. It is only now that we are beginning to discover the truth of the positive part of that reflection, eccentric with respect to all authorities and all academic moral and political philosophies, a reflection that, in its time, was almost entirely dismissed by the powerful as insanity.

We also have to put the legacy of Bloch, vindicated today by impatient Christians and critical Marxists, into context. Perhaps the most serious criticism of the positive utopian spirit and the notion of hope present in Bloch was made by Günther Anders, that ludic, critical, subversive, and desperate thinker, still little known, who put Benjamin's manuscript of the theses on the philosophy of history into the hands of Bertolt Brecht. Asked by Mathias Greffrath in 1979 about what nourishes consolation, courage, and hope after so much suffering, barbarism, and failure in calling the people to react, Anders responded: *Distress your neighbor as you would yourself.* And he added: "In principle, I do not know hope. Because my principle is: while there is still the smallest chance to intervene constructively into this enormous mess we have made for ourselves, then one must. My commandments for the atomic age conclude with a principle that says: *If the situation is desperate, so what?*" Anders related despair to what he had called the obsolescence of human beings, and he maintained that one of the causes of this was the species' blindness to apocalypse. Typical of his manner of reasoning is the comparison he establishes between the notions of *hell* and the *dialectic*: "Considering the immense role the dialectic has played, it sounds strange to hear that the nineteenth century lacked the negative. But if one compares the dialectic's negativity with that implied by the concept of hell, it is clear that the dialectic has 'positivized' the negative, transformed it into a ferment."[31]

We have here the highest level of comprehension of the necessary subjectivity from a secular futurological prospective that denies the usual notion of progress but still does not renounce the betterment of the world, even if it acknowledges that human beings have become obsolete. But is this the last word on positive utopia? There remains, of course, a problem Anders only touches on.[32] Is this desperate and pessimistic conception of the blindness of the species, what Anders calls "Promethean shame," only the consciousness of tragedy shared by the select few, or is it a truth *communicable* to majorities, to those who are at the threshold of hunger and misery, trying to satisfy the most basic human needs? Are Benjamin, Anders, and many others really contemporaries of those others who have lived and live the hunger, suffering, and disgrace that accompany misery and illiteracy? Is not the immense difficulty of communicating to these others, the wretched of the earth, a pessimistic, hopeless conception of natural illusions, a limitation of contemporary secular consciousness? These are some of the questions intellectuals must ask themselves if they really want to relate to the prevailing mood while being conscious of their privileged situation.

Conscious of this problem, a friend of the people, wherever a people exists at this dawn of the century and millennium, will feel morally comfortable using the word "utopia" in a very precise sense: the ideal, illusion, hope, daydream, illumination, premonition, or regulative idea of an alternative to the world of neoliberal globalization as we know it, a society that is at once freer, more egalitarian, more fraternal, more just, more humane, more hospitable, more harmonious. He or she will not mind being called a "utopian" in this precise sense because, although it is true that every utopia can turn, in time, into its opposite, it is truer that what exists has already turned into the opposite of what utopia wants. Rebellion must have an internal limit, surely, but in order to speak about the limit of rebellion one has to have been a rebel. The opposite is voluntary servitude. The friend of the people will feel uncomfortable when confronted with the use of the term "utopia" in its generic sense of a convenient illusion, ideal, or dream, like a never-never land, a place we will never get to see. Because in that usage the principle of imaginative desire clashes with the reality principle and is turned into literature and limits itself to the literary. While appealing in literary figures, it conflicts with the exigencies of those others, the downtrodden, whom it is meant to benefit. The horizon of utopia can be individual—there is nothing wrong with that—but its lining, the lining of that horizon, will be closer to us to the extent that the alternative proposed is more social and collective.

Finally, the friend of the people, wherever he or she exists, will feel uncomfortable, I believe, when the word "utopia" is used to designate ideas, theories, anticipations, or intentions that are not realized exactly as they were meant to be by their proponents. This is because the dominant ideology calls everything that falls beneath its paving stones "utopian": More as much as Fourier, Marx as much as Gandhi, Luxembourg as much as Guevara. To systematically call all of history's defeated "utopians" is to deny half of history. And it is precisely that other half of history that the friend of the people has to recover for the people itself to come to realize that the rights it has today, considered utopian by those who ruled earlier, are owed to the (temporarily) defeated of history. In sum, the history of utopia in the twentieth century should teach us to distinguish between deluding ourselves and having hope. Or, as Leopardi said when speaking of what he called "natural illusions":

> Few can be great (and in art and poetry perhaps no one) unless they are governed by illusions.
>
> The half-philosopher combats illusions precisely because he is deluded; the true philosopher loves them and proclaims them because he is not deluded.
>
> How many great illusions conceived in a moment either of enthusiasm or of despair or indeed of exaltation are, in fact, the most real and sublime truths, or their forerunner?[33]

NOTES

Originally published as part of *Utopías e ilusiones naturales* (Barcelona: El Viejo Topo, 2007). This translation is by Manuel S. Almeida.

1. For detailed information on *Utopia* (and Thomas More's life and works in general), including images, reproductions of original manuscripts, information on editions, university centers and associations dedicated to the study of his work, bibliographies, and articles, see www.thomasmorestudies.org/, www.shu.ac.uk/emls/iemls/conf/texts/marius.htm, www.thomasmorestudies.org/library.html, http://webdoe.gwdg.de/edoe/ia/cese/artic96/wenzel/10_96.htm#Morus, as well as gracewoodo.tripod.com/freemanmore.html.
2. See Demetrio Ramos Pérez, "Sobre el origen de la utopía de Tomás Moro," in *Homenaje a Antonio Maravall* (Madrid: Centro de Investigaciones Sociológicas, Consejo Superior de Investigaciones Científicas, 1985), 3:221–235.
3. For more detail on influences, see André Prévost, "Introduction," in *L'Utopie de Thomas More* (Paris: Nouvelles Éditions Mame, 1978), xxii–xxix; Dominic Baker-Smith, ed., *More's Utopia* (London: Harper Collins Academic, 1991), chaps. 1, 2, and 3.
4. Nicola Bottiglieri, "Colombo, Vespucci e le prime immagini del nuovo mondo," *Scoperta e conquista dell'America*, special issue of *Dimensioni e problemi della ricerca storica* 2 (1992): 105–127. See also Francesco Guicciardini, *Storia d'Italia* (Milan: Garzanti, 1988), 642ff. And also Carlo Ginzburg, *El queso y los gusanos* (Baltimore: Johns Hopkins University Press, 1980).
5. López de Gomara, Fernández de Oviedo, and Bartolomé de las Casas thought the same; later, Francis Bacon too subscribes to this idea that the new continent was the Atlantis that Plato spoke of in the *Timaeus* when he wrote the *New Atlantis*.

6   Sir Thomas More, *Utopia* (Durham: Duke University Classics, 2012), 60.
7   Ibid., 66.
8   Peter Matheson, ed., *The Collected Works of Thomas Müntzer* (Edinburgh: T and T Clark, 1988). See also Ernst Bloch, *Thomas Münzer als Theologe der Revolution* (Munich: Kurt Wolff, 1921); Marianne Schaub, *Müntzer contre Luther: Le Droit divin contre l'absolutisme princier* (Paris: Armand Collin, 1984).
9   Biographical information from Silvio Zavala, *Recuerdos de Vasco de Quiroga* (Mexico City: Porrúa, 1987), 98–99.
10 Ibid., 12.
11 Ibid., 39–46.
12 Vasco de Quiroga, *Información en derecho*, ed. Carlos Herrejón (Mexico City: Secretaría de Educación Pública, 1985). Quiroga himself called the work "a salad of what I had written and thought over many days."
13 Other authors influenced by More in the Spain of the sixteenth and seventeenth centuries were Herrera, Ribadeneyra, and Quevedo. See Silvio Zavala, "Nuevas notas en torno de Vasco de Quiroga," in *Recuerdo*, 97.
14 Paz Serrano Gassent, *Vasco de Quiroga*: *Utopía y derecho en la conquista de América* (Madrid: Universidad Nacional de Educación a Distancia—Fondo de Cultura de España, 2001).
15 On the Valladolid controversy, see Fernández Buey, *La gran perturbación: Discurso del indio metropolitano* (Barcelona: El Viejo Topo, 2000).
16 Such was at least the opinion of Marcel Bataillon: see Bataillon, "Vasco de Quiroga y Bartolomé de las Casas," *Revista de Historia de América* 33 (1952): 83–95. Bataillon believes one can find an echo of *De debellandis indis* in Miguel de Arcos's *Parecer*. René Acuña has discussed this hypothesis in the "Preliminary Study" to his Spanish edition of a brief anonymous treatise that has been conserved in fragmented form among the papers of Bartolomé de las Casas, which he identifies as the lost work of Vasco de Quiroga: *De debellandis indis* (Mexico City: Universidad Nacional Autónoma de México—Instituto de Investigaciones Filológicas, 1988).
17 Bataillon reproduces and analyzes the letter in his *Études sur Bartolomé de las Casas* (Paris: Centre de Recherches de l'Institut d'Études Hispaniques, 1965), 226, and in *De debellandis indis*. René Acuña reproduces it in the "Preliminary Study" to his edition of *De debellandis indis*.
18 Ibid., 157 and 169.
19 Ibid., 181.
20 There is now a considerable bibliography on the work of Quiroga. On the Mexican phase, see Fintan B. Warren, *Vasco de Quiroga and His Pueblo-Hospitals of Santa Fe* (Washington, DC: Academy of American Franciscan History, 1963); Francisco Martin Hernández, "Don Vasco de Quiroga, Protector of the Indians," *Salmanticiensis* 34 (1987); Ramón Xirau, *Idea y querella de la nueva España* (Madrid: Alianza, 1973), 123–124 (this text includes an anthology of writings); Carlos Herrejón, "Introduction," in *Información en derecho* (Mexico City: Secretaría de Educación Pública, 1985), 9ff.; Herrejón, ed., *Humanismo y ciencia en la formación de México* (Mexico City: El Colegio

de Michoacán, 1984); Paulino Castañeda Delgado, *Don Vasco de Quiroga y su Información en derecho* (Madrid: José Porrúa, 1974); Silvio Zavala, *Recuerdo de Vasco de Quiroga*; Mauricio Beuchot, *La querella de la conquista: Una polémica del siglo XVI* (Madrid: Siglo XXI, 1992), 73–83.

21 Sometimes even incorrectly interpreting Francis Fukuyama. This is well observed by Rafael Vidal Jiménez, "La utopía después del 'fin de la historia': Pensar un futuro abierto más allá del progreso," www.cica.es/aliens/gitteus/R.%20Vidal.htm.

22 See Octavio Paz, "In Search of the Present," acceptance speech for the Nobel Prize for Literature, 1989. http://nobelprize.org/literature/laureates/1990/paz-lecture.html.

23 Translator's note: *libertarianism* (*libertarismo*) or *libertarian* here refers to radical, emancipatory and anti-statist movements and thought and has no relation to the American ultraliberalism that goes by the same name. It is synonymous with anarchism.

24 Herbert Marcuse, "The End of Utopia," trans. Jeremy Shapiro and Shierry M. Weber, in *Herbert Marcuse: Five Lectures* (Boston: Beacon, 1970).

25 Hans Heinz Holz, Leo Kofler, and Wolfgang Abendroth, *Gespräche mit Georg Lukács* (Reinbek: Rowohlt, 1967).

26 I have analyzed the objectives, aims, and the debates of the World Social Forum, as well as those of the *movement of movements* in *Guía para una globalización alternativa: Otro mundo es posible* (Madrid: Ediciones B—Byblos, 2005).

27 William Morris, *A Dream of John Ball* (London: Nonesuch, 1948), 214.

28 Peter Sloterdijk, "La utopía ha perdido su inocencia," interview with Fabrice Zimmer, trans. Ramón Alcoberro, *Magazine Littéraire* (May 2000).

29 Fredric Jameson, "The Politics of Utopia," *New Left Review* 25 (2004): 35–55.

30 "L'Homme est un animal utopique: Entretien avec Miguel Abensour," *Mouvements* 45–46 (2006): 72–87.

31 Günther Anders with Mathias Greffrath, "Wenn ich verzweifelt bin, was geht's mich an?," in *Die Zerstörung einer Zukunft: Gespräche mit emigrierten Sozialwissenschaftlern*, ed. Mathias Greffrath (Reinbek: Rowohlt, 1979). Anders published the first volume of *The Obsolescence of Man* in 1956 and the second in 1980. Besides a philosopher and journalist, he was a renowned antiwar and antinuclear activist.

32 And of what has been said by another author who was no friend of utopias, E. M. Cioran, *History and Utopia*, trans. Richard Howard (1960; New York: Seaver, 1987).

33 Giacomo Leopardi, *Zibaldone*, ed. Michael Caesar and Franco D'Intino, trans. Kathleen Baldwin et al. (New York: Farrar, Straus and Giroux, 2013), 15, 782, 832.

II

QUESTIONING UTOPIA

4

MARX AND UTOPIA

FRANCK FISCHBACH

Before any discussion of the relation between utopia and Marxism, it is necessary to consider Marx's own relation to utopia. Let us start by recalling that the philosophical, notably Hegelian, tradition inherited by Marx is very hostile to utopianism. Marx knew by heart the preface to the *Elements of the Philosophy of Right*, in which Hegel virulently opposed those who, in matters of political philosophy, build castles in the air, which is to say, think or imagine the political and social world as it should be, and thus dispense with knowing it as it is.[1] Marx had incontestably inherited this Hegelian antiutopian tendency, which we find expressed in one of the few definitions of communism he gives, namely, in *The German Ideology*: "communism is for us not a *state of affairs* which is to be established, an *ideal* to which reality [will] have to adjust itself. We call communism the *real* movement which abolishes the present state of things."[2] One can hardly think of a more antiutopian definition of communism! Communism does not designate for Marx an ideal society or a future one to which we would be led by this real movement and effective process—less a process of construction than a movement of destruction of the existing state of things.

Let us remember that communism is for Marx first of all the name of the process that leads us there through different phases or periods, essentially three, the first being *destructive* (the famous "*revolutionary* dictatorship of the proletariat"), the second again *negative* (the first form of communist society that still carries "the birthmarks of the old society from whose womb it emerges"), and only the third and final stage or period being positive and affirmative.³ If Marx and Engels are critical of the utopians in the *Manifesto of the Communist Party*, it is primarily because utopianism is focused on the positive content of the society to come and neglects or ignores what, in the eyes of the *Manifesto*'s authors, is essential, that is, the process that is likely to lead us there.

That is why Marx and Engels's critique throughout the *Manifesto* does not bear on the utopian content of the socialists (Saint-Simon, Owen, Fourier), on "their positive proposals concerning the future society" (propositions that Marx and Engels were quick to reprimand them for), but on the fact that these utopian socialist thinkers see in the proletariat only "the spectacle of a class without any historical initiative or any independent political movement."⁴ This is surely the point on which Marx and Engel's diagnosis homes in: the fact that the socialist utopias were constructed and elaborated in the heads of philosophers without any relation to the political and social movement specific to the proletariat—to the extent that the authors of the *Manifesto* came to think that there was a connection between the abundance of socialist utopias and the absence of a movement and political organizations belonging to and internal to the proletarian itself. The existence of socialist utopias becomes for Marx and Engels the very symptom of the proletariat's political and historical weakness.

In other words, our two authors are not critical of utopias as such; they are critical of them to the extent that they do not come from the proletariat itself, that they are not borne by it and immanent in the very movement of its self-organization, that is to say, immanent also in class struggle. Well after the *Manifesto*, Engels returned to the question of utopia, though not to say anything substantially different from what he said with Marx in 1848. In 1880, in *Socialism: Utopian and Scientific*, Engels again welcomes the "breadth of view" and the "grandeur" of the three great, above-named utopians. But he also maintains the idea that these utopias had been formulated in an era when the proletariat was "as yet quite incapable of independent political action."⁵ It is the very same argument as in the *Manifesto*: the utopias of the socialist thinkers are inseparable from the historical moment of their formulation and are the visible signs of an era in which the proletariat had not yet deployed a political and thus theoretical energy that was its own.

In this way, a utopia can basically be defined as revolutionary thought that is not the theoretical expression of political and social practice that is itself revolutionary, and thus as revolutionary thought that does not testify to the activity and self-organization of an agent engaged in revolutionary practice. In turn, if there is something more Engelsian than Marxian here, it is the opposition between "utopian socialism" and "scientific socialism," an opposition incidentally absent from the *Manifesto*. One can nonetheless appreciate that the expression "scientific socialism" certainly has meaning for Marx as well, but on the condition that we understand by it a doctrine or a theory based at once on a materialist conception of history (according to which history is the history of the unfolding of human practical, material activity) and on a critique of political economy (unmasking the illusions engendered specifically by a capitalist economy). These are the two elements that give specificity to Marx's socialism. But if one understands by "scientific socialism" the theory of historical evolution, *necessary* because subject to *laws* (themselves resembling laws of nature), toward a socialist society, then in this case I think one moves away from Marx and closer to Engels, and even to Kautsky. Marx, for his part, had taken care to specify the meaning of "scientific socialism": the term only has meaning "in opposition to utopian socialism, which wants to attach the people to new delusions, instead of limiting its science to the knowledge of the social movement made by the people itself."[6]

Should we conclude that his rejection of utopia also explains Marx's hostility to anarchism? If, as Gérard Bensussan and Georges Labica say in their *Dictionnaire critique du marxisme*, anarchism can be considered the "congenital enemy" of Marxism, it is certainly because the connections between them are as strong as the conflicts, and without a doubt because there is an anarchistic element in Marx's own thought, which he continued to make explicit in the years following the Paris Commune: "All socialists see anarchy as the following program: Once the aim of the proletarian movement—i.e., abolition of classes—is attained, the power of the state ... disappears, and the functions of government become simple administrative functions."[7] The modern bureaucratic state with its army of functionaries (and its army as such) is for Marx clearly a "parasite feeding upon, and clogging the free movement of, society."[8] From 1843, the date of his commentary on the *Elements of Hegel's Philosophy of Right*, right up until the end, Marx held to the fundamental idea that society is the foundation of the State and not the reverse. On this basis, the perspective of a classless society is indissociable from that of a society able to move beyond the State—a perspective that one can genuinely say would constitute the content of utopia specific to Marx, since it has, according to him, seen the start of the realization of its being, in the form of the Paris Commune.

We have here occasion to recall that Marx himself did not use the expression "historical materialism": he speaks instead of a "materialist conception of history," and when determining the nature of his own philosophical position he describes himself as a *"practical* materialist."[9] In other words, Marx's conception of history does not imply that the development of the latter is subject to necessary laws. Marx did not pretend to have uncovered necessary laws that the historical succession of modes of production obeys. His specific objective was to study the capitalist mode of production, and thus to comprehend what it is about this mode of production that makes it *specific* relative to all other modes of production. These other modes that have existed in history can be grasped retrospectively *starting from* the study of capitalist society. Marx said only that there comes a moment in the history of society when the social relations of production become a hindrance to the further development of productive forces, and that, when this moment comes, the relations in question "are exploded." But when it comes to knowing when exactly and in what way precisely they are "exploded," on this point Marx is carefully imprecise: that depends on historical action that, in itself, is unforeseeable.

This is indeed why the materialist conception of history that is Marx's cannot be reduced to determinism pure and simple: to say that it is cumbersome and tends to slow development in the history of human societies, and that these tendencies are social, or in other words that they escape *individual* decision, is one thing, but to say that such tendencies develop necessarily, that they obey necessary laws absolutely constraining all human will, including collective will, is another thing, and nowhere affirmed by Marx. On the contrary, according to him, men make their own history, collectively to be sure, and certainly also in conditions that they have not chosen and that they have inherited from the past, but they do make it; clearly they do not make it "just as they like," that is to say, on the basis of their own individual free will; neither do they make it out of nothing, that is to say, as though there were no preexisting conditions into which one must insert one's action.[10] That is why we should take equally seriously the label "materialism of practice," which Marx himself expressly gave to his approach. It means that the basis of all things, for him, is men's real activity as they produce and work, but also as they trade, exchange, speak, communicate, think, know, desire, create, and so on. This real, multiform activity of an essentially social nature is the fabric of which human history is made: considered positively, this activity is fundamentally affirmative, productive, and even creative, but, at least so far, it also possesses a negative side, in the sense that it too is an activity that constantly gives rise to, in contradiction with itself, obstacles, stumbling blocks, and breaks to its full and complete unfolding (in addition to what nature already sets against it). These are the obstructions and obstacles to be exploded.

This brings us to the observation that Marx is in effect very grudging when it comes to describing, "in pictures" or not, the communist society to come. But this is precisely because he knows that the creativity of human action renders impossible all prediction (in the literal sense) of the exact form future society is likely to take. It is precisely because determinism does not rule in matters of history that it is also not possible to anticipate the future beyond uncovering certain tendencies already at work in the present. And this is what Marx himself did in his analysis of the tendency leading to "great industry," the massive investment in physics and chemistry in the industrial process, opening up, for him, the perspective of a development of productive forces in proportion to which human work would no longer be the measure of value, and productive tasks could be carried out by the machines directly derived from applied science, liberating even more men from their tasks and procuring for them leisure they could devote to their formation as "social individuals."[11] To say this in 1858, on the sole basis of an analysis of immanent tendencies of modern industry, and in a period when peasants made up the vast majority of the population of European countries, is more powerful than any utopia.

Recall that Marx is not in fact interested in the construction of a utopia, but in laying bare, through the study of capitalism itself, tendencies working to bring about conditions that contradict the internal logic of capital and that, insofar as they are taken up in political practice, can become conditions of impossibility of capitalism.[12] The fundamental idea, in any case, is that these conditions do not fall from the sky and that they arise within the social process of work and production.

As for the theme of Marx's messianism, in connection with utopia, we know well that more than a few have dreamed and continue to dream of it. As for me, I am quite skeptical on this point. There is certainly evidence of messianism in a text like *Introduction to the Critique of Hegel's Philosophy of Right*, published in 1844, where it is a question of the crow of the Gallic rooster[13] and of the proletariat as the class that is no longer a class because it suffers a universal and absolute wrong. But this text seems for the most part to have remained without sequel in Marx's oeuvre. Such messianism seems to be characteristic not so much of Marx's own thought as of the spirit of this period, which the Germans call *Vormärz*, that is, the lead-up to 1848. If Marx, still young, gave in to these messianic tendencies that were in a sense in the air at the time, I believe that the failure of 1848 definitely put an end to them. It is strange that it is still—including today, and perhaps even more today than earlier—hard to allow that Marx, personally, could have been someone who really had done with all forms of religious consciousness, messianic or not. Now, that his thought has subsequently been able to give birth to secularized forms of the religions of history, even to forms of historical messianism, is another matter, and more complicated that it appears. Let us keep in mind that, in the terms of the Internationale itself, "there are no supreme saviors."

All this leads me to think that the only possible Marxian recuperation of the concept of utopia is without a doubt a negative one. Let me explain: if utopia can make sense from a Marxian point of view, it is not, as is often thought, by virtue of its relation with the future, but with the present, and more precisely its relation to what in the present constitutes an active negation of the current state of things. If utopia, then presently and actually, in every sense of the latter term, namely, in a present and active way. In other words, if there is a concept of utopia in Marx, it is less temporal than spatial—the concept of utopia itself being, as Jameson reminds us, a spatial and not a temporal one (in which case one would have to speak not of utopia but of uchronia). Utopia refers in this sense to what in the present social space constitutes a negation of the work of the current order of things. In this respect, there would be in Marx a thought not only of what is really possible in the present situation, but also of what actively negates that situation. Let us take a simple example: thought that remains faithful to the inspiration and spirit of Marx would be capable of being a thought that shows—as does notably that of Antonio Negri—that the form taken by work in the post-Fordist era that is ours is a form in and through which work recovers the autonomy that it had lost and that constitutes an active negation of work's real subjection to capital. In short, utopia in this sense is the uncovering of what is anticapitalist, that is to say, what constitutes *already actualized* forms of the negation of capitalism in our contemporary capitalist societies. It is not only the possible; it is the possible that appears as such mainly because it is the negation of the work of the real and the actual. What this implies on a purely philosophical level is the elaboration of a form of negative ontology, an ontology of the negative or the "not yet," which Bloch was able to see and explain better than anyone. I will only add that Bloch's thought took shape largely in a struggle against all the deterministic, mechanistic, and necessitarian versions of Marx's thought, and that Bloch's oeuvre is philosophical in its own right, and not a simple continuation of, or even less a commentary on, Marx: it is also an oeuvre in which Marx's thought is only one source among others, notably alongside Jewish and Schellingian strands.

The question of utopia in Marx leads us finally to the question of the place and role of morality, to the extent that the construction of utopias can rest on a moral condemnation of present society. On this point, we must remember that there is certainly morality in Marx, including in his mature writings, notably *Capital*, where certain passages evince a true indignation from Marx the individual that seems to be very much on a moral register. But what is certain is that for Marx the philosopher morality is never the ground: it is neither his starting point nor the basis for his critique of capitalism. The critique of capitalism in Marx is first of all the critique of a determinate social system and, as such, a critique of illusions that this system engenders about itself in the social agents living with it. His critique is not a critique of evil, any more than of injustice; it is primarily a critique of illusions, thus a demystification that aims to increase our degree of consciousness, knowledge, comprehension, and hence also our power to act. It is here that Marx comes close to Spinoza: neither the one nor the other believes in the abstraction (produced by the imagination, thus an imperfect knowledge) of what is called "evil." They prefer the concept of the harmful (Marx says this clearly in *The Holy*

Family), that is to say, the idea that there are things, circumstances, and individuals that we naturally avoid because they harm us, and others toward which we equally naturally incline because they are favorable and useful to us. One leaves here the realm of morality to rejoin that of ethics, in the Spinozist sense of that term. In this realm there is absolutely no need for "humanism"; a simple naturalism such as that of Spinoza or Marx is more than sufficient. Like all natural beings, men aspire to live in conditions that allow them to live better, they flee misery and poverty, they aspire to the satisfaction of essential and vital needs (food, fluid, shelter, warmth, education, care, cultivation, personal growth, and so on). To be sure, this implies urgency that one can say has to do with justice, but the norm of this justice is never, according to Marx, external and from above relative to the real life of men and practical relations in which they are engaged with one another. Such a norm cannot be defined independently of the relations themselves, even in the case when this norm is defined *against* the actual form of these very relations.

We know that Karl Mannheim, in *Ideology and Utopia* (1929–1931), explained that ideology is the deed of the dominant (with a view to perpetuating their domination) just as utopia is the deed of the dominated. What remains to be said is that utopia is itself also always an ideology, without being conservative, justifying the current state of things; on the contrary it is a driving ideology of history, the ideology that moves things along beyond the current state of things. To this I will add simply and in conclusion that, if utopia can be considered a driving ideology, it is uniquely to the extent to which it subtends and is itself borne by the practices that produce in the *here and now* the conditions of *impossibility* of maintaining the current order of things.

NOTES

1   "Since philosophy is *exploration of the rational*, it is for that very reason the *comprehension of the present and the actual*, not the setting up a *world beyond* which exists God knows where.... As a philosophical composition, it must distance itself as far as possible from the obligation to construct a *state as it ought to be*; such instruction as it may contain cannot be aimed at instructing the state on how it ought to be, but rather at showing how the state, as the ethical universe, should be recognized." Georg Wilhelm Friedrich Hegel, *Hegel: Elements of the Philosophy of Right*, ed. Allen W. Wood, trans. H. B. Nisbet (Cambridge: Cambridge University Press, 1991), 20, 21.

2   Karl Marx and Friedrich Engels, "The German Ideology," in in *Marx/Engels Collected Works* (*MECW*) (Moscow: Progress, 1975–2005), 5:38.
3   Karl Marx, "Critique of the Gotha Program," in *MECW* 24:86.
4   Karl Marx and Friedrich Engels, "Manifesto of the Communist Party," in *MECW* 6:514.
5   Friedrich Engels, "Socialism: Utopian and Scientific," in *MECW* 24:289.
6   Karl Marx, "Conspectus of Bakunin's *Statism and Anarchy*," in *MECW* 18:630–636.
7   Karl Marx, "Fictitious Splits in the International (Private Circular from the General Council of the International Working Men's Association)" (1872), in *MECW* 23:123.
8   Karl Marx, "The Civil War in France," in *MECW* 22:333.
9   Marx and Engels, "The German Ideology," 5:38.
10 Karl Marx, "The Eighteenth Brumaire of Louis Bonaparte," in *MECW* 11:103.
11 Karl Marx and Friedrich Engels, "Grundrisse," in *MECW* 29:90–94.
12 "The productive forces and social relations—two different aspects of the development of the social individual—appear to capital merely as the means, and are merely the means, for it to carry on production on its restricted basis. In fact, however, they are the material conditions for exploding that basis." Ibid., 29:92.
13 Karl Marx, "Contribution to a Critique of Hegel's Philosophy of Right," in *MECW* 3:13.

5

GENERAL WISH OR GENERAL WILL?

Political Possibility and Collective Capacity
from Rousseau Through Marx

PETER HALLWARD

In well-run oligarchic societies, the best and simplest way to dismiss egalitarian challenges has long been to deride them as impracticable or "utopian"—and I use the word "utopian" here in the most banal sense, to mean an abstract notion or project that might be viable only in another place or time, or if undertaken by actors unlike ourselves.[1] A society without exploitation, hierarchy, or discrimination might be all very well in theory, but appropriately maintained ideological reflexes ensure that everyone knows that such fancies are not feasible in practice, here and now. Egalitarian ideals seem too demanding for selfish and shortsighted human beings, and inconsistent with the patterns that underlie their historical development. Anyone who understands these patterns, and these beings, is also supposed to understand that there is no viable alternative to the prevailing order of things.

Ever since the need for more robust anticommunist measures began to recede with the fading of the Cold War, our triumphant oligarchs have subjected their populations to a steady stream of variations on this theme, designed to bury the notion of egalitarian emancipation once and for all. Marx and his most committed followers were, for obvious reasons, the main initial targets of this campaign, which relished the failure of China's Great Leap, the futility of post-Cuban guerrilla campaigns in Latin America, the collapse of repeated experiments in African socialism, and many other comparably "utopian" ventures. All of these projects were demonstrably motivated by demanding ideals, whose realization called for little less than an appeal to what Che Guevara called *el hombre nuevo*— the "new people" of a virtuous and equitable social order, who could be trusted to prefer moral to material incentives in the workplace, and to opt for direct confrontation over complacent "coexistence" in their dealings with imperialism. Their failure appeared to confirm the apparent identity of utopian theories and barbaric practices, and helped to consolidate the prevailing neoliberal order of things as the only viable game in town. Any revolutionary desire for radical social change, in short, could be both dismissed as idle fancy and condemned as totalitarian crime, often in the same breath.

Dismissal of emancipatory practice as wishful thinking goes back to well before the neoliberal turn against Marx and his legacy, of course. In a modern European context the paradigmatic antiutopian reaction remains the counterrevolutionary backlash against the French Jacobins and their primary source of inspiration: Rousseau. Once the Jacobin threat to the old social hierarchies had been contained, relieved liberals like Benjamin Constant on the one hand and reactionary ideologues like Joseph de Maistre on the other (to be followed in due course by François Guizot and Hippolyte Taine, as by Charles Maurras and Maurice Barrès) could afford to indict Rousseauist notions of freedom, equality, and the common good as an ominous mixture of social leveling and pie-in-the-sky fantasy. Obsessed by the memory and implications of the Jacobin Terror, Constant set a lasting pattern in the reception of Rousseau's work when, after confusing the autonomous activity of a general will with passive submission to the dominant whims of a ruling clique, he denounced Rousseau's conception of sovereignty as "the most terrible auxiliary of every kind of despotism."[2] There are good reasons why a long list of more recent liberal critics of revolutionary democracy like Jacob Talmon, Isaiah Berlin, Hannah Arendt, or François Furet identifies Rousseau, before Marx or Lenin, as the founding father of the "authoritarian" and "messianic" tradition they attack.[3] This Rousseau figures, in Berlin's words, as "one of the most sinister and most formidable enemies of liberty in the whole history of modern thought."[4] Rather more nuanced and more sympathetic versions of a similar critique have since recurred across a wide spectrum of work on Rousseau, from Judith Shklar to Jacques Derrida.

The same is true of variations on the charge of utopia. Scornful dismissal of Rousseau's conception of an egalitarian social order as impracticable and anachronistic goes back as far as the earliest public responses to his writings, and quickly became an abiding preoccupation of his own participation in the debates they provoked. Edmund Burke anticipated what soon became the standard liberal response to Rousseau when he dismissed his project as "so inapplicable to real life and manners, that we never dream of drawing from them any rule for laws or conduct."[5] An emphasis on Rousseau's lack of "realism" and his "fanatical" attachment to absolute principles has been a recurring feature in the critical literature ever since, from the substantial studies by Lester Crocker and Jean Guéhenno through to the recent "big picture" contributions by Joseph Schwartz and Michael Sandel.[6] Shklar sums up what still remains the prevailing view when she dubs Rousseau "the last of the classical utopists," and "one of the greatest nay-sayers" and denouncers of the established social world.[7]

From the left too, Rousseau's political theory has been regularly attacked as abstract and ahistorical, confined within an individualistic "ideal order" that serves only as a mask for the emergent interests of a rising bourgeoisie.[8] Building on Marx's parenthetical critiques of Rousseau and the Jacobins as regressive utopians, Louis Althusser's influential reading of the *Social Contract*, for instance, culminates in the diagnosis of an ultimate and irreconcilable "discrepancy of theory with respect to the real," a *décalage* that reduces Rousseau's position to an empty exercise in "moral preaching," without practical purchase on any social actuality. In the end, Althusser argues, once there is "no further flight possible in reality itself," Rousseau finds himself obliged to compensate for the impasse of his political philosophy by projecting its "impossible theoretical solution into the alternative to theory: literature." The sophisticated readings of Rousseau's fictional and confessional writings offered by critics like Jean Starobinski, Bronisław Baczko, and Paul de Man each in their own way serve to echo Althusser's admiration of the "fictional triumph" of Rousseau's "unprecedented writing"—precisely as the underside of his theoretical failure.[9] It would not be long before even a neo-Maoist critic of Althusser like Guy Lardreau could conclude that Rousseau's social contract represents only a dystopian "nightmare" that liquidates all individuality, integrity, and dissent.[10]

Rousseau's notion of a general will, in particular, with its combination of a far-fetched call to "change human nature" and its threat to "force people to be free,"[11] has now long figured as the prototype of a fascist *Volkswille* at worst, or as fictional if not utopian escapism at best. In practice, and especially in recent practice, has not the very notion of a general will been exposed as little more than a general wish, if not simply rejected as extrapolitical tout court? As Arendt puts it, compressing a long-running argument:

> That the faculty of will and will-power in and by itself . . . is an essentially nonpolitical and even antipolitical capacity is perhaps nowhere else so manifest as in the absurdities to which Rousseau was driven and in the curious cheerfulness with which he accepted them. Politically, this identification of freedom with sovereignty is perhaps the most pernicious and dangerous consequence of the philosophical equation of freedom and free will.[12]

I want to argue here, on the contrary, that insofar as we can indeed distinguish it from mere notions of wish or whim, the notion of a general or political will should remain central to our conception of emancipatory theory and practice.[13] In addition to Rousseau and his Jacobin followers, I think this argument can also draw, more controversially perhaps, on some aspects of Marx[14] and on those we might call the "neo-Jacobin" followers of Marx, like Lenin, Gramsci, Mao, or Che, whose resolve to "continue the revolution" quickly returns them, in effect, to problems first confronted by Rousseau. What distinguishes this broadly Rousseauist conception of the will is precisely its defining association with autonomous *capacity*, the capacity to realize one's own consciously chosen end or purpose, free from coercion or submission to another's will. In a political context, such a capacity must by definition become a collective power, and thus involve capacities for association, assembly, and organization, along with capacities to access reliable information about a situation, and to participate in unhindered public consideration or deliberation about what should be done to change it.

Although the one may emerge through the transformation of the other, we need to remember this essential difference between the mere wish or aspiration for a goal and the will to realize it, for, as Gramsci notes, the aims of any political actor will remain "empty, bombastic whim, until it possesses the means to act, until whim has been converted into will."[15] The distinction between wish and will is not absolute, of course, no more than the capacities of the will itself. It is more a matter of dialectical transition, a conversion from quantity to quality, than of rigid demarcation. In terms that are broadly consistent with Ernst Bloch's distinction between an "abstract" (or impracticable) and a "concrete" utopia ("a dream which lies in the historical trend itself"),[16] Gramsci rightly recognizes the "importance of utopias and of confused and rationalistic ideologies in the initial phase of the historical processes whereby collective wills are formed,"[17] but his particular concern, early and late, is always with the dynamics of "concrete will, that is, the effective application of the abstract will or vital impulse to the concrete means which realize such a will."[18] In keeping with the truism that Gramsci, Trotsky, and so many other revolutionary writers have confirmed, "whoever genuinely wills an end must also will the means," and to will the means involves acquiring the ability to make use of them.[19] On this basis, Gramsci will strive "to put the 'will' (which in the last analysis equals practical or political activity) at the base of philosophy," insofar as it is a matter of a "rational, not an arbitrary, will, which is realized in so far as it corresponds to objective historical necessities"—that is, insofar as it serves to specify and undertake what needs to be done in order to pursue the "progressive actualization" of our political goals.[20]

If Rousseau and tacitly Rousseauist disciples of Marx like Gramsci or Che help us to distinguish will from whim or wish, they also remind us of the essential difference between voluntary self-determination and submission to the apparent laws of economic or historical necessity. The great virtue of the "voluntarism" for which these and related thinkers are so routinely attacked is precisely its capacity to take full stock of what Walter Benjamin summarized, in the last years of his life, as "the experience of our generation: that capitalism will not die a natural death."[21] Late in his life Benjamin himself, influenced in part by that most vigorously (and one-sidedly) voluntarist of nineteenth-century revolutionaries, Auguste Blanqui, drew some of these conclusions in his reflections "On the Concept of History": "Nothing has corrupted the German working class so much as the notion that it was moving, with the current."[22] Anticipating Benjamin, soon after the Russian Revolution Gramsci realized that "the gravest mistake of the socialist movement" was to allow itself to go with the prevailing historical flow: "As they participated in the general activity of human society, within the State, the Socialists forgot that their position ought to be essentially one of criticism, of antithesis. They allowed themselves to be absorbed by reality, rather than dominating it."[23] They forgot, in other words (as Gramsci allowed himself to say in one of his more enthusiastic moments), that our priority must be to "forge a social, collective will" strong enough to control the economic forces that have hitherto controlled us, "until this collective will becomes the driving force of the economy, the force which shapes reality itself, so that objective reality becomes a living, breathing force, like a current of molten lava, which can be channelled wherever and however the will directs."[24] Che would later make a similar point, in a more measured but scarcely less exalted tone, when he recognized that "centralized planning is the mode of existence of socialist society, its defining characteristic, and the point at which man's consciousness finally succeeds in synthesizing and directing the economy toward its goal: the full liberation of the human being within the framework of communist society."[25] Since his work offers a striking synthesis of Rousseauist and Marxian themes, I will come back to Che in the final pages of this chapter.

ROUSSEAU AND VOLUNTARY SELF-DETERMINATION

To his credit, Rousseau consistently rejects any approach to political problems that aims to resolve them simply through a protopositivist appeal to the prevailing order of things, any attempt "to establish right by fact," in keeping with a logic that favors actually existing tyranny. Just as consistently, he tries both to "take men as they are" and to treat laws and conventions as they actually *could* be, and thus "to ally what right permits with what interest prescribes," without any appeal to a state of perfect (and certainly impossible) disinterest.[26] Rousseau recognized that aspirations to organize executive or administrative power (as distinct from legislative or sovereign power) on a harmonious democratic basis certainly *were* utopian,[27] as were hopes that conflicts between the private and the public might one day be overcome, or anticipations (to evoke Engels's phrase) that the state might one day simply "wither away." Anyone who seeks "to form a durable establishment," he recognizes, should not "dream of making it eternal."[28]

Rather than an abstract utopia, another vision of that "land of chimeras" explored in Plato's *Republic* or More's *Utopia*, Rousseau claimed to have modeled his *Social Contract* on the concrete example once set by his native Geneva, before it fell prey to the machinations of its own ruling oligarchs—and it is precisely because these oligarchs can recognize his account as a critique along these lines, Rousseau suggests, that they now go out of their way to attack it as a genuine threat to the recently corrupted order of things.[29] And rather than pretend that the corrosive forces of greed and self-interest might somehow be banished from a perfectly "transparent" community, Rousseau busies himself with schemes whereby these irreducible tendencies might be channeled, through forms of emulation or sublimation, into forms of esteem more conducive to the collective good.[30] He urges the Poles, for instance, "never to shake up the machine too brusquely. . . . Since it is impossible to create new citizens all at once, one has to begin by making do with those there are; and offering their ambition a new avenue is the way to incline them to follow it."[31] As for his notorious readiness to insist that "whoever refuses to obey the general will shall be constrained to do so by the entire body," this is the step Rousseau takes—and the step that so many revolutionary leaders subsequently found themselves obliged to take—precisely in order to lend the social compact genuine political actuality, to ensure that it is not reduced to an "empty formula," by equipping it with a capacity that alone can give strength or "force to the rest."[32]

Far from conceiving his social contract as the abstract blueprint of an impossible future, Rousseau's outline is inspired by the exemplary achievements accomplished in the past, since these testify to what we might still be capable of in the present. He invites us "to consider what can be done on the basis of what has been done." If Rousseau is a political 'visionary', it is only insofar as he seeks to envision what might still feasibly be achieved through systematic effort and a resolute determination to *prevail*—the sort of determination that would find its champions, in due course, in Robespierre, Saint-Just and their associates. Rousseau knows that his call for mass participation in civic assemblies will be rejected by his cynical contemporaries as an implausible "chimera," but reminds them of situations in which citizens could and did do everything necessary to subordinate private inconvenience to the common good.[33]

Critics who dismiss his account of the general will as utopian, in other words, too rarely remember that what is at stake is indeed a practice of autonomous *willing* as such, that is, a matter of deliberate striving and purposeful capacity, as distinct from ineffectual wish or ephemeral whim. "It is only our lukewarm will which causes all of our weakness," Rousseau maintains, "and we are always strong enough to do what we strongly will [*veut*]. *Volenti nihil difficile* [nothing is difficult for him who wills]."[34] In keeping with this logic, Rousseau insists that "the limits of the possible in moral matters are less narrow than we think. It is our weaknesses, our vices, our prejudices that shrink them."[35]

The practical priority of Rousseau's work can be summarized quite simply, then, as the pursuit of popular or collective empowerment. Negatively, what is at stake is emancipation from any servitude, any submission to external constraint or to a heteronymous will—and from this perspective, Rousseau will argue that a person's freedom is less a matter of "doing merely what he wishes" than of "never doing what he does not want or will to do; and that is the freedom I have always laid claim to, often preserved, and that most scandalized my contemporaries."[36] Positively, the issue turns on the coordination, in actual practice, of willing and doing, of *vouloir* and *pouvoir*. Unlike the monarch who depends on the obedience of those he dominates, from Rousseau's perspective "the only person who does his own will is he who, in order to do it, has no need to put another's arms at the end of his own.... The truly free man wills or wants only what he can do and does what he pleases. That is my fundamental maxim."[37] Although Rousseau is often accused of introducing tensions, if not contradictions, into the relation between the individual and collective dimensions of social existence, in principle his maxim applies—as will the maxims that orient Marx's conception of communism—to both individual and collective: the freedoms that socialized individuals can exercise must have a collective or popular dimension as a matter of course. On their own, as Rousseau's maxim suggests, individuals' freedom is confined to the scope of their own limited abilities, but once combined with that of others, the freedom of socialized individuals expands at the same time and for the same reasons as their collective power or capacity. Isolated individuals can do little more than try to fulfill their immediate bodily needs; socialized individuals acquire the capacity to act independently of such needs, and to do what is necessary to transform their collectively created world.

Rousseau conceives of free will as a defining capacity of human beings, a capacity grounded in human nature and human psychology, and he dismisses any effort to find some deeper foundation for this ground as futile speculation. Freedom or a free will figures here as a constitutive principle of explanation rather than as something to be explained.[38] Since he affirms freedom as "a consequence of man's nature" pure and simple,[39] "it always appears peculiar to me," he admits, "to ask a free people why it is free. It is as if one asked a man who has his two arms why he is not one-armed. The right to liberty is born from itself, it is the natural state of man. This is not the case for domination, whose right needs to be proved when it exists."[40] Rousseau's mouthpiece in *Émile* likewise posits as a matter of "dogma," or as an "article of faith," that "there is no true action without will."[41] Reflecting on his capacities for action in comparison with those of other animals, he discovers that "by my will and by the instruments in my power for executing it, . . . I have more force for acting on all the bodies surrounding me, for yielding to or eluding their actions as I please, than any of them has for acting on me against my will by physical impulsion alone; and by my intelligence I am the only one that has a view of the whole."[42] Understood as a practical capacity in this sense, the will is neither an obscure metaphysical mystery nor an absolute freedom that operates in some sort of supranatural or noumenal sphere, beyond the boundaries of experience. On the contrary, the will is a banal, "this-worldly" capacity that all human beings have as a matter of course, and whose relative power varies from one individual to another according to the degree to which this capacity has been cultivated and practiced together with other individuals.

Apart from criteria immanent to freedom and volition themselves, Rousseau insists that there is nothing about human nature, or the subsequent socialization and history of human beings, that puts any restrictions on its exercise. The main effect of his famously controversial evocation of a plentiful and premoral "state of nature" is to secure the freedom of such a deliberately and contingently socialized will from any intrinsic, necessary, or timeless social orientation (for example, toward hierarchy or deference), apart from the minimal criteria of a voluntary or positive freedom itself. Any actually constituted social order is based on chosen conventions, not intrinsic natural norms,[43] even though our natural capacity for free choice itself provides a normative basis for our choosings. Rousseau's reconstruction of social development is likewise designed to secure the subsequent exercise of free will, and not to evoke a lost Eden or inaccessible utopia. For Rousseau, unlike Montesquieu, a people is less the result of natural influences rooted in geography or climate than an ongoing process of deliberate self-constitution. A society takes on a particular political shape mainly because the people who rule it have willed it thus—and what has so far been willed one way can in the future be willed another. The social configuration of a group of people, in other words, is not something that expresses their (racial, ethnic, cultural, immemorial) essence: it is something that they *institute*, precisely, or that they bring upon themselves, for specific reasons over a specific time.

It is Rousseau's prescriptive conception of autonomous will, in other words, that accounts for his conception of society and politics, and not the reverse. The conclusion of Rousseau's Savoyard Vicar makes the basis of his political theory perfectly explicit: "The principle of every action is in the will of a free being. One cannot go back beyond that. It is not the word freedom which means nothing; it is the word necessity. . . . Man is therefore free in his actions" and "if man is active and free, he acts on his own," in relative independence of natural inclination, historical tendency, or providential direction.[44] The idea that human actions and intentions might be understood simply on the basis of material processes and the play of "necessary motion," Rousseau admits, is one "of which I have never made any sense."[45] He recoils in horror from the logic which, appealing to the "law of necessity," argues that "nothing is free, that all is forced, necessary, inevitable; that all the movements of man, directed by blind matter, depend on his will only because his will itself depends on necessity: that there are in consequence neither virtues nor vices, neither merit nor demerit, nor [any] morality in human conduct."[46]

Rooted in its primordial, species-defining affirmation of freedom, the human will seeks most fundamentally "to break the bonds constraining it"—the bonds of appetite and sensibility, as well as the bonds of servitude and dependence.[47] "I hate servitude," Rousseau wrote a few months after his *Social Contract* was condemned as subversive by the archbishop and the Parlement of Paris, "as the source of all the ills of human kind," and "in the relations between man and man the worst that can happen to one is to find himself at the other's discretion."[48] As a rule, "anyone who depends on someone else and does not have his resources in himself cannot be free."[49] Confined within a finite "body that impedes the majority of its faculties," at every moment "the human soul wants to break open its prison," and thereby joins "an almost divine audacity" to its mortal frailty.[50] Thanks to this power or "force" that animates and incites us, we are entitled to assume that "it depends only on us to maintain ceaselessly in this condition of freedom . . . [this] energy of our faculties that detaches itself from their earthly bonds." By the same token, everything depends on our actual capacity to maintain this condition, and to exercise the faculties it enables.

There is thus an essential difference between a disabling dependence on a master or patron on the one hand, and on the other enabling, empowering relations of solidarity with free and equal coparticipants in a shared project or community.[51] Since for Rousseau association with others is itself something achieved or acquired, since it is not an originary dimension of human nature, when it occurs the "act of association" generates an entirely new "moral and collective body made up of as many members as the assembly has voices, and which receives by this same act its unity, its common self, its life and its will."[52] As a result of such association, the individual that in isolation remains merely a "stupid and limited animal" can be "elevated" to become "an intelligent being and a man":

> This transition from the state of nature to the civil state produces a most remarkable change in man by substituting justice for instinct in his conduct, and endowing his actions with the morality they previously lacked. Only then, when the voice of duty succeeds physical impulsion and right succeeds appetite, does man, who until then had looked only to himself, see himself forced to act on other principles, and to consult his reason before listening to his inclinations.[53]

In the first substantial account of this process he provides, Rousseau explains that wherever a group of people assembles and combines themselves to form a single community or "body politic," this virtual body is constituted as "a moral being that has a will."[54] What sustains such a being is the power and integrity of its common will, insofar as this "general will always tends to the preservation and the well-being of the whole [community] and of each part."[55] Thus defined, "the general will is always on the side most favourable to the public interest, that is to say, the most equitable," and so "the first and the most important maxim of legitimate or popular government, that is to say of government that has the good of the people as its object, is then, in all things to follow the general will."[56]

An egalitarian collective actor or "people" comes into existence, in other words, insofar as its members combine together, unite, and resolve to pursue collectively determined ends. Such a people endures insofar as it cultivates the abilities required to sustain and implement its common will, and thereby retains the means to overpower the will of those who might oppose, exploit, or divide them. "So long as several men united consider themselves a single body, they have but a single will, which is concerned with their common preservation and the general welfare," and the more the pursuit of this common interest excludes the play of partial, privileged, and "contradictory" interests, the more self-evident its principles and transparent its practice.[57]

Sovereignty is here nothing more, or less, than the political and thus collective exercise of a free will, and popular sovereignty governs a situation insofar as the people who inhabit it are able and prepared to assume full, deliberate command of a common purpose and to pursue the goals they choose, rather than persist in a condition that they suffer. "Since it is nothing but the exercise of the general will, sovereignty can never be alienated" or coerced, without dissolving itself; for the same reason, its volition cannot be necessitated in advance, determined from without, or shackled by its own past decisions. Since law-giving will, unlike executive power, cannot be transferred or delegated, the "sovereign, which is nothing but a collective being, can only be represented by itself," and consists solely in its own voluntary, self-determining practice.[58] Moreover, since the freedom acquired through emancipation from dependence consists first and foremost in "not being subject to someone else's will" and since a will evaporates as soon as it abandons its capacity to determine its own ends, as soon as a "people promises simply to obey [a master], it dissolves itself by this very act, it loses its quality of being a people; as soon as there is a master, there is no more sovereign, and the body politic is destroyed forthwith."[59] Again, "sovereignty, which is only the exercise of the general will, is, like it, free, and is not subject to any kind of engagement. Every act of sovereignty, like every instant of its existence, is absolute, independent of the one that precedes it; and the sovereign never acts because it willed [in the past,] but because it *wills*," in the present.[60] The sovereign is the free and ongoing self-determination of a common will, or it is nothing all.

The crucial question to ask of any political action, then, regardless of scale or configuration, is simply this: Do the members of the collective actor involved actually participate, yes or no, in a common will? Either a "will is general or it is not; it is either the will of the body of the people, or that of only a part." A will is either egalitarian and inclusive and thus sovereign, or it is merely imperious and thus capricious and tyrannical. Since "the Sovereign, by the mere fact that it is, is always everything it ought to be," the essential question is just whether or not it exists, or persists.[61] All other questions are secondary.

COLLECTIVE CAPACITY AND POLITICAL VIRTUE

Although freedom is an originary human capacity, the actual exercise of this capacity must be acquired. The free adult may do what she wants to the degree that she wants or wills [*veut*] what she can do and vice versa, but a child—and the political equivalent of a child—is unable to do or will very much.[62] We must learn to do what we are capable of doing, at the same time that we learn to will what it is that we should do. We are all capable of freedom, but everyone must learn how to practice it. Along the same lines, Marx will suggest, it is by gaining the capacity to formulate a conscious "purpose" and then by submitting to the disciplined forms of practice and attention its accomplishment requires that people participate over time in the historical and distinctively human, more-than-animal practice of working or laboring; whatever project we engage in, "a purposeful will is required for the entire duration of the work."[63]

"Virtue" is the general name Rousseau gives to the practices that enable a general will to take control of its destiny and determine its own ends. Without an egalitarian, collectively oriented, or virtuous will we are left to drift this way and that, at the mercy of what others do and think, subject to the whims or wishes of the others who might influence or oppress us—"floating on this sea of human opinions," as Rousseau's vicar puts it, "without rudder or compass and delivered to their stormy passions without any other guide than an inexperienced pilot who is ignorant of his route and knows neither where he is coming from nor where he is going."[64] So long as we are deprived of a clear principle and a "sure goal" we are condemned to "flit about from one desire to another," "victims of the blind inconstancy of our hearts."[65]

More precisely, the term "virtue" applies to those principled and deliberately instituted practices that serve to orient individual wills toward their common rather than their partial or private ends, and that thus overcome what Rousseau calls the typically "bourgeois" tendency to prefer selfish or whimsical penchants over demanding public duties.[66] Virtue is precisely a matter of "will-power" in the sense that it lends the will the power it needs to overcome the obstacles posed by both social corruption and "natural" temptation. Since "every man is virtuous when his particular will conforms in all things to the general will," if you want to ensure that the "general will be carried out" you need to simply arrange things so "that all particular wills take their bearings by it," or "to say the same thing in a word: make virtue reign."[67] Virtue is nothing other than the practice of egalitarian political will, and it is itself a thoroughly practical question. "The ardour for doing good is also the means for doing it," just as "it is in doing good that one becomes good; I know of no practice more certain."[68] The ideal social arrangement would thus be one where, "in order to do what one ought, it suffices to think that one ought to do it"; a contrario, "it is useless to preach to anyone who has no desire to act rightly."[69]

Rousseau's account of virtue as the practice of political will has several distinguishable but overlapping and mutually reinforcing aspects, all of which return, in one guise or another, in later contributions to neo-Jacobin politics.

First of all, at the most basic level, and as its etymology suggests, virtue is a matter of effort and struggle, of "fortitude" and strength (*force*). This is why Rousseau can write, in keeping with republican tradition, that a "single thing" is enough to defend a country against any danger of subjugation: "the love of *la patrie* and of freedom animated by the virtues inseparable from that love."[70] Rousseau never forgets that the "word virtue means *force*. There is no virtue without struggle, there is none without victory."[71] "My child," Emile's tutor explains,

> there is no happiness without courage nor virtue without struggle. The word virtue comes from strength. Strength is the foundation of all virtue. Virtue belongs only to a being that is weak by nature and strong by will. It is in this that the merit of the just man consists; and although we call God good, we do not call Him virtuous, because it requires no effort for Him to do good. . . . Up to now you were only apparently free. You had only the precarious freedom of a slave to whom nothing has been commanded. Now be really free. Learn to become your own master. Command your heart, Emile, and you will be virtuous.[72]

To will an end is to take command of the means to achieve it. It is not the quality of a passion per se that makes it morally good or bad, but the relation of mastery or command between a passion and a person, between a desire and a person's control of the means to achieve it. "All the sentiments we dominate are legitimate; all those which dominate us are criminal."[73]

Since it is a matter of force and actual practice, it follows as a matter of course that the exercise of virtue cannot be delegated to others or undertaken by proxy. Here is a second feature. Citizens either will and do what their duty prescribes or they do not. This is why delegates can be chosen to execute collective decisions, but not to make them. Where it exists, sovereignty is unalienable and unrepresentable as a matter of principle, and as we have seen, the sovereign "can only be represented by itself; power can well certainly be transferred, but not will." For exactly the same reason, any group or agent that apparently seeks to represent sovereignty actually seeks to usurp it. "Sovereignty consists essentially in the general will, and the will does not admit of being represented: either it is the same or it is different; there is no middle ground. The deputies of the people therefore are not and cannot be its representatives, they are merely its agents." Rousseau recognizes that even the smallest and most concentrated peoples will need to delegate the actual execution of their decisions to particular agents, but when it comes to its sovereign or law-making power, "the instant a People gives itself Representatives, it ceases to be free; it ceases to be."[74]

Third, Rousseau assumes that virtuous self-mastery can only be acquired collectively, rather than in isolation. Although natural or solitary man has an innate capacity for virtue, this potential becomes actual only through its social and thus postnatural institution. "All the virtues arise from the different relations Society has established between men," and "it is only by becoming sociable that he becomes a moral being, a reasonable animal, the king of the other animals, and the image of God on earth."[75] Since social interaction is the source of "all [our] moral being," "where there is no society, there can be neither Justice, nor clemency, nor humanity, nor generosity, nor modesty, nor above all the merit of all these virtues."[76] It is the community or *patrie* (or the mobilization, the union, the party) that gives the individual both a reason to be virtuous and the means to become so. One way or another, therefore, "good social institutions are those that best know how to denature man, to take his absolute existence from him in order to give him a relative one and transport the I into the common unity, with the result that each individual believes himself no longer one but a part of the unity and no longer feels except within the whole."[77]

In the *Social Contract*, Rousseau again stresses the collective, social, and more-than-natural dimension of collective empowerment, in a passage that deserves to be quoted at length:

> Anyone who dares to institute a people must feel capable of, so to speak, changing human nature; of transforming each individual who by himself is a perfect and solitary whole into part of a larger whole from which that individual would as it were receive his life and his being; of weakening man's constitution in order to strengthen it; of substituting a partial and moral existence for the independent and physical existence we have all received from nature. In a word, he must take from man his own forces in order to give him forces which are foreign to him and of which he cannot make use without the help of others. The more these natural forces are dead and destroyed, the greater and more lasting are the acquired ones, and the more solid and lasting also is the institution: So that when each Citizen is nothing and can do nothing except with all the others, and the force acquired by the whole is equal or superior to the sum of the natural forces of all the individuals, the legislation may be said to be at the highest pitch of perfection it can reach.[78]

The more complete the substitution, the more virtuous and more forceful the practice that results, and the more united the community it sustains.

Political virtue is thus the social practice that seeks to unite and uphold the common interest in the face of whatever might tend to divide or obscure it. This is a fourth characteristic. Virtue unites, vice divides. Unity is not to be confused with uniformity, of course, and well before he had established his reputation as Europe's most remarkable literary eccentric, Rousseau's first significant publication already bemoaned the fact that "a vile and deceiving uniformity prevails in our morals, and all minds seem to have been cast in the same mould: constantly politeness demands, propriety commands: constantly one follows custom, never one's own genius."[79] Precisely because he surveyed his society from the perspective of a critical and isolated outsider, and because he considered his social "superiors" not as leaders who might benefit from "reform" or "improvement" but as parasites to be overthrown, few philosophers have had as acute a political appreciation of the significance of embattled popular unity and solidarity as Rousseau. You must "above all come together" and "deliberate with your Fellow Citizens," Rousseau advises his Genevan compatriots, "and do not count the votes until after having weighed them. . . . You are ruined without resource if you remain divided."[80] To preserve the unity of an assembly, you must ensure that whatever question it considers, rather than individual, class, or factional will, it is "the general will [that] is always consulted, and that it always replies."[81]

The easiest way to integrate individual and collective, naturally, is through direct proximity and congregation. It is a bitter but unavoidable fact that "the league of the stronger is a natural one, and what constitutes the weakness of the weak is *not* to be able to league together this way. Such is the destiny of the people, always to have its opponents as judges inside and out."[82] To compensate for this weakness, the people have no other recourse than to invent and preserve more elaborately and purposefully institutionalized means of combination that might allow them to overpower their "natural" superiors and the governments that represent them. The more scattered or dispersed a population, the more difficult it normally is to "take concerted action quickly or in secret." Tyranny thrives across the distances that separate isolated subjects, whereas "the people's force," as Rousseau puts it in an arresting metaphor, "acts only when concentrated, it evaporates and is lost as it spreads, like the effect of gunpowder scattered on the ground and which ignites only grain by grain."[83]

The fact that Rousseau draws most of his own examples of virtuous association from ancient history would not prevent his subsequent admirers from addressing this problem in distinctly modern forms, from Jacobin Clubs and industrial combinations to vanguard organizations of the working class. Alongside his familiar references to homogeneous communities on the Spartan model, we shouldn't forget that Rousseau himself offers the ongoing Jewish diaspora as perhaps the most striking example he can give of an autonomous, self-legislating community:

> It is an amazing and truly unique spectacle to see an expatriate people, without either location or land for nearly two thousand years; a people that has been modified, oppressed, and mingled with foreigners for even longer . . . a scattered people, dispersed over the earth, subjected, persecuted, scorned by all nations, and yet preserving its customs, its laws, its morals, its patriotic love, and its initial social union when all its links appear broken. The Jews give us this amazing spectacle. The laws of Solon, of Numa, of Lycurgus are dead; those of Moses, far more ancient, are still alive. . . . How strong must a legislation be to be capable of producing such marvels; capable of facing conquests, dispersions, revolutions, centuries; capable of surviving the customs, laws, dominion of all nations; which promises, finally, through the trials it has sustained, to sustain them all, to conquer the vicissitudes of human things and to last as long as the world?[84]

In a different context, the dispersed and subjugated people of Poland offer a similar spectacle of unyielding solidarity: confronted by successive oppressors, they have learned to compensate for their lack of centralized organization through daring innovations in "what is known as guerrilla warfare, . . . the art of sweeping over a country like a torrent, to strike everywhere without ever being struck, always to act in concert even though separated."[85]

This brings us to a fifth characteristic, an echo of the first. As an expression of *force* or strength, the exercise of virtue includes a readiness to do whatever is needed to express and impose the general will. Virtue must be as forceful as it needs to be—on this, Rousseau broadly agrees with Machiavelli. In societies organized around the pursuit of private gain, "evil and the abuses from which so many people profit find their way in by themselves; but what is useful to the public hardly finds its way in except by force, considering that private interests are almost always opposed to it."[86] As so often in Rousseau, the problem could not be simpler: "The goal of the government is the realization of the general will; what prevents it from achieving this goal is the obstacle of private wills."[87] In such circumstances, if the only way to overcome private or class resistance is through expulsion or compulsion, then reluctance to take the necessary measures is itself a clear expression of affiliation, and a betrayal of the general for the particular. To be merely "gentle out of indifference for good and evil" is no virtue, and no ruler "can be good . . . if he cannot be terrible to the wicked."[88] Nowhere is the conjunction of virtue and duty more obvious and more painful. "To be just, you have to be severe: to tolerate the wickedness that you are entitled and empowered to repress is to be wicked yourself."[89] It is only a short step from here to Robespierre's notorious assertion that, in the circumstances of class struggle or civil war, "virtue without terror is powerless."[90]

It remains the case, for both Rousseau and his followers, that if violent measures are "sometimes necessary [they are] always terrible" and can only become legitimate once alternatives have proved futile, in "the final extremity, only for your defence"; every unjustified punishment is itself an admission of weakness.[91] Short of such extremity, the only forms of social "compulsion" that Rousseau advocates are intended to be thoroughly consistent with volition as such. In the first draft of the *Social Contract*, anticipating the logic later invoked by Che Guevara and Fidel Castro (see below), Rousseau identifies this sort of "voluntary coercion" with the will itself:

> As the State or city constitutes a moral person whose life consists in the cooperation and union of its members, the first and most important of its concerns is that of its own preservation. This concern requires a universal, compulsory force to move and arrange each part in the manner best suited to the whole. Thus, just as nature gives each man absolute power over his members, the social compact gives the body politic absolute power over its members; and it is the exercise of this same power, directed by the general will, which as I have said bears the name sovereignty.[92]

Rousseau's subsequent reformulation of this point, in the published version of his book, yields the most illiberal (and therefore most vilified) passage in his work. Although only voluntary commitment associates them to the common interest, "the Sovereign would have no guarantee of the subjects' engagements if it did not find means to ensure their fidelity." Since "each individual may, as a man, have a particular will contrary to or different from the general will he has as a Citizen," for it "not to be an empty formula, the social compact tacitly includes the following engagement which alone can give force to the rest, that whoever refuses to obey the general will shall be constrained to do so by the entire body: which means nothing other than that he shall be forced to be free; for this is the condition which, by giving each Citizen to the Fatherland, guarantees him against all personal dependence."[93] Here as everywhere, Rousseau rejects any conflation of will and whim, of freedom and caprice; collective freedom implies collective discipline.

Although virtue can only be acquired and internalized through disciplined constraint, it thus remains, and for this very reason, a matter of active freedom and volition. For Rousseau as for Kant (whose practical philosophy owes much to Rousseau), willing freedom and autonomy or self-legislation are opposite sides of the same coin. "The impulsion of mere appetite is slavery, and obedience to the law one has prescribed to oneself is freedom."[94] The opposite of freedom is not discipline or obedience but, more precisely, forced obedience to a will *other* than one's own. "It is certain that if someone can compel my will, I am no longer free"—but I am no more free if I cannot compel my own actions to conform to what I decide or command.[95] Unless it is freely or willingly assumed as a moral imperative, no law has the power to overcome the "wicked" tendency of private or factional will to evade the constraints of general will. "Wickedness is basically only an opposition of the private will to the public will, and it is for this reason that there could not be any freedom among wicked men, because if each one acts according to his own will, it would thwart the public will or that of his neighbour and most of the time both; and if he is constrained to obey the public will, he would never act according to his own will."[96]

Precisely because virtuous or moral action can only result from an act of free will, however—and this is a final characteristic of Rousseau's account of virtue—it does not involve any appeal to some merely ascetic suspension of interest. Virtue has nothing to do with any sort of otherworldly disinterest or dispassion, let alone a cultivated and disempowering indifference—"as soon as someone says about affairs of State, 'What do I care?', the State has to be considered lost."[97] We can no more renounce our innate self-interest or *amour de soi* than we can renounce freedom itself. Rousseau fully accepts that "people can be moved to act only by their interest," but sees no need to appeal to an angelic disinterest in order to overcome antisocial forms of self-interest. Anyone and everyone can learn, in principle, how it serves "his own better understood interest . . . to become just, beneficent, moderate, virtuous."[98] A true political commitment is a response to a true political interest. "The commitments which bind us to the social body are obligatory only because they are mutual, and their nature is such that in fulfilling them one cannot work for others without also working for oneself. Why is the general will always upright, and why do all consistently will each one's happiness, if not because there is no one who does not appropriate the word each to himself, and think of himself as he votes for all?"[99] By contrast, the private pursuit of private gain yields only private gain pure and simple. Contrary to Mandeville, Smith, and other protoliberal thinkers, therefore, Rousseau (like Marx or Che after him) insists that social goals must be achieved by directly social rather than by individual means. Collective interests require a collective capacity for action, spurred by "great desires, great hopes, great positive motives for acting."[100] Any revolutionary or "historical act," to anticipate Gramsci's terms, "can only be performed by 'collective man,' and this presupposes the attainment of a 'cultural-social' unity through which a multiplicity of dispersed wills, with heterogeneous aims, are welded together with a single aim, on the basis of an equal and common conception of the world."[101]

MARX *VOLONTARISTE*?

The gulf that separates Marx from Rousseau is wide and familiar, and it should go without saying that Marx cannot be read simply as an extension or radicalization of the Jacobin project. Marx's emphasis on the historical and economic dynamics that create and then shape the proletariat as a tendentially universal class is already enough to distinguish his project from any neo-Rousseauist project of virtuous generalization. The young Marx was already sharply critical of the sort of "merely" political will he associates, in different places, with Robespierre, Hegel, Bauer, or Blanqui, and as any number of critics have pointed out, Marx's antivoluntarism occasionally encourages him to downplay questions of proletarian agency and purpose in favor of an analysis of "*what the proletariat is*, and what, in accordance with this *being*, it will historically be compelled to do."[102] Similar priorities will later lead him to assume, with remarkable brevity and nonchalance, that "capitalist production begets its own negation with the inexorability of a natural process."[103] Even if Marx himself may underestimate the depth of his own debt to Rousseau (for reasons that have never been properly explained), there can be no denying the distance that separates the prophet of proletarian revolution from the champion of civic virtue.

It would be just as mistaken, however, to underestimate the significance and extent of quasi-voluntarist aspects of Marx's own work and, more importantly perhaps, the way these aspects are later taken up and radicalized by some of his most resolute disciples, in terms that often suggest an effective (though invariably tacit) fusion of Marx and Rousseau—I've already mentioned the example of Gramsci, and I will end this chapter with a brief evocation of Che. While it may be forcing the issue to characterize Marx's own perspective as voluntarist, there is certainly a neo-Rousseauist or neo-Jacobin voluntarist dimension that persists *through* Marx's legacy, and recurs in the work of Lenin, Luxemburg, Trotsky, Mao, and many other revolutionary figures of the twentieth century.

This is not the place to consider in detail the relative importance of voluntarist themes in Marx's own work, but it is clearly a mistake to assume that just because he insists that social being determines consciousness rather than vice versa, we might then be entitled to read his conception of social being as a rigidly determinist one, as if human behavior is more or less mechanically governed by material processes. The young Marx insists on the distinctive way that, unlike other animals, "man makes his life activity itself an object of his will and consciousness,"[104] and in a crucial chapter of *Capital* the older Marx insists in comparable terms on man's "sovereign power" and capacity to "change his own nature," his ability consciously and deliberately to determine his own ends and to sustain the disciplined, "purposeful will" required to realize them.[105] The young Marx, furthermore, insists on "the self-determination of the people," and emphasizes the unique virtues of democracy as the political form of a fully "human existence," one in which "the law exists for the sake of man" rather than vice versa,[106] is formulated as "the conscious expression of the will of the people, and therefore originates with it and is created by it";[107] the older Marx will likewise embrace the Paris Commune of 1871 (inspired and organized in large part by Blanqui's supporters) as an exemplary instance of precisely this sort of democracy in action, an illustration of our capacity to invent a political lever that can wedge its way *underneath* the so-called material base of social being, "a lever for uprooting the economical foundation upon which rests the existence of classes, and therefore of class rule."[108] This material base itself, moreover, is both shaped by the irreducibly political inflection of class relations and sustained by the irreducibly "human" and thus purposeful and inventive character of the forces of production. Especially during periods of revolutionary opportunity, as in 1871, or 1848–1850, what takes pride of place in Marx's political perspective is not any sort of inexorable historical determinism so much as a strategic need for vigorous and lucid action, carried out by an independent, resolute, and fully conscious political actor.[109]

The chief target of Marx's critique of bourgeois ideology in general and of bourgeois political economy in particular is precisely the way they discourage such resolution and consciousness by disguising capitalist forms of compulsion and command. One of the recurring priorities of Marx's economic writings is to expose the violence and deceit implicit in the "voluntary" submission of labor to those who control, employ, and exploit labor: once it has completed the brutal work of its "originary accumulation," capital's "command of unpaid labour" binds it not with the flagrant chains of slavery but with the "invisible threads" and "silent compulsion" of dependence and precarity.[110] Early and late, Marx understands communism as a definitive end to all such compulsion and dependence, and thus as "the true appropriation of the human essence through and for man," "the true resolution of the conflict . . . between freedom and necessity."[111] What is at stake in the revolutionary transition from capitalism to communism is nothing other than the "development of all human powers as such,"[112] together with "the control and conscious mastery of these powers, which, born of the action of men on one another, have till now overawed and governed men as powers completely alien to them."[113] Once we understand the ways we determine our social relations, Engels will add in an almost openly Rousseauist vein, "it depends only upon ourselves to subject them more and more to our own will, and, by means of them, to reach our own ends. . . . Man's own social organization, hitherto confronting him as a necessity imposed by Nature and history, now becomes the result of his own free action" and confirms "the ascent of man from the kingdom of necessity to the kingdom of freedom."[114]

HASTA LA VICTORIA . . .

If I conclude this chapter with a nod to Che Guevara, it is because he (after Lenin, Gramsci, and Mao, and at roughly the same time as Fanon and Giáp) helps to illustrate how Marxian and Rousseauist priorities can combine to ground a coherent account of revolutionary political will. The shortcomings of Che's particular formulation of such an account are well known and there is no need to go through them again here. Perhaps no modern political actor, however, did more to test the hyperbolic principle (which the young Ernesto Guevara jotted down as early as 1947) that "willpower can overcome everything."[115] What determines any emancipatory struggle, Che would soon realize, is "the essential will [*voluntad*] for liberation" that directs and sustains it,[116] and if the Cuban "revolution has always acted with the will of the entire people of Cuba" it is precisely because this people has proven itself willing to do what is required "to liberate ourselves at any price."[117] Whereas established and reactionary regimes of power seek to "freeze the present" in line with the past, "to conquer the future is the strategic element of revolution"—which is a fine way of summarizing the generic purpose of political will.[118]

Although Rousseau exercised little or no direct influence on Che, what is striking about Che in relation to the orthodox Marxist tradition is his emphasis on several neo-Rousseauist dimensions of revolutionary practice. First of all, Che never forgets that a revolution is first and foremost a matter of conquest—of winning or taking political power, and of establishing popular sovereignty in the teeth of imperial and oligarchic resistance. "National sovereignty means . . . the right of a people to choose whatever form of government and way of life suits it. That should depend on its will," to the exclusion of other wills. However, since many fragile pseudodemocracies "actually depend on the all-embracing will of the United Fruit Company" or of other imperialist monopolies, "the people cannot even dream of sovereignty unless there is a power that defends their interests and aspirations." Hence Che's insistence, in terms more reminiscent of Rousseau or Blanqui than of a revisionist version of Marx, on the strategic priority of political over economic considerations: "revolutionary power or political sovereignty is the instrument for the conquest of the economy and for making national sovereignty a reality in its broadest sense."[119]

Since hitherto powerless and dependent peoples cannot afford to "sit back and wait for the objective and subjective conditions—which are formed through the complex mechanism of the class struggle—to meet all the necessary requirements for power to fall into the hands of the people like ripe fruit," they must resolve to do what is necessary to seize it as quickly as possible.[120] If guerrilla warfare presents itself as the quickest and clearest way of seizing power in Latin American countries, it is partly because it goes straight to the decisive question: which group, the exploited or the exploiting, will command the means and arms to impose its will upon society as a whole? As Cuba's example illustrates, moreover, such warfare can *win* the battles it engages in—in other words, it appears to offer a practicable strategy for the conversion of wish into will. Cuba's mobilization and capacity to prevail change the balance of political possibility, and show conclusively that "popular forces can win a war against the army,"[121] even one backed by today's "monster" of imperialism, the United States. As Che told the OAS in 1961, "a country can take up arms, destroy an oppressing army, form a new popular army, stand up to the invincible monster, await the monster's attack, and defeat it also. And that is something new in the Americas, gentlemen."[122] Properly planned and executed, guerrilla warfare thus meets the two "subjective conditions" that Che posits as crucial to any emancipatory project: it fosters "awareness of the need to effect urgent social change in order to do away with the situation of injustice, and the certainty that it is possible to bring about that change."[123]

It is Che's steadfast insistence on the primacy of subjective conditions and "virtuous" moral practice that most emphatically aligns him with our neo-Jacobin voluntarist tradition. In the great socialist revolutions of the twentieth century, Che observes, "it was not capitalism's internal contradictions that, having exhausted all possibilities, caused the system to explode," but rather "the struggle for liberation from a foreign oppressor" or from neocolonial dictatorships, combined with "conscious action" and resolute determination.[124] As Fidel Castro saw very well when he came to mourn Che's death in October 1967, what set him apart from his comrades was his unyielding affirmation of "revolutionary virtues," his "boundless faith in moral values" and in our conscious capacity to assert them.[125] What is primary for Che is certainly the "moral" and "ideal" dimensions of struggle, but not in an abstract or idealist sense; what lends the practical determination and self-sacrifice of the guerrilla vanguard its "heroic" and "positive" edge is the fact that

> each guerrilla fighter is ready to die not just to defend an ideal but to make that ideal a reality. This is the basis, the essence of guerrilla struggle. The miracle is that a small nucleus of men, the armed vanguard of the great popular movement that supports them, can proceed to realize that ideal, to establish a new society, to break the old patterns of the past, to achieve, ultimately, the social justice for which they fight.[126]

The decisive factor, then, is the set of practices that enable such determination to endure over time, to cope with discouragement and exhaustion, and to persevere in "struggle no matter what the economic consequence of our actions may be."[127]

Like Rousseau, Che thus insists on the subordination of economic to political considerations, and of political considerations to moral ones. Virtuous practice, if undertaken with sufficient dedication and discipline, can enable a united but self-critical collective capacity to change the world, overcome imperialism, and herald the creation of a new society. This is again a matter of practice and capacity. Anticipating predictable accusations of "utopian" deviation, Che addressed what soon became the standard objection to his approach. "If someone says we are just romantics, inveterate idealists, thinking the impossible, that the masses of people cannot be turned into almost perfect human beings, we will have to answer a thousand and one times: Yes, it can be done; we are right. The people as a whole can advance."[128] We can advance insofar as we pursue "our political work with dogged determination to rid ourselves of the lack of internal motivation, that is, the lack of political clarity, which translates into things not getting done."[129]

For Che as for Rousseau, the way to cultivate such virtuous practice is through forms of political education that reinforce the sufficiency of "moral incentives." The paradigm of such practice, for both thinkers, is the disciplined solidarity of comrades in arms, the "heroic" phase of struggle "in which combatants compete for the heaviest responsibilities, for the greatest dangers, with no other satisfaction than fulfilling a duty." Political education instigated by a virtuous vanguard (and then subsumed by a self-educating society) is the answer to otherwise intractable social or economic problems. "Society as a whole must be converted into a gigantic school" in order to enable "the gigantic change in consciousness necessary to tackle the transition" to a socialist economy.[130] This transition will fail, sooner or later, unless "social duty" and commitment to the common good come to prevail over the corrupting and divisive motivations that prevailed in our "wretched past—a past that strangled man."[131] If capitalist relations of production have long required material incentives to induce people to perform tasks they despised, the goal of the new virtuous society is to allow work to become both creative and fulfilling on the one hand, and a matter of public pride on the other. Just as Rousseau's patriots labor on behalf of society as a whole, Che's workers are motivated primarily by selfless enthusiasm, "the moral incentive of being at the head of the people, of being recognized as exemplary workers."[132] Pending the full generalization of virtuous practice, both Rousseau and Che admit that there can be no avoiding the preliminary (though soon to be overcome) dualism, implied by any pedagogical model, of "the educator and educated"—of *législateur* and *citoyen* for Rousseau, or of *vanguardia* and *pueblo* for Che. So long as there is a transitional need to force some people to be free, as Rousseau might have put it, there will be a need for "moral compulsion"[133]—and whether we trace this back to Kant or to Castro, this sort of autonomous, self-imposed obligation is and has always been part and parcel of any account of political will.

As with some other revolutionary voluntarists who have effectively combined aspects of Rousseau and Marx in their political practice, if

Che's theory falls short it is not through *excès de zèle*. As with Lenin and Trotsky before him, the problem with Che's account is not that it is too idealistic or too voluntarist, but that his voluntarism is mediated and partially oriented by some quasi-determinist historical assumptions. It is Che's hasty reading of the "objective" tendencies at work in Latin America that leads him to conclude that "life and death" polarization of the continent is already irreversible, and to assume that, while the precise course of revolution may be contingent, he can still "predict its advent and triumph because it is the inevitable result of historical, economic and political conditions."[134] If we have since learned to expect less of history, this need not discourage us from acknowledging a political point that both Rousseau and Che liked to make: the power of a good example.

NOTES

1   This is what Ernst Bloch dubs a merely "abstract" utopia, one that lacks the actualizable "power of anticipation" characteristic of (socialist, historically mediated) "concrete utopia." See Ernst Bloch, *The Principle of Hope*, trans. Neville Plaice, Stephen Plaice, and Paul Knight (Cambridge: MIT Press, 1995), 1:17–18, 145, 157.

2   Benjamin Constant, *Cours de politique constitutionnelle*, ed. Edouard Laboulaye (Paris: Guillaumin, 1872), 2:280; see also Joseph de Maistre, *Against Rousseau: On the State of Nature and on the Sovereignty of the People* (1795), ed. Richard A. Lebrun (Montreal: McGill-Queen's University Press, 1996).

3   See, in particular, Jacob Talmon, *The Origins of Totalitarian Democracy* (London: Secker and Warburg, 1960), 38–50; and Lester G. Crocker, "Rousseau et la voie du totalitarisme," in *Rousseau et la philosophie politique*, ed. Pierre Arnaud et al. (Paris: Presses Universitaires de France, 1965). More recently, Jonathan Israel has added his authority to this old chorus, presenting Rousseau as a critic of the genuinely "radical" (that is, materialist-atheist) Enlightenment and as an enemy of representative democracy and free speech; the "darker side" of the French Revolution, he adds, "was chiefly inspired by the Rousseauist tendency. The crass demagoguery and murderous violence directed by Robespierre and the Jacobins did not hesitate publicly to condemn all the *philosophes* and the whole Enlightenment." Jonathan Israel, *A Revolution of the Mind* (Princeton: Princeton University Press, 2009), 231.

4   Isaiah Berlin, *Freedom and Its Betrayal* (Princeton: Princeton University Press, 2009), 2, 49; see also Robert Nisbet, *Community and Power* (Oxford: Oxford University Press, 1967), 153. For Berlin's correspondent Karl Popper, Rousseau's Romanticism likewise figures as "one of the most pernicious influences in the history of social philosophy." Karl R. Popper, *The Open Society and Its Enemies* (London: Routledge, 2002), 658n20.

5   Edmund Burke, "A Letter to a Member of the National Assembly" (1791), in *The Works of Edmund Burke* (Boston: Little, Brown, 1839), 3:310.
6   Lester Crocker, *Jean-Jacques Rousseau*, vol. 2, *The Prophetic Voice* (New York: Macmillan, 1973); Jean Guéhenno, *Jean-Jacques Rousseau*, vol. 2, *1758–1778*, ed. and trans. John and Doreen Weightman (New York: Columbia University Press, 1966), 262; Joseph Schwarz, *The Permanence of the Political: A Democratic Critique of the Radical Impulse to Transcend Politics* (Princeton: Princeton University Press, 1995), 10 and passim; Michael Sandel, *Democracy's Discontent: America in Search of a Public Philosophy* (Cambridge: Harvard University Press, 1998), 319–321.
7   Shklar, *Men and Citizens: A Study of Rousseau's Social Theory* (Cambridge: Cambridge University Press, 1969); see also Alfred Cobban, "New Light on the Political Thought of Rousseau," *Political Science Quarterly* 66, no. 2 (1951): 283.
8   See for instance Karl Marx, "Critical Marginal Notes on the Article 'The King of Prussia and Social Reform,' by a Prussian" (1844), in *Marx/Engels Collected Works (MECW)* (Moscow: Progress, 1975–2005), 3:199.
9   Louis Althusser, "Sur le *Contrat social* (Les Décalages)," *Les Cahiers pour l'Analyse* 8 (1967): 42. See also Jean Starobinski, *Jean-Jacques Rousseau: La Transparence et l'obstacle* (Paris: Gallimard, 1971), 49–50; Bronisław Baczko, *Rousseau: Solitude et communauté* (Paris: Mouton, 1974); Baczko, *Lumières de l'utopie* (Paris: Payot, 1978). See also Irmgard Hartig and Albert Soboul, "Notes pour une histoire de l'utopie en France au xviiie siècle," *Annales historiques de la Révolution française* 224 (1976): 177–178.
10 Guy Lardreau, "Une théorie totalitaire," *Le Monde: "Le Monde des livres,"* April 7, 1978; see also Guy Lardreau and Christian Jambet, *Le Monde* (Paris: Grasset, 1978), 89–92.
11 Jean-Jacques Rousseau, "Social Contract," in *The Social Contract, and Other Later Political Writings* (Cambridge: Cambridge University Press, 1997), 2:7; 1:7. Hereafter cited as "SC." References to the *Social Contract* are to book and chapter: SC 2:4 refers to book 2, chapter 4. Rousseau cited from *Œuvres complètes*, 5 vols., Pléiade ed. (Paris: Gallimard, 1964–1995). Hereafter cited as "OC." I have generally used Victor Gourevitch's translations for Rousseau's main political works, published by Cambridge University Press, and Christopher Kelly's comprehensive, multivolume edition of Rousseau's *Collected Writings* (Hanover, N.H.: Dartmouth College Press, 1992–) for other texts. Hereafter cited as "CW." Significant changes to translations are indicated. Here are the other abbreviations used in the chapter: "C," *Constitutional Project for Corsica* (in OC 3), trans. Christopher Kelly and Judith Bush, in CW 11; "CS," *Confessions* (in OC 1), trans. Christopher Kelly, in CW 5; "DAS," *Discourse on the Arts and Sciences* (in OC 3), trans. Victor Gourevitch, in *The Discourses, and Other Early Political Writings* (Cambridge: Cambridge University Press, 1997); "DOI," *Discourse on the Origin of Inequality* (in OC 3), trans. Victor Gourevitch, in *The Discourses*; "DPE," *Discourse on Political Economy* (in OC 3), trans. Victor Gourevitch, in *The Social Contract, and Other Later Political Writings*; "GM," *Geneva Manuscript* (in OC 3), trans. Judith Bush, in CW 4; "JNH," *Julie, ou La Nouvelle Héloïse* (in OC 2), trans. Philip Stewart and Jean Vaché, in CW 6. "LA," *Letter to d'Alembert on the Theater* (in OC 5), trans. Allan Bloom, Charles Butterworth, and Christopher Kelly, in CW 10; "LB," *Letter to Beaumont*

(January 1, 1763) (in *OC* 4), trans. Christopher Kelly and Judith Bush, in *CW* 9; "LF," *Letter to M. de Franquières (January 15, 1769)* (in *OC* 4), trans. Victor Gourevitch, in *The Social Contract, and Other Later Political Writings*; "LG," *Letter to Grimm* (*OC* 3), trans. Judith Bush, in *CW* 2; "LM," *Letters Written from the Mountain* (in *OC* 3), trans. Christopher Kelly and Judith Bush, in *CW* 9; "ML," *Moral Letters* (in *OC* 4), trans. Christopher Kelly, in *CW* 12; "N," *Narcissus*, preface (in *OC* 2), trans. Victor Gourevitch, in *The Social Contract, and Other Later Political Writings*; "OL," *Essay on the Origin of Languages* (in *OC* 5), trans. John T. Scott, in *CW* 7; "P," *Considerations on the Government of Poland* (in *OC* 3), trans. Victor Gourevitch, in *The Social Contract, and Other Later Political Writings*; "PF," *Political Fragments* (in *OC* 3), trans. Judith Bush, Roger D. Masters, and Christopher Kelly, in *CW* 4, and references are to the section and number of the *Fragments* as arranged in the Pléiade edition, followed by the page number, for example, "PF 4:7, 493" refers to fragment 7 of section 4, on page 493 of volume 3 of the *Œuvres complètes*.

12 Hannah Arendt, *Between Past and Future* (New York: Viking, 1961), 164; see also Arendt, *On Revolution* (New York: Viking, 1963), 77–79. And François Guizot, who was one of the first to anticipate and spell out some of the conservative social implications of an anti-Rousseauist, antivoluntarist position: "What is true of the child and the fool is true of man in general: the right to power is always derived from reason, never from will. No one has the right to lay down the law because he wills it; no one has the right to refuse to obey it because he does not will it; the legitimacy of power resides in the conformity of its laws to eternal reason, and not in the will of the man who exercises power, nor of him who submits to it." Guizot, *Histoire des origines du gouvernement représentatif en Europe* (Paris: Didier, 1851), 2:109.

13 For a preliminary overview, see Hallward, "The Will of the People," *Radical Philosophy* 155 (2009): 17–29.

14 See Andrew Levine, *The General Will* (Cambridge: Cambridge University Press, 1993); Luc Vincenti, ed., *Rousseau et le marxisme* (Paris: Sorbonne, 2011).

15 Antonio Gramsci, "Our Marx" (1918), in *Pre-Prison Writings*, trans. Virginia Cox, ed. Richard Bellamy (Cambridge: Cambridge University Press, 1994), 57.

16 Bloch, *Principle of Hope*, 2:623.

17 Antonio Gramsci, "The Modern Prince," in *Selections from the Prison Notebooks*, trans. Geoffrey Nowell Smith (London: Lawrence and Wishart, 1999), 194.

18 Ibid., 360.

19 Antonio Gramsci, "Workers' Democracy" (1919), in *Pre-Prison Writings*, 99. And Trotsky: "Who aims at the end cannot reject the means." Trotsky, *Terrorism and Communism* (1920; London: Verso, 2007), 25; cf. Leon Trotsky et al., *Their Morals and Ours: The Marxist View of Morality* (1938; Sydney: Resistance, 2000), 28.

20 Antonio Gramsci, *Selections from the Prison Notebooks*, 345.

21 Walter Benjamin, *Arcades Project*, trans. Howard Eiland and Kevin McLaughlin (Cambridge: MIT Press, 2002), 667.

22 Walter Benjamin, "On the Concept of History," in *Walter Benjamin: Selected Writings*, ed. Howard Eiland and Michael Jennings (Cambridge, Mass.: Harvard University

Press, 2003–2006), 4:392; see also Hallward, "Blanqui's Bifurcations," *Radical Philosophy* 185 (2014): 36–44.

23   Antonio Gramsci, "The Conquest of the State" (1919), in *Pre-Prison Writings*, 110.
24   Antonio Gramsci, "The Revolution Against Capital" (1917), in *Pre-Prison Writings*, 40.
25   Ernesto Che Guevara, "On the Budgetary Finance System" (1964), in *Che Guevara Reader: Writings on Politics and Revolution*, ed. David Deutschmann (Melbourne: Ocean, 2003), 201.
26   *SC* 1, introduction; *OC* 3:351.
27   *SC* 3:4; *OC* 3:404.
28   *SC* 4:9; *OC* 3:424. Rousseau had no reason to write out the strikingly pessimistic sequel to his *Emile* (the unpublished *Les Solitaires*), moreover, if he wanted to imply that a virtuous education, by itself, was sufficient to ensure happiness and fulfillment.
29   Rousseau, *Lettres écrites de la montagne*, sec. 6; *OC* 3:810.
30   Rousseau, *Projet de constitution pour la Corse*; *OC* 3:937–938. *Considérations sur le gouvernement de Pologne*; *OC* 3:958–961. "De l'honneur et de la vertu," in *Fragments Politiques* 5:3; *OC* 3:503.
31   *Considérations sur le gouvernement de Pologne*, *OC* 3:1040–1041.
32   *SC* 1:7; *OC* 3:363–364. Other recent readings that reject the characterization of Rousseau as utopian include Joshua Cohen, *Rousseau: A Free Community of Equals* (New York: Oxford University Press, 2010), 10–12, 178n6; Ethan Putterman, *Rousseau, Law and the Sovereignty of the People* (Cambridge: Cambridge University Press, 2010), 1–2, 122ff.; Kevin Inston, *Rousseau and Radical Democracy* (London: Continuum, 2010), 71–73, 168; Lelia Pezzillo, *Rousseau et le contrat social* (Paris: Presses Universitaires de France, 2000), 6–7; James Swenson, "Rousseau, the Revolution and the Republic," in *Rousseau and Revolution*, ed. Holger Ross Lauritsen and Mikkel Thorup (London: Bloomsbury, 2011), 189. See also Jean Fabre, "Réalité et utopie dans la pensée politique de Rousseau," *Annales Jean-Jacques Rousseau* 35 (1962): 215–222.
33   *SC* 3:12; *OC* 3:425. "Repose and freedom seem to me to be incompatible; we must choose between them." *Considérations sur le gouvernement de Pologne*, *OC* 3:955.
34   The edition is Rousseau, *Emile, or, On Education*, trans. Allan Bloom, vol. 13 of *Collected Writings*, ed. Roger D. Masters and Christopher Kelly (Hanover, N.H.: University Press of New England, 2010), 817–818, 650–651. The pagination refers to the standard French edition (the Pléiade *Œuvres complètes*, vol. 4), which is included in this English edition. Hereafter cited as "*E*."
35   *SC* 3:12; *OC* 3:425.
36   Rousseau, "Reveries of the Solitary Walker," in *OC* 1:1059; see also "Letter to Malesherbes," January 4, 1762, in *OC* 1:1132.
37   "*L'homme vraiment libre ne veut que ce qu'il peut, et fait ce qu'il lui plaît.*" *E* 308–309.
38   Rousseau is quite happy to accept, for the same sort of reasons Kant will accept after him, that the will needs to be approached as a practical rather than a theoretical question. "It is no more possible for me to conceive of how my will moves my body than it is to conceive of how my sensations affect my soul," and "just as the action of the soul on the body with respect to man's constitution is unfathomable in philosophy, so the action of the general

will on the public force with respect to the constitution of the State is unfathomable in politics." *E* 576; cf. *E* 574, 586; *GM* 296–297; "Fragment on Freedom" (c. 1750), in *CW* 4:12).
39 *SC* 1:2; *OC* 3:352.
40 Rousseau, "History of the Government of Geneva," in *OC* 5:519.
41 *E* 576.
42 *E* 581–582; cf. *LB* 954–955.
43 See also *SC* 1:1; *OC* 3:352.
44 *E* 586–588.
45 *LF* 1135.
46 *LF* 1145.
47 *E* 585.
48 Rousseau, "Fragments of the Letter to Beaumont," *OC* 4:1019; *DOI* 181. In the so-called confession recorded by his daughter Jenny in 1865, Marx identified "servility" as the vice he most detested, "gullibility" as the vice he was most ready to excuse, and "to fight" as his idea of happiness. Marx, "Confession," in *MECW* 42:567.
49 *C* 903.
50 *ML* 1098, 1101.
51 See, in particular, Joshua Cohen, *Rousseau: A Free Community of Equals* (New York: Oxford University Press, 2010).
52 *SC* 1:6; *OC* 3:361.
53 *SC* 1:8; *OC* 3:364.
54 *DPE* 245. A "moral being," Rousseau explains elsewhere, is "a being that is intelligent, free . . . [and] endowed with reason." Ibid., 124.
55 *DPE* 245; cf. *LM* 807.
56 *DPE* 247.
57 *SC* 4:1, *OC* 3:437.
58 *SC* 2:1, *OC* 3:368; cf. *LM* 808.
59 *LM* 842. *SC* 2:1; *OC* 3:368–369.
60 *PF* 3:11; *OC* 3:485, my emphasis.
61 *SC* 2:2; *OC* 3:369. *SC* 1:7, *OC* 3:363.
62 This, parenthetically, might be Rousseau's answer to Guizot's criticism, cited above.
63 Marx, *Capital*, trans. Ben Fowkes (London: Vintage, 1977), 1:284.
64 *E* 567; cf. *JNH* 493.
65 *ML* 1087.
66 *E* 250.
67 *DPE* 254, 252.
68 *PF* 13, 544; *E* 544.
69 *DPE* 252; *PF* 4:7, 493.
70 *P* 1018.
71 *LF* 1143.
72 *E* 817–818; see also Rousseau, "Discourse on Heroic Virtue," in *OC* 2:1272.
73 *E* 818–819.
74 *SC* 2:1; *SC* 3:15; *SC* 3:15.

75 Rousseau, "Discourse on Heroic Virtue," in *OC* 2:1270; *PF* 2:8, 477; cf. *P* 973.
76 *PF* 5:6, 505.
77 *E* 249.
78 *SC* 2:7; *OC* 3:381.
79 *DAS* 8.
80 *LM* 896.
81 *SC* 4:1.
82 *LM* 892.
83 *SC* 3:8; *OC* 3:418–419.
84 *PF* 4:24; *OC* 3:499–500.
85 *P* 1017–1018.
86 Rousseau, "Judgment of the Plan for Perpetual Peace," in *OC* 3:599.
87 *PF* 3:11, 485.
88 *LG* 73. "The genuinely tolerant person does not tolerate crime." *LM* 701.
89 *DPE* 254.
90 Robespierre, *Œuvres complètes* (Paris: Leroux, 1910), 10:356.
91 *LM* 851; *DPE* 249–250; see also *P* 1039–1040.
92 *GM* 305–306.
93 *SC* 1:7; *OC* 3:363–364.
94 *SC* 1:8; *OC* 3:365.
95 *DPE* 248.
96 *PF* 3:7, 483–484.
97 *SC* 3:15; *OC* 3:429.
98 *PF* 2:12, 480.
99 *SC* 2:4; *OC* 3:372.
100 *C* 937.
101 Gramsci, *Selections from the Prison Notebooks*, 349.
102 Marx and Engels, "The Holy Family," in *MECW* 4:37; cf. Marx and Engels, "The German Ideology," in *MECW* 5:52.
103 Marx, *Capital*, 1:929.
104 Marx, "Economic and Philosophical Manuscripts," in *Early Writings*, trans. Rodney Livingstone and Gregor Benton (London: Penguin, 1992), 329.
105 Marx, *Capital*, 1:283–284.
106 Marx, "Critique of Hegel's Doctrine of the State," in *Early Writings*, 89, 88.
107 Marx, "The Divorce Bill," in *MECW* 1:309.
108 Marx, "Class Struggles in France," in *MECW* 22:334.
109 See in particular Marx et al., "Address of the Central Committee to the Communist League" (March 1850), in *MECW* 10:277–287.
110 Marx, *Capital*, 1:719, 899. If someone "relates to his own activity as unfree activity, then he relates to it as activity in the service, under the rule, coercion and yoke of another man." Marx, "Economic and Philosophical Manuscripts" (1844), in *Early Writings*, 331.
111 Marx, "Economic and Philosophical Manuscripts," in *Early Writings*, 348; cf. Marx, *Capital*, 3:959.

112 Marx, *Grundrisse*, trans. Martin Nicolaus (London: Penguin, 1993), 488.
113 Marx and Engels, "German Ideology," in *MECW* 5:51–52.
114 Engels, "Anti-Dühring" (1877), in *MECW* 25:266, 270.
115 Che Guevara, poem of 1947, cited in John Lee Anderson, *Che Guevara: A Revolutionary Life*, rev. ed. (New York: Grove, 2010), 44.
116 Guevara, *Guerrilla Warfare* (1961; Lincoln: University of Nebraska Press, 1998), 9, translation modified.
117 Guevara, "Speech to the Latin American Youth Congress" (1960), in *Che Guevara Reader: Writings on Politics and Revolution*, ed. David Deutschmann, expanded ed. (Melbourne: Ocean Press, 2012), 240; Guevara, "Create Two, Three, Many Vietnams," in *Che Guevara Reader*, 353.
118 Guevara, "Tactics and Strategy of the Latin American Revolution" (1962), in *Che Guevara Reader*, 295.
119 Guevara, "Political Sovereignty and Economic Independence" (1960), in *Che Guevara Reader*, 99–100.
120 Guevara, "A Party of the Working Class" (1963), in *Che Guevara Reader*, 171.
121 Guevara, *Guerrilla Warfare*, 7.
122 Guevara, "The OAS Conference at Punta del Este" (1961), in *Che Guevara Reader*, 245.
123 Guevara, "The Cuban Revolution's Influence in Latin America" (1962), in *Che Guevara Reader*, 286.
124 Guevara, "Socialism and Man in Cuba" (1965), *Che Guevara Reader*, 216.
125 Che, Castro continues, "had a boundless faith in the consciousness of human beings. And we should say that he saw, with absolute clarity, the moral impulse as the fundamental lever in the construction of communism in human society." Castro, "Memorial Speech for Che Guevara," October 18, 1967, in Fidel Castro, *Fidel Castro Reader*, ed. David Deutschmann and Deborah Shnookal (Melbourne: Ocean Press, 2007), 323.
126 Guevara, *Guerrilla Warfare*, 14, translation modified.
127 Guevara, "Reminiscences of the Revolutionary War," in *Che Guevara Reader*, 57.
128 Guevara, "To Be a Young Communist" (1962), in *Che Guevara Reader*, 167. It is rather the architects of state capitalism, as Che can argue with some justification, who in their very "pragmatism" may be most guilty of idealism. "The pipe dream that socialism can be achieved with the help of the dull instruments left to us by capitalism (the commodity as the economic cell, profitability, individual material interest as a lever, etc.) can lead into a blind alley," and if it is laid along neocapitalist or neocolonialist lines then the new "economic foundation" will be sure to "undermine the development of consciousness" and with it the revolution in general. Guevara, "Socialism and Man in Cuba," in *Che Guevara Reader*, 217.
129 Guevara, "Against Bureaucratism" (1963), in *Che Guevara Reader*, 181.
130 Guevara, "Socialism and Man in Cuba," in *Che Guevara Reader*, 213, 217.
131 Guevara, "On the Budgetary Finance System" (1964), in *Che Guevara Reader*, 200; Che Guevara, "A New Culture of Work," in *Che Guevara Reader*, 146.
132 Ibid., 149.

133 See in particular Guevara, "Socialism and Man in Cuba," in *Che Guevara Reader*, 220–221.

134 Guevara, *Guerrilla Warfare*, 153. As so often in the early 1960s, here again Che and Castro are on the same page, most notably in this prediction from Castro's "Second Declaration of Havana" (February 4, 1962), cited by Che: "In many Latin American countries revolution is inevitable. This fact is not determined by the will of any person. It is determined by the horrifying conditions of exploitation under which the Latin American people live, the development of a revolutionary consciousness in the masses, the worldwide crisis of imperialism and the universal liberation movements of the subjugated nations." *Che Guevara Reader*, 73.

6

AFTER UTOPIA, IMAGINATION?

ÉTIENNE BALIBAR

It seems to me that the main problem facing us at the turn of the century consists of taking leave of utopia while setting free the powers of the imagination. This thesis is not original, I freely admit, but it could be that it would allow us to get beyond the sterile oppositions between an ethics of conviction and an ethics, or politics, of responsibility. My reason for this will be developed on three, tightly connected registers. First of all, utopia—be it individualist or collectivist—traps us and the imagination within the alternative of realism and unreality, whereas realism is profoundly unreal and in another sense the unreal, even the "impossible," is that without which no reality can be tolerated in history. Next, we are obliged to observe that with the process today designated by the name of "globalization," which for my part I prefer to call the "globalization of the globe," the very bases of the classical utopia have been radically destroyed. On the other hand, the question of institutional change, with its inevitable fictional component (the invention of rights, new techniques for the expression and representation of the collective interest, the transmutation of values that articulate the "private" and "public" spheres), has become unavoidable. In particular it concerns the forms and content of "citizenship" beyond the crisis of the nation-state that we are experiencing today.

This allows me to make a detour by way of formulations we have inherited from Karl Marx and Michel Foucault, the incompatibility of whose philosophies at the end of the day renders their convergence that much more significant. Very early on, we know, Marx chose "utopian socialism" as his target. But the meaning of this critique has been obscured by the false alternative of "utopian socialism" and "scientific socialism," with effects we all know. Scientific socialism, it must be said, is not the opposite of utopian socialism (just as scientific capitalism, that of the Nobel Prize for Economics, is not the opposite of utopian capitalism, in which individual interests naturally harmonize). The meaning of the Marxian critique of utopia must not be sought on the side of science (the interest in which is completely different, namely, knowledge), but on the side of practice and its revolutionary conception. It must be sought in the "transformation of the world," or better still, in an alternative solution to the seemingly ineluctable evolution of the world as it is objectively inscribed in its contradictions and struggles, in the impossibility of the dominant tendencies being realized without intolerable constraints for larger and larger masses of people, and therefore in the resistance they provoke.

For his part, Foucault (for whom the thought of resistance was far from foreign) opposed to utopia not transformative mass movements, but what he called "heterotopia," the very real varieties of which he sought to describe and classify. They are generally situated at the margins of society, but they in turn act on it and fulfill an essential function in its regulation of differences, on a large or small scale: spaces of exclusion or, on the contrary, of experimentation, normalization, and deviance. Brothels, camps and colonies, theaters, prisons, museums, gardens . . . in the end we ask ourselves what institution does not have a heterotopic dimension, and what institution could live without one. What is important is the emphasis that is placed not on the contradiction of becoming, on irreconcilable conflicts, but on the irreducible heterogeneity of social behaviors, rebellious to any normalization, more complex or more marked by foreignness than any rule. But, it must also be noted, Marx and Foucault each explore in their way an essential dimension of politics: the emergence of subjectivity in the social field, not as its absolute "other," but as its intimate, necessary difference, the counterpart of its ineluctable mobility, of its "historicity."

What then has become of utopia and its critique in the contemporary world? I will say, very quickly, that globalization has sounded the death-knell for the great classical forms, particularly to the extent that they are inscribed within a "cosmopolitan" horizon: the extension of the harmonious dream of the *città ideale* to the limits of the world; the horizon of every modern idea of progress, which we can imagine as the domination of the planet; the unification of the human species within a single space of intellectual communication and division of labor that would coincide with the resolution of racial and national antagonisms; the elimination of the most unacceptable forms of inequality and of man's oppression of man. This is what, before our eyes opened by the end of the antagonism of the "camps," by the growing interpenetration of the populations of the North and the South, by the bloody failures of the New World Order and its humanitarian prostheses—in short, everything that is called globalization—has completely dissolved. It appears in effect that the unity of the human race has finally been realized within a single world, subject to the same economic regulations, facing the same environmental problems, and it looks more like the "war of all against all" described by Hobbes as a state of nature than a civic or civil space. It even seems that the multiplication of "virtual worlds" of communication has continually promoted indifference to the sufferings closest to us, which are transformed into spectacles (as we saw with Bosnia, Rwanda, and Algeria), and has re-created the division between "subhumans" and "superhumans" that we thought we had definitively abolished.

There are no more utopias, then, because we have in reality gone beyond the conditions for their realization. This is perhaps why they have survived intellectually only in the most degraded, mutually opposed forms: technocratic programs and messianic preaching. For my part I do not conclude from this that the imagination no longer has a place in politics or that we must be content to manage the inevitable, to adjust it at the margins or minimize as best we can its human costs. But I am thinking of an imagination of the present rather than an imagination of the future. Above all, I believe that it is necessary once again to exercise this imagination in the field of institutional creation, with its collective, practical dimension and its juridical, symbolic dimension. For example, undertaking to democratize the institution of borders, this antidemocratic condition par excellence of democracies themselves, is not a small matter. This is what I call fiction in the full sense of the term, it being understood that fiction is the production of the real on the basis of experience itself, knowledge and action indissociably mixed, insurrection leading to constitution (and the transformation of existing constitutions).

The most important thing, no doubt, for the reinvention of politics in today's world as an individual responsibility and as a scheme of communication among groups, is to find experimentally the places of fiction. The immediate present reveals a few sites, without being restricted to them: the status of foreigners in the "nation" or the difference between nationals and foreigners, which certainly cannot be abolished, but which must go from being a function of discrimination to one of reciprocity and local opening on the basis of the solidarities but also the conflicts of the global space. This is only an example, no doubt, and one that we cannot isolate from other struggles concerning work or cultural identity and religion, but it is one that, all things considered, when we take stock of the road already traveled in the last ten or twenty years, allows us to resist nihilism.

NOTE

Originally published as "Après l'utopie, l'imagination?," *Le Monde*, November 24, 1997.

7

A STRANGE FATE FOR POLITICS

Jameson's Dialectic of Utopian Thought

JOHN GRANT

Must utopia remain utopian, or can it be achieved without at the same time announcing its own end? This question helps to orient an examination of Fredric Jameson's engagement with utopia and the critical insights about society that come with it. In early work such as "Reification and Utopia in Mass Culture" (1979), Jameson articulates how cultural artifacts contain twin utopian and ideological components, with the latter never managing to preclude the former. In more recent work such as "The Politics of Utopia" (2004), Jameson claims that utopian thinking flourishes when we find politics has been suspended. This raises a host of questions: Is politics in fact suspended, as Jameson contends? What is utopian thinking meant to disclose to us about our society? Indeed, what do we turn to utopia for?

In this chapter I examine Jameson's shifting responses to these questions using evidence from four different decades of his career. My aim is to show that while Jameson's early hermeneutic involving ideology and utopia is convincing as a mode of critique, his ongoing negotiations involving a dialectic of politics and utopia are compromised by the "strange fate for politics" that I identify in his work. His hesitations regarding politics approach the old danger that Louis Althusser called "theoreticism": a one-sided insistence on theory that is itself an obstacle to radical change. Even in those moments where Jameson's dialectical approach seems as fluid as ever, switching between negative and positive valences, it remains unclear how either valence is possible given his analysis of existing conditions, or which one is most desirable from the perspective of radical politics. As Jameson indicates, thinking the positive and negative together is what a dialectical approach demands. Yet to do so successfully should not merely open the space required for an articulation of radical politics; it should take up that very task. This is where Jameson wavers more often than not, and it is why the suspension of politics that he worries so much about applies at least as much to his own work as it does to Western society.

UTOPIA, IDEOLOGY, AND MASS CULTURE

Jameson's engagement with utopia is now more than forty years old. One of his most noteworthy contributions remains his article "Reification and Utopia in Mass Culture," in which various arguments are rehearsed through readings of hit movies from the 1970s, *The Godfather* (parts 1 and 2) and *Jaws*. One of the main insights we should take from this article is Jameson's demonstration that there are utopian and ideological components in all works of art. Products of mass culture in particular cannot have ideological features without having utopian ones as well. The term "ideology" designates two important and related functions for Jameson: the presentation of social and historical phenomena as natural, and the displacement of objects that we ought to critique with objects of significantly less importance.[1] Both of these functions are examples of "ideological manipulation" that exploits the interests of the masses by playing on their anxieties for conservative and counterrevolutionary purposes.

And yet the success of ideology in mass culture actually depends on an accompanying utopian dimension that offers the public something it genuinely wants. Mass culture cannot be so ideologically pernicious that it treats people as dupes and nothing more, since this would increase the risk of critical backlash. The analysis of utopia—or the utopian—remains available, precisely because "utopia" designates those dimensions of mass culture that are negative and in one way or another are critical of the existing social order. It is no surprise, then, that Jameson thinks utopia has a transcendent function, though it is not entirely clear whether this means "actual" transcendence—that is, radical changes to our material conditions and how we relate to others—or transcendence in a lesser sense of having one's life outlook transformed but where material conditions themselves would not qualify.

The best example of Jameson's exploration of ideology and utopia involves his treatment of the first *Godfather* film.[2] Condensing considerably, Jameson sets out the ideological aspects of *The Godfather*, notably its displacement of viewers' anger at big business onto organized crime. By presenting the mafia as the corrupt underside of legitimate business interests, the business world is portrayed as law-abiding and fair. Not only that, but notice the register on which the comparison is taking place: the fact that America's welfare is put at risk by nefarious business practices is presented as an ethical matter, not an economic one.

Yet there is more to the mafia than just corruption, profiteering, and financial gain. The mafia, or more precisely the mafia *family*, is the site of a utopian moment for viewers. The Corleone family offers a vision of social—and ethnic—belonging that is tightly knit, secure, and well ordered thanks to its strictly enforced patriarchal order. Such circumstances exist only as fantasy for the majority of Americans, whose reality combines anomie and atomization with greater permissiveness and an erosion of authority. According to Jameson: "The drawing power of a mass cultural artifact like *The Godfather* may thus be measured by its twin capacity to perform an urgent ideological function at the same time that it provides the vehicle for the investment of a desperate Utopian fantasy."[3] Notice, however, that in this instance the utopian fantasy is scarcely a radical one. Retreating to the family does nothing to address the (post)modern social and economic forces—from the disorientations caused by global capitalism to the opaqueness of the modern state to a generally diminished sense of belonging—that give rise to such an impulse in the first place. The result is that in instances such as this one, even the utopian components of mass culture are ideological because they offer false remedies.

UTOPIA, CRITIQUE, AND POLITICS

I turn now to a number of Jameson's works and examine them in light of the questions I posed at the outset about the state of politics, the insights that utopian thinking offers, and our motivation for turning to utopia in the first place.[4] Jameson's article "The Politics of Utopia" makes a number of useful distinctions, beginning with that between utopias that focus on the root of all evil as against political utopias.[5] The former are usually backward-looking, regressive, and wistful for a time of uncorrupted innocence. The latter tend to be forward-looking and progressive yet also largely anonymous, shorn of any existential sense of lived experience. Another related distinction is that root-of-all-evil utopias are motivated by wish-fulfillment, whereas political utopias should be seen as constructions akin to "model railroads of the mind."[6]

What is more interesting—and more controversial—about this article is the relationship Jameson sees between utopian thinking and politics (or "the political"—he uses the terms interchangeably). The two are negatively related because "utopia emerges at the moment of the suspension of the political."[7] There are two reasons for this: First, despite the turbulence of the real world, changing our political system and its institutions appears impossible—and therefore stands as a profoundly limiting preoccupation that forces us into the ruts of reformism or worse. Second, in any instance when popular demands for change become louder and unrelenting, our attention is directed to ever-more specific matters. The result is that a sufficiently collective utopian impulse can give rise to the very type of precise political demands—a program, even—that act to close down the utopian impulse. "At such a moment" Jameson contends, "the utopian imagination no longer has free play."[8] The strange fate for politics that emerges in Jameson's work begins to take shape here. The next passage is worth quoting in full:

> We need, then, to posit a peculiar suspension of the political in order to describe the utopian moment: it is this suspension, this separation of the political—in all its unchangeable immobility—from daily life and even from the world of the lived and the existential, this externality that serves as the calm before the storm, the stillness at the centre of the hurricane; and that allows us to take hitherto unimaginable mental liberties with structures whose actual modification or abolition scarcely seem on the cards.[9]

Jameson's claim is that a political storm is building but will not arrive at all soon. In the meantime, the utopian will flourish under the conditions of politics' absence.

This may well be so, but Jameson's regret about the impossibility of change has been secondary throughout his career to his utter dismay at our supposed inability to imagine change at all. Take these representative examples. In "Progress Versus Utopia; or, Can We Imagine the Future?" (1982) he contends that the vocation of science fiction is "to demonstrate and to dramatize our incapacity to imagine the future," a circumstance he attributes to "the atrophy in our time of what Marcuse called the *utopian imagination*."[10] Nine years later in his grand book on postmodernism he affirmed that "the question of Utopia would seem to be a crucial test of what is left of our capacity to imagine change at all."[11] The introduction to his full-blown examination of utopia—*Archaeologies of the Future* (2005)—includes the same argument:

> What is crippling is not the presence of an enemy but rather the universal belief, not only that this tendency [the right-wing rollback of progressive achievements] is irreversible, but that the historic alternatives to capitalism have been proven unviable and impossible, and that no other socio-economic system is conceivable, let alone practically available.[12]

The consistency with which Jameson holds this position does not prevent awkward problems from emerging. There is no misinterpreting his claims that utopia will flourish when politics has been suspended, and that this suspension has taken place. Why, then, does he insist on our incapacity to imagine alternative futures at precisely the moment when, according to his own account, such thinking should thrive? Why are we denied the promise of utopian thinking? One response to Jameson is to point out that it is not politics but radical politics that has been suspended—or, even more accurately, radical politics on the Left. For Jameson has no difficulty listing all kinds of regressive neoliberal policies that—it bears recalling—began as the utopian aspirations of neoliberal intellectuals in the 1930s and 1940s, long before neoliberalism's ascendancy in the 1980s.[13] Thus, the problem is not that utopian thought finds politics as such to be immobilized, or is itself fossilized; it is that prospective utopian thinkers on the Left find *their* politics to be generally unthinkable, not to mention impossible from a practical standpoint.

Jameson's exaggerated sense of politics' absence raises a related issue concerning what he thinks utopia is meant to disclose about society. Any indication that utopian thought is beginning to thrive should tell us, in

Jameson's view, that we are in the grip of regressive, reactionary forces that make politics impossible. But in *Archaeologies* Jameson describes how utopia's "very existence or emergence certainly registers the agitation of the various 'transitional periods' within which most Utopias were composed."[14] Jameson sees no contradiction in suggesting that the initial agitations of radical politics can occur while the larger political system remains seemingly unchangeable. While I think this is right, it does not resolve the dilemma that Jameson has introduced. Does utopia register the *absence* of radical thinking and change or, as he also claims, the *preliminary disturbances* that they cause through actual politics? For it does not seem consistent, temporally, to claim that it does both. If utopia blossoms while politics is suspended, should it not recede as politics emerges onto the scene? Surely such dialectical equivalence is implied by Jameson's argument quoted above that precise political demands and programs restrict the utopian imagination. In any case, I would contend that it is not utopia but politics itself—that is, collective action—that registers against the system's frozen core. But even this formulation is not quite right. The active and ongoing assault by neoliberalism I mentioned above means that Jameson's language about the stasis, blockage, and absence of politics entices us into imagining an altogether misleading model of political reality. The emergence of radical left politics does not confront an unchangeable system; it enjoins a battle over an ever-changing system that has been dominated and reshaped by right-wing politics for close to four decades.

It is worth spending some time now to consider exactly what Jameson thinks we should turn to utopia for. Jameson insists on multiple occasions that we should treat utopian thought as a negative diagnostic tool, one that uncovers our blind spots as well as our general mental imprisonment in relation to our present circumstances.[15] And he performs exactly such an analysis in his reading of *The Godfather*. It is certainly a success for theory, and a vivid demonstration of how ideology and utopia are dialectically intertwined.

Elsewhere, however, Jameson modifies his restriction that we should use utopia only as a negative tool and is more open to judging the positive content and representations of utopian visions. He has suggested full, universal employment as the most radical utopian demand that can be made today (or at least in 2004).[16] He has also posited that "the most urgent task seems to me the defense of the Welfare State,"[17] the nonutopianism of which he justifies by pointing out that such a defense will fail and in so doing drive home the inadequacies of mere social democracy. More interesting is his interest in the idea of abolishing money: "It is the decision to abandon money, to place this demand at the forefront of a political program, that marks the rupture and opens up a space into which Utopia may enter."[18] Here utopia is not so much about our blind spots, and certainly not about a utopian society, as about the break between our infernal present and an alternative future. For Jameson: "Disruption is, then, the name for a new discursive strategy, and Utopia is the form such disruption necessarily takes."[19]

Suddenly political demands and even programs are no longer separate from the purpose of utopia in Jameson's view. Has he resolved his anxiety about whether or not "the achievement of utopia will efface all previously existing utopian impulses"?[20] It is certainly unexpected to find him arguing that radical political demands and policy-specific programs will open up space for utopia to enter, for, as I showed, his long-standing position (in no way disavowed) is that utopian thinking chisels out narrow openings for radical politics. The result, I contend, is unclear. Is utopian thinking the route to radical politics, or is a radical program the advance sentry of a more expansive utopian imagination? Treated separately, each option seems possible. But as strategies, Jameson has always insisted more strongly on the former, largely because he has tended to treat utopian political programs as antithetical to the utopian impulse or imagination. Indeed, he *had* to do so because of his certainty that our utopian faculties have been gravely impaired. If in fact radical demands and programs can and should come first, then it is conceivable that our impairment is not as terrible as Jameson believes.

UTOPIA AND DIALECTICS

I will return to the question of utopia and politics shortly. First, it is necessary to expand on the issue of dialectical thought in Jameson. There are moments where the very possibility of dialectical thought—and of critique itself—seems lost for Jameson. This is no more so the case than when he claimed, in his book on Adorno, to sense "some dawning apprehension of an intellectual landscape in which the negative, or 'critical theory,' will have definitively become a thing of the past."[21] Certainly this supports his view that the negative is, at best, deeply buried within late capitalism's ideological commitments. In *Valences of the Dialectic* (2009) and its chapter titled "Utopia as Replication," we encounter this position but also its virtual opposite. Initially Jameson affirms the necessity of the negative as a clue to our present confinement by dismissing the idea of accommodating utopian thought to positive, representational thinking: "what is important in a Utopia is not what can be positively imagined and proposed, but rather what is not imaginable and not conceivable."[22] Very quickly, however, he revises this stance, saying that he *does* see a place for representational utopias because they "destabilize our stereotypes of a future that is the same as our own present."[23] This is not a fleeting consideration for Jameson, he suggests, adding that this argument builds on the one in *Archaeologies* discussed above, in particular his view that positive political claims can produce new intellectual space for utopian thought to develop.

The most obvious way to negotiate Jameson's different positions is to treat them as the unfolding parts of a dialectic that is simultaneously negative and positive. There is no doubt that Jameson is aware of the advantages and drawbacks of a purely negative or positive dialectic and it is not surprising that he hopes to avoid both extremes. Nevertheless he shows a decided preference for the negative, the consequences of which need to be explored.

One of the ways Jameson stages positive and negative is by counterposing what he terms the "utopian impulse" against "utopian politics," with the latter amounting to a utopian program.[24] The utopian impulse rehearses the same type of hermeneutic found in the article from 1979. It involves a relentless search for the negative and resists the positivity not just of utopian politics, but of all politics. Where the utopian impulse is open, expansive, and daring, politics—even of the utopian variety—is confining, perhaps even small. Such an outcome seems unavoidable to the extent that every utopian program amounts to a totality and therefore "must posit limits"[25] as to what it involves and excludes.

Recall that I began this chapter by considering Jameson's hermeneutic of ideology and utopia in mass culture. Then I examined how Jameson finds reason to allow utopia to be not only representational but explicitly political, despite his reservations. In *Valences* he introduces an entirely new third option: "I consider the Utopian 'method' outlined here as neither hermeneutic nor political program, but rather something like the structural inversion of what Foucault, following Nietzsche, called the genealogy."[26] Jameson describes genealogy as the attempt to articulate the conditions of possibility, both past and present, for a particular phenomenon to emerge, without saying that this emergence was preordained. His "structural inversion" replaces genealogy with utopia as a method or operation intended to express not a history of the present, but a contemporary account of alternative futures. This involves "experimentally" declaring "positive things which are clearly negative in our own world" and isolating "specific features in our empirical present so as to read them as components of a different system."[27]

At first glance it might appear as if Jameson has come full circle and is now willing to elaborate the type of program he has so diligently avoided. Instead, it becomes clear that this is nothing more than a recapitulation of his belief that utopia is essential for a critique of the present, but that this critique has little to do with politics:

> This kind of prospective hermeneutic is a political act only in one specific sense: as a contribution to the reawakening of the imagination of possible and alternate futures, a reawakening of that historicity which our system—offering itself as the very end of history—necessarily represses and paralyzes. . . . Such a revival of futurity and of the positing of alternate futures is not itself a political program nor even a political practice: but it is hard to see how any durable or effective political action could come into being without it.[28]

It is telling that in the space of two pages in *Valences*, Jameson distinguishes his new utopian method from a hermeneutic and then confirms their essential equivalence. These passages reinforce the view that he has scarcely deviated from where we began, namely, with his resignation to the apparent fact that we are unable to imagine a different world and must rely on utopia to help us do so. In this light, the earlier excursion in *Archaeologies* into political demands and even program-making looks like nothing more than a temporary aberration. Recall his enthusiasm for the political demand to eliminate money: it was that demand, and the decision to place it "at the forefront of a political program," that supposedly opens up space for utopia, and is "how Utopia recovers its vocation."[29] Essentially Jameson has claimed that politics is the means by which we make utopia possible again. But why would we need to recover utopia when the political demands that do so are already utopian?

Jameson's use of politics as a means to rescue utopia amounts to working backward, contrary to his principal aim of using utopia to galvanize politics. Further, it is the ultimate demonstration of his tendency to favor theory over politics. I mentioned at the outset that Jameson's privileging of theory risks becoming what Louis Althusser called "theoreticism." Here is Althusser's most thorough explanation of the term:

> Theoreticism here means: primacy of theory over practice; one-sided insistence on theory; but more precisely: *speculative-rationalism*. To explain only the pure form: to conceive matters in terms of the contrast between truth and error was in fact *rationalism*. But it was *speculation* to want to conceive the contrast between established truths and acknowledged errors within a General Theory of Science and Ideology and of the distinction between them.[30]

To be sure, Jameson's work does not contain a "thick" version of theoreticism. There is no speculative rationalism or attempt to separate science from ideology like we find in Althusser. Neither does declining to elaborate on radical political claims amount to theoreticism. But a charge of thin or weak theoreticism does apply when appeals to theory interfere with the work of radical politics. The claim that only by undertaking extensive theoretical work will we possess the mental space needed to conceive of radical politics in the first place is particularly suspect. This is the dominant tendency in Jameson to be sure, but he can be ambivalent on this question, no more so than in *Archaeologies*, when he reverses his typical priority and considers whether hard political demands ought to precede the theoretical work of utopia. (His occasional support in *Valences* for positive utopias is less demanding by comparison.) But this ambivalence only underscores his theoreticism. For if Jameson actually thought that politics and political demands had primacy, his strategy would be different. There would be less emphasis on our inability to imagine a radical future and a greater commitment to making the kind of political demands that appear sporadically in his work. And certainly there would be little concern for using radical politics to rescue utopia so it can remain his interrogative mode of choice. Instead, we find that politics becomes a pragmatic tool when confined to offering single strikes against orthodoxy as part of a utopian impulse, but becomes unacceptably limiting to the imagination and even suspect the moment we turn to praxis.

By way of conclusion, consider the following passage from *Late Marxism*:

> No future is conceivable, however, from which the deeper ideological commitment to politics—that is to say, left politics—is absent . . . and even a fully postmodernized First World society will not lack young people whose temperament and values are genuinely left ones and embrace visions of radical social change repressed by the norms of a business society.[31]

Jameson would hardly be the first person whose hopes and optimism of the will are at odds with their pessimism of intellect. Nevertheless, this statement encapsulates the strange fate of politics in Jameson's work. Politics is simultaneously *hoped for* as a way to overcome capitalism and domination, and *expected* as an irrepressible mode of resistance against existing power relations, yet perpetually *absent* thanks to the iron grip of late capitalism and its political and cultural supports. Fidelity to this last belief demands that theory take precedence over praxis despite Jameson's occasional suggestions to the contrary. The fact that Jameson issues these dissents against his own positions suggests an alternative path, one that conceives of radical politics and utopian imagination as entering into a dialectical relationship of coproduction rather than negative reciprocity.[32]

NOTES

1. Fredric Jameson, "Reification and Utopia in Mass Culture," *Social Text* 1 (Winter 1979): 142–143.
2. Ibid., esp. 145–146.
3. Ibid., 147. Jameson makes this same point thirty years later in *Valences of the Dialectic* (New York: Verso, 2009), 415–416.
4. In 1998, the journal *Utopian Studies* (vol. 9, no. 2) devoted a special section to examining Jameson's work on utopia. While the articles are illuminating, they are now dated because of how much he has published since then.
5. Fredric Jameson, "The Politics of Utopia," *New Left Review* 25 (January-February) 2004: 37–40.

6   Ibid., 40.
7   Ibid., 43.
8   Ibid., 44.
9   Ibid., 45.
10 Fredric Jameson, "Progress Versus Utopia; or, Can We Imagine the Future?" *Science-Fiction Studies* 9, no. 2 (1982): 153, italics in original. This article has been reprinted in *Archaeologies of the Future* (2005).
11 Fredric Jameson, *Postmodernism, or, The Cultural Logic of Late Capitalism* (London: Verso, 1991), xvi.
12 Fredric Jameson, *Archaeologies of the Future: The Desire Called Utopia and Other Science Fictions* (London: Verso, 2005), xii; see also p. 231.
13 Rachel S. Turner, "The 'Rebirth of Liberalism': The Origins of Neo-Liberal Ideology," *Journal of Political Ideologies* 12, no. 1 (2007): 67–83.
14 Jameson, *Archaeologies*, 15.
15 For two such examples, see Jameson, *Archaeologies*, xii; and Jameson, *Valences*, 361. See note 21 for additional examples.
16 Jameson, "The Politics of Utopia," 37.
17 Jameson, *Valences*, 299.
18 Jameson, *Archaeologies*, 231.
19 Ibid.
20 Jameson, "The Politics of Utopia," 52.
21 Fredric Jameson, *Late Marxism: Adorno, or, The Persistence of the Dialectic* (New York: Verso, 1990), 245. See Grant, "The End of Critique? Ideology as Replication in Adorno and Jameson," *Culture, Theory and Critique* 55, no. 1 (2014): 1–16.
22 Jameson, *Valences*, 413; see also Jameson, *Archaeologies*, 12; and Jameson, "The Politics of Utopia," 46.
23 Jameson, *Valences*, 415.
24 Ibid.
25 Ibid.
26 Ibid., 433.
27 Ibid., 434.
28 Ibid.
29 Jameson, *Archaeologies*, 231.
30 Louis Althusser, *Essays in Self-Criticism*, trans. Grahame Lock (London: New Left, 1976), 124n19, italics in original. See also Grant, *Dialectics and Contemporary Politics: Critique and Transformation from Hegel Through Post-Marxism* (London: Routledge, 2011), 43–44, 48.
31 Jameson, *Late Marxism*, 251.
32 Does Jameson take up this path in his book *An American Utopia: Dual Power and the Universal Army*, (London: Verso, 2016), which arrived too late to be incorporated above? Uncertainly at best. "I can't be sure whether I am proposing a political program or a utopian vision, neither of which, according to me, ought to be possible any longer" (2).

III

UTOPIA AND RADICAL POLITICS

8

THE REALITY OF UTOPIA

MICHÈLE RIOT-SARCEY

Utopia unsettles. Even in the writing of history one has tried to sort out impossible reforms from signs of progress, the illuminism of the former from the realism of the latter. As Miguel Abensour underlines concerning the Marxist critique of utopias, "the critique of utopia is situated at the culmination of a real theoretical revolution—the production of a theory of history,"[1] and, whatever the political options or ideological choices of historians, this critique strongly marked the schools of historiography. Utopia in the doctrinal sense is itself a partial criticism of society, incomplete and, by the same token, unable to formulate economic and social relations that could be integrated into the science of history. Yet utopias have most often been analyzed in the spirit of doctrines. One sought to read in them the premises of social organization: the premises of association turned union organization and the premises of individual identity, in the sense that persons would now be defined by their functions, based on their work. On this basis, people have been confused with the social category to which they are assigned by virtue of their role, even their nature.

Our entire understanding of the past is read within these economic, social, and ideological frames of reference. The continuity of history depends on them. The meaning of history does not depend on social actors, to whom it no longer belongs, for it is revealed in the evolution of ideas and things. In the representation imposed on them, men and women become objects of historical knowledge based on the activities they carry out or according to the ideas that guide them. Individuals pass away, but the materiality of things and words remains: it is materiality that gives history its rhythm. Yet the hopes as well as the excesses of innovators escape both temporalities and historical "scansions": gaps remain, soon transformed into errors, since these "utopias" only attain reality through their effects, through the ideas that take hold of individuals who act in the present instant. Unintegrated, or rather removed from what makes sense in the reality of the moment, they appear like so many parasites in the course of history.

While the topicality of utopia evades the factual continuity of narrative accounts, its visible traces are politically exploited. Thus, the economic and financial work of the Saint-Simonians acquires a meaning in the general, progressive evolution of financial and industrial institutions. Economic history as well as the history of technology can easily incorporate these troublemakers of the 1830s. Condemned by what became common opinion after the elimination of "heresy," social reformers were absorbed by the philosophy of progress. As long as scattered fragments of their works remained, they could be included in the narrative as symptoms of illusions without destabilizing preconceived classifications. Or else, their reforms were lumped with others after their singularity had been taken from them: they dissolved in the collective universe.

For a long time in history books, the Saint-Simonians, like the actors of 1848, represented the female part of socialism, to which the subversive aspect of the "free woman" was relegated. Conversely, the misogyny of a man like Proudhon was overshadowed by his standing as the father of modern socialism and anarchism.[2] Of the questions central to contemporary discourse—in the eyes of the *Globe*'s correspondents and other contemporaries, as seen through their diatribes and the trials they underwent—social problems remained in the margins of history. They were always the themes to exceed the apparatus of doctrinaire morality. Above all, what was feared was the knowledge of utopia held by the people. In every risk encountered by the established order, there, too, is utopia.

Despite the large number of scholarly works on utopia, to which historians have contributed their share, questions persist. Most of the questions posed by Louis Marin in 1979 linger without satisfactory answers. "What allows us to speak of a genre of discourse called *utopia*? By what textual, discursive traits is it recognized? What allows us to speak of a semiutopian discourse, comprised of utopian elements?"[3]

Forever between two temporalities, between the real and the ideal, between the ungraspable "present instance" and a positivist representation of society, between individual desire and the construction of a dream community, between the refusal of the moment and a refuge in the imaginary, between critical theory and the utopian genre, utopian discourse has constantly been placed outside historical time. Yet if one sticks to the analysis of doctrines, the set of questions posed by Marin does find an answer: in the prison of communitarianism where the individual is lost, in the elsewhere of an ideal island separated from the continent of history, in the concordance of the present and its representation.[4] The distance created by the different utopian systems between a factual positivity and the absence of effectiveness gives utopias a textual or visual representation that never allows them to attain concreteness. That seems enough to inscribe them all in a nonplace, an elsewhere confined to the frontiers of the imagination. If, however, we try, as I do, to reestablish the historicity of utopias in the concrete effects they provoked, it becomes easy to trace the discourses that took them as their object, in particular their representation by the partisans of order, the declared adversaries of social criticism. At least when it comes to the utopias of the nineteenth century, the concept of utopia appeared forged by men of power seeking to perpetuate relations of domination. Thus, from my perspective, utopias belong to history, to the reality in which they arose.

Much has been written about the invention of the social, the birth of social relations, and the genesis of socialism.[5] Researchers have by and large confronted these questions, which emerged in the nineteenth century at the heart of political contradictions. These problems are at the same time recurrent and insoluble, more often than not rethought in a reconstructed continuity—from the present back to the past.

From the beginning of that century, the struggle against individualism led to critiques of the primacy accorded to individual liberty by the preceding generation. Fired by this conviction, most men of knowledge sought to organize the human community by rethinking relations among people as harmonious bonds among individuals in the service of objectives shared by the whole of humanity. The discovery of the force of public opinion, capable of exercising reason enough to destabilize regimes; the consciousness of a social power whose existence seems evident without being precisely identified; the will to structure disparate groups using uncontested representation; the need to construct communities by reconstituting social relations—all of this contributes to emphasizing the importance of the community over the individual. This valorization gives birth to social thought.

Because of the precedence of the idea of society over that of the individual and the individual's participation in the creation of the social realm, the individual in the nineteenth century is subordinated to the collective body and the right of each is subsumed under the law of all. In this mode of common thinking, we see that different doctrines compete to impose on the collectivity of free men their vision of the sovereign organization of society, one no longer founded on popular sovereignty but on the sovereignty of law; in other words, an organization that encompasses men with their consent while avoiding their active participation. This is a difficult wager, since once individualism is overcome, it is impossible to return to the idea of liberty acquired in the Revolution, according to which all think themselves free—actually free, or becoming so.

It is moreover necessary for authorities, whose aim is to make themselves understood by people capable of reason, to make themselves heard by all. Auguste Comte, one of the most advanced representatives of the century's thought, made it his ambition to try to define the true laws of humanity. The elaboration of common laws, whose reality is imposed not by constraint but by consent, presupposes that these laws are supported by a discourse of truth.

The elaboration of this discursive apparatus was the essential task of the political. In accordance with this objective, the political is first of all conceived as an exercise of power: the power to convince so as to articulate rules respected by all, the power to speak in order to act. Thus, from a historical point of view, it is as difficult to conceive of the social as a product of the political as it is to reduce the political to the state of existing social relations. The new force, or, if you prefer, motor of history, is shifted in the first decades of the nineteenth century to the side of the materiality of things and the creative capacities of men. It is this that Saint-Simon understood very well, that liberals sought to organize and channel, and that socialists chose as a lever of transformations to come.

Nonetheless, despite the power of these ideas, the social fact or rather social force thus foreseen, feared, or awaited, fled or sought after, remained in the realm of thought—an abstraction, one not always well understood. Guizot's courses on the "History of Civilization in Europe," his remarks on liberty, his views on the superiority of reason, his reflections on political legitimacy, and his discoveries concerning the meaning of history were heard and understood by an informed public. In the same way, the "Exposition of the Doctrine of Saint-Simon" was warmly received by the enlightened and critical part of the public. The eminent reason of Jouffroy was discovered, as was the importance of the humanism of Ballanche. The regeneration of humankind was considered possible without, for all that, being envisioned practically; the exploitation of man by man was considered over and done with without being denounced concretely; history indeed appeared "as a succession of relations of forces" without these forces being grasped in the reality of the poverty of the time, which was waiting to be revealed by those subjected to it.

If social thought was at the heart of the creative ideas of the first decades of the nineteenth century, it nonetheless remained an abstraction, limited to debates in which different doctrines clashed in the apprenticeship of democracy, rushing to put across their truths about society. Social thought participated in new ideas without being received as potentially destabilizing, even if the will to transform the order of things and reorganize the hierarchy of men did appear here and there.

With the advent of the social, the risk of the existing order being overturned emerged not from the revelation of poverty in the inquiries of 1830 to 1840, but from the awareness of a force emanating from "the most numerous and poorest class." Just as the words of Shelley apropos Peterloo—*Ye are many, they are few*—could provoke panic in England, the reality of the presence of numerous poor men and women capable of insurrection brought to the surface an unexpected political fact that materialized in this power that had been sensed in poorly understood origins. The social question exploded owing to an event staged by a group whose political potential had, until that point, been dissolved in the idea of a movement of history inscribed in social relations conceived in abstract terms. That is my analysis of the significance of November 1831. It was not only the autonomy of the working class that became manifest in the worker uprising (the First Canut Revolt); it was the confirmed will to make the right to live freely known to that part of the population entirely subjected to "free men."

It was only at that moment, in the temporal concordance between social practices and discursive developments, that reformist thinking corresponded to necessities thrown into relief by the event. It is here that we find the *reality of utopia*: when possible reforms are concretely envisioned. It is no longer a question of becoming better, in a reasonable philosophy of progress, but of an expected disruption of relations of domination through a reorganization of labor, a new redistribution of property, a reconceived allocation of wealth. This possibility, presented to the critical wisdom of enlightened men, offered the conditions for realizing the hopes of the "most numerous and poorest class." Likewise, it allowed women to perceive the end of a subjection said to be anchored in the specificity of female nature. *In that moment, the reality of utopia created the revolutionary spirit*, not with a view to seizing power but with a will to reestablishing the rights of all, which implied structuring society otherwise. Here was utopia's impossible integration into history, from the hitherto privileged point of view of spokesmen who reinforced power before thinking of the transformation of social relations.

This *reality of utopia* was not integrated into doctrines, be they Saint-Simonian or Fourierist. Rather, it can be found in what is conventionally called concrete utopias. It becomes actual with the recognition of reformist ideas by men and women who are confident in their expectation of a better future, but who demonstrate, above all, a will to radically transform relations among individuals. Consequently, it is not utopian doctrines that the moral and political authorities fear; it is the hopes they engender in the actuality of a social event, the index of political dysfunction. From a sense of division among the ruling classes, every strategy is deployed to reject projects of reform as illusory and impossible by elaborating a discourse of the nonplace. The construction of utopian origins in the 1840s is all the more important since the working masses become aware of the idea of a reorganization of labor by the producers themselves.

At the core of this discursive configuration, the separation of the political from the social became a major preoccupation. It was a matter of dissociating the rights of the poor from the process of political representation reserved for ostensibly free men. The social question was thus all about timing, education, and moral improvement, under the control of a would-be representative political system.

There has been too great a tendency until now to take as objects of study doctrines whose abstract constructions could be tied to the utopias of the ancien régime. Yet this rapprochement, far from being a given, is the product of a political strategy that can be grasped in its historicity. The doctrines first elaborated on the basis of critical reflection on civilization following the Revolution entered into political actuality not in the form of dreams, but through the practice of men and women convinced of the well-founded radicality of the reforms they sought to realize, avoiding, if possible, the (obligatory) passage through power relations. Indeed, this actuality excluded even the idea of revolution, considered as the running board of men aspiring to power, according to the view of Jean Deroin, prototype of a utopian if ever there was one. Thus, another sense of history took shape, far from teleological visions; its reality imposed itself on the confluence of events, reformist ideas, and needs clearly exposed as soon as they can be heard. But the hearing was constrained by the event and extremely brief, since political discourses promptly imposed their interpretation by implementing a strategy of recuperating conflicts—the very object of the political.

Whence the difficulty of restoring these singular moments—a task all the more important as they participate in the movement of history—hidden beneath the traces of words spoken by those who show us the past they have rewritten. Critical potentials, like the prospects of transforming social relations made possible by the perception of dysfunction, disappear beneath interpretive writings speaking "the truth" of the event in the name of political realism. The discourse of truth, founded on the appropriation of universality, denounced as false in this brief time misunderstood by history, was reconstituted thanks to the sum of interests it defended. In its recuperating and hence totalizing vision, it absorbed the particularities of innovative proposals by projecting them into the future under cover of an industrial progress that advances in a slow but cumulative march toward expected improvements. This is why, outside this projection of a social development entirely subjected to the political system, the *reality of utopia* appears as a determining factor in a possible subversion; its intervention is not inscribed in a projected future but in the daily present of "the most numerous and poorest class."

Are historians, then, called upon to look into political discourses that aim to render conflicts historically insignificant, calling them "social" to this end? Understood according to customary criteria, from Guizot to Marx, the continuity of history can be read through political transformations stemming from relations of forces. But the *reality of utopia*, which does not take effect through the seizure of power, cannot be translated into the dominant terms of political language; it only allows aspirations for a better life, situated precisely outside relations of domination. Consequently, this *reality* cannot attain historical visibility. Public discourses develop above the plurality of reformist projects, becoming incomprehensible in the face of political signifiers that designate them as nonsense.

In this way democracy, which at one time signified the exercise of popular sovereignty, was convicted of being utopian when faced with the practice of representative democracy exercised by a privileged minority. In this way liberty, demanded by all those, male and female, who did not possess it, was identified, in its political signification, with property. In this way, finally, the democratic and social republic saw itself qualified as utopian after the failure of the insurrection of June 1848.

Nonetheless, despite the tireless production of the dominant strain of political discourse, the polysemy of concepts, even when they are instrumentalized, persists, if only by reference to their becoming concrete. Consequently and unavoidably, the *reality of utopia* interferes in a punctual way in lifeless political thought by resisting it through practices and words used in other senses, which are closer to universality. All the same, indeterminacy is unacceptable for a political system formed between universal principles and practices of power. The object of the political is first of all to confer a dominant meaning on the references that establish its legitimacy. Political interlocution exists only among equals, individuals who give words identical meaning. The rest, destined for an indistinct crowd, is only a discourse of domination. From this arises, for a historian, the necessity of reconstituting the historicity of concepts and words to allow the reader to understand the conflicts that reveal the production of meaning.

Faced with this all-encompassing unity of linguistic formations produced by the political, the researcher is left with nothing but a multiplicity of isolated, disparate interventions that cannot be united in an arrangement equivalent to political discourse, which denies them any proper meaning. These interventions are removed from history, evacuated to the nonplace of utopia. For these reasons, political history can only be written by re-creating the tension between constructed discourses and singular interventions of refusal and resistance—interventions that derive all their meaning from discontinuities in the political process.

Outside the genre of literature, beneath or beyond the reconstruction of the world they project, utopias—which I would rather call "critical ideas," historically specific, contemporaneous with the development of representative democracy—contribute de facto to the movement of history. If speech, dreams, and subversive or simply reformist proposals are soon covered over by normative discourses, once order is restored they persist and spread at the foundations of appearances. Diffused, interpreted, commented upon, and reappropriated, they are exchanged without any necessary continuity of aim in the present concerns of a receiver or speaker. As subterranean ideas, they resurface thanks to other interrogations, other impasses, other dysfunctions, perceived individually or experienced collectively. Latent, they always arise as a potential risk to the existing social hierarchy and the preservation of order. Moreover, whether they are made into object lessons or designated as sources of unrest, it is always these critical ideas that serve as fixing points in reconstructing and updating the political apparatuses necessary for ordering society. Moral values and social norms as well as discursive practices are reinvented so as to be operative and convincing in the face of a destabilizing gap afforded by an alternative practice or project.

Politics unfolds in this space between the excess of criticism and assimilable values and norms: at the close of every civil or class war, at the end of each revolution, particularly in the nineteenth century, the goal of political confrontation was to integrate some or all of the actors of the conflict into the orderly framework of representative democracy, rejecting the excess as utopia. In 1830, the renewed Charter allowed the dismissal of some killjoys, who were understood as republicans. But the integration of a divided middle class was a time of hesitation, ripe for so-called utopian propaganda. It was only in the 1840s that things took a definitive direction, in setting priorities by distinguishing between the social and the political. From then on, the spokespeople of different classes were convinced that social transformations happen above all through the expansion of suffrage, that is to say, by going through the stage of the political. From that moment, in 1848, it became obvious that, with "universal" suffrage secured, class war was too much. Inassimilable, it was then represented as an excessive expression of the utopias born in February of the same year. A collective silence accompanied the ordering of the Second Empire, but individual voices made themselves heard—strange, profoundly dissonant voices, such as that of Joseph Déjacque, already heard by Valentin Pelosse, inaudible within the framework of the political system and workers' organizations soon considered representative by the powers that be. Nevertheless, at the margins of legality, critical thoughts always spread in different ways; they would surge anew, though never identically, in the moment of the Paris Commune.[6] Here was utopia according to Joseph Déjacque, "a dream unrealized, but not unrealizable."[7]

It would be possible to follow the subterranean path of critique right up to our day. It is there—present, diffuse, not always articulated, and for this reason little known by certified representatives. Despite its rhetorical quasi-absence, this critique belongs to the current project of European construction; it serves as a reference point for both those who are dissatisfied with one-track thinking and those men and women in power who are attentive to the risks of popular overflow and hence concerned to reactivate values believed to have fallen into disuse, such as the *nation* or *republican principles*. Restored citizenship, a local endeavor, is lost in the labyrinth of its instrumentalization. Today, concrete sovereignty, where everyone can exercise a freedom they have won, still looks like utopia.

NOTES

Originally published as the conclusion to *Le Réel de l'utopie: Essai sur le politique au XIXe siècle* (The reality of utopia: An essay on the political in the nineteenth century) (Paris: Albin Michel, 1998), 259–270.

1. Miguel Abensour, chapter 1 of this volume, 9.
2. The updated *Dictionnaire biographique du mouvement ouvrier français*, le "Maitron," edited by Claude Pennetier, Jean Risacher, and Michel Cordillot, allows us to fill this gap by restoring to Proudhon his misogyny.
3. Louis Marin, "Le Maintenant utopique" (The utopian now), in *Stratégies de l'utopie: Colloque organisé au Centre Thomas More* (Paris: Galilée, 1979), 246, proceedings from a colloquium organized by Pierre Furter and Gérard Raulet.

4   On this point, see articles by Gérard Raulet, Michel de Certeau, and André Reszler in *Stratégies de l'utopie*.
5   It is impossible to cite all the work on this question. Let us mention, however, Pierre Macherey's "Aux sources des rapports sociaux: Bonald, Saint-Simon, Guizot," *Genèses* 9 (1992): 25–43 ("Conservatism, Liberalism, Socialism"). There is no disputing that the "discovery" of "the social," in particular by Saint-Simon and his disciples, greatly contributed to inflecting the course of nineteenth-century ideas and hence weighed on conceptions of social relations. But whatever the pertinence of modern ideas, they only ever have an impact when animated by a political practice that always interprets and redirects their object, originally conceived in the abstract.
6   On this, see the two articles by Abensour published in *Textures* (both in this volume).
7   Joseph Déjacque, "Qu'est-ce que l'utopie," in *À bas les chefs: Écrits libertaires (1847–1863)*, ed. Valentin Pelosse (Paris: Champ Libre, 1971), 131.

9

NEGATIVITY AND UTOPIA IN THE GLOBAL JUSTICE MOVEMENT

MICHAEL LÖWY

The global justice movement is without a doubt the most important phenomenon of antisystemic resistance of the beginning of the twenty-first century. This vast, nebulous "movement of movements," which has taken visible form since the regional or world social forums and the great protest demonstrations—against the WTO, the G8, or the imperial war in Iraq—does not correspond to the usual forms of social or political action. A large decentralized network, it is multiple, diverse, and heterogeneous, joining trade unions and peasant movements, NGOs and indigenous organizations, women's movements, as well as ecological associations, intellectuals, and young activists. Far from being a weakness, this plurality is one of the sources of the movement's increasing and expansive strength.

The international solidarities born inside this vast network are of a new type, somewhat different from those that have characterized the internationalist mobilizations of the 1960s and 1970s. At that time, solidarity was mobilized in support of liberation movements, whether in the global South—the Algerian, Cuban, or Vietnamese revolutions—or in Eastern Europe, with Polish dissidents or the Prague Spring. A little later, in the 1980s, it was solidarity with the Sandinistas in Nicaragua or Solidarność in Poland.

This generous and fraternal tradition of solidarity *with* the oppressed has not disappeared in the new movement for global justice that began during the 1990s—far from it. An obvious example is the sympathy and support for the Zapatistas since the uprising of the indigenous peoples of Chiapas on January 1, 1994. But this also marks the appearance of something new, a change of perspective. In 1996, the Zapatista Army of National Liberation convoked in the mountains of Chiapas, an international encounter—ironically designated as "Intergalactic" by Subcomandante Marcos—against neoliberalism and for humanity. The thousands of participants from the forty countries participating in this meeting—which can perhaps be considered the first sign of what would later be called "global justice"—*also* came, to be sure, out of solidarity with the Zapatistas, but the objective of the meeting, defined by the latter, was much greater: the search for convergences in the common struggle against a common adversary, neoliberalism, and the debate about possible alternatives for humanity.

Here is the new character of the solidarities developing within or around the movement of global resistance to capitalist globalization: the fight for immediate common objectives common to all—for example, the failure of the WTO—and the common search for new paradigms of civilization. In other words, more than solidarity *with*, it is solidarity *among* diverse organizations, social movements, or political forces from different countries or continents that help one another and join together in the same struggle, against the same planetary enemy.

To give an example, the international peasant network Via Campesina gathers movements as diverse as the French Peasants' Confederation, the Landless Workers Movement of Brazil, and the great peasant movements in India. These organizations mutually support one another, exchange their experience, and act in common against neoliberal politics and against their common adversaries: agribusiness multinationals, seed company monopolies, producers of GMOs, large property owners. Their solidarity is reciprocal and together they constitute one of the most powerful, active, and energetic elements of the worldwide movement against capitalist globalization. One could give other examples, in the areas of unionism or feminism—the Women's World March—environmentalism or politics. Of course, the process of revitalizing old solidarities and inventing new ones is still in its infancy. It is fragile, limited, uncertain, and quite incapable, for the moment, of threatening the crushing domination of global capital and the planetary hegemony of neoliberalism. It constitutes only the strategic link to the internationalism of the future.

The dynamics of the global justice movement comprise three distinct but complementary moments: *the negativity of resistance*, *concrete proposals*, and *the utopia of another world*.

The first moment, the movement's point of departure, is *refusal*, protest, the imperative of resisting the existing state of things. It constitutes in fact that *International of Resistance* Jacques Derrida appealed to in his book *Specters of Marx* (1993). The initial motivation of the crowds that mobilized in Seattle in 1999 was the will to oppose, actively, not "globalization" as such, but its capitalist and liberal form, corporate globalization with its pageant of injustices and catastrophes: rising inequalities between North and South, unemployment, social exclusion, destruction of the environment, imperial wars, crimes against humanity. The movement was, moreover, born with a cry, issued by the Zapatistas in 1994: *¡Ya basta!* Enough is enough! The force of the movement comes above all from this *radical negativity*, inspired by a profound and irreducible *indignation*. Celebrating the dignity of indignation and the unconditional refusal of injustice, Daniel Bensaïd wrote: "The burning tide of indignation is not dissolved by the tepid waters of consensual resignation. . . . Indignation is a beginning. A way of getting up and getting going. One is outraged, one rises up, and then one sees."[1] The movement's radicality results, in large measure, from this capacity for revolt and insubordination, this intractable tendency to say *no*. The movement's critics and the conformist media strongly insist on the excessively "negative" character of the movement, its "purely" protest nature, the absence of alternative "realistic" proposals. One ought to resolutely refuse this blackmail: even if the movement did not have a single proposal to make, its revolt would be no less totally justified. The street demonstrations against the WTO, the G8, or imperialist war are the concentrated expression, visible and undeniable, of this defiance toward the rules of the game imposed by the powerful. The movement is proud of its active negativity, its core of protest and rebellion. Without this radical feeling of refusal, the global justice movement would not exist.

Against which enemy is this refusal directed? Is it the international financial institutions (WTO, IMF, World Bank)? Or neoliberal policies? Or the great multinational monopolies? All these forces, responsible for the marketization of the world, are targets of the movement. But the movement is even more radical. The word "radical" signifies, as we know, going to the root of problems. But what is the root of the totalitarian domination of banks and monopolies, of the dictatorship of financial markets, of imperial wars, if not the capitalist system itself? Certainly, not all the elements of the global justice movement are ready to draw this conclusion; some still dream of a return to neo-Keynesianism, to the postwar boom or regulated capitalism, with a human face. These "moderates" have their place in the movement, but it is undeniable that a more radical tendency tends to predominate. Most of the documents coming from the movement question not only neoliberal and warmongering policies, but also *the power of capital* itself. Let us take as an example the "World Social Forum Charter of Principles," written by the Brazilian Organizing Committee—on which sit not only trade unions and peasant movements, but also NGOs and a representative of the Catholic Church's Commission for Justice and Peace—and approved, with some modifications, by the International Council of the World Social Forum. This document, among the global justice movement's more representative and "consensual," affirms: "The World Social Forum is an open meeting place for reflective thinking, democratic debate of ideas, formulation of proposals, free exchange of experiences, and interlinking for effective action, by groups and movements of civil society that are opposed to neoliberalism and to domination of the world by capital and any form of imperialism, and are committed to building a planetary society directed toward fruitful relationships among mankind. . . . The alternatives proposed at the World Social Forum stand in opposition to a process of globalization commanded by the large multinational corporations."[2] The movement's main watchword, "the world is not a commodity," is not so far from the ideas of a certain Karl Marx, who wrote, in the *1844 Manuscripts*: in the capitalist system, "the worker becomes an ever cheaper commodity the more commodities he creates. The devaluation of the world of men is in direct proportion to the increasing value of the world of things."[3] The radicalness of global justice refusal concerns the capitalist nature of domination.

Even so, contrary to what the pen pushers of the official consensus claim, the movement does not lack *alternative proposals* that are concrete, urgent, practical, and immediately realizable. To be sure, no authority approved a "common program," and no political force imposed "its" project. But one can see coming into view, in the course of the forums and debates, a set of claims that are, if not unanimous, at least largely accepted and taken up by the movement: for example, the abolition of Third World debt, the taxation of financial transactions, the suppression of tax havens, a moratorium on GMOs, the right of people to feed themselves, the effective equality between men and women, the defense and extension of public services, the priority of health care, education, and culture, the protection of the environment. These claims have been elaborated by international global justice networks—the Women's World March, Attac, Focus on Global South, Via Campesina, Committee for the Abolition of Third World Debt, and the like—and by different social movements and have been debated in the forums. One of the latter's great qualities is to enable the meeting and exchange between feminists and trade unionists, believers and nonbelievers, activists from the North and from the South. This process of mutual confrontation and enrichment is not free of disputes, but little by little one can see the outlines of a set of common proposals.

Are these proposals "realistic"? The question is badly posed. In the existing relation of forces, the elites and the dominant classes refuse to consider them en bloc; they are unimaginable to neoliberal dogma, they are intolerable to the representatives of capital—or, in the hypocritical version of social liberals, they are "unfortunately unfeasible." But it is enough that the relation of forces changes and that public opinion mobilizes for those "responsible" to be obliged to draw back, to make concessions, all the while trying to void them of substance. But the important thing about these proposals is that they are expandable: any partial victory, any conquest, any advance, lets us move to the next stage, to a higher stage, to a more radical claim. It is a "transitory" dynamic, different in form from that of the traditional workers movement, that leads, eventually, to questioning the system itself.

We touch here upon the third moment, just as important as the previous two: the movement's *utopian dimension*. It too is radical: "another world is possible." It is not simply a matter of correcting the excesses of the capitalist/industrial world and its monstrous neoliberal policies, but of dreaming and fighting for *another civilization*, another economic and social paradigm, and another form of living together on the planet. Beyond the many concrete and specific proposals, the movement includes a more ambitious, more "global," more universal transformative perspective. Of course, there too one searches in vain for a common project, a consensual program of reform or revolution. Global justice utopia manifests itself only in the sharing of certain common values. They are what outlines the contours of this other "possible world."

The first of these values is *the human being itself*. The movement's utopia is resolutely humanist; it demands that the needs and aspirations of human beings become the vital core of a reorganization of the economy and of society. Its revolt against the marketization of human beings and their relations, against the transformation of love, culture, life, and health into commodities, presupposes another form of social life, beyond reification and fetishism. It is not by accident that the movement addresses itself to all humans, even if it privileges the oppressed and the exploited as actors of social change. The defense of the environment—it too is humanist in inspiration: preserving ecological equilibria, protecting nature against the predations of capitalist productivism, is the precondition of ensuring the continuity of human life on the planet.

Another essential value of global justice utopia is *democracy*. The idea of participatory democracy as a superior form of the exercise of citizenship, beyond the limits of traditional representative systems—because it allows the population direct exercise of its power of decision and control—is one of the movement's central themes. It is a case of a "utopian" value to the extent that it calls into question existing forms of power, but at the same time it is already put into practice, in experimental form, in various cities, beginning of course with Porto Alegre. The great challenge, from the perspective of a project of an alternative society, is to extend democracy into the economic and social realm. Why grant an elite exclusive power in *this* domain when one rejects it in the political sphere?

Capital has replaced the three great revolutionary values of the past—liberty, equality, fraternity—with more "modern" concepts: liberalism, equity, charity. The global justice utopia takes up the values of 1789, but gives them a new reach. Thus, liberty is not only the freedom of expression, organization, thought, criticism, demonstration—achieved with difficulty through the centuries of struggle against absolutism, fascism, and dictatorship. Rather, it is also, and today more than ever, the freedom from another form of absolutism: that of the dictatorship of financial markets and the elite of bankers and heads of multinational enterprises who impose their own interests on the whole planet. As for equality, it concerns not only the "social division" between the wealthy and the dispossessed, but also the inequality between nations, ethnic groups, and men and women. Finally, fraternity—which seems to be limited to brothers (*frates*)—should be replaced by *solidarity*, that is to say, the relations of cooperation, sharing, mutual aid. The expression "civilization of solidarity" is a nice summary of the movement's alternative project. It signifies not only a radically different economic and political structure, but also, above all, an alternative society that celebrates the ideas of the common good, general interest, universal rights, and free access.

Another important value of global justice is *diversity*. The new world that the movement dreams of is the complete opposite of a homogeneous universe, where everyone should imitate a single model. We want "a world in which many worlds have their place," say the Zapatistas. The plurality of languages, cultures, music, cuisines, forms of life is an immense wealth that ought to be cultivated.

These values do not define a paradigm of society to come. They furnish the paths, openings, windows to the possible. The way to utopia is not all mapped out; it is the marchers themselves who chart it.

For many of the participants of forums and demonstrations, *socialism* is the name of this utopia. It is a hope shared by Marxists and left-libertarians, Christians and left-environmentalists, along with a significant number of activists from workers, peasant, feminist, and indigenous movements. A socialist democracy means that the major socioeconomic choices, investment priorities, the fundamental direction of production and distribution are democratically discussed and established by the population itself, not by a handful of exploiters or the so-called laws of the market (or, again, in an already bankrupt variant, by an all-powerful policy bureau). It is not a question of imposing socialism as the movement's program, but the debate about socialism is a legitimate element of the confrontation of ideas about alternatives. At the second World Social Forum, in February 2002, the international network Via Campesina, with the participation of thousands of delegates, organized a three-day cycle of conferences on socialism.

At any rate, it is not a matter of the movement waiting for the "singing tomorrows,"[4] but of working, here and now. Every Social Forum, every local experiment in participatory democracy, every collective occupation of the land by peasants, every internationally concerted action against war is a prefiguration of the global justice utopia, and is inspired by its values, which are those of a civilization of solidarity.

NOTES

Originally published as "Négativité et utopie du mouvement altermondialiste," *Contretemps* 11 (September 2014): 44–50.

1. Daniel Bensaïd, *Les Irréductibles: Théorèmes de la résistance à l'air du temps* (Paris: Textuel, 2001), 106.
2. Appendix to Bernard Cassen, *Tout a commencé à Porto Alegre* (Paris: Mille et une nuits, 2003), 166.
3. www.marxists.org/archive/marx/works/1844/manuscripts/labour.htm.
4. *Les lendemains qui chantent* was a slogan of the French communist party, indicating the future toward which they were working—Editors' note.

10

UTOPIANISM AND PREFIGURATION

RUTH KINNA

For anarchists, utopias are about action. As Uri Gordon argues, utopias are "umbilically connected to the idea of social revolution."[1] The kind of action utopia describes is a matter of debate. This essay examines how utopian thinking shapes anarchist thought and highlights some recent shifts in the political uses of utopia. Utopianism is not treated as an abstract concept or method, or as a literary genre or place—because that is not how anarchists have understood the idea. Utopia, Gordon notes, "has always meant something more than a hypothetical exercise in designing a perfect society." As a revolutionary idea, utopia is instead linked to the principle of prefiguration.

Prefiguration has been identified as a core concept in contemporary anarchist thinking and it is increasingly invoked to highlight the distinctiveness of anarchist practices, actions, and movements. In 2011, two months after the start of Occupy Wall Street, David Graeber identified prefigurative politics as one of the movement's four characteristically anarchist principles, the other three being direct action, illegalism, and the rejection of hierarchy. Hinting at the utopianism of the concept, he described Occupy as a genuine attempt "to create the institutions of the new society in the shell of the old." Pursuing the idea, he linked prefiguration to the creation of "democratic General Assemblies," consensus decision making, and a range of mutual aid, self-help institutions—including "kitchens, libraries, clinics, media centres."[2] The spontaneous emergence of these bodies and practices attested to the practicality of radical aspirations, in ways that might be deemed to be at odds with the traditional idea of utopia as an imaginary realm of ideal nonexistence or impossibility. Yet insofar as actions like Occupy expose the flimsiness of official dismissals of egalitarian social change, captured in the mantra TINA, they are also utopian.

While there is little dispute about the centrality of prefiguration in anarchist literatures, there is considerable variation about the utopian politics that prefigurative action variously encourages and rules against. The essay shows how blueprint utopianism (associated with mid-nineteenth-century utopian socialists) serves as a foil for contemporary anarchism. It also touches on Miguel Abensour's well-known framing of "utopia as desire" in order to illustrate the dovetailing of antiutopian utopianism with some recent conceptions of anarchist utopianism. By examining debates about the interrelationship of these two concepts and, in particular, the continuities and discontinuities in the history of anarchist thought, it is possible to capture the spectrum of utopian political practice that prefiguration describes, extending from a utopian commitment to a sociological framing of alternatives to a dystopian embrace of a psychology of desiring.

PREFIGURATION

For Benjamin Franks, prefiguration is the principle anarchists use to assess the legitimacy of actions, and he defines the concept in terms of a relationship between ends and means. A core anarchist commitment, he argues, is that "means have to prefigure ends."[3] In normative political theory, the commitment to prefiguration leads anarchists to reject both consequentialism, the idea that the outcomes of actions are the proper measures of rightness, and deontology, which instead considers the justness of actions in terms of duty or conformity with established norms or laws.[4] Prefiguration, Franks argues, steers anarchists toward virtue ethics, a position that grounds morality in character or behavior and the intentions of actors. In addition, Franks associates prefiguration with what he terms "pragmatic ethics." This means that anarchists reject instrumentalism, or the principle that "the success of a plan is determined by its efficiency in meeting the objectives."[5] Franks associates instrumentalism with Max Weber. However, his elision of instrumentalism with consequentialism leads him to identify a range of exponents, from J. S. Mill to Lenin, and even to apply it to doctrines that seek to decouple the evaluation of action from considerations of rightness by the substitution of mere "necessity." Machiavellianism and Nechaevism are examples. In contrast to this broad body of thought, anarchist prefiguration collapses the distinction between means and ends. In terms reminiscent of Gandhi's anarchist-friendly precept to be the change you wish to see, Franks argues that actions "embody the forms of social relation that actors wish to see develop."[6] The political implications are that everyday behaviors are central to anarchist practice and that the choices individuals make in the conduct of their lives provide a primary locus for anarchist actions. This understanding is echoed by Cindy Milstein. Prefiguration, she argues, is

> the idea that there should be an ethically consistent relationship between the means and the ends. Means and ends aren't the same, but anarchists utilize means that point in the direction of their ends. They choose action or projects based on how these fit into longer-terms aims. Anarchists participate in the present in the ways that they would like to participate, much more fully and with much more self-determination, in the future—and encourage others to do so as well. Prefigurative politics thus aligns one's values to one's practice.[7]

The priority attached to intention as a standard of rightness is not new in anarchist thought. The nineteenth-century anarchist Peter Kropotkin defended the assassins of Alexander II in 1881 in precisely these terms.[8] Similarly, anarchism has long been associated with the rejection of instrumentalism: Weber framed his critique of Tolstoy in terms of the priority anarchists attached to the "ethics of ultimate ends" over the "ethics of responsibility."[9] Yet the term "prefiguration" does not appear in nineteenth-century anarchist discourses, at least not commonly. For some contemporary writers this absence is significant, and its emergence in the last two decades or so captures the sense that there has been a shift in thinking, or perhaps in emphasis, in contemporary anarchist thought in the post-Second World War period.¹⁰ Indeed, some tie the concept tightly to recent activism. The strong association sometimes made between labor organizing and historical anarchism, on the one hand, and the dichotomy between social and lifestyle anarchism, on the other, has encouraged this view (though proponents of prefiguration overwhelmingly reject the critique of lifestyle that Murray Bookchin advanced when he cemented this distinction).¹¹ To give one example, in "Trying to Occupy Harvard" Philip Cartelli notes:

> Since the beginning of Occupy Wall Street, much has been made of its prefigurative politics—an increasingly popular mode of political organization and practice among grassroots movements of the Left over the past half-century that models the kind of democratic society in which they aspire to live. In my experience, however, such radical lifestyle politics are more likely to appeal to activists outside of traditional political groupings such as labor unions or specific issue and policy-oriented organizations.¹²

Marianne Maeckelbergh offers a similar account, tracking prefiguration through postwar feminism, "the anti-nuclear and peace movements, the racial justice movements in the US, anti-colonial and anti-developmentalism movements in the global South, and later the do-it-yourself and environmental movements—all of which fed into the alterglobalization movement that challenged the right of multilateral organizations (WTO/WB/IMF/G8) to rule the world."¹³ In this context prefiguration is an expression of countercultural politics, which disappeared at the end of the 1960s to reemerge in recent anticapitalist campaigns. And rather than attach to "anarchism" as such—a doctrine suggestive of thick ideological commitment and defined practice—prefiguration is instead linked to practices free from specific content. Maeckelbergh finds the contrast in old-style programmatic politics:

> The practices today find their predecessors in movements of the 1960s, when activists questioned on a large scale the need for a unitary political program of revolutionary change (in other words, the need to determine ahead of time the one thing your movement is "for"). These ideas often took the form of practicing "participatory democracy" and building "autonomous" social relations.¹⁴

The narrowly workerist assumptions about the character and composition of the historical movement are contestable. Moreover, the identification of prefigurative politics with particular waves of activity or forms of practice betrays a tendency to historicism that is difficult to reconcile with the types of agency that prefiguration spotlights. The significance of the means-ends dynamic in prefigurative politics is not that it maps actions to a prescribed set of approved forms, but that it rules against judgments based on the consideration of outcomes or, at least, results determined by anyone other than the "local agent."[15] Similarly, the weight attached to the choices that activists make when engaging in action is not that prefiguration results in moral consensus or political uniformity, but only that it supports direct action: the power of transformation is placed in the hands of individuals, acting by themselves or in collaboration with others.

In current discourse, prefiguration is used to describe the creative power of collective struggles,[16] the project of building a new world in the heart of the old, in the ordinary sense, as a foreshadowing,[17] or to describe ways in which revolutionary desires are expressed in respect of the intimate relationship between social transformation and action in the present.[18] Like Franks, Graeber places the commitment to direct action in everyday life at the heart of prefigurative discourses.[19] Prefiguration is linked to creativity, subversion, and playfulness and to the development of alternative relationships and ways of living. Prefigurative politics, Federico Campagna and Emanuele Campiglio argue, "go hand in hand with the desire for long-term, broad-horizon imagination"; prefiguration is about "the continuous exercise of testing the imaginary landscapes against the necessities and the subterranean flows of daily life."[20]

In all these senses, prefiguration contests the frequent and unthinking association of anarchism with destruction, and instead stresses the experimental, productive, and innovative characteristics of anarchist practices that seek to replace or challenge hierarchical and oppressive social forms. As Franks argues, prefigurative politics describes the rejection of vanguardism and the "scientific" certainties on which revolutionary elitism has been constructed as well as the repudiation of the varieties of socialism that vanguard strategies have produced—classless but nevertheless highly centralized and industrialized dictatorships.[21] Just as it refuses the imposition of even fleeting, temporary dictatorial means, prefiguration embraces actions that achieve nothing more than transitory, momentary gains in autonomy. The local, direct actions that bring these gains about foster behaviors that are transformative. In sum, prefiguration rules out certain approaches to social change, but leaves the specification of behaviors open to activists. In this respect, and in the context of debates about the continuities and discontinuities of the historical and modern anarchist movements, Franks's approach to prefiguration appears malleable to the politics of the nineteenth century, to post-Second World War campaigns, and to contemporary forms of activism. Nevertheless, as the relationship between utopianism and prefiguration reveals, the utopianism of the historical movement appears to rule against this application. In Franks's terms, the suspicion is that this form of utopianism admits a gap between means and ends, compromising prefiguration by directing action toward the realization of predetermined goals.

PREFIGURATION AND UTOPIANISM

It is common to find contemporary anarchists describe prefiguration as a utopian politics. In *Anarchism and Its Aspirations*, Cindy Milstein argues that envisioning a world "beyond hierarchy" is "part of prefiguration." And, hinting at the continuity of anarchist thought, she suggests that by adopting prefigurative politics, contemporary anarchism "retains a utopian impulse."[22] Milstein's defense of anarchist utopianism is advanced explicitly as a rejection of two other types. Utopia, she argues, is neither "a thought experiment. Nor is it a blueprint or rigid plan." Franks makes a similar point. Prefiguration, he argues, is compatible with utopianism, but he qualifies the ways in which it is so; and he shares Milstein's worry that utopias typically fall into one of two main types: abstract ideal or blueprint. The first runs counter to prefiguration by stripping action of practical content and the second by enforcing an ideal social arrangement that renders prefigurative engagement impossible. Returning to the dynamic of the means-ends relationship, Franks argues that the role of utopian thinking cannot be to delineate the "end" or purpose of action, for this encourages both consequentialism and statist thinking: both the idea that the prospect of the end mitigates the harm of the means deployed for its achievement and, in the first place, that the goal can be predetermined.

The conception of utopianism that Franks and Milstein are most concerned to resist is the one painted by antiutopian liberals, which links utopianism to rigid social planning, moral perfectionism, and the totalitarian determination of individual well-being. In these schemas, utopians often appear as dangerous fantasists, completely out of touch with reality and blind to the social costs of their ideals. In critical literatures on anarchism, this kind of utopianism is typically inscribed in portraits of Bakunin.[23] Milstein's response is to treat utopia as a method linked to practice rather than a descriptor of a social condition. Anarchist utopianism "dreams up ways to embody its ethics, and then tries to implement them."[24] Parecon, Michael Albert's model of participatory economics, might be considered an example of this approach, though it is not an example she cites.[25] Franks follows a similar tack. In prefigurative politics, he contends, utopia might illustrate anarchist principles, model their practical operation, inspire actions, or provide a springboard for the development of new critical discourses, as long as it does not serve as the end itself.

In addition, Franks develops a psychology of action. Anarchist utopianism, he argues, might be regarded as a myth, comparable to Sorel's myth of violence. Like the Sorelian myth, anarchist utopianism is unaffected by the failure of its achievement:[26] to borrow Milstein's neat formulation, "anarchists are used to loss."[27] In this guise, the myth indicates an eternal willingness to endure the impossibility of success as a condition of struggle. In addition, anarchist utopianism shares the Sorelian myth's irrational qualities, which Franks captures in the notion of desire. In light of antiutopian liberal critique, the invocation of Sorel appears odd; as Mark Antliff argues, both the Janus-faced nature of Sorel's thought and his appeal to anesthetized violence are deeply problematic. Nevertheless, Antliff's careful analysis of Sorel also helps explain why myth remains attractive to contemporary activists as "a catalyst for revolutionary inspiration." For Sorel, Antliff notes, "myths presented the public with a visionary ideal whose stark contrast with present reality would agitate the masses." His invocation of the myth was a marker of the role he attached to emotion and intuition in social action. It was also a sign of his rejection of "rational planning" and, more pointedly, of the idea, which he associated with socialist reformism, of using social blueprints to delineate policies of incremental action.[28]

A strong tradition of critical anarchist thinking, stretching back to Proudhon's refusal of all systems, attests to the antiutopianism Franks and Milstein describe. Anarchism's antiutopianism was cogently restated by Rudolf Rocker.[29] Nevertheless, the association of anarchism with abstraction and blueprint utopianism infuses a lot of contemporary anarchist thinking. The title of Christian Marazzi's preface to *What We Are Fighting For*, "Exodus Without Promised Land," hints at the persuasiveness of anarchist self-criticism.[30] More pointedly, Uri Gordon, Simon Tormey, and Saul Newman have advanced the critique and sought to distance contemporary anarchism from dominant nineteenth-century doctrines. Kropotkin is often identified as an exponent of the wrong sort of utopianism: a form that is inflexible, focused on the destination rather than the journey, and rooted in abstract, essentialist conceptions of nature and human flourishing. In Newman's recent work, the relevant distinction is between

> "scientific utopianism," in which a future anarchist society is founded on scientific and rational principles and will be the inevitable outcome of a revolution against the state; and another that might be termed "utopianism of the here and now," in which the focus is less on what happens after the revolution, and more on a transformation of social relations within the present.[31]

Franks's discussion of twentieth-century utopian political theory helps uncover the reason why historical anarchist traditions have been persistently identified with blueprint utopianism. His view—that anarchists are more open to engagement with postmodernism than other types of socialists (specifically Leninists) because of the fluid conceptions of utopia that postmodernism supports—points to theoretical developments in the field of utopian studies. Miguel Abensour's scholarship has been extremely influential here. In a recent discussion, which Newman recommends, Abensour defines "utopianism" as an idea of "becoming," a term he uses to describe an ontological condition linked to the creativity, individuality, and inventiveness of desire. There is a broad sense in which utopianism captures a particular desire, but it is not one that can be given content. Persistent utopias, in distinction to "eternal forms," designate "a stubborn impulse toward freedom and justice—the end of domination, of relations of servitude, and of relations of exploitation." This impulse is an "orientation toward what is different, the wish for the advent of a radical alterity here and now."[32]

These innovative developments in utopian studies tend to historicize forms of utopian antiutopianism, largely in the critique of vulgar Marxist traditions, much in the same way that contemporary activists historicize prefigurative politics. Yet the divergence of anarchist and Marxist historical traditions is rarely noted and the result is that the convergence of anarchist utopianism and contemporary utopian antiutopianism is not treated, as Franks argues, as a shift in utopian thinking, but as a revision of anarchism. Thus, for Newman, their dovetailing informs the rejection of two currents: one that associates nineteenth-century socialist traditions with workerism and a second that treats socialism as an enlightenment philosophy that automatically places utopian visions in a box marked abstraction or blueprint. However, another reading of history is possible and the openness of contemporary "here and now" anarchist utopianism to forms of postmodern thinking that Newman and others link to parallel modifications in historical anarchism can equally be explained by the critical distance between anarchist utopian thought and other forms of socialist utopianism. As David Leopold has argued, the conventional "utopian" and "antiutopian" dressing of nineteenth-century socialism conceals significant differences in the structure of revolutionary political thought.[33]

In the nineteenth century, arguments about utopianism were often rehearsed in the context of an extended debate about the role of the state's repressive tools as instruments of revolutionary transformation. Divisions on this issue became markers of ideological commitment. Anarchists and other antiauthoritarians firmly rejected the idea that the state's powers might be used in this way, and argued that the contrary position assumed a model of change that was elitist and therefore self-defeating. Babeuf and Blanqui were identified as the progenitors of this strategy. The strategies that anarchists proposed in response were utopian, but not in the sense in which authoritarians usually painted utopian traditions—typically by referring to fantastical and pointless blueprints. The important indicator of utopianism as an alternative to the elitism of authoritarian socialism was the expression of anarchist ideals through direct actions that plotted the means consistently to the ends of struggle. For example, in Bakuninist insurrectionary models of change, the destruction of individual ownership rights—recorded in land registers—was often identified as a means of revolutionary change and it mapped onto a particular end: the abolition of private property. The destruction of the registers was a symbolic act through which the landless rid themselves of the formal legal protections that supported property rights and the system of rural exploitation and oppression they served to sanction. The idea of the general strike followed a similar logic, but instead of burning records of property ownership, workers took immediate, direct control of the land and factories and abandoned for-profit production. The Tolstoyan model was rather different, involving multiple individual acts of refusal, in addition to collective actions, notably of participating in the systems of conscription and the regimes of punishment. Here, action was directed toward the realization of peaceful coexistence, and nonviolence was the required means. For Kropotkin, revolution had an insurrectionary aspect but was underpinned by a principle of collective withdrawal. The ends were captured in the principle of mutual aid. The appropriate means was the construction of political, social, and economic networks, organized beyond the reach of the state, which would ensure both that activists had access to basic necessities in periods of violent repression and intense combat, and that the social relations capable of sustaining anarchist practices were brought into being prior to the state's collapse.[34]

Just as anarchists accused authoritarians of focusing on issues of efficiency or necessity in developing revolutionary strategy—the same critique that Franks attaches to Leninism—they were also wary of abstraction. In Bakunin's, work the means-end relationship was underpinned by an understanding of conceptual contestability. Socialists, he argued, were united in their commitments to "equality, freedom, justice, human dignity, morality and the well-being of individuals." But these were not ends as such, since the meaning of these abstract ideas was always open to interpretation: they took on a particular hue when they were "mapped by a few sages or savants."[35] The utopian element of his anarchism was filled out by a vision of ordinary people negotiating conceptual meanings through struggle and the process of self-organization, having once thrown off the shackles of their enslavement in a direct act of insurrection.

Kropotkin and Gustav Landauer developed their utopian alternatives through the critique of socialist theories of history, which they considered abstract.[36] Their special concern was to highlight the structure of Marx and Engels's scientific socialism and show that anarchist utopianism stood some distance from it. Marx, they argued, denied he was a utopian yet he conjured a vision of the future by rooting socialism in a theory of change that assimilated prevailing norms, practices, and institutional forms and ridiculed other, imaginative visions as impractical or whimsical dreams. The hallmarks of their utopianism were, first, the possibility of working practically toward the realization of a different politics and, second, the space that existed for creative thought and moral judgment in shaping that politics. In this, Kropotkin aligned himself with early nineteenth-century utopian socialists—particularly with Charles Fourier—both to show the continuity of anarchism with these traditions and to probe the possibilities of realizing a better (more beautiful, emotionally rich, humane, convivial) future than the one that history, without intervention, seemed most likely to otherwise deliver.[37] However, in appealing to conceptions of desire, he explicitly rejected the phalanstery and the classification of personality types that Fourier's science defined.[38]

As Franks suggests, contemporary anarchists recognize an affinity with forms of utopianism that reject scientism, a pervasive feature of dominant forms of historical socialism. Yet the consistent feature of anarchist thinking about utopianism is the prefigurative framing of social transformation—a framing that in different ways was designed to challenge principles of certainty and inevitability. Utopia was not held up as "the end" in the means-ends relationship, but invoked in order to assert the possibility of different alternatives, each dependent on direct action and the principle of desire. As utopians, anarchists elaborated strategies for change consistent with their antiauthoritarian principles precisely in order to resist unspecified abstract utopias and blueprints.

Acknowledging the open-textured character of historical anarchist utopianism and its consistency with contemporary prefigurative politics suggests a possible recasting of Franks's conception of prefiguration. Franks defines prefiguration in dyadic terms and argues that anarchism collapses the distinction between means and ends. His recognition of the utopian element in prefigurative politics indicates that prefiguration describes a triadic relationship and that anarchist utopianism mediates the means and the ends of anarchist action, injecting it with a set of possibilities that make sense of their ethical interrelationship. In a discussion of the Committee of 100, Nicholas Walter made the point in this way: "unilateral nuclear disarmament as the end, and mass non-violent action as the means." The utopian idea that brought the end and the means into a prefigurative relation was the vision of Britain that embraced revolutionary solutions to existing social problems, had banned the bomb, left NATO, disengaged from the Cold War, and adopted "positive neutralism," rejecting "colonialism abroad and racialism at home."[39] Utopianism might have different flavors, but in order to be prefigurative anarchist recipes for the cookbooks of the future must include it as an ingredient.

Questioning the conjunction of historical anarchism with rigid utopianism also challenges the contention that the shifts that Franks observes within utopian studies map neatly to an evolution within anarchism from abstract or blueprint utopianism to "here and now" utopianism. By resetting the relationship between anarchism and utopian studies, it is possible to locate the significant shifts in the anarchist politics of utopia elsewhere. Even though there are considerable overlaps between historical and contemporary forms of prefigurative politics, the detectable change lies in the psychology of action that Franks refers to in his discussion of Sorel. In other words, the distancing of contemporary from historical anarchism has encouraged a move away from positively utopian aspiration and toward the dystopian framing of utopian desire.

ANARCHISM AND THE POLITICAL USES OF UTOPIA

Removing anarchist utopianism from the binominal taxonomies that distinguish historical, workerist, ideological anarchism from contemporary anti-ideological horizontalism reveals the existence of a spectrum of utopian, prefigurative practices and suggests a number of distinct political uses for utopia in contemporary activism. Utopias might be fleshed out sociologically at one end of this spectrum and appear as nebulous possibilities, vehicles for the principle of desire, at the other. The danger of invoking a harsher historicized transformation of anarchist utopianism, crystallized in the concept of prefiguration, is that a particular set of approaches to social change is valued at the cost of others. Recognizing the spectrum of anarchist utopianism admits a diversity of prefigurative practices.

Contemporary literature shows that utopianism supports diversity in activism. Among the prefigurative practices that contain strongly sociological currents are a number of grassroots community projects. Shaun Chamberlain, for example, describes the "force for a better future" in a project of community building, fostering a collective psychology of hopefulness. In a discussion of the Transition movement, he argues that, "if despair is perceiving an undesirable future as inevitable, one glimpse of a realistic, welcome alternative transforms our despondency into a massive drive to work towards that alternative."[40] In a similar spirit, Mark Smith advocates a form of practical utopianism that models ecological ways of living through the estimation of global risk.[41] There is at least a hint of Proudhon and Kropotkin in these approaches and a resounding echo in Franco "Bifo" Berardi's conception of utopian possibility:

> As Force and Reason have failed as principles of social change and political government, I think that we should adopt the point of view of the tendency, not the point of view of the will. Tendency is not an ideal, a utopia, it is not the projection of a rational order that force would eventually implement. Tendency is a possibility implicated in the present state of things, a possibility that cannot currently be deployed because the present paradigm of social relations . . . makes such deployment impossible.[42]

Utopias that prioritize psychologies of action often revolve around the creation of autonomous space and the transformation of everyday social relationships. Dreams and visions still have a place in these strands of prefigurative practice. Ben Lear and Ralph Schlembach's recent discussion of hope and despair includes a central demand, "luxury for all," which is reminiscent of William Morris's call for wealth and the abandonment of riches. Utopia provides a way of moving beyond the despair that capitalism induces by providing a "basis of our hope, not in capitalist development, but in its confrontation and eventual abolishment." Their antiutopian utopianism bears some other hallmarks of Morris's utopian romance:

> Our hope is ... non-utopian in the sense that we are not in the business of painting detailed pictures of what a post-capitalist society will look like. That does not mean that we cannot imagine or experiment with social relationships that are not dominated by the logic of accumulation and valorization.... What we do say when we talk about an alternative is that we reject the logic of capital. The vision of a post-capitalist world is not one of paradise; ... we can, and must imagine a future where the production of wealth is no longer tied to class divisions and the labour relation.[43]

Nevertheless, a striking trend in prefigurative politics is toward dystopian escape, rather than utopian achievement. Lear and Schlembach's conclusion is that indignation can be powerfully brought to bear on change, and that the "unwillingness to imagine bigger political alternatives" contributes to the "sense of despair and rage" that activists feel. In other activist writing, the idea is taken a step further. Utopia captures a boundless politics, but one described negatively as the desire to resist, reject, or destroy. Mark Fisher evokes an idea of perpetual motion, rooted in a psychological drive against death, or stasis. "As desiring creatures," Fisher notes, "we *ourselves* are that which disrupts organic equilibrium," or the tendency toward regulation, direction, and control.[44]

Paul Goodman's discussion of utopianism offers a useful way of thinking about this recasting of prefigurative politics. In a discussion of grief and anger, Goodman linked utopianism to patience. Patience, he argued, did not mean calm. On the contrary, utopianism was also a trigger for violent passions: anger, about the obstacles to the realization of utopian desire, and grief, for things understood to be absent through the identification of that desire. Utopians were patient in the sense that they were prepared to wait for the emergence of felt desire, through their anger and grief. This meant that utopian desire always had an object and it involved effort in the present in order to secure its attainment—Goodman's anticipation of prefiguration.

In contemporary activism, the positive value attached to the ability to tap negative passions—despair, indignation, hatred, and particularly rage—does not suggest that utopian patience has been eclipsed. But their invocation suggests a narrowing of contemporary anarchist utopianism and of the notion of prefigurative practices open to activists. John Holloway's discussion of anticapitalist rage captures the mood. His concern is to channel the forces of destruction rather than confront their negativity:

> Break the windows of the banks, shoot the politicians, kill the rich, hang the bankers from the lampposts. Certainly, all that is very understandable, but it does not help very much. It is money we must kill, not its servants. And the only way to kill money is to create different social cohesions, different ways of coming together, different ways of doing things. Kill money, kill labour. Here, now.[45]

This most negative casting of the means-end relationship remains prefigurative and is perhaps reminiscent of Bakunin's famous declaration that the passion for destruction is a creative passion too. The difference is that the righteous expression of rage, indignation, or despair often appears in contemporary literature as a condition of being rather than of doing. Moreover, it depends on the conjuring of powerfully dystopian images of existing society, which variously ensnares, entraps, and enslaves individuals. In the light of this dystopian imagery, the generalized emotions that radicals seek to release increasingly resemble those that Paul Goodman cautioned against when he contrasted desire "without its object" and the adoption of "the role of being angry" to the desire for something and the ability to blaze against the obstacles to its achievement. The ends of change are not only described with deliberate vagueness, even when linked to practical activities, but the analysis of means is developed as pulling away, less a pushing toward. Goodman explained the enraging desire to desire as a sense of lost paradise or the idea of "paradise not yet," but rather than endorsing this idea as an impulse to eternal struggle, as Abensour suggests, he rejected it as a cause of continuous frustration.[46]

The negativity and dystopianism of contemporary prefiguration change the focus for action, tend against the specification of hopes and desires, and undercut the positive charge that Bakunin excludes in his destructiveness. The power of this imagery might well help facilitate common actions, masses, occupations, and demonstrations, and the new types of social cohesion that Holloway advocates, even while the ends and means of protest are defined in a variety of different ways. Yet it is difficult to accommodate the horizontal practices and behaviors expressed through mutual aid in protest organizations and community campaigns in these dystopian frameworks, for they seem to exist "outside" the real world in a manner that makes their operation appear partial or compromised or impossible. Linked to a more positively utopian politics, this kind of activity might support a variety of ends and means and might even remain indeterminate, but in any of its forms, it would be possible for everyone—participant and observer, friend and enemy alike—to appreciate the complex ways in which actions might be designed to prefigure utopian goals. Looking again at anarchist history helps uncover some political uses of utopia that might contribute to such an approach.

NOTES

1. Uri Gordon, "Utopia in Contemporary Anarchism," in *Anarchism and Utopianism*, ed. Laurence Davis and Ruth Kinna (Manchester: Manchester University Press, 2009), 260.
2. David Graeber, "Occupy Wall Street's Anarchist Roots," *Al Jazeera Opinion*, November 30, 2011.
3. Benjamin Franks, *Rebel Alliances: The Means and Ends of Contemporary British Anarchisms* (Edinburgh: AK Press and Dark Star, 2006), 13.
4. Ibid., 17–18.
5. Ibid., 101.
6. Ibid., 114.
7. Cindy Milstein, *Anarchism and Its Aspirations* (Edinburgh: AK Press/IAS, 2010), 68.
8. Peter Kropotkin, "Anarchist Morality," in *Kropotkin's Revolutionary Pamphlets*, ed. Roger Baldwin (New York: Dover, 1970), 100.
9. On Tolstoy and Weber see Sam Whimster, ed., *Max Weber and the Culture of Anarchy* (Basingstoke, UK: Palgrave Macmillan, 1999).
10. Prefiguration is a familiar term in English-language anarchism but it does not feature in Daniel Colson, *Petit lexique philosophique de l'anarchisme de Proudhon à Deleuze* (Paris: Librairie Générale Française, 2001).
11. Murray Bookchin, *Social Anarchism of Lifestyle Anarchism: An Unbridgeable Chasm* (Oakland: AK Press, 1995).
12. Philip Cartelli, "Trying to Occupy Harvard," in the series Occupy, Anthropology, and the 2011 Global Uprisings, ed. Jeffrey Juris and Maple Razsa, *Cultural Anthropology* (2012), http://culanth.org/fieldsights/63-occupy-anthropology-and-the-2011-global-uprisings.
13. Marianne Maeckelbergh, "Horizontal Decision-Making Across Time and Place," *Cultural Anthropology*, ed. Jeffrey Juris and Maple Razsa, 2012.
14. Ibid.
15. Franks, *Rebel Alliances*, 114.

16 Christian Marazzi, "Exodus Without Promised Land," in *What We Are Fighting For: A Radical Collective Manifesto*, ed. Frederico Campagna and Emanuele Campiglio (London: Pluto, 2012), viii–ix.
17 The Anarchist FAQ talks about "the future in the present"; see the discussion of blueprints at http://anarchism.pageabode.com/afaq/secI2.html, January 31, 2014.
18 Uri Gordon defines prefigurative politics as a practice: the "actual implementation and display of anarchist social relations." Gordon, "Anarchism and Political Theory: Contemporary Problems," PhD diss., University of Oxford, 2007, chap. 3.
19 David Graeber, "The New Anarchists," *New Left Review* 13 (January/February 2002): 62; Campagna and Campiglio, "Introduction: What Are We Struggling For?," in *What We Are Fighting For*, 5.
20 Campagna and Campiglio, "Introduction: What Are We Struggling For?," 5.
21 See, for example, Carl Boggs, "Marxism, Prefigurative Communism, and the Problem of Workers' Control," at http://libcom.org/library/marxism-prefigurative-communism-problem-workers-control-carl-boggs.
22 Milstein, *Anarchism and Its Aspirations*, 66.
23 For a recent discussion of liberal antiutopianism, see Lucy Sargisson, *Fool's Gold: Utopianism in the Twenty-First Century* (Basingstoke, UK: Palgrave/Macmillan, 2012), 22–31.
24 Milstein, *Anarchism and Its Aspirations*, 67.
25 For a recent, pithy description of Parecon, see Michael Albert, "Participatory Economics from Capitalism," in Campagne and Campiglio, *What We Are Fighting For*, 11–17.
26 Franks, *Rebel Alliances*, 105.
27 Milstein, *Anarchism and Its Aspirations*, 65.
28 Mark Antliff, "Bad Anarchism: Aestheticized Mythmaking and the Legacy of Georges Sorel," *Art and Anarchy* 2 (2011): 162–163.
29 Rocker argued: "Anarchism is no patent solution for all human problems, no Utopia of a perfect social order (as it has so often been called), since, on principle, it rejects all absolute schemes and concepts. It does not believe in any absolute truth, or in any definite final goals for human development, but in an unlimited perfectibility of social patterns and human living conditions which are always straining after higher forms of expression, and to which, for this reason, one cannot assign any definite terminus nor set any fixed goal." Rudolf Rocker, *Anarchism and Anarcho-Syndicalism*, https://libcom.org/library/anarcho-syndicalism-rudolf-rocker-chapter-1.
30 Uri Gordon, "Utopia in Contemporary Anarchism," in *Anarchism and Utopianism*, ed. Laurence Davis and Ruth Kinna (Manchester: Manchester University Press, 2009), 266; Simon Tormey, "From Utopian Worlds to Utopian Spaces" *Ephemera* 5 (2005): 394–408.
31 Saul Newman, *The Politics of Postanarchism* (Edinburgh: Edinburgh University Press, 2011), 162.
32 Miguel Abensour, "Persistent Utopia," *Constellations* 15 (2008): 406–421.
33 David Leopold, "The Structure of Marx and Engels' Considered Account of Utopian Socialism," *History of Political Thought* 26, no. 3 (2005): 443–466.

34 Peter Kropotkin, "Anarchism: Its Philosophy and Ideal," in Baldwin, *Kropotkin's Revolutionary Pamphlets*, 140.
35 Michael Bakunin, "Stateless Socialism: Anarchism," in *The Political Philosophy of Bakunin*, ed. G. P. Maximoff, http://dwardmac.pitzer.edu/Anarchist_Archives/bakunin/stateless.html.
36 Ruth Kinna, "Anarchism and the Politics of Utopia," in Davis and Kinna, *Anarchism and Utopianism* (Manchester: Manchester University Press, 2009), 221–240.
37 For a discussion of Marx's utopianism, see Leopold, "The Structure of Marx and Engels' Considered Account of Utopian Socialism"; and David Leopold, "Socialism and (the Rejection of) Utopia," *Journal of Political Ideologies* 12, no. 3 (2007): 219–237.
38 For a discussion of Kropotkin and Fourier, see Matthew Adams, "Rejecting the American Model: Peter Kropotkin's Radical Communalism," *History of Political Thought* 35 (2014): 147–173.
39 Nicholas Walter, "The Committee of 100: Ends and Means," in *Damned Fools in Utopia, and Other Writings on Anarchism and War Resistance*, ed. David Goodway (Oakland: PM, 2011), 79.
40 Shaun Chamberlain, "The Struggle for Meaning," in Campagna and Campiglio, *What We Are Fighting For*, 45.
41 Mark J. Smith, "Practical Utopianism and Ecological Citizenship," in Campagna and Campiglio, *What We Are Fighting For*, 82.
42 Franco "Bifo" Berardi, "The Transversal Function of Disentanglement," in Campagna and Campiglio, *What We Are Fighting For*, 144. Kropotkin argued in very similar terms. In "Anarchist Communism" he wrote: "As to the method followed by the anarchist thinker, it entirely differs from that followed by the utopists. The anarchist thinker does not resort to metaphysical conceptions ... to establish what are, in his opinion, the best conditions for realizing the greatest happiness of humanity.... He studies society and tries to discover its *tendencies*.... He distinguishes between the real wants and tendencies of human aggregations and the accidents (want of knowledge, migrations, ward, conquests) which have prevented these tendencies from being satisfied." In Baldwin, *Kropotkin's Revolutionary Pamphlets*, 47.
43 Ben Lear and Ralph Schlembach, "If You Don't Let Us Dream, We Won't Let You Sleep?," in *Occupy Everything: Reflections on Why It's Kicking Off Everywhere*, ed. Alessio Lunghi and Seth Wheeler (Brooklyn: Minor Compositions, 2012), 43–44.
44 Mark Fisher, "Post-Capitalist Desire," in Campagne and Campiglio, *What We Are Fighting For*, 135.
45 John Holloway, afterword to *What We Are Fighting For*, 204.
46 Paul Goodman, "On the Intellectual Inhibition of Grief and Anger," in *Utopian Essays and Practical Proposals* (New York: Vintage, 1962), 93–109.

IV
PERMANENCE OF UTOPIA

11

THE SENSES AND USES OF UTOPIA

JACQUES RANCIÈRE

I will present here a few very general hypotheses concerning a simple question, the simplest that could be asked about utopia: that of its prefix. I will leave to one side the question of whether this *u-* comes from *ou-* or *eu-*, whether the word "utopia" originally meant the *nonplace* or the *good place*. If the former interpretation is already established, it is because the *good place* was not thought except as a *nonplace*. The problem crystallizes around the sense of a negation. How can we interpret its virtue? What is the topos denied or displaced by u-topia?

There are two classic responses. According to the first, utopia is a simple negation of reality, a work of pure theory or imagination. Here is how the *Littré* defines it: "Plan of *imaginary* government, where everything is perfectly regulated for the happiness of all, and which in practice most often yields results contrary to those hoped for." One will have noticed that this timeless definition includes *failure* as always already given, verified in advance. Utopia is then framed by the reality that it negates and is negated by.

The second response goes on to determine this "reality." According to it, utopia is a negation of the present. It is that which makes visible present reality as nonnecessary and another reality as possible. Utopia is a fable or allegory that suspends adherence to a given and proposes a question rather than a program. It is essentially anticipation. It activates a fundamental anthropological characteristic: the manner in which being is moved by that which carries it beyond itself, the presence of that which is not yet in any act, its power to arouse the potentials of human action.

These two responses seem to me to miss an essential point: u-topia is not a simple negation, but a double negation. It is not only the nonplace of a place, but the nonplace of a nonplace. The utopian is not he who says, "Let's flee reality." The utopian is he who says, "Enough of utopia. Let's have done with words, chimeras, ideology. Let's devote ourselves to things that are real." This is, for instance, the lesson of the most eloquent of the Saint-Simonian preachers, Émile Barrault: "To work, then, to work! Ideas, doctrines, theories should finally be succeeded by actions, practice, realization." Only this kind of proclamation, an appeal to quit the fog of words for the things themselves, presupposes a particular capacity: to designate the "thing itself" as a very particular thing, as the incarnation of its own sense. Contrary to the superficial visions that identify utopia with a dream, the fundamental utopian gesture is to show, to designate, the sensible presence of the sense as manifested by a thing resembling the word that designates it. So it is, for example, that the Saint-Simonian missionaries on the ground refute the accusation of being the destroyers of property in practice, by bringing the village fire under control: "You who have spread or peddled against us such calumnious imputations, you who accuse us again of wanting to destroy property, come, come and see us amid the flames of Brazay, come and see us defend property against fire and save from the blaze goods we respect because they are the fruit of man's labour. It is no longer with words that we respond to you, but with actions!"[1]

The anecdote is exemplary: the utopian is he who speaks not through words thrown on paper or into the wind, but through actions that impose their meaning on visible things. He is then a speaking being of a particular type: a speaking being who speaks no more, who has eliminated the "nonplace" of language, that is, the absence of things in words. The utopian traces sense, communication, community in things themselves. The utopian "nonplace" is in fact the sur-place of a hyperwriting.

This point can be illustrated by a work of fiction composed by a novelist who had no sympathy for Saint-Simonian utopians but who, at least once, cast the very characters of the Saint-Simonian system—the priest, the engineer, the woman, the proletarian—in order to draw a lesson formally very much like theirs. I speak of Balzac and *The Village Priest*. The book tells the story of Véronique Sauviat, daughter of a scrap merchant from Limoges grown rich on the traffic in National Property [Church property nationalized during the Revolution—*trans.*], but who nonetheless continues to live a simple life on the outskirts of town. The existence of the little "virgin of the suburb" is disturbed by two isolated incidents: one visible, the small pox that destroyed or, rather, interiorized her beauty; the other invisible and more destructive, the purchase of *Paul and Virginia*[2] from an open-air stall. Véronique is henceforth given to dreaming of chaste and celestial loves. She designates a little island on the Vienne situated across from her window as the Île-de-France of the novel. And she imagines herself liberating with her pure love one of the workers who pass beneath that same window. This young woman's dreams seem, however, to vanish when Véronique, amply provided for by her father's hidden fortune, marries a hard-up banker: hardly a happy marriage, to a husband as miserly as he is ugly, for which, however, she compensates by frequenting select company and all kinds of good works. During her pregnancy, the village is shaken by a criminal affair. A gentleman of modest but independent means is robbed and killed. The murderer is soon found and turns out to be a young worker with an excellent reputation, Jean-François Tascheron, who, however, defies the magistrate by his refusal to say where he hid the stolen treasure, and the clergy by his curses and blasphemies. The opinion spreads in the village that his crime and strange behavior can only be explained by a mad passion for a woman from a higher class whose secret he wants to protect. The criminal having been condemned to death, the Church sets itself to imposing upon him an edifying end and for this purpose sends for the Curé Bonnet, the holy priest who brought religion to Tascheron's home village of Montégnac. Thanks to his intervention, the condemned dies reconciled with God and promises the restitution of the money. The money is recovered from its burial place on the bank of the island on the Vienne, the very same island Véronique contemplated from her window.

The episode that follows shows Véronique, mother but soon widow, retiring on a property her husband purchased in the village of Montégnac. There, under the direction of the Curé Bonnet, she leads a life of village benefactress. Her great work, inspired by the curé and carried out by a young polytechnician resembling the companions of Enfantin, is the construction of a system of canals that captures water from the hills that has hitherto been wasted, transforming arid soil into flourishing pastures. Near the end of her life, Véronique makes a public confession in which she admits what the reader has long since understood—that she was the woman for whom the unfortunate Tascheron brought about his own downfall—and who "inscribed her repentance on the soil of Montégnac in indelible letters."

At the center of the story, in exemplary fashion, stand two opposing configurations of place, which are also two configurations of the relation between the earth and water: the island and the canals. There is a configuration that brings prosperity to those close to the land, and there is another that brings them to perdition. This baleful configuration is the island: the island that hides the fruit of crime because it was the cause of the crime in the first place—the island of fiction projected onto the reality of a laborious life, the utopia disrupting lives dedicated to domestic work. The utopia of the island is not the land of Cockaigne proposed to simple folk. It is quite simply the island of the book in general. It is not only the story of a happy island that provokes the catastrophe. It is the book as an island, the book in general, in its materiality as an available object, exposed in the public square, in an open-air stall. The "crime" is, first of all, the encounter between society's two dispositions toward place, two distributions of the sensible. There is the "normal" disposition of places and functions, of ways of doing, being and speaking, that harmonize in one way to occupy their place in the common space, to perform the function attached to this place, and to manifest the *ethos* specific to the exercise of this function in this place. In this disposition, in particular, all words are emitted by a voice, a body, directed toward another body, and have to do with actions to be performed. All speech has a destination, a determinate point of origin and determinate destination. Every statement is accompanied by a body oriented toward this destination.

But there is also the second disposition, a "perverse" one, where the space of distribution of bodies in their place and in their function is traversed, penetrated by spaces with an indeterminate destination, for example, the places of promenade, the marketplaces that provide buyers merchandise of a particular kind: published speech, folded back into the volume of a book (the "spiritual instrument" of Mallarmé, which is in no way the privilege of aesthetes); the insular words, organized in the space proper to speech, where they are addressed by an absent subject to a certain destination, subtracted from the normal play of nominations, from the presence of speech that designates, indicates, orders. These insular words, then, themselves organize a space proper to them that comes to superimpose itself onto the "normal" disposition—the body in community—and to reorganize, little by little, every system of relations between words and things, between the visible, the sayable, and the doable.

It is this first negation, the first nonplace, that will denounce the second negation of utopia. It is easy to recognize in the fable proposed by Balzac the obsessive preoccupation of his time. It is a fable of democracy, but democracy as ontological disorder more than as a particular regime of government. Balzac's is a Platonic fable of democracy. It begins with the revolution that has overturned the order of conditions, making a millionaire of a modest scrap merchant. In Plato, the son of a stingy oligarch is a sensual and prodigious democrat. In Balzac, the daughter of an enriched scrap merchant abandons herself and delivers her admirer to a more dangerous perversion, that of ideality. It is not material joys that carry them off, but the joys of speech and thought. The name of this perversion was constantly brought up in the eighteenth and nineteenth centuries. It is *déclassement*. It is the evil of all the proletarian sons seized by writing and diverted toward another distribution of the sensible world by the efficacy of certain words and phrases folded back upon their insularity: words of poetry, words of politics. The fundamental problem with the "antiutopian" utopia is this: the problem of productive or reproductive life seized and diverted from its path by the immaterial that adumbrates another place, a place without place.

It is this original problem that is signified by the word "democracy." Democracy is not first of all a regime of government or a state of the social. It is first of all the pure inscription of a place without place, a place that disturbs the natural order of places and functions. Such is the paradox of the *demos* as the philosophers originally described it. The *demos* is a supernumerary part, a void part that adds itself to the count of the real parts of society until it identifies itself with the whole of the community. Under the name of *demos*, the people of no means, those who in the city count for nothing, identify themselves with the whole of the community. And yet it is this paradox that makes it so that there is politics and not simply domination or management. There is politics because there is a part that has no part, a count whereby all the people who have nothing superimpose themselves on the real count of the parts of society or on the enumeration of its functions.

The first nonplace, the baleful island denounced by the Balzacian and the Saint-Simonian utopia alike, is this empty part that superimposes onto the natural order of places and functions another distribution of the sensible, determined by the efficacy of certain words (the people, liberty, equality) and phrases that stage them, instituting in this way an inconsistent and polemical community. What utopia dreams of, and the reason utopias of the Saint-Simonian age are still attracted to the Platonic archi-utopia, is the replacement of this community defined on the basis of an empty space by a community without a gap, without dead time or lacunae, where words ("the people" or others) could institute their sphere of appearance. The essence of the Platonic republic is the being of a community without a *demos*, with neither time nor space where this signifier could penetrate. The utopian community is a saturated community. The artisans of the *Republic* do not have time; the citizens of the *Laws* constitute a chorus enchanted without a break by the living rhythm of the community. The utopian project is a project of the complete aestheticization of the community. It requires that the meaning of the community not have any separate space of inscription, and that it be felt in every place at every instant in every gesture of every member of the community. This principle is in strict opposition to that which founds the democratic nonplace, namely, writing. The appearance of the *demos* and the miscount it introduces into the communitarian body are tied to the problem of writing. And the Balzacian fable is a fable of the misdeeds of literature, a modern version of the Platonic *Phaedrus* myth, opposing the living *logos* to the dead letter. The dead letter was for Plato at the same time mute (incapable of rendering what was said) and overly talkative—indefinitely susceptible to rolling to the right and the left and speaking to anyone, without distinguishing between those to whom one should and should not speak. The evil of writing is the trajectory of the statement no longer accompanied by a voice and a body that legitimates it, by a soul that commands and carries it to a destination. Democracy, as ontological reality and not as a simple form of government, is suspended in this problem of writing's availability, openness to being seized by anyone for any purpose. The sickness of writing is the disease of disembodied bodies giving over to their contingency every legitimate position of speech and every functional order of the communitarian body. The democratic perversion is to identify this sickness with the normal regime of life, this problem of legitimacy, with the very principle of legality: the written law and its indifference to differences, this written law that, as Plato says, resembles a prescription a doctor departed for somewhere far away would leave for all future illnesses. The principle of the Platonic republic is, then, not simply to impose communitarian law on democratic facticity and turbulence. It is to oppose a community of the living *logos* with a community founded on the exteriority of writing, a community where the living law exists as *ethos*—as the way of being and the character of the community and each of its members—as an occupation of workers, as a tune that sings in their heads, a movement that spontaneously animates the body and turns minds toward a certain comportment and way of thinking. The community of the living, incarnate law is thus opposed to the community of writing.

But the corrective for the problem of writing is not its suppression; it is another kind of writing. The utopian principle links the vitality of the communitarian body to the idea of another kind of writing: less than written or more than written. Less than written: a pure trajectory of the breath unarrested by words and without risk of being diverted by them. Such is already that oracle of the wind in the leaves at Dodona of which Socrates reminds Phaedrus. Such is the communitarian symphony as the moderns imagine it: rhythm more than speech, marking the natural respiration of the common spirit. Conversely, more than written: the writing of truth minus the fragile supports and ambiguous written signs, traced indelibly and unfalsifiably in the very texture of things. This writing that is "more than written" separates modern utopia from the Platonic community. The legislator of the *Laws* should have vocalized the laws, mixing them with his voice, with his admonitions. But, when all is said and done, this supplement of the voice is always a supplement of writing. Modern utopia has at its disposal a double paradigm of writing that is more than written. It is first of all the Christian paradigm of the Word incarnate, of the letter becoming truth by becoming flesh. The Saint-Simonian living law and the new Book[3] inscribe themselves into the logic of the Book, which becomes truth by becoming flesh. In this way the beginning of *The New Book* shows us the disposition of apostles around Enfantin as a living disposition of the pages of the Book with their two columns. The paradigm of incarnation and that which renews it, the sacrament, is at the center of the institution of the Saint-Simonian community.

The second modern paradigm is that of writing in things, of materiality as the manifestation of the spirit outside of itself. Thus, everything sensible appears blessed with a capacity for self-presentation that is at the same time the presentation of its "spirit." "Each thing," says August Schlegel, "first of all presents itself, that is to say, reveals its interior by its exterior, its essence by its manifestation (hence it is a symbol of itself); it then presents that with which it has the closest relations and which acts upon it; finally, it is a mirror of the universe."[4] According to this Romantic theory of the symbolism of language, writing more than written is everywhere, which makes meaning and community to the very extent that it is mute. There is the mute life of the spirit, which is the mute life of the community and which materially refutes the gap of writing: the gap between words and the things they name and the bodies that utter them. From this derives a principle of the general sensibilization of the communitarian essence. Utopia, I have said, is fundamentally a generalized aesthetic. It implies that the sense of community is felt in each gesture of each of its members. And yet what gives us the Romantic theory of language is precisely this: the virtual identification of every bodily position with a way of signifying the corporal community. What it founds is the aesthetic saturation of the communitarian body: the absence of the void or interval (leaving no empty space is the principle of the Saint-Simonian missionaries' demonstration):[5] the absence of nonsignification. This latter virtue is, to be sure, a virtue that cuts both ways: it is only in madness that everything makes sense and Enfantin does not refrain from making fun of his companions from Ménilmontant who examine celestial signs to know if God bids or forbids them to go and cut up a pumpkin from the vegetable patch. Beyond these comical episodes, however, the power of the idea of writing in things is to connect a very old hermeneutic to technological modernity. And the Saint-Simonians put this marriage that thus weds a religious to a technological idea to exemplary effect. Here the new channels of communication are given the religious mission of replacing the old community of speaking beings. One can think of Michel Chevalier's statements concerning the Egyptian expedition. To those political parties that make everything "ideology and as vaporous and mystical as possible" he opposes the Saint-Simonian way of tracing in things themselves the links of communication at the same time as the demonstrations of thought. We trace our arguments, he says, on a geographic map.[6] And *The Book of Acts* explicitly opposes two kinds of writing: that of the ancient Egyptian priests who conceal the meaning in their signs from laymen and that of the new engineer-priests whose signifying activity is indissolubly an activity that produces wealth and community; "We do not decipher old hieroglyphs of its past grandeur. But we engrave on its soil the signs of future prosperity."[7] The railways and canals that *link* distant territories and populations are writing in things themselves. They trace the *religious* and effective forms of links between men, links that unite the community and make it prosper.

It is clearly the same for Balzac, even if he puts the same idea in the service of the old religion and the old dreams of a pastoral government of men. The irrigation system conceived by the Abbé Bonnet is a writing in things themselves that founds a community of meaning and prosperity in place of the writing that leads individuals and communities to their doom. The new "book of life" thus has a double existence. On the one hand, it is realized in the breath of the communitarian chorus. On the other, it is traced on the very territory of the community in lines that link men together and fertilize the common wealth. The community's infrastructure is both the way in which the sense of community is defined and the forms of linkage uniting bodies with bodies.

It is now possible to systematize the sense of the "negation of the negation" particular to utopia by defining three orders of the constitution of community. There is first of all the order of domination, the order that assigns bodies to determinate places based on what they have to do, based on their attributions and destinations. This order, which I have elsewhere defined as the police order,[8] is the distribution of the sensible that divides those who are to be obeyed from those who are to be commanded, those who deal with the particular of manual work from those occupied with the general of thought. This assumes the division of occupations into those belonging to the sphere of the visible and those belonging to obscurity, and of phonic articulations into those considered a discourse emitted by a thinking brain and those considered noise emitted by a satisfied or suffering body. It is the immemorial and forever-young logic of domination that makes it so that in the grievance of plebeians, proletarians, women, and others, the dominant hear only the formless noise of suffering, a rage and a stubbornness of a body without the capacity for thought.

There is, secondly, a political order that tears the fabric of the first. The political act interrupts the police order by imposing a supernumerary count of the uncounted that disrupts the distribution of functions by suspending the forms of perception and attribution that gave it its sensible self-evidence and linguistic manageability. The political act makes visible those who have no place to be seen. It makes heard as speaking beings those who were meant only to make noise. It suspends the self-evidence of relations between names, bodies, places, and functions. It inscribes litigious places (litigious in a double sense) within the territory of the political order. These places, first of all, no longer delimit places destined for categories possessing properties adapted to occupy this place. They are spheres of appearance defined by the names of supernumerary subjects, subjects without property: people, citizens, proletarians . . . And, second of all, these litigious subjects are not simply the "excluded" who manifest their contention and their right to be counted; they are subjects whose very identity is the exercise of contention about the count of identities and about the properties of the visible and the sayable that authorize this count. They are subjects whose own subversive act is to play in the gap between words and things, whose junction constitutes the sensible universe, the self-evident universe of domination.

The utopian project, for its part, comes third, and the theory of the "three estates" is, in sum, a theorization of this third position. It wants to bring to a close the "critical" age, the "protestant" age of writing and politics. It proposes to return consistency to the inconsistent community of politics, to eliminate the distance between the names of political subjects and actual social functions and groups. It wants, by the same stroke, to eliminate the wrong as the constitutive conflictual principle of the political community. It proposes an order where bodies are in their right place, according to their true capacities and connected by true links, where the scriptural gap between words and things is replaced by a continual presentation of the community to itself. This order presupposes, as we have seen, a thorough refiguration of relations between the visible and the sayable, an order where the vanity of language gives way to the sensible presentation, in bodies and in the links that unite them, of the sense of community.

On this basis we can understand that the singular relations of the engineers of utopian souls with these workers fit the presentation of the new community, which speaks through their gestures, prays through their works, and establishes the links of interhuman communication through their industrial achievements. These workers are in fact in the same position as the characters in *The Village Priest*: the sons and daughters of the iron race, creatures of an obscure world for whom the accidental encounter with the book made for a radical experience: that of a confrontation between two distributions of the sensible—a "natural" division based on the distribution of occupations, the separation of *estates* and ways of being fitted to them, and another, based solely on the circulation of the letter, which courses anywhere, solely on the equality of speaking beings, whoever they are. It is to the likes of Véronique Sauviat and Jean-François Tascheron that the Saint-Simonian proposal is addressed. And here is what they propose to them: pass directly to the third stage, to the organic community identifying speech with life, place, and bond, renounce the book and its island in order to work to inscribe upon the soil the communitarian law of communication among men.

On this basis we can understand the fascination and the resistance they arouse and the reasons resistance carries the day. This resistance of the workers whom they solicit is not the preserve of practical men before exalted theorists. For these workers who only entertain them halfway often prove to be ready to follow beliefs at least as extravagant as those of the Saint-Simonians' *New Book*. They refuse to yield on the status of belief itself, on its "unreality," on the gap between words and things, that is to say, on the power of rupture and the obligation of words as such, the power of the "dead" letter over the spirit become flesh.

This distance could be illustrated by the opposition between city-utopias and utopias of the future. The city elaborated by Enfantin and his fellows in *The New Book* is a city-body: an organicist and religious model of the living spirit become flesh is superimposed on the Vitruvian relation of geometrical proportion and the proportions of the human body. The city invented by the Saint-Simonian Gauny, the most faithful of the doctrine's faithful, is distinguished by two essential characteristics. On the one hand, it is a city with tortuous streets, a labyrinth inaccessible to the gaze and to the canons of tyranny. On the other hand, it is a nonfunctional space, a space marked by the circulation of speech—a space strewn with empty spaces destined for walking and conversation and temples of philosophy, a space overloaded with memorial inscriptions of contention: the rights of man and reminders of violations of these rights visible on columns at every crossroads; the rights of tenants and the obligations of landlords posted on every building; each street bearing a plaque with its history; and so on.[9] It is a place entirely marked by the eradication of tyranny, in the secrecy of its many folds as in the openness of its spaces of speech and its overabundance of memorial writings. To the city of the engineers of souls that presents its sense on its body, its sense as a body, stands opposed this city of writing in which the body is covered in inscriptions that speak the partition of two worlds. In short, the democratic Saint-Simonian worker restores the playfulness of that in which he embraces the doctrine—that is to say, the *words*. The Saint-Simonian utopia establishes its nonplace as a negation of the democratic nonplace. The Saint-Simonian worker reinstates the former in the latter.

In the same way, one could oppose two ideas of the temple. *The New Book* imagines a temple that in its technical reality and sensible form is a material symbolization of the community: a temple of the industrial future, built of colossal magnets; a prodigious temple of technology, an encyclopedia of the world and of history, a total work of art. Gauny insists on reveries of old Greek temples and peristyles propitious for philosophical perambulation. He insists on such vignettes as Stoic porticos or the gardens of Anacreon, places reserved for philosophy, but also concealed from philosophy by those not "destined" for it by birth. He insists also on reveries of a place he calls the belvedere, the "ideal" place, which changes one's perception, which dominates the city, from which one sees the future, but also a place easily realized in every empty apartment where he performs the solitary task of the floor layer. The belvedere is a place where one occupies an undecided position so as to observe a spectacle of the sensible that is itself undecided. An undecided position: the space of work leaves its identity, is identified with the space intended for that activity which, in Platonic philosophy as in the Christian apologues of Martha and Mary, is structurally opposed to it: contemplation. An undecided spectacle: the city embraced from the belvedere is at once an aesthetic space for a disinterested gaze (in the Kantian sense of that term), but also the place of the division of conditions, the place encumbered by the constructions of tyranny. But precisely the views, like the spaces, come to slide one over the other. The belvedere is a place that allows contention to be aestheticized—or, conversely, spectacle to be polemicized—and to be held, in this contemplation, on the edge of the future.

On the edge of the future, but not in the future. The belvedere is the place of a mobile refiguration, of a translation of spaces. This mobile and divided space of perception where the division of spaces and times plays out is then opposed to the engineers of souls' city of the future. Its heterotopia is opposed to utopia conceived as a place of covering words with actions and of the integral sensibilization of the sense of community. There would thus be two ways of using utopia: a utopian way that aims to replace the nonplace, to constitute a space materially saturated by the inscription of the sense of community; and a heterotopian way, where utopia serves to constitute divided spaces, to vary perceptions of the world, to make another one appear, to constitute the scene of opposition between two worlds. One could evoke here a tension of spaces of the same kind: that presented by the utopian America of the Icarians. America is, in one sense, the place of a utopian concordance of book and reality, the virgin land where Cabet brought his disciples, the cloth from which to cut the future, hence a place that is nothing more than the stuff of communal work-time. But then the Icarians make very different use, or rather uses, of this place—uses that evade the realization of the book of life by being either on the side of life or on the side of the book. One can in fact betray the book of life in two ways. The first, simpler one—also the most convenient for a simplistic theorization of the "end of the utopian dream"—is to exchange it for a simple pursuit of fortune to be made in the new world. It is a simple confusion of the spiritual gold of the Icarian community with the material gold of Californian rivers. But there is another way, more honest but also more insidious—for the utopian and for the historians—to betray the book of life. It is to treat the latter simply—which is also to say absolutely—as a book. Now, there are a thousand ways of treating a book—of reading and appropriating it: as a pastime or as a cult object; as a rigorous demonstration or a fabulous story; as the Bible or as *Robinson Crusoe*; by enjoying its deferred expectations or beginning at the end; by taking it literally or figuratively; by believing or not believing it; by not believing *and* believing it. The use of a book consists of the variable combination of these choices that can also strip it of their alternative character. It is in this way that one inserts it into the writing of one's own life as the refiguration of the common distribution of the sensible. It is also in this way that individual and communitarian heterotopias take shape, making a place of the utopian nonplace and a nonplace of its places.

NOTES

Originally published as "Sens et usages de l'utopie," *Raison Présente* 121, no. 1 (1997), reprinted in *L'Utopie en questions*, ed. Michèle Riot-Sarcey (Saint-Denis: Presses Universitaires de Vincennes, 2001), 65–78.

1. *Mission de l'Est* (Paris, 1833), 35; Jacques Rancière, *Short Voyages to the Land of the People*, trans. James B. Swenson (Stanford: Stanford University Press, 2003).
2. Popular novel by Jacques-Henri Bernardin de Saint Pierre, published in 1787—Editors' note.
3. Barthélemy Prosper Enfantin's *Le Livre nouveau* was conceived as a replacement for the Bible. The unpublished manuscript is stored at the Bibliothèque de l'Arsenal in Paris—Editors' note.
4. A. W. Schlegel, *Leçons sur la littérature et l'art*, quoted in Philippe Lacoue-Labarthe and Jean-Luc Nancy, *The Literary Absolute: The Theory of Literature in German Romanticism*, trans. Philip Barnard and Cheryl Lester (New York: State University of New York Press, 1988).
5. *Foi nouvelle: Livre des actes, publié par les femmes* (Paris: A. Johanneau, 1833), 35; Rancière, *Short Voyages*, 44.
6. Michel Chevalier, *Politique industrielle et système de la Méditerranée* (Paris: Everat, 1832), 24.
7. *Livre des actes*.
8. See Jacques Rancière, *Disagreement: Politics and Philosophy*, trans. Julie Rose (Minneapolis: University of Minnesota Press, 1998).
9. See Gabriel Gauny, *Le Philosophe plébéien* (Saint-Denis: Presses Universitaires de Vincennes, 1985); Jacques Rancière, *The Nights of Labor: The Workers' Dream in Nineteenth-Century France*, trans. John Drury (Philadelphia: Temple University Press, 1989).

12

REALISM, WISHFUL THINKING, UTOPIA

RAYMOND GEUSS

The short monograph *Philosophy and Real Politics* represents my attempt to give a sketchy answer to the question of how a political philosophy that can be taken seriously might look today.[1] As an explicitly programmatic work, the book certainly does not claim to contain a complete political philosophy, if completeness would even be a meaningful demand in this domain. Rather, it includes only a few positive and a few negative pointers: positive pointers as to where one could possibly continue the investigation, and negative pointers concerning approaches and modes of inquiry that have proven to be not especially promising, or indeed blind alleys.

As long as our political life is not completely ossified,[2] "completeness" is as little to be expected in political philosophy as "absolute clarity," absolute precision, or absolute predictability.[3] On the other hand, there is no reason, through dogmatically pregiven disciplinary boundaries like the alleged boundaries between political science, political theory, and political philosophy, or between historical and systematic considerations, to be scared off in advance from mobilizing all possible intellectual resources when it is a matter of how we should engage in political action.

As is well known, in his early writings Marx broke with a long philosophical tradition that goes back to Plato and argued for the priority of real history over mere conceptual analysis and practice over theory. "We know only a single science," as it is put in *The German Ideology*: "the science of history."[4] This in turn means that the idea that there can be a substantial, freestanding philosophical ethics is an illusion. This is not to say that there can be no systematic knowledge of valuable and less valuable action, for "ethics" is not necessarily discredited when it is accorded an appropriate—one could almost say "honorable"—albeit subordinate place as part of a historically oriented social science. Conceptual analysis, too, can, within certain limits, such as when it is conducted historically, prove to be a serviceable method, if not one that is completely satisfactory on its own. One can understand the history of political philosophy in the twentieth century as a long trench warfare between the followers of a Platonic tradition that has been "rehabilitated" in one way or another (for instance, by Frege) and a diverse group of historically oriented philosophers, such as Nietzsche, Dewey, Adorno, or the late Wittgenstein. For thinkers of this second group there is no timeless "essence" of politics in a Platonic sense and no conceptuality prescribed by the nature of things; in this sense they are antiessentialists. Various practical problems that involve concrete human beings and arise in a context of historically evolved institutions, power relations, and value judgments in the end constitute the starting point for every theoretical reflection, and concept formation too has a historical context that must be explained. Since we actually live in a society with an advanced division of labor, the problems that concern philosophers "professionally" have often been only very indirectly connected to forms of action. This of course does not do away with the need to take into account the developmental context of related problems. The same holds for the future prospects of theoretical work. Constructing a political theory means intervening in political life itself. For this reason theorists are also held accountable for the consequences that can be expected from the "solutions" they propose, even when these apparently have an only conceptual character.

In *Philosophy and Real Politics* a series of different tasks of political philosophy are named and briefly discussed, without any claim for completeness being made for this list. First, political philosophy must fulfill the condition that has become canonical for every science by offering a correct, comprehensible, and clear description and explanation of complex states of affairs. Thus, for example, much of what we these days usually call "political life" plays out in a sphere that is essentially structured by a system of states. This raises a series of questions it is the task of political philosophy to answer. What is a "modern state," and what distinguishes it from a Greek polis, a medieval kingdom, or a northern Italian Renaissance republic? How has it arisen? How does it work? Under what conditions is peaceful coexistence possible with neighboring states that are in economic competition?

Since our need for practical orientation is not satisfied by understanding alone, we rightly also expect political philosophy to ask questions concerning the evaluation of institutions, practices, decisions, and so on—and, as far as possible, to answer them. It also seems entirely justified to expect help from political philosophy with practical questions, that is, questions that have the form "What is to be done?" Is a strong currency good for the profitability of domestic heavy industry? Should the free market be developed, limited, or abolished in higher education or health care? Will pensioners be better off if the new finance bill passes? Would the legalization of the drug trade have social advantages? What should we make of genetic engineering? Should we participate in the invasion or not? Under modern conditions, asking this kind of question quickly becomes reflexive. What does "better off" mean here? How can we measure "social advantages"? Can and should these standards not themselves be investigated? What do we do in the case of conflicting values?

Since the end of the eighteenth century the theory of the division of "is" and "ought," that is, between facts and values, has been dogmatically established in leading philosophical circles. For those under the reign of this dichotomy, it is clear that the two tasks named above must be kept separate and that the division must be supported by an appropriate philosophy of science. This opens the way for the development of an apparently purely positivist "political science" on the one hand, and an equally apparently "pure normative theory" on the other. In the fully realized form of this position, which we frequently encounter in contemporary analytical philosophy, it is assumed that empirical political science is philosophically irrelevant. Political philosophy should be a normative enterprise that proceeds on the basis of "ideal theory." This ideal theory refers in the first instance to the practical circumstances and moral characteristics of individual human beings. Political philosophy is accordingly "applied ethics."

Both presuppositions of current analytical political philosophy are theoretically dubious and practically completely useless. First, the strict division between facts and values is a meaningful starting point neither for solving political problems nor for understanding and explaining social states of affairs, institutions, and events. For one thing, in political life "evaluations" are inextricably intertwined with complex assumptions about the structure of society, human possibility, and the expected course of our actions. An unprejudiced observer would also very quickly come to the conclusion that people behave as they do because they strive to realize certain values in the circumstances in which they happen to find themselves. Occasionally, of course, the only empirically satisfactory explanation one can find is that apparently obvious possible courses of action are out of the question (for whatever aesthetic, moral, or other reasons) for the subjects in question. The second presupposition—namely, the idea that in the end political philosophy is nothing other than applied individual ethics—has in my view never really been fully justified, but is rather at best dogmatically adopted and passed on. The most by way of justification that anyone ever gives is a mere gesture at one or another version of a program of reduction that has so far never been carried out. Because, however, societies are in some sense "composed" of individuals, it by no means follows that politics can be "reduced" to a matter of individual ethics. The apparent self-evidence that still often clings to this presupposition probably goes back to the unexamined repercussions of the Western religious tradition, where what counts above all is individual salvation and choice.

As long as human practice remains open to the future, problems will arise that we can grasp barely, or not at all, with the concepts and theories that have been handed down to us. Concepts like "the state,"[5] "sovereignty," or "division of powers" were, after all, deliberately introduced in the early-modern period in order to deal cognitively with problems that had hitherto not existed. The practically motivated invention of *new* concepts is a third legitimate task of political philosophy. These concepts should not only retroactively depict existing if also novel states of affairs; they should also help shape reality in a penetrating way. The modern state thus presupposed a factual concentration of power, the existence of an appropriate administrative order, and a series of further social conditions, but it cannot be understood as mere fact in the sense of the positivists. The modern state in the full sense of the word only "exists" if it is recognized by its inhabitants and by the other members of the international state system. This implies that the people involved in specific respects know *what* is to be recognized and what "recognition" means here. If Max Weber's analysis is right, a state only "exists" insofar as a power apparatus with a de facto monopoly on the use of force within a given geographic area makes a specific claim (to "legitimacy") that is in fact accepted by the inhabitants of the relevant area (and by legal and diplomatic authorities of other states).[6] Thus, for the state as an institution to be fully realized, one must have at one's disposal at least a crude concept of the state. Since they have a proleptic character, preliminary concept formations of this kind can either succeed, if they come to be established in ordinary and scientific linguistic usage and anchored by corresponding social institutions that are based on them, or fail and be forgotten outside historical reports. "Church" (as a designation for a new kind of religious community of Christians arising in late Antiquity), "evil," or "the United Nations"[7] are successful new creations; "dictatorship of the proletariat," "*phalanstères*," and "New American Century," on the contrary, for different reasons that could be investigated historically, did not make it. From this perspective, political philosophy can be regarded as a kind of (conceptual) experimental science, as it was conceived by, for instance, Dewey, Nietzsche, or Brecht.[8]

In modern politics one can distinguish at least analytically between two dimensions. On the one hand, political life is structured by visible and hidden power relations of different kinds. Lenin's diagnosis was completely right: the eternally recurring question in our political life is "Who whom?"—that is, who can arrest, free, convince, influence, bribe, and so on whom? A political philosophy that makes it possible to disregard the question of power entirely has completely lost contact with reality and has become mere literature or "poetry." But if power is the first and last word in politics, it is certainly not, in its most naked form, the whole of the story in between. For human beings are also "evaluating animals" who can distinguish the good and the better from the less good, the bad, and the unbearable, who have expectations and make various claims on one another, and who are sometimes in the position to reject these claims as badly justified or simply unacceptable. Whoever has power automatically has an interest in proceeding with at least the appearance of legitimacy, since successful legitimation makes the possession of power more secure and its exercise easier. Thus, modern politics is characteristically about, among other things, the relationship between power and legitimation, and the ways in which one is brought to bear on the other. The question always arises: Is this relation in a given case transparently arranged or not? There will be a recurring temptation to fall back into the old error mentioned above of distinguishing too sharply between "ought" and "is" and corrupting the analytically useful distinction between power and legitimacy by epistemologically reifying it, as if it were a matter of two totally separate spheres with completely different rules, principles, and laws.[9]

Another task of political philosophy, ideology critique, is located here.[10] Ideology critique tries to illuminate nontransparent combinations of claims to power and knowledge as well as legitimacy. To be sure, factually existing situations in which power is systematically used to uphold distorted structures of knowledge or to feign legitimacy are neither dissolved nor done away with through insight alone, but groups of people who have acquired the appropriate "insight" are in most cases probably better positioned to perceive their interests in realistic ways and to work toward dismantling objectionable power structures. To underline the point once again: sometimes we can come to see that the existence of certain power relations has the effect of distorting our view of the world, and in some cases we can also see that power relations produce the mere appearance of legitimacy where no real legitimacy exists. Neither of these facts, though, should be taken to imply that there could be any such thing as a realm of human affairs from which power relations were completely absent, a kind of human knowledge for the full understanding of which an analysis of social power relations was irrelevant, or a form of "real legitimacy" that was in any sense absolute. These are all fantasies, which critics of ideology can also see through and to which they need not themselves be subject.

The ideology critique we know from the nineteenth and early-twentieth century refers to a specific historical situation: society is divided into two groups, capitalists and proletarians. The capitalists possess factories, ships, machines, and railways, and have disposal as a class over highly extensive economic and therefore also social and political power; the proletarians, by contrast, possess only their own labor power. The society constituted by the unmoving, in a sense fast-frozen, radically asymmetrical power relations between these two groups keeps itself alive among other ways by producing and disseminating ideologies, that is, false forms of consciousness that stabilize the existing economic order. Since flexibility is a great advantage, it is no wonder that the nineteenth and twentieth century featured a wide array of different kinds of ideological products: the current form of economy is especially rational and incomparably productive, it corresponds to the "natural order of things" and is based on inalienable "human rights," the owners have "earned" their position, and so on. These are all pure, content-free illusions, up to and including the clause about "productivity." Statements about the productivity of an economic form presuppose complex assumptions about boundary conditions and measurement procedures that are themselves in principle wholly questionable, although it was in fact simply assumed by friends of ideology critique that something like the capitalist economy of the eighteenth and early-nineteenth century was more productive than all other economic forms.

Of course, the statement "x is more productive than y" can, even when specified appropriately and well founded, assume an ideological function if its epistemological status is not specified and it is *not* specifically and explicitly presented as a merely historical observation of fact. The members of *both* classes, capitalists and proletarians, may possibly suffer equally and in the same way from delusion, the only difference being that the relevant illusions serve the capitalists' interests in upholding the present order while they make it more difficult for proletarians to perceive their own real interests. A capitalist who supported laissez-faire in 1820 could with good reason feel comforted by his illusions and they could contribute to his sense of well-being. A laissez-faire proletarian, in contrast, would be a sad case: to his ideological delusion would have to be added the baleful damage to his own interests.[11]

For this reason ideology cannot simply be identified with the somewhat different phenomenon of wishful thinking. I am subject to wishful thinking when my own drives, desires, goals, tendencies, or preferences overwhelmingly, unduly, or in an inappropriate way influence the processes through which I develop my ideas about the character of the world around me. What exactly "overwhelmingly," "unduly," or "in an inappropriate way" mean must for the moment remain open. But the use of these expressions need not presuppose that one can say *positively* how in general a completely "appropriate" relation between the structure of our wishes and our epistemic apparatus would have to be constituted. And *complete* appropriateness is probably also a mere fantasy. Of course it also does not presuppose that human knowledge plays out in a hermetically sealed, dust-free space in which our drives, wishes, and goals have in principle no role.[12] But the designation "wishful thinking" refers unambiguously to the properties of a process of belief-formation, not to its result. An idea that is based on wishful thinking can therefore turn out to be true, as in the case of someone who is completely and stubbornly convinced that next time he will win the lottery. It may happen that one day he wins; but, unless he has bribed the people who run the lottery, his conviction is based not on a realistic appraisal of his environment, but on a drive-based hope.

To the extent that they have reached a certain cultural level and are not victims of pathological personality development, human beings have a very strong tendency to cling to an affirmative self-image, that is, to see themselves, their character, their properties, their intentions and actions in a positive light. Nietzsche suggests that we think of this drive to self-affirmation in anthropomorphic terms: it is a clever but devious impulse that likes to hide and camouflage itself, sometimes presenting itself as the opposite of what it is, that is, as a form of self-abnegation rather than self-aggrandizement. It is adept at finding hidden channels and pursuing its ends through an almost untraceable sequence of detours, reverses, and switchbacks. To say this is not to give a negative moral judgment on this human characteristic. That I have a tendency to entertain ideas that are flattering to myself can be harmless. Within certain limits it can even have a positive significance, if human life is in fact so unbearable that one must hold on to illusions in order to survive[13]—assuming, naturally, that survival has a value. But "tendencies" are not always irresistible. Even if it is true that there is a remnant of illusory self-centeredness so deeply rooted in us that it is practically ineradicable, that would be no reason to be content with our tendency to develop illusions that flatter us rather than, to the extent that we can, to check and combat them.

Wishful thinking of course exists not only on a small scale, but also as a collective phenomenon. Small groups as well as whole societies often work assiduously to make their own actions, attitudes, decisions, or properties appear externally to members of other groups in the best light, but also struggle to convince members of their own "we-group" of their own praiseworthy particularities.[14]

In colloquial language the expression "wishful thinking" rightly has negative overtones, but they are often based on a seriously skewed image of the relations between the structure of wishes and "reality," whereby more substantial determinateness is attributed to reality than is warranted. If one has a complete account of the facts, then wishes are in fact no help. If my friend has really died, the wish that he might still be alive is impotent and for most people probably does not even have psychological value, for example, as "comfort." But here we should not overlook the fact that what we in hindsight call "reality" was in the past often a highly indefinite future, and that this indefiniteness plays a large role in human life.[15] When an objectively indefinite future (or present) is involved, the balance is not always so clear. Our attitudes can under certain conditions themselves in whole or in part come true by helping to produce the reality we wish for. Those with illusions about the friendliness of the world who encounter others under all circumstances in a friendly way will naturally occasionally have very bad experiences, but they may possibly in some situations have a greater chance of being received in a friendly way than a cool, distanced skeptic.

After all, there are some goals one can only achieve if one has a belief in oneself, one's abilities, and one's luck that exceeds what can be proven, and thus a belief that in some sense must be irrational. There can be cases like that of a man who is psychologically unable to buy a lottery ticket for fun or on the off chance, but could only take a shot if he imagined that this time he would definitely win.[16] If he is for no reason convinced that he will win the lottery next time, he is clearly the victim of wishful thinking. But of course it can also "accidentally" turn out that this time he does in fact win. His firm but baseless conviction did not itself conjure up this success, but had he not had this unjustified belief, he would not have bought a ticket, and without the ticket he surely would not have won.

In paradigmatic cases wishful thinking can be distinguished from ideology in two respects. First, wishful thinking is a matter of active conative structures, that is, "preferences," tendencies, while ideology critique is about "interests,"[17] that is, structures that at least make a claim in the longer run to be oriented toward a good that is allegedly not merely subjective. Second, the "wishes" that are involved in the paradigmatic case of wishful thinking are *self-referential* wishes: *we* wish for the whole world to find *us* great, and adjust our knowledge about ourselves accordingly. We are the bearers of a *mission civilisatrice*, and not, for instance, an occupying army that uses torture against the native population (France in Algeria, 1954–1962); we are protecting peaceful settlers, and are not mass murderers (the United States during the Indian Wars of the eighteenth and nineteenth centuries); we are introducing "freedom" and "democracy," and are not a colonial power (likewise the United States in the twentieth century in the Philippines, central American, Vietnam, and so on). Even if outsiders are able to see through these narcissistic mental structures, the illusions to which they give rise can still reinforce a positive self-evaluation on the part of those who fall prey to this kind of wishful thinking. In contrast, it is characteristic of ideologies that many victims of ideological delusion do not promote their *own* interests, but precisely the "objective" interests of a completely different group. An ideology would be of very little value for capitalism if *no* proletarian and *no* member of the smaller classes that have not yet been dissolved (such as small, still independent craftsmen or shopkeepers) ever took it seriously in any way. The trick in developing an ideology sometimes consists in tapping into the motivational potential of self-reflective wishful thinking and using it for the identification with certain ideological positions. Thus, the most exploited members of the British proletariat in the nineteenth century, for instance, when they had served in the colonial army, regarded themselves as the betters of Indians or Africans *because* they identified within certain limits and under certain conditions with the masters of the global empire. In this way they contributed to the consolidation of an imperialist ideology that only to a highly restricted degree was compatible with their own, longer-term interests.

Another task of political philosophy emerges in connection with the writings of Michel Foucault. In everyday political life we often refer to theoretical complexes that count for us as obvious unities. One speaks of the free and democratic legal order or the liberal-democratic state as if each was a seamless web of elements that "naturally" complement one another and belong together. This semblance of natural unity is, however, an illusion.[18] One can show by historical analysis that conceptual elements that apparently "naturally" refer to one another (like "democracy," "liberalism," the "state") originally had little to do with one another or were even mutually antagonistic. Thus, in the seventeenth century the concept of the "state" was introduced as a theory-laden designation for a coercive apparatus that had not yet fully developed in political reality but the prospect of which seemed especially reasonable and desirable. This concept had precisely the meaning of clamping down on democratic aspirations.[19] It is widely known that historically "democracy" and "liberalism" were antagonists: either the full assembly had the last word (democracy) or it was under no circumstances allowed to violate certain rights-based principles like tolerance, individual freedom, and so on (liberalism). Genealogical analysis sets out to show how historical processes, which were contingent as well as occasionally violent, brought together incompatible things (like democracy, liberalism, and the state) and how the appearance of the quasi-normative obviousness of the artificial unity thus produced spread.

Using the terminology of German Idealism, we can say that the last three tasks—the critique of wishful thinking, ideology critique, and genealogy—all amount to analyses of deficits of reflection, be it psychological (wishful thinking), sociological (ideology critique), or historical (genealogy). Political philosophy has the task, in each case somewhat different, of recognizing and undoing misleading abstraction.

In *Philosophy and Real Political* I put forth the thesis that a large share of the current ideas that have been articulated in the most various works of analytical philosophy either express wishful thinking, turn out to be ideologies, or cannot withstand serious genealogical investigation.

Unfortunately, in *Philosophy and Real Politics* I used the word "realism" to designate a political philosophy that aims to proceed in the most "reflective" possible way—that means a philosophy that works with ideology critique and genealogy and constantly checks its own basic concepts with respect to their possible origin in wishful thinking. Since the word "realism" is highly ambiguous, in retrospect it is no wonder that its use in central places in *Philosophy and Real Politics* has given rise to misunderstandings.

The word "realism" has at least four different meanings, depending on the context. "Realism" is used first in a metaphysical or epistemological sense. A philosopher represents a "realistic" position in metaphysics when, for example, he argues, in opposition to nominalism, for the real existence of universals ("*universalia ante res*"), or when he asserts, in opposition to idealism, the existence of the familiar world around us independent of mind. The epistemological "realist" is convinced that we have unmediated access to our world through our sense perception.

In international relations theory (IR), however, "realism" has a completely different meaning.[20] In the first place it is a thesis about the kind of explanation to be sought in political contexts; then of course it often becomes a normative thesis. Political decisions, according to the realists, are to be explained with reference to the concrete (material) interests of the respective actors or to the efforts that can be assumed to exist among them to secure and expand their own power. *Moral* reasons that are given are always at best pretexts and have explanatory power only insofar as they, for instance, are used to deceive or influence naïve others who are susceptible to such arguments. The "normative" variant thus has it that political powerholders should never be distracted from pursuing their own political goals (expanding their power and satisfying their interests) by moral reasons. In the most benign subvariant, "expanding their power" is understood as "expanding the room for maneuver of one's own state vis-à-vis other states" and "satisfying their interests" as "the maximal satisfaction of the interests of all citizens," but there are naturally much less benign readings. The de facto primary antagonists of "realists" in the existing IR literature are called "liberals," but one can easily imagine a whole range of "nonliberal" theories of politics that are incompatible with the basic principles of the "realism" sketched above.

There is also a third, more colloquial use of "realism," where "realism" is set in opposition to utopianism. The realist is someone who never undertakes anything that is not "possible" in a given situation, or even one who attempts always to restrict his own wishes to what can be achieved in the existing situation. Of course it may be significantly more difficult than it initially appears to distinguish attitudes that are "realistic" in this sense from utopian ones, since concepts like "in the given situation" and "possible" are so indefinite. Moreover, the determination of what is "fundamentally possible" for me or for us in most cases depends at least in part on my or our other preferences, character traits, values, and attitudes. To what extent am I—or are we—prepared to pursue my—or our—goals stubbornly, bitterly, and without compromise, to exert and apply my—or our—power? To what extent am I—or are we—ready to neglect or even damage other values and possibly to accept painful losses?

In any case, one can estimate what is "possible" for us only if one knows who all is meant by "we." If I identify with other citizens of the European Union, all sorts of things that would be unachievable for me as a private individual might be "possible" for "us." If "we" refers to the human race, "we" have even further possibilities.

In *Philosophy and Real Politics* "realism" is used in a fourth sense. According to this usage, a "realistic" assessment of a situation would be one in which the agent's view was not limited, impeded, or distorted by wishful thinking or ideology. Finally, "realism" in this sense would require that the assessment in question not depend on taking for granted problematic identities or forms of valuation just because they are presupposed in everyday life. "Realism" in this sense is by no means necessarily antiutopian. Those who argue against wishful thinking do not after all necessarily want to abolish or restrict wishes themselves. Someone who takes into account the world we live in with a sober eye might still without difficulty also harbor "utopian" wishes, that is, wishes he knows are not to be realized. Indeed, it is completely open to the realist to depict utopian conditions in all their particulars if he has a mind to. Wishes or wish-images of this kind can, despite their utopian character, play an important role in our psychological household, our common projects, our political actions, and so on. The point is not to confuse them with reality and not to be confused about their epistemic standing. The difference between "realism" in this fourth sense and "realism" as it is used in the IR literature should probably also be clear. The realist in question here need by no means claim that politics is *really* only about power and material interests, but can rather point out that the concept "*material* interest" is completely indeterminate and accordingly as good as useless. Of course the behavior of many people, including the political behavior of great states, cannot be explained if one does not consider their ethical or "normative" ideas, and the realist has nothing against this, as long as these ideas are really action-motivating. On the other hand, power relations are so obviously important that a political philosophy that systematically disregarded them would automatically have to be suspected of being ideological.

An especially influential strand of analytical philosophy that goes back to the works of Rawls stands, according to the main thesis of *Philosophy and Real Politics*, under a very strong suspicion of being ideology because

Rawls's whole procedure is directed toward making power invisible. The same suspicion applies to two further presuppositions of Rawlsian philosophy, namely, the idea that there can be a completely freestanding ethics and the thesis that political philosophy can best be understood as applied (individual) ethics.

To repeat it once more in conclusion: realism properly understood is opposed to ideological, not to utopian, thinking. Rawlsian theory is *both* insufficiently realistic *and* insufficiently utopian. It is insufficiently utopian because the basic structure of the North American social and economic order is simply presupposed and never really questioned. The highest flight of fancy Rawls ever managed was to envision a small redistribution of goods within the presupposed political, social, and economic system. Without too much exaggeration one could say that the socially transformative potential of Rawlsian theory is exhausted by tax reform. Rawlsian philosophy is insufficiently realistic because social reality appears in its theory only in a peculiarly distorted form, cleansed of all power phenomena and deformed by wishful thinking. Beyond this it imagines that its decidedly modest reform proposals could in principle be realized within the reality it analyzes—as that reality, as it were, "really is," not merely as it appears in the theory. Hegel, Marx, Nietzsche, Weber, Lenin, Dewey, Adorno, and Foucault are better models for contemporary political philosophy than Kant, Rawls, Nozick, Dworkin, or Habermas.

NOTES

Originally published as "Realismus, Wunschdenken, Utopie," *Deutsche Zeitschrift für Philosophie* 58, no. 3 (2010): 419–429.

1. Raymond Geuss, *Philosophy and Real Politics* (Princeton: Princeton University Press, 2008).
2. Max Weber, "Objectivity in Social Science and Social Policy," in *Max Weber on the Methodology of the Social Sciences*, ed. and trans. Edward Shils and Henry Finch (Glencoe, Ill.: Free Press, 1949), 84.
3. Raymond Geuss, "Vix intellegitur," in *A World Without Why* (Princeton: Princeton University Press, 2015), 22–44.
4. Karl Marx and Friedrich Engels, "The German Ideology," in *Marx and Engels: Selected Writings*, ed. Lawrence H. Simon (Indianapolis: Hackett, 1994), 107.
5. Quentin Skinner, "The State," in *Political Innovation and Conceptual Change*, ed. Terrence Ball (Cambridge: Cambridge University Press, 1989), 6–23.

6   Max Weber, "Politics as a Vocation" (1919), in *The Vocation Lectures*, ed. David Owen and Tracy Strong, trans. Rodney Livingstone (Indianapolis: Hackett, 2004); and Weber, *Economy and Society*, ed. Guenther Roth and Claus Wittich, trans. Ephraim Fischoff et al. (Berkeley: University of California Press, 1978), 31–38.
7   On *evil*, see Friedrich Nietzsche, *On the Genealogy of Morality*, ed. Keith Ansell-Pearson, trans. Carol Diethe (Cambridge: Cambridge University Press, 1997). On the United Nations, see Mark Mazower, *No Enchanted Place* (Princeton: Princeton University Press, 2009).
8   John Dewey, "The Quest for Certainty," in *The Later Works*, ed. J. A. Boydston, vol. 4 (Carbondale: Southern Illinois University, 1988); Friedrich Nietzsche, *Beyond Good and Evil*, trans. Walter Kaufman (New York: Vintage, 1989); Bertolt Brecht, *The Measures Taken* (1930), trans. Carl R. Mueller (London: Methuen, 1977).
9   Michel Foucault, *Discipline and Punish*, trans. Alan Sheridan (New York: Vintage, 1975).
10 Raymond Geuss, *Glück und Politik* (Berlin: BWV, 2004), 111–121.
11 "The propertied class and the class of the proletariat present the same human self-estrangement. But the former class feels at ease and strengthened in this self-estrangement, it recognizes estrangement as its own power and has in it the semblance of a human existence. The class of the proletariat feels annihilated in estrangement." Karl Marx, "The Holy Family," in *Marx/Engels Collected Works* (*MECW*) (Moscow: Progress, 1975–2005), 4:35.
12 Nietzsche, *On the Genealogy of Morality*.
13 Friedrich Nietzsche, *The Birth of Tragedy*, trans. Douglas Smith (Oxford: Oxford University Press, 2008).
14 See, for example, Robert Musil, *Der Mann ohne Eigenschaften* (Reinbek: Rowohlt, 1952), 18, 19, 35.
15 Bernard Williams, "Moral Luck," in *Moral Luck* (Cambridge: Cambridge University Press, 1981), 20–39.
16 In the 1970s and 1980s my now deceased former colleague David Lewis always insisted that the Princeton Philosophy Department would only be able to fill a position when (a majority of) the members of the department were convinced not only that one candidate was better qualified than all others, but *also* that all other candidates who might somehow come into question were *not* qualified. He himself held this attitude to be immoral in the highest imaginable degree, and he explicitly presented his thesis not as a general social-psychological law, but as something that held *for this institution alone*.
17 Raymond Geuss, *The Idea of a Critical Theory* (Cambridge: Cambridge University Press, 1981), 45–54.
18 John Dunn, *Setting the People Free* (London: Atlantic, 2005); Raymond Geuss, *History and Illusion in Politics* (Cambridge: Cambridge University Press, 2001).
19 Skinner, "The State."
20 Raymond Geuss, *Politics and the Imagination* (Princeton: Princeton University Press, 2010), 31–42.

13

DESIRE AND SHIPWRECK

Powers of the *Vis Utopica*

ÉTIENNE TASSIN

"The world has long dreamed of possessing something of which it has only to be conscious in order to possess it in reality," writes Marx in a letter to Ruge from September 1843.[1] For the dream to become reality, it is sufficient that, here and now, humanity be aware of its ancient desire in order to give it existence, to actualize and see the birth of a new society."

In this letter to Ruge, Marx opposes this becoming-aware to the utopian projects of Étienne Cabet.[2] There is no need for a *Voyage to Icaria* to create from scratch, in the New World, in the form of an experimental community that breaks totally with the past, a future that cannot be anticipated here in the old. What the Icarian utopia presupposes is that this world, with its past of oppression and domination, injustice and inequality, is not pregnant with a future. It is dead to all promise. It is necessary to leave and begin anew from scratch, elsewhere, to create new communities founded on the true principles of justice and equality. One could obviously then hope that the experiences of utopian communities spread throughout the world would end up providing evidence that a community based on their true principles could give rise to social life freed from oppression and domination.

What Marx suggests, to the contrary, is that *this* world bears within itself an old dream that has been repressed, but can emerge. This, then, supposes that

1. the future is not elsewhere, in another world, but here in the real world—or, in other words, that there is not an old and a new world but *one* world;
2. it is a matter of transforming this world by giving flesh to its dream, of waking it from its dogmatic slumber rather than dogmatically constructing a new world, or trying to make one elsewhere, outside this world; and
3. political criticism therefore has a specific task: effecting this actualization of the dream by becoming aware.

The task of a philosophy involved in political struggle is "the ruthless criticism of all that exists." "We do not dogmatically anticipate the world, but only want to find the new world through criticism of the old one," Marx writes. While anticipation projects a new world into an improbable future, discovery reveals in the past its promises for the future. While anticipation of the future is dogmatic and technological (making a new society starting from a tabula rasa), discovery is critical and reflexive (actualizing the powers of the dream). While Cabet's communism is a dogmatic abstraction, it is left to us, Marx writes to Ruge, to "show the world what it is really fighting for. . . . The reform of consciousness consists *only* in making the world aware of its own consciousness, in awakening it out of its dream about itself, in *explaining* to it the meaning of its own actions." Our motto will therefore be, he adds, "reform of consciousness not through dogmas, but by analysing the mystical consciousness that is unintelligible to itself." In short, "it is not a question of drawing a great mental dividing line between past and future, but of *realizing* the thoughts of the past."[3]

Marx thus opposes the realism of political criticism to the dogmatism of Cabet's utopian socialism. But perhaps what he announces here is less an alternative between the dogmatic utopia of Icarian communities and the realism of a political struggle that aims to awaken the sleeping consciousness of subjugated and exploited peoples than an alternative between two regimes of desire—which is also to say, two conceptions of utopia. For what is in fact expressed here are desire's two dimensions: the desire for an elsewhere-to-come, condemned to meet only with its own wreckage as the price of its realization; and the desire for justice that, self-aware, can take reality as the consciousness of injustices and the desire to combat them. In this exchange with Ruge, does Marx not invite us to think the difference between the actualization of desire (its consciousness-raising, we can say) and the realization of its object (the creation of Icaria); or, further, the difference between a reflective utopia that makes the dream conscious and gives flesh to the imagination and a productive utopia that submits the dream of justice to the concrete, constraining forms of a reputedly perfect social order?

This is the question I would like to raise. There is no utopia that is not the expression of a desire, no thought of utopia that is not a meditation on desire, and thus on its relation to reality. I propose to examine the tension within utopian desire between the actualization of the dream as dream and the realization of its object. Is not the very real efficacy of utopia to give existence to the dream as dream and not to destroy reality and the dream by pretending to realize the dream? What, then, is the power proper to the *vis utopica*, utopia's specific efficacy?

I will begin by returning to Socrates's argument concerning the desire for the just city in order to examine the division within utopia in the nineteenth century, a division I propose to illustrate by the image of the shipwreck, with which various parties bore witness to the failures of utopian communities. Perhaps we will then finally be able to understand the properly utopian dimension of Marx's critical project in 1843: "We do not confront the world in a doctrinaire way with a new principle: Here is the truth, kneel down before it! We develop new principles for the world out of the world's own principles."[4]

OF UTOPIAN DESIRE: THE PARADOX OF THE UNREALIZABLE CITY

There is no politics without the desire for a society that can be called just and without the projection of what is desirable. But it is still necessary to distinguish the wished-for ideal from the realized ideal, or the desire for the ideal from the desire to realize it. The definition of a political ideal is not to be confused with the project of realizing it. The desire that aims at the ideal is not illusory. It is only the claim to realize it that creates or maintains an illusion, for, as Freud writes, "we call a belief an illusion when wish-fulfillment is a prominent factor in its motivation."⁵ It is not an illusion to desire what we judge to be worth wishing for, for it would be inconceivable for us to wish for something without desiring it. To the contrary, illusion resides in the belief that what is worth wishing for is *to be realized* and that it is *realizable*.

In a now-classic analysis, Leo Strauss argued that what characterizes modernity is not so much its conception of an ideal, which we find already formulated by the ancients, as the belief in the realization of this ideal, in its possible realization.⁶ Between the ancients and the moderns, therefore, the status of utopia changes. We could say that Greek political thought conceives of the ideal city without deducing from this the necessity of realizing it, whereas modern political thought does not conceive of an ideal that would remain purely ideal. For the Greeks, the desire for justice does not imply the desire to realize it. The best regime in speech (in *logos*) is not destined to become the best regime in fact (according to historical conditions). This is what Socrates makes clear in Plato's *Republic*.

Having referred to the lost city of Atlantis, in the *Republic* Plato sets out the principles of the just city, a city conceived as an ideal—in words, according to *logos*—as that which answers to the rational criteria of universally shared justice. But he immediately introduces a doubt as to whether this city, defined ideally as the "best regime in speech," could be in any way realized. Indeed, it seems destined to remain an Idea, not only because its realization would not be *possible*—it would be extremely difficult for men and women to achieve the necessary conditions to make it—but, moreover, because this realization is perhaps not, in the end, *to be wished for*. We cannot realize the desirable city; even more, we cannot even desire that it be realized.

In the first place, Socrates has to take on three arguments to prove that the realization of this perfect city cannot be *envisioned*: we must first of all accept that women be integrated into the guardian class on equal terms with men; we must then accept a community of women and children; and finally we must accept that philosophers will consent to go back down into the cave and concern themselves with the affairs of the city.⁷ Each step of the argument reinforces the doubt we feel from the beginning that the realization of the city is nothing but a pious wish.⁸ To be sure, having multiplied the hesitations as to the status of this idea and its effectiveness[9] along with certain reservations,[10] Socrates carries on *as if* the city he finally describes "is not altogether a daydream" and everyone can agree that, "though it is difficult, it is in a way possible."[11] But the alert reader cannot underestimate either Socrates's reticence or what it signifies. As Strauss shows, if Plato writes so as to let it be understood that the resistances can be eventually overcome, as if the just city could be realizable in fact, all the while suggesting to his perceptive readers that it could not be at all, it is because it is necessary to let the vulgar among them think that it could be. By way of these perplexities, by letting the vulgar think that a perfect city can be realized, Socrates in fact lets the philosopher understand the higher point that no one should try to implement the idea of a just city.

For Socrates puts forth, in the second place, another argument that indicates, at the very moment it shows the means of putting it to work, why the realization of the just city is not *to be wished for*. To realize a city that corresponds to the requirements of justice that have been defined in words, it would be necessary for the philosophers who have been called on to govern the city to act as tyrants. In order to build their just city, there would be no other solution than to take the children of Athens and send them deep into the countryside so that they can receive, far from their current homes, the education needed to make them citizens of the perfect city.[12] The rejection of the family structure, the second of the arguments that make the city hard to wish for, requires that children be removed from their parents' authority by force because the latter maintain the morals that must be broken for children to be raised according to the rules of the just city. It is through intolerable violence that philosophers, no longer kings but tyrants, could bring about the city defined in words. Now, instead of the idea serving as a yardstick by which to measure the injustice of real cities, it becomes the "boss," the model to be executed, and thus requires, as Hannah Arendt shows, the violence that every work does to its material, be it human or other.[13] In going from being an idea to be contemplated to an idea to be applied, there is a slide that subjects political action to technical work and transforms free action into constrained and constraining fabrication. Socrates warns us against this as he carefully underlines in passing: "A pattern, then, was what we wanted when we were inquiring into the nature of ideal justice and asking what would be the character of the perfectly just man. . . . We wished to fix our eyes upon them as types and models, so that whatever we discerned in them of happiness or the reverse would necessarily apply to ourselves.... *Our purpose was not to demonstrate the possibility of the realization of these ideals.*"[14]

This, then, is the paradox Socrates reveals: the just city could be realized only by recourse to the most unjust means; realized perfection would justify tyranny. To see the just city realized is an enterprise that does not belong to human beings because they could claim it only by making themselves into demiurges, at the price of intolerable violence that would contradict the perfection of the desired city. The desirable cannot be realized without destroying what makes it desirable. Thus the paradox starts again: that which is most to be wished, the just city, is so only owing to its unreality; what is most desirable *in speech*—according to *logos*—is not so *in fact*. We are not allowed to desire the realization of the desirable. Conversely, those who truly desire justice cannot want this city that has been recognized as being just ideally to exist in fact. Those who truly desire justice cannot desire that it be realized. All they can want is for people to seek it, limiting their efforts to a struggle against injustice; they cannot desire that people give themselves the means to actualize this possibility since that would be to desire tyranny, even if only as a means to achieving justice. Thus, the unjust means would contradict the end. We will never be able to attain justice by means of injustice, even if, conversely, only the injustice of the means could actualize—that is, realize—justice.

We understand that the just city cannot exist as a "thing" that could be built, which we could bring into existence by certain appropriate means. Justice exists only as the object of a continual and infinite struggle, never as an achieved work, as a good that could be possessed or forged by human means. Justice exists only as so many just actions that carry it out but do not reify it into any relation that claims to be objectively just. It cannot be a "work" produced by a *tekhnē*.

This status of the just city—or of justice in itself—depends, in Strauss's language, on what for the Greeks *is*—that is, some particular imperfect and still unjust city, whatever its virtues—never being equal to what it must or should be, namely, the perfect city. The Greeks, says Strauss, knew that the chasm between being and what should be could not be filled and that it was not the role of human beings to claim to do so—a lesson in modesty, or in wisdom. The good in itself always transcends the good realized, so that we will never stop trying to realize it. We will never be done with the politics that tries to make the city more just. But the fact that we know that we will never be done with it does not imply that we give up our desire for justice as a vain task. On the contrary, it implies that we never slacken in our efforts although their goal is never attained. No one can call himself just in the sense that he embodies justice; no society could claim that it has finally done with justice, that it has realized it once and for all. And we can say the same thing about equality or freedom. The temporality of the political is in-finite, a beginning that does not end, of indefinitely beginning again.

The consideration of the just city—or, in our language, the utopian imagination—teaches us that politics contradicts the technologies of domination and the management of the social.

THE REALIZATION OF UTOPIAN DESIRE: DESPOTISM

The *Republic* allows us to appreciate what separates the ancients from the moderns on this point. Everyone knows the famous allegory of the cave, which describes unenlightened humanity as a group of prisoners chained to their prejudices and errors, taking appearances for reality and ineluctably condemned to illusion. The allegory stages the paradox of illusion: those who are subject to it, subject to the cave, cannot leave it. They would have to be outside to know that they are inside, since they would have to be in truth in order to know that they are in error. But those who are chained to and within this inside can never reach a position of clarity that would allow them to recognize their status as prisoners and escape the illusion by destroying the error they take for the truth. We can only be pulled out of this paradoxical situation, which does not contain a solution within itself, by some external remedy—that of the philosopher who, detached from all illusion, having reached the outside where he encounters the truth, delivers us from our error.[15]

The allegory is easily translated into politics. Only an enlightened despot (a philosopher-king or a king-philosopher) can emancipate the people from their illusions. The condition: having himself had access to truth itself (to the true idea of justice, to justice in itself), he has, by acquiring the truth, acquired the principle for verifiably distinguishing between appearance and reality, error and truth, illusion and science. There is a political lesson here, a lesson that puts us on guard precisely against enlightened despots and the illusion that moves them to be those whom destiny has named to emancipate the people from its illusions. For if the philosopher, as he who possesses the truth, is delivered from illusion, it is still not permissible for him to deliver the people from it.

Why can the supposed possessor of truth not deliver the people from their illusions? For two reasons.

On the one hand, it is because the people, imprisoned within their own illusions, do not want it. (Plato writes that they put to death the philosopher who risked himself by going back down into the cave in the hope of freeing the prisoners.)[16] The people are imprisoned by their illusions not because they take their desires for reality, but because they take the poor appearances that shimmer before their eyes for the object of their desire; the object of their desire is appearance. The people cannot desire truth; truth is not popular. The people cannot desire beyond what they see, what they possesses. What the people lack, which holds them in servitude, is the power of the desire that corresponds to what Ernst Bloch called "the utopian surplus."[17] Utopia is excessive. It is to desire more than can be wished for; it is to desire the impossible, what cannot be done. The people, prisoners of the consuming images that are delivered to their view and bridle their imagination, curb their desire and shackle the movement by which they could imagine having more than what they have been persuaded they have a right to, being more than the place and the role to which they have been assigned.

On the other hand, for his part, the philosopher does not want to go back down into the cave. In a delicious paradox, all the sophistical art of a Thrasymachus is required to persuade the philosopher to give up the contemplation of truth in order to go convince the idol-worshipers in the cave that they are subject to illusion. But this victory of sophistry over philosophy would be a victory of persuasive power, which is illusory, over the convincing force of truth. For the people can only be delivered from their illusions at the price of the victory of an illusion. Here every Leninist theory of the avant-garde party—the modern revolutionary version of the theory of the philosopher-king—is invalidated in advance: it rests on this illusion. The party-king "knows" only what the people ignore, and the people can only follow at the price of this illusion.

On one side, then, the people lack the surplus of utopian desire to emancipate themselves by themselves. On the other, the excess of confidence—power's claim to possess the legitimate means to emancipate the people by means of the capacity they believe they have to transform them—maintains the despot (king, government, or party) in the illusion of justified omnipotence.

How does it happen that the people cannot desire beyond the visible and the feasible, and that the emancipatory power of power is really an illusion? The *Republic* does not invite us to reproduce among those who govern—despots or parties who feel they are invested with an emancipatory mission—the illusion in which the people are supposed to be trapped, the logic of which they are content to reverse. Making of the truth (of the ideal city known in its truth) the object of practical, political desire, an ideal to realize—such is the inverse but symmetrical face of the illusion that characterizes the ignorant people. Those who believe that the just city, which is by definition of the order of the "should-be," should and can be realized are subject to an illusion equal to that of the people who believe that the only reality is the one they live and see. Political emancipation requires, first, that the people give itself over to the utopian surplus by freeing itself from the realism of images and, second, that power free itself from the excess of realism that justifies its claim to power by recognizing the indeterminable character of the people and giving itself over to the indetermination of history.

At bottom, Plato's lesson would be the following: in politics, the worst illusion is to believe that we can realize our desire, be it for justice or for freedom, wealth, ethnic purity, and the like, in the form of a historically constructed society that would correspond to the idea we can make for ourselves of the just city. In short, the worst illusion would be to believe that, through a scientifically established and judiciously shaped politics, people can unite what should be with what is, so that real cities are made on the model of the ideal city and real, imperfect cities give way to the perfect city. We could put it another way: the most dangerous political illusion is to deny utopia in its utopian dimension so as to pretend to realize it in fact.

THE TWO FACES OF MODERN UTOPIA:
THE STRAIGHT PATH AND THE OBLIQUE

Arendt writes in *The Origins of Totalitarianism* that those who claimed to realize heaven on Earth in fact produced hell.[18] In wanting to realize heaven on Earth, human beings made a hell. The reversal of heaven into hell is brought about by the passage from the heavens to the Earth, by the movement that pretends to realize the ideal, to give substance to desire. The ideal is ideal in the heavens; on Earth it is abhorrent. Conventional wisdom attributes this function of illusion to utopia. Utopia is dangerous, it says, insofar as it invites us to configure social and political reality on the model of the ideal city, which, constructed *in abstracto*, turns out to be more rational and geometric the more it turns up its nose at the concrete circumstances and accidents of history. It could also be said that Plato was the precursor of totalitarianism, just as Rousseau was the precursor of Stalinism, or the cities imagined by the utopians prefigured the worst authoritarian plans for society. On this basis it would be the utopians, more than others and more dangerously than others, who carried illusion to its highest and most murderous extremes. Now, we need to reverse this judgment, not by reversing the relation but by showing that there are at least two ways of thinking utopia, and two uses of utopia: one that holds the surplus of desire at a distance from its realization and another that, because it seeks to be carried out, brings about the wreckage of the ideal.

As Miguel Abensour points out, utopia first of all fulfills a critical function.[19] Far from describing the realizable, far from simply inviting us to work toward realizing the cities they describe, in their very writing modern utopias, on the contrary, drive home the distance that separates Utopia from the historical world, so that the extreme difficulty of reaching the land of Utopia in turn signals the incongruity of a transport from Utopia to this world or a transposition of Utopia into this world. Further, far from being univocal, utopia covers its tracks the better to reveal the gap between the irreducible plurality of political possibilities and the reductive univocity of political positions that can be undertaken. This ambiguity is vouched for by More's *Utopia*, right down to its elusive title: "*Utopia*, the place that is nowhere; *Udetopia*, the place without time; or *Eutopia*, the happy place where everything is good—a plurality of meanings, inspirations, and forms."[20] For there is indeed in More's work, as Abensour shows, a positive relation to folly, a Machiavellian strategy of writing, and a recourse to trickery as the supreme value of *humanitas*—in short, a deliberate choice of an "oblique path" that makes it impossible to reduce *Utopia* to "an institutional project or a dogmatic plan for a future society."[21]

Yet it is not a matter of putting all utopias in the single category of disillusioned figurations of the political. Rather, we must think that the genre of utopia is itself permeated by a tension between two poles: that of a geometric and statist figuration of social order and the space of living together, and that of a disorganizing force, a resistance to any static form, to any fixing of the social order in the name of what, within the human, appeals to and at the same time transcends living together politically. In addition, we could, as Abensour invites us to do, distinguish between two types of utopia, and, within these utopias themselves, between two poles that establish an irreducible tension that could be the proper, unlocatable place of the political.

Some "direct their utopian energy (the *vis utopica*) toward the state in the name of the harmonious organization of society and, . . . haunted by the search for the perfect constitution, fold this force back onto the state form." These utopias that "aim at positive organization" are "haunted by the *illusion of a good regime*, which tends toward application, toward building an immediate relation with practical politics."[22] With them, the desire for perfection seeking realization always risks being reversed into tyranny. Others, conversely, "detach desire from the state," aiming at the "completely other social"[23] and inviting us to never reduce the human bond and political action to the sole level of organization or institutional form. In this case, desire, keeping its distance from positive application, exerts a critical and inventive force that the political cannot do without. The latter group, we could say, are not subject to the illusion of realizing their desire, of positively applying it. They inscribe the alterity of desire, the "completely other" social (the *no-where*) within the *hic et nunc* (the *now-here*) of acting together in such a way as to welcome into the present place of society this nonplace to come that undoes in advance the fantasy of a perfect organization of the social.

Instead of accusing utopia of being the matrix of totalitarian representations and projects for society, it would be better to ask "what relation should we posit between utopian projections and the social practices" that are historically deployed against them.[24] Considered from this angle, the utopian tradition is diversified. With utopias that "are inscribed, in the Jacobin tradition, within a global strategy for creating a political party," fabulation "is reduced to a merely ornamental function" and the utopian dimension "becomes a program, it decays into solutions." There then emerges the figure of power as the place and mode of the institution of social relations, the figure of good government that possesses knowledge of the social and claims to bring about good organization. The Icarian communities furnish an illustration of this despotic figure of utopia, a fusion of socialism and the state, in the form of realizing desire, a statist application of the dreamed city. However, as Abensour notes, it is within the same utopian tradition that the critique of this political illusion is born: "Déjacque against Cabet or Louis Blanc, William Morris against Bellamy."[25]

For it is a completely different tradition that opposes the revolutionary model born of 1793, of state revolution, with an ambition that is more subversive than constructive, whose originality in the nineteenth century was noted by Martin Buber.[26] What characterizes it is an antistatist strategy, the opening of a horizontal space of social experimentation, the proliferation of decentralized microcommunities as well as places of heterogeneous modes of socialization that resist the vertical organization of state power and give rise to a "society of societies."[27] Far from feeding the illusion of the rational achievement of the perfect city in history, utopia understood in this sense, on the contrary, invites us continually to deepen the gap between the utopian society and its institutions, on this basis introducing the idea of the constant modification of what is dreamed or desired.

There would thus be a strange historicity to the critical, nonprogrammatic realization of dreams of insurrectional utopias in the course of actions and social struggles that are not organized in advance by a centralized or organizational power. The key to this strange historicity is provided by William Morris: "men fight and lose the battle, and the thing that they fought for comes about in spite of their defeat, and when it comes turns out not to be what they meant, and other men have to fight for what they meant under another name."[28] Morris suggests a historical dynamic in place of a statist stasis, a dynamic that will never complete (satisfy and extinguish) desire, but ceaselessly carry it back from the incompletion of our efforts to realize it so that desire never concludes, never ends, since its object, which is never possessed, is always revived and pursued again. We could say, following Jacques Derrida, that desire deferred in time is reborn, to be sure, but differently. Taken up by others under other names, the object of desire is taken up in a "différance,"[29] and this différance is in principle the same as utopia as understood by Morris. The struggles we wage to achieve what we desire, which always partly fail, are nevertheless unceasingly reborn, the same and yet different, maintaining desire beyond successes and failures. These utopias of différance are temporizations and spacings, not plans and mandates.

This understanding of the nature of political struggle is at once critical and profoundly utopian. Desire is not realized by being provided with a structure of domination, an organization, by submitting it to power and using coercive means on its behalf. It is realized through action, not work; through struggle, not administration: an indefinite, interminable achievement, since utopia conceived in this way can only realize desire by leading it back to its original home, thereby establishing that no finished political form can satisfy it without contradiction. And this desire can only struggle to be realized by struggling at the same time against itself, against its own tendency to desire power, domination, and servitude, since, after all, power and organization are themselves always struggling against the powers of desire. This is what makes Fourier the perfect utopian: he turns the desiring passion back against the desire for order that desire always harbors as it is realized. Only the differant and deferred desire of critical utopia rises up against the statist forms of planned utopias that destroy the *vis utopica*.

SHIPWRECKS, OR REAL POLITICS

The discourses, doctrines, and political programs that proclaim their realism or pragmatism enclose the order of the possible within the allegedly rational and constraining net of reality. These realist discourses abound and are always right, since they invoke the reality principle and shunt off excessive desires to the pleasure principle. They always make one and the same argument: that of applied rationality, that is, "feasibility." This formula—trivial, antiutopian—is in reality antipolitical and supports a double illusion concerning the political: that politics is a matter of *domination*, of power exercised over individuals, groups, and institutions; and that politics is a matter of *managing* social relations, of an equilibrium or economy among antagonistic forces that must be harmonized. These are the illusions of sovereignty and governmentality. The two go together, transforming politics into a matter of strategic or economic calculation—"police" in Jacques Rancière's terms—and trying to push back the hard-to-control insurrectional powers of utopian desires, which they denounce as illusory and dangerous.

But it could be said, conversely, that there is only politics because of the utopian dimension of a desire for something else that knows that this desire is unrealizable. The much-mocked slogan in the opening of May '68 speaks the strict and happy truth of utopia: "Be realistic, demand the impossible." This formula contains the counterintuitive truth of utopia. It is in fact completely unrealistic to demand the possible, which is to say, the realizable. The possible can only be realized by ceasing to be what it is. There may be no greater or more dangerous illusion in politics than circumscribing demands by the domain of the possible. For with this, the forces of order believe they have succeeded. Utopian realism, this way of demanding the impossible, of desiring in excess of any real and of holding on to this unrealizable desire that makes *nowhere* and *now-here* coincide, enchants the real world with desire itself. It is the lucid and critical consciousness of the wide-awake dream. Far from awakening from this dream, utopia attempts, on the contrary, to awaken reality to its dream, as Marx says to Ruge.

All the same, a large share of the communitarian experiments of the nineteenth and twentieth century consisted in more or less rigorously planning the future by organizing the present. This is what Cabet did in Icaria, in the colony of Nauvoo, which ended up after a few years dividing and reproducing within itself the oppositions of values and interests at work in all societies.[30] As Buber recalls, the colony underwent schism after schism—on the one hand, because Cabet proved to be an authoritarian, but, on the other hand and above all, because he "made a bid for dictatorship in the form of dogmatic planning."[31] Thus, on the night of February 3, 1856, a scene from the French Revolution, the Tennis Court Oath, was repeated. It would of course have soon condemned the community to an irreparable divide that would have led to a new ninth of Thermidor, with Cabet in the role of deposed dictator.[32] In the history of the dissolution of the Icarian communities of Nauvoo and Corning, we see the paradox of utopian communities built on the idealization of a well-ordered society that gives substance to the desire for the just city. Because of the order they claim to impose equality, fraternity, and justice, they irresistibly reproduce the balancing act between the authoritarianism of dictatorships and the disorders of democratic societies, with their trail of rivalries and conflicts. The concrete, extraordinary realization of the desire for justice ends up in the ordinary shipwreck of society.

This wreck is not the privilege of Icarian communities. The Fourierist community of Reunion, Texas, for instance, supported by Victor Considerant, ended up in the "shipwreck" described by Dr. Savadan.[33] Why a shipwreck? Not just owing to a lack of preparation or favorable circumstances such as soil and climate, but fundamentally because of the fatality that is life for many and that no government, no city however justly conceived, can overcome. All social organization has a history, which has a double effect: while, little by little, by groping and successive compromises, it comes up with solutions to the divisions that cannot fail to emerge, at the same time it accumulates, as if by sedimentation, motives for conflicts and maintains them from day to day, making power indispensible and its effects of subjection, exploitation, and inequality inevitable. This is the story Jules Verne tells in his novel *The Survivors of the "Jonathan,"*[34] which concerns a misanthropic anarchist exiled in Tierra del Fuego, virgin territory not yet divided between Chile and Argentina, who is forced to become the uncontested ruler of a community of failed colonists on the shores of Cape Horn. Here the shipwreck is upstream, explaining why the colonists are cast, despite themselves, on the hospitable and fertile lands where they found their community; but it is also downstream, since the divisions within the new society soon force the colonists to turn to an anarchist dictator (in the ancient sense of the term) in order to put an end to the conflicts that divide them. It is as if, Verne suggests, neither those who flee power in the name of the slogan "Neither God nor master," nor those who want to go beyond it in the name of the wise administration of things, can in reality escape it because of the fatality that unites them. It is inevitable that concretized utopias end up reproducing the divisions that permeate every society. It is therefore also against these divisions that utopian desire is erected, the spring of freedom and equality against power.

As Maximilien Rubel suggests, Marx did not oppose his scientific socialism to the utopian socialism of his predecessors. He thought the utopian dimension of socialism in all its radicalness where certain utopians, who claimed to realize their utopia scientifically, had disavowed the utopian surplus and led desire into shipwreck.[35] From this perspective, we can read Marx in the way Ernst Bloch understood utopia, a way that he saw appearing in Marx himself and that, we could say, is entirely contained in the letter to Ruge. Whereas Icaria was a unitary and homogeneous edifice, whose experimental communities in Illinois and Missouri furnished a model destined to prefigure the future of France, Marx sought to awaken the utopian germs of the future in the dreams of the old Europe. This is the utopian task par excellence, according to Bloch: discovering in the present the traces of a past that summon a future, which bring about, on the condition that we become aware of them, what is not yet of the order of being. To such a critical vision, "the rigid divisions between the future and the past thus themselves collapse, unbecome future becomes visible in the past, avenged and inherited, mediated and fulfilled past in the future."[36] The past seized in dreams of justice becomes a "living source for revolutionary action, for a *praxis* oriented toward the utopian future."[37] This is Marx the utopian, the dream-spotter in Walter Benjamin's sense. "The dream-spotter," writes Abensour, "is not there to inspect the perhaps very perilous character of the dream of justice in relation to the existing order; he stands there to be on the lookout for the dreams of the collective—against the mythical forces that work to prolong the sleep of the capitalist universe—the fragile glimmer that suddenly awakens us and tears us out of the ill fate of the nineteenth century."[38] If dreams secretly await awakening, as Benjamin says, then Marx the utopian appears here as a technician of awakening who records the collective dream, gives society an opportunity to wake up rather than give itself over to the seductive myths of power and of the just society. Such would be the properly utopian dimension of Marx's critical project in 1843, and such would also be the principle of any utopia:

that "we develop new principles for the world out of the world's own principles."[39]

That is said in its own way by this poem written during the Maple Spring:

> that the now would look beyond the end of its nose
> that it would invent a horizon at frontiers that are not yet visible
>
> ...
>
> they reply to me that we are dreaming
> and that they do not dream
>
> ...
>
> and I no longer know how to respond
> to this hollowed-out Québec
> which frightens me
> and makes us want to create a new one
>
> out of breath
> and of statistics
> I note my ignorance and am delighted with it
> I still have space to build
> and virgin dreams[40]

NOTES

1. Karl Marx, Letter to Arnold Ruge, September 1843, in *Marx/Engels Collected Works* (*MECW*) (Moscow: Progress, 1975–2005), 3:145.
2. Ibid., 3:144. Étienne Cabet's *Voyage in Icaria* was published in 1840.
3. Marx, Letter to Ruge, 3:145.
4. Ibid.
5. Sigmund Freud, *The Future of an Illusion*, trans. James Strachey (New York: Norton, 1961), 31.
6. Leo Strauss, "What Is Political Philosophy?," in *What Is Political Philosophy?, and Other Studies* (Chicago: University of Chicago Press, 1959).
7. Plato, *The Republic*, trans. Paul Shorey (Cambridge: Harvard University Press, 1969), V 457a, 457d, 473a.
8. Ibid., V 450d, VII 540d.
9. Ibid., V 471c–473e.
10. Ibid., VI 502c: "Our present opinion, then, about this legislation is that our plan would be best if it could be realized and that this realization is difficult yet not impossible."

11 Ibid., VII 540d.
12 Ibid., VII 541a.
13 Hannah Arendt, "What Is Authority?," in *Between Past and Future* (New York: Viking, 1961).
14 Plato, *Republic*, V 472c–d, my emphasis.
15 How the first philosopher left the cave will forever remain a mystery.
16 Plato, *Republic*, VII 517a.
17 Ernst Bloch, *Spirit of Utopia*, trans. Anthony A. Nassar (Stanford: Stanford University Press, 2000).
18 Hannah Arendt, *On the Origins of Totalitarianism* (New York: Houghton Mifflin Harcourt, 1973); and Arendt, "The Image of Hell," in *Essays in Understanding, 1930–1954* (New York: Knopf, 2005).
19 Miguel Abensour, *Le Procès des maîtres rêveurs* (Arles: Sulliver, 2000).
20 Ibid., 37.
21 Ibid., 40–41. See also Abensour's analysis of More's *Utopia* ("More, *L'Utopie*," in *Dictionnaire des œuvres politiques*, ed. Francois Châtelet, Olivier Duhamel, and Evelyn Pisier [Paris: Presses Universitaires de France, 1986], 582–601) and Abensour, *L'Utopie de Thomas More à Walter Benjamin* (Paris: Sens et Tonka, 2000).
22 Abensour, *Le Procès des maîtres rêveurs*, 42, 48.
23 Ibid., 42.
24 Ibid., 48.
25 Ibid., 49.
26 Martin Buber, *Paths in Utopia* (Syracuse, N.Y.: Syracuse University Press, 1950). See also Emmanuel Levinas's preface to the French edition of *Utopie et socialisme*, trans. Paul Corset and Francois Girard (Paris: Aubier Montaigne, 1977).
27 Abensour, *Le Procès des maîtres rêveurs*, 49–50.
28 William Morris, *A Dream of John Ball* (London: Nonesuch, 1948), 214.
29 Jacques Derrida, "Différance," in *Margins of Philosophy*, trans. Alan Bass (Chicago: University of Chicago Press, 1982). "Différer" in Derrida's sense means both to differ and to defer. "Différance" thus names "the process of scission and division through which different things or differences are produced" in time and space.
30 In his *Voyages and Adventures of Lord William Crisdall in Icaria*, published under the pseudonym Th. Dufruit in 1839 and republished the following year under his own name as *Voyage in Icaria*, Cabet proposes an egalitarian, rational, planned city submitted to an order that restricts time as much as space, morals as much as work. It was in 1847 that he launched a recruitment campaign through an article in the newspaper *Le Populaire* ("Let's Go to Icaria") that would carry the Icarians to Nauvoo, Illinois.
31 Buber, *Paths in Utopia*, 76.
32 Jean-Christophe Petitfils, *Les Communautés utopistes au XIXe siècle* (1982; Paris: Pluriel, 2010), 320.
33 Contacted by Albert Brisbane while he was in Brussels in exile after May 1849, Victor Considerant agreed to demonstrate the validity of Fourierist doctrines by going to a community near Dallas. Considerant's book, *Au Texas*, appeared in 1854 and, after the

disappointments of 1848, enjoyed success equal to Cabet's *Voyage in Icaria*. Four years later, Dr. Savardan's narrative described in minute detail the vicissitudes of the new colony: *Un Naufrage au Texas: Observations et impressions recueillies pendant deux ans et demi au Texas et à travers les États-Unis d'Amérique* (*A shipwreck in Texas: observations and impressions collected over two and a half years in Texas and around the United States*) (Paris: Garnier Frères, 1858).

34 Jules Verne, *The Survivors of the "Jonathan"* (Paris: Hachette, 1979), published as *Les Naufragés du Jonathan* in 1909, written in 1891. The novel was rewritten by Michel Verne after his father's death. The original version, long unpublished, recently appeared under the title *En Magellanie* (Paris: Folio, 2012).

35 Maximilien Rubel, *Marx critique du marxisme* (Paris: Payot, 2000): "Marx is the most utopian of the utopians: little concerned with the future society, he is exclusively occupied with the destruction of the present society. But he raises revolution to the rank of an absolute demand" (419). See also p. 342n2: "Marxian socialism feeds on the same 'utopian reason' as is precursors and, . . . at bottom, Marx saw himself in Saint-Simon, Fourier, Weitling, and Owen precisely because these thinkers gave him a complete vision of a free society."

36 Ernst Bloch, *The Principle of Hope*, trans. Neville Plaice, Stephen Plaice, and Paul Knight (Cambridge: MIT Press, 1986), 1:8–9.

37 Michael Löwy and Robert Sayre, *Romanticism Against the Tide of Modernity*, trans. Catherine Porter (Durham: Duke University Press, 2001), 180.

38 Miguel Abensour, "Walter Benjamin, le guetteur de rêves," in *L'Utopie de Thomas More à Walter Benjamin*, 127.

39 Marx, Letter to Ruge.

40 "Que le maintenant regarde plus loin que le bout de son nez / qu'il se crée un horizon aux frontières encore invisibles / . . . / on me répond que nous rêvons / et qu'ils ne rêvent pas / . . . / et je ne sais plus quoi répondre / à ce Québec affaissé / qui me fait peur / et qui nous donne envie de nous en créer un nouveau / à bout de souffle / et de statistiques / je constate mon ignorance et je m'en réjouis / j'ai encore de l'espace à construire / et des rêves vierges." Sara Dignard, "Je ne sais plus quoi répondre," *Fermaille* 10 (April 22, 2012): 8–9, reprinted in *Le Printemps québécois: Une Anthologie* (Montréal: Ecosociété, 2013), 133. Used with permission of the author.

CODA

UTOPIA, ALIBI

S. D. CHROSTOWSKA

What is quite common? Hope. When all is gone, there is still hope.
—THALES

The ear of wheat (in Latin spica, *obsoletely* speca, *from* spe, *hope) should not be the only hope of the husbandman; its kernel or grain (*granum *from* gerendo, *bearing) is not all that it bears. How, then, can our harvest fail?*
—HENRY DAVID THOREAU

A POLITICS OF HOPE?

Our problematic in this volume on the "uses of utopia for politics" brings together what commonly comes in separate packages. To be sure, mainstream readings of modern Western political history support the attribution of a utopian dimension to left-radical politics, and, conversely, of radical, if covert, political motives to utopia. The historic conflation of utopianism and political radicalism does not, however, explain the internal crisis of the Left any more than it explains today's generalized political apathy. Neither does it absolve this apathy's dispirited sufferers of their tendency to equate legitimate politics with a crude, calculating realism, one that discredits as utopian and idealistic real struggles against state institutions and transnational capitalist hegemonies that have a hand in state politics or stand to gain by it.

Those of us who give history a closer look will recognize here a banal rhetorical shortcut: rather than acknowledge these struggles' existence as vital, contend with their subjective necessity, and evaluate their actual efficacy, critics of all stripes point to the fiction that sustains them and dismiss this silver lining as a "hopeless" weakness, an "impossible dream," which in fact is often no more concrete or audacious than a desire to make things better. In making this tried-and-true rhetorical move, they construe the effect of such transgressive efforts in terms only of extremes—as either recklessly accelerating or else setting back the clock of progress. (It would be easy, for instance, to make the case for the excluded middle: that the greatest contribution of radicalism, right and left, is its *destabilizing* political energy, largely benign when not subject to reprisals, an energy that puts the rest on the defensive, further entrenching the ideology of "natural" steady progress in increasing contradiction with reality.)

Old rhetorics die hard. Yet where not long ago *hope* was only for the foolhardy disaffected—neoliberalism's skeptics, dissenters, vandals, losers, and victims—in an ironic reversal it is now in demand just about everywhere. The steady growth of a *salve*-mentality alongside a hope industry of sorts means that demand for the stuff is barely being met; it may be at an all-time high. A salve for the decent and depressed, whose ranks are swelling, it comforts with sharing the same boat, local and translocal community-building, and occupying pell-mell some scrap of public space. There is much to be said for this expansive solidarity-in-precarity, among not just those who can "afford" it but also those in the middle income brackets who, until recently, had been content with a marginal advantage they could call their own. Others get their fix of hope through a range of custom channels: the proliferation of bit causes, go-to activist streams, and revamped platforms as so many opportunities to get involved (no "quick fixes" these, fixing little). Still others take their hope in private; here the zeitgeist is less obliging, and refined cultural fare harder to come by. Even some once hopeless diehards have started to come around—so easy it is nowadays to become hooked on hope.

All this would be well and good were the supply of hope not all but without a *political* edge. In a climate of political enervation, the cynicism of Occupy,[1] the virtual battles of hacktivism, or any international protest movement that shies away from programs and overt demands is easier than ever to shrug off as a passing trend, distraction, and nuisance. Mainstream indifference, on the one hand, and short-lived buzz, on the other, are mirrored in the movements' own unwillingness to take political risks, their group-therapism and creeping defeatism, or, on the contrary, their inflated morale; to this extent, too, many participants either do not recognize their own radicalism or, enamored of theoreticism and catchphrases like "Hope in Common,"[2] contemplate their own direct-democratic staying power before fizzling out.

Despite what official politics would have us believe, no *rhetorical* conflation of radical politics with "the principle of hope" can eliminate the productive tension between them—a mutual suspicion that is a lasting legacy of Marx and Engel's critique of utopian socialism (Owen, Saint-Simon, Fourier).[3] For one aware of this history but boasting firsthand (grassroots-democratic) experience, radicalism and utopia may be difficult to separate like children who insist on sitting together only to have it out under the table.

Calling attention to this enduring yet routinely overlooked tension invites the following question: Why is it so hard to couple radical politics with a utopia worthy of the name? After all, utopianism has come a long way from what Judith Shklar called nineteenth-century "activist" quasi-utopias (even as she questioned their status as utopias, seeing them, *pace* Karl Mannheim, as ideologies),[4] let alone from what many others also regarded as, at best, protoutopian fantasies: primitive, vulgar, popular, pleasure-driven "body utopias" foundational to "social dreaming" proper.[5] But, rather than adding to our bafflement, this longer historical view may offer a key to the difficulty of a rapprochement. It should be noted that none of the possible relations obtaining between politics and utopia— not only those A. O. Hirschman identified for progressive ideas in general, namely, *futility* and *perversity*, but also those of *compatibility* and *inevitability*—amount to a real *working* relationship. And conceiving of such a relationship may precisely be the best guard against the conceptual reduction of utopia to politics, radical or otherwise, opposed by a chorus of thinkers, among them Ruth Levitas and Étienne Tassin.

A liberal theorist of utopia, Shklar took its political character for granted, even if this did not entail for her any particular political practice or form. " 'Utopia' stands for political hope," she wrote, meaning the hope that politics will take us somewhere far better than where we are. Its uncoupling from politics was for her a matter less of essential difference than of historical contingency. Since utopia is of "little use" to politics in the wake of ideological struggle hot and cold, the apparent decline of utopian writing is hardly surprising and nothing to be concerned about. Yet while utopia (qua political hope) is not necessary "to think creatively about politics at all," its disparagement and banishment from the state may impair thinking critically and creatively about improving that state. "One might ask at the end of the twentieth century," Shklar concludes, "why anyone would yearn for transformative politics, but if one does [*yearn* for it], then utopia remains very useful, perhaps indispensable. If, however, we do not identify hope with transformation, then it is neither necessary, useful, nor particularly stimulating."[6] Thus, if nothing else, Shklar's defense of utopia against its accusers should convince us of the need to realign utopianism and radicalism. (As for her own ideological position, back in the day of body-political radicalism she might have made an accepting hostage.)

The set of claims I am advancing can be summed up as follows. Radical politics has distanced itself from utopianism in order to obtain political results and be recognized as a force in real politics. Its operation, as action in the world, tends to be conceptualized within an actualist ontology, for which everything possible is actual—while that of utopia, as a critical and imaginative challenge to the necessity of the given world, has long been committed to possibilism and, specifically, to theoretical or technological physical possibilia that are not (yet) actual. In light of this metaphysical difference, politics and utopia appear fundamentally at odds. It would therefore be shortsighted to attribute their conceptual distance to specific discursive legacies: that of Marxism, which emphasizes the efficacy of radical politics, but also that of liberalism, which questions such politics' legitimacy. The problem of this distance, insofar as one recognizes it as worth solving, needs to be tackled in two steps. First, politics must be returned to the body of the political actor. This step has already been taken with the emergence of groups that are beginning not only to theorize but to show us the way back to *somatics*, or concrete body-politics. Second, this properly *political* body must be conceptually restored to utopia. This latter and smaller step is my task here. And, small though it is, it requires turning against the classical utopian tradition beginning (at least in retrospect) with Plato. Perhaps the first part of the problem—that politics and body do not quite go together—cannot be remedied except by taking a page from the anarchist recipe book and throwing some "primitive" utopianism into the mix.

A BODY OF HOPE

The great hope realized in the French Revolution was that the minor bodies making up the "masses," whether seen as an aggregate of individual wills or as a profane *bona voluntas*, could transmogrify into a powerful political agent of their own self-emancipation and a measure of the *bien commun*—effecting what we might call a new *physicalization* or *somatization* of politics.[7] The development of this insurgent mass politics of the working class was concurrent with and counter to the "anatomo-political" practices of states aiming to contain, discipline, and optimize the functionality of corporal individuality.[8] In response to the bodily flooding of the West's political stages, a new secularizing discourse tried to demarcate legitimate from illegitimate politics and (*pace* Weber) politics from violence, by and large disqualifying the latter from politics proper. The consequences of this progressive abstraction of *nomos* and marginalization of *physis* in the nineteenth century are most clearly seen in the power of political ideologies to *concentrate*, culminating in authoritarianism, but they are still perfectly in evidence today in the repressive apparatus, symbolized by the riot police, for controlling public assemblies.

The understandable aversion to physical harm among the latest generation of Western activists stands in sharp contrast not just to the movements of the 1960s and 1970s, "the decade of anarchy," not to mention the history of the workers' movement, but to the waves of bodies hurling themselves upon the gears of hostile apparatuses in the Arab world. While it signaled the definitive death of hope in the body of one man, Mohamed Bouazizi's self-immolation in Tunis went beyond social protest; it was a *utopianizing* statement. Unpacked, it might run: *I give up my body because life has become unbearable. This body cannot exist without hope for a future in which it and those it supports could be significantly better off, and live in freedom and dignity.* Bouazizi's fatal "sacrifice" returned *mere bodies* to center stage, reminding us of their power to ground claims and draw public attention to them. What else if not bodies gives rise to that basic despair that has nothing to lose but itself, and that then, through some chain reaction, becomes a mass struggle? Individually and collectively vulnerable, their injury flagging injustice, they are deployed and exposed in the politics of disobedience and provocation. Compared with humiliated, hopeless life, in which utopia has no place and cannot make up for political impotence, death suddenly appears preferable. Such suicides, no matter how they are framed, no matter where they are performed, no matter whom they affect or what they set in motion, remain nonetheless *unrecognizably* political. The centrality of bodies to radical struggles thus remains opaque unless we grant protest suicide, including martyrdom with targeted damage to human life and property, the status of a political act.[9]

Even if propaganda for antistate body-politics—violent, nonviolent, or autoviolent—exceeds such politics' transformative efficacy, the degree to which citizens can and do body forth "unreasonable" political hopes and galvanize them was manifest in the popular radicalism sparked elsewhere in the region and its resonance abroad. It has become a commonplace that these days practice outstrips theory, that "Each wave of struggle," past and present, "confronts theory with its own limitations."[10] Impatience with revolutionary theory appears directly proportionate to the political currency of bodies—the embrace of revolutionary *physics*. In the words of the anarchist-communist collective behind *Tiqqun*, "Zones of Offensive Opacity do not have *to be created*. They are already there, in any kind of relation that brings about a veritable putting into play of bodies"—a "*Conspiracy of bodies*. Not critical minds, but *critical corporealities*."[11] The *critical body* returns in more recent anarchist works, such as Claude Guillon's *Je chante le corps critique*, a tome taking the temperature and measure of the body as the battleground of contemporary struggles for utopia.[12]

Whatever we might think of the desires that motivate some to take their own lives in protest, our lingering disinclination to consider such acts as protest suicide as political points more directly to our difficulty in thinking utopia and politics together than does our often uneasy recognition of the politics of Western activism. Then again, perhaps the utopian character of such acts is not so unmistakable either. A bequest of the failure of prescriptive, picture-book approaches to social transformation, our going conception of utopia elides bodily realities. By contrast, the "utopian" dimension of collective action eschewing concrete political demands seems unproblematic and, in its organizing and goals, comparatively more sophisticated, if ultimately unthreatening.

Here I can only sketch the historical *mentalization* or *spiritualization* of utopian writing, stemming from its loss of grounding in the body and its needs, which Rousseau deemed the "foundations of society."[13] Theoretical utopia's loss of corporality correlates with its dissociation from political practice (particularly, it would seem, from the transformative kind, in *yearning* for which it can be, as Shklar said, "very useful," and from the bodily kind just mentioned, to whose utopianizing the world can be blind). The progressive evacuation of the body from utopia correlates also with discursive utopianism's corresponding alliance with critiques of politics.[14] For, indeed, the hoped-for day when Enlightened politics, trumpeting the right to the pursuit of happiness, would yield eupsychian bodies did not break. At the height of revolutionary fervor, Sade's notorious call (*Français, encore un effort . . .*) to radicalize republicanism by way of boundless sexual freedom went unanswered. Medicine's political consciousness, mobilized around the Revolution by the dream of restoring the social body "to an original state of health"—bracketed by the overhaul of the state and later its constitution—soon faded, and with it the myth of the total, politico-physical cure followed by real, lasting equaliberty.[15] Further deepening utopia's estrangement from politics was an aftermath of mutual disappointments (most notably, 1848 and 1871). The body, meanwhile, once a rivet between them, gradually underwent devaluation in each.

This estrangement also derives from isolated social-utopian experiments. Take the Owenite rationalist management of the welfare of workers in New Lanark, pressing their morally edified souls and fortified bodies into the service of industry—without, that is, contesting the ideology of progress of the many through the prosperity of the few. In exchange for this improved lot, the rank-and-file producer of wealth gained the moral superiority of being content with the satisfaction of immediate needs. (Given his emphasis on physical economization and regimentation, it seems clear why Owen's stepped-up, political-utopian project in American New Harmony, where "intelligence and happiness increased an hundred-fold," was doomed to failure.)[16] Even as the masses began to grasp desire's universality and universal rightness, going beyond basic needs, they lacked sufficient means to satisfy their own cravings, the natural "appetites of the mind."[17] The expansion, on the one hand, and, on the other, the *education* of this universal desire in the suffering masses became the social-utopian formula for eventual emancipation. In reality, however, utopian dreaming intensified alongside, and partly no doubt owing to, proletarianization, which left little time and energy for political capacitation. The harnessing of the body in the "age of work" thus sapped its power as utopian agent, stamping out collective dreams. The bourgeois pursuit of material happiness, meanwhile, was going public with mass advertising, even as the bourgeois body tended to be kept private, mastered, or sublimated. (By the time socialist and liberal utopias of plenty competed in serving up new fantasies of security through industrial surplus and consumer goods, the actual needs and longings of the body had largely lost their status as utopian catalysts; they were widely believed to have been satisfied.)

Vestiges of body-centered utopia continued to play a role in scenarios for radical social reconstruction. They were essential in Charles Fourier's passional "rehabilitation of the flesh" (a Saint-Simonian expression), his complex effort to center utopia in politics via sensuality,[18] in Joseph Déjacque's anarchist-utopian evocation of animated passionality,[19] or, somewhat later, in William Morris's Arts and Crafts movement, animated by desire for pastoral utopian romance, and focused on moving the vulnerable body beyond politics.[20] Corporality was, as I have suggested, increasingly dissociated from political action in the century after Fourier, and utopianism—in a failed effort to make itself politically relevant—followed suit. The age of the social question, primarily one of the provision of basic necessities to bodies (increasingly marshaled by the "working day" and losing their power of resistance), was also the great age of capitalism. For those in search of wealth, attention to the body came with time to be aligned not with feeding and dressing, which were taken for granted, but with hedonism and the "private utopias" of money-driven excess. Satiety of this sort, as unlikely as it was, did not guarantee sharing; if anything, it was predicated on individual possession. The insatiable greed of those historically favored to work up ever-greater appetites through sheer surfeit made of the overfed body the symbolic enemy of the alienated dispossessed, who drove the surplus economy that left them without means or hope. The pursuit of utopias of immoderation (as far from the delicacy and decadence of the aristocrat as it was from the frugality of felt need), demanded by a body grown monstrous and unruly, freed from "natural" limits, became a social evil—secretly coveted, outwardly condemned.

Passing over for the moment Marx and Engels's well-known polemic against utopian socialists in the *Communist Manifesto*, the wedge between politics and utopia was driven still deeper by the popularity in the utopian heartlands of France and Germany of largely unpolitical *naturisme* and *Körper-* and *Freikörperkultur* (lit. "free body culture"). A practice-oriented reaction to the urban materialist middle class, the movement that sprang up at the end of the nineteenth century—the culture of communal nudity and the lifestyle reform for which it stood—eventually spanned *völkisch* romantics (like the *Wandervögel*) and nationalists, socialists and anarchists, nondogmatists and apoliticals. Among them were founders of intentional communities like the Himmelhof commune in Austria. Its utopian overtones are unmistakeable: the bather in light and air (*Licht-Luftbäder*) was the "New Man." Established in 1933 on the Île du Levant, the first *village naturiste* was named Héliopolis, city of the sun. The *labile* body drawing its energy from nature fell between the well-fed body of the utopian imagination and the abused able body of capitalist industry. Yet the politics and the utopianism in its conception proved too weak. Under National Socialism the German naturist movement became depoliticized and adapted to totalitarian reality, promising utopia through the *Gleichschaltung* of collective athletic and sexual discipline—an unfortunate alliance of social nudity and dystopia.[21] The obverse of this grim corporal apotheosis, the abysmal experiments conducted in utopia's name, from compulsory sterilization programs to industrial-scale repurposing of corpses, underscored the defenselessness of the body, framed accordingly in subsequent scientific-utopian thinking (prior to the emergence of transhumanism, functional bodily optimization was the province of military R and D). Eugenics, or "good birth," and the presumed good life obtaining from it, as well euthanasia, or "good death," found their crooked reflection in genocide. In Europe at least, concrete utopianism after Auschwitz was lastingly compromised.

But the fallout from these developments did not end there: reformist naturism aggravated the spiritualization of Victorian culture, helping it to clarify its opposition to public nudity. The Victorian body responded by detaching itself from, on the one hand, sexuality and, on the other, the natural world—robbed of their innocence and familiarity by libidinal interrogations and clinical handling. Translated into domestic terms, this entailed a strict division between the reproductive and productive spheres of the bourgeois household, as well as a voluntary sacrifice of "light and air" to progress, curtailing the satisfaction of elementary needs and forms of freedom like physical comfort, freedom of motion, and mobility—all in return for respectability. In the process, the body's abusive mastery in the name of economic domination also became normalized among the affluent.

Utopia focused in and on the body thus came to evoke either "aristocratic" corruption by capital or a primitive fantasy of social leveling, with the bonds of law and morality loosened only to reinforce feudal structures in the end; it signified, in other words, the downfall of the autonomous individual through money and power, the ideological subjugation of will. The body was not just susceptible, it was addictive. In Aldous Huxley's dystopia from 1932, "there is always *soma*, delicious *soma*"—"body" in Greek—"half a gramme for a half-holiday, a gramme for a weekend, two grammes for a trip to the gorgeous East"; the "utopian" "body" drugs and abolishes the actual body in its everyday unhappiness.[22]

Utopia, conversely, could only be redeemed from its political-economic misadventures by being reconceived as unreality, an ethics of social justice, collective wishful thinking projected onto the widest screen, or an expression of pure, bodiless will, a "politics of the spirit."[23] But to the philosophical apologists for utopianism, the more impracticable and abstract it was, the more benign and attractive; the more politically abstinent and exclusively critical, the greater its power to unite. The strongest line of defense against conservative and radical critics (the first in the name of past and potential victims of dictatorships, the second in the name of Marxist science) was to stress the plurality of the utopian tradition's emancipative energies, its value as social exploration, experimentation, movement, becoming.[24] (Whether this theoretical "rehabilitation" can be had without depoliticizing utopianism altogether is another matter.)

Utopia survived, then, not as a comprehensive solution to social ills, but for the most part as *spirit*, increasingly disembodied, grasped in mystical, negative-theological, ethical, or normative outline.[25] These contours came to function defensively, as the opposite of its former incarnation, as a nonpolitical *alibi*, literally "elsewhere," after the nineteenth and twentieth centuries. Arguably, it did not yet need one in Thomas More's jocoserious and "Platonic" method of indirect political council, written as a comic dialogue to friends—a discourse that refers sympathetically back to *Plato's* distancing of philosophy from the realm of politics and law, notwithstanding the "utopian" *politeia* being ruled by philosopher-kings. It was not so much political neutrality, which would expose it to charges of covert collaboration, as it was an abrogation or a total innocence of politics; this utopia, to quote one of Georges Duveau's utopian aphorisms, was "distance, so as not to get dirty."[26] There was no *corpus delicti*, so, for all one knows, no crime. A utopia that did no harm, did not fail, did not incur moral opprobrium; a place to put oneself imaginatively, leaving the real world alone. If this is not escapism for "beautiful souls," what is? Recoiling from the atmosphere of a trial, utopia here walks away free. And it is not because *political* utopias did not deliver; it is because, when they were made to deliver (on a simplistic view), they did not deliver what was promised, proving disastrous and indistinguishable from ideologies.

Conversely, the body—wanton, mistrusted after decades of political manipulation, mowed down in battlefields, reduced to the physical, the creaturely suffering of the Muselmann, the docile biopolitical subject-object, the victim of global neoliberal exploitation, tool and raw material in illicit economies, exiled from utopia—bore the full weight of reality. In this context, Hannah Arendt's long-uncontroversial distrust of the body as the unshareable, unpolitical "quintessence of all property" is entirely comprehensible:

> Nothing, in fact, is less common and less communicable, and therefore more securely shielded against the visibility and audibility of the public realm, than what goes on within the confines of the body, its pleasures and its pains, its laboring and consuming. Nothing, by the same token, ejects one more radically from the world than exclusive concentration upon the body's life, a concentration forced upon man in slavery or in the extremity of unbearable pain.[27]

Just as the scope of postwar politics contracted without bodies—bodies sacrificed for the collectivist cause, resisting and strong in numbers, staked on a common end, repressed and mistreated by state organs—so utopia, in renouncing bodies, grew impoverished, not to say malnourished. Given these developments, is it so surprising that radicals should eventually take up corporality as the most valuable, because long untapped and unsuspected, *political* instrument available to them?

In 1966, Michel Foucault, father of "heterotopology," went on the air to revisit embodied utopia. The title of his broadcast, "Le Corps utopique," establishes the body as the dialectical source of utopian thinking: it is the chronologically and ethically primary topos of utopian desire, but "it is against [the body] and as if to efface it" that utopias were born.[28] The world never satisfies living bodies well or long enough; we nourish the fantasy of being independent in avatar form, even rid of the body itself. And yet this body, routinely "salved, scraped, burned, cut, torn, and emptied,"[29] is not simply wretched, not simply opposed to utopia. Lack and the horizon of its fulfillment, bodily wholeness, turn the body into the topography of utopia, the no-place that cannot be glimpsed entire but only in parts, in its sites of wanting, its sensory relays. In the course of his reflections, Foucault arrives at the body as "sovereign utopia" insofar as it "is the point zero of the world—there, where paths and spaces come to meet, the body is nowhere. It is at the heart of the world, this small utopian core from which I dream, speak, advance, imagine, perceive things in their place and also destroy them with the indefinite power of the utopias I imagine."[30] The body is the point of departure for utopia, but also the utopian destination. The body of the utopian return is transfigured by the world (which achieves therein a fragile, finite totality) and figured as a corpse, the site of an imaginary total gratification.[31]

The persistence into adulthood of a personal bodily "autopia" (Foucault's term) owes less to individual memory of childhood fantasies than to their place among cultural archetypes and myths. Its value for world-altering scripts as a "blueprint" for the good society is negligible. Lest we reify this fantastic, sensually open body as a privileged (because prepolitical, preethical, presocial) site of utopia, let us remember that, even for Adorno, the positive, hopeful imagination of the child at play exists within a bad totality, with which it interacts from the start, and which both stirs and taints the dreams it is capable of. Society's demands both inspire and interfere with bodily wants whose gratification makes up a large share of adult happiness. Uncensored sensual pleasure shrinks to the private realm of friends, family, and servants and to intimate interior spaces, where it is still normal to shut out the world, where we can let go and indulge the bodies that, outside, are chiefly sensors of our discontent.[32]

If the body is the point zero of utopia, the complex desiring source of our conscious being in the world, it is also that which the conscious mind can never fully inhabit, a thing of appetites that satisfies itself through other bodies, to which it remains bound by debts incurred for its daily provision. It is forced to reach out to the world to renew itself as best it can. As long as it cannot hope for self-sufficiency, it dreams precisely of self-sufficiency. But even if they lack a general history in lacking serious (as opposed to playful) articulation, its dreams are widespread enough to be shareable, even social, utopias.[33] The age-old politico-ethical objections to such dreaming would make one believe it is without restraints, as though its economic and societal bounds counted for nothing, when in fact these largely delimit political claims (if not exactly moral imperatives).[34] The body dies of its own too-much in more ways than one. The "denaturing" or hyperextension of desire comes at the cost not only of well-being but of meaning, drawn from natural and social orders.

There is no *politics* as we know it in traditional proto- and classical-utopian projections; the Golden Ages and Isles of the Blessed, Edenic paradises, Arcadias and Cockaignes, New Atlantises and Kallipoleis, Eldorados and Thélèmes are either pre- or postpolitical, transcending what is inherently opposed to peaceful felicity. Morris's account of politics in England in the "epoch of rest" is all of three words: "We have none." Where politics formed part of the process of getting there, its relation to utopia has always been that of a means to an end. From the vantage of ideal society, the object of revolution is "to make people happy," and it is "hope and pleasure [that] put an end to" war and violence.[35] It is the elision or abbreviation of the process of transformation, its eclipse by the utopian design itself, that bore the brunt of Marx and Engel's critique of utopian socialism as a fantasy that jumps the cue of the historical-materialist process (rather than "hacking the dialectic," as the revolutionary should).[36] Due to their practical-ideological character, post-1848 utopias like Morris's, incorporating some of the critical backlash against them, broadened their strokes and emphasized the historical process along with the politics that would lead to the new society. The popular body was an increasingly silent constant in radical debates about social inequality and the apparent chief beneficiary of the revolutionary ferments that were their expression.

The twentieth century would deal these high-minded progressivist schemes a near-fatal blow. The failure of attempts to realize a perfected or at least significantly better society, on the one hand, and, on the other and in reaction to this, the post-World War I emergence of a practically disembodied conception of utopia as *critical spirit*[37] ensured that, for a while, the body's happiness all but vanished from revolutionary models of social transformation in the West. It was soon replaced by such focal points as identity and human rights. While actually existing socialism and liberal democracy vied for first place in the race for affluence, radicals were busy exposing the damage done to its contestants, false consciousness and surplus repression, government corruption and murderous campaigns at home and abroad. In these struggles, bodies were wagered and harmed. The more Western-style material comforts and social conventions were equated with political conformism, the more radicalism adopted an ethos of material depredation in the name of oppositional political objectives.

Utopianism ran on a parallel track by providing the theory of the totality and its reflective negation. Bodies had proven too volatile and insensible in real politics, putty in the hands of ideologues near the sources of power. Adorno's iconoclastic minimalism in conceiving a utopia where "no-one shall go hungry anymore" is symptomatic of this caution.[38] While it appears to say that utopia is nothing if not a world of sated bodies, this minimum, colored by the experience of the first part of the century, hardly conjures a happy place. Indeed, our relationship to the body is the "most mutilated of all"; modern Western culture has enslaved the flesh to its basic needs, selling it as base labor.[39] Utopianism in this form thus set itself up as the ethical watchdog for the political abuse of defenseless corporality. In 1960, the dissonance between the early Marxian position on the positive happiness-content of materialism—the "affirmation of the material satisfaction of men"[40]—and capitalism, with unions cooperating with employers, could still be ignored. A heady mix of psychoanalysis, politics, and critical theory showed how everyone whose bodily needs were ostensibly met was cheated out of their freedom. "False happiness" was traded in for collective resistance to the encroachment of the state and capital, to the allure of instant gratification, individualism, and body image-based self-fulfillment. More positively and practically (in the groundswell of utopian, body-friendly communes of the 1960s and 1970s in North America, but also in the French "communism of desire"), this meant the preservation of alternative social relations and value systems, where bodies would be shared without being wasted. With the unbridling of capitalism, material attachments—configured by (and seemingly inseparable from) the capitalist economy and value system—diverged much more sharply from any technical and intellectual capacity to "turn the world into the opposite of hell," as Herbert Marcuse put it in 1967 (hopeful for the "end of utopia" in its realization).[41] With the sharpening of inequality and the general political failure to remedy it came an increasingly global consciousness of *lack*. Whether in the form of unchosen privation, voluntary doing without, or a deep sense of something immaterially missing, lack became an index uniting a wide range of radical and utopianizing emancipatory projects equally disillusioned with state socialism and late capitalism, and ranging from the radical democratic and countercultural strands of the New Left to liberation theology's "preferential option for the poor" to the degrowth, environmentalist, and counterglobalization movements. The desire for stuff, having been learned, could be unlearned.

The self-ennoblement of left radicals through identifying, and identifying with, conditions of lack in order to fight it more effectively is nothing new: in addition to its "theological premium,"[42] want has long come with moral and radical-political credit. If there is one belief cherished by *bien pensants* concerning those they want to help liberate, it is that the poor and oppressed (two sides of one coin) are somehow inherently *for* a better world, united in their misery on the side of utopia. Poverty gives birth to a spiritualizing longing for salvation where it does not utterly demoralize (its appeal lies in these extremes, its reward in saving those in desperation from an unjust fate, its pathos in making this difference). The poor are not merely *closer* to a better because more morally defensible world; raised morally by imagining its possibility, they have already placed one foot *inside* utopia.

It is good to hear their complaints as long as one does not give them what they want. The value of the ethos of lack—rather than involuntary destitution[43]—depends on such ironic, self-critical distance from necessity-as-virtue, especially in moments of solidarity with the poor. Doing more with less (being creative, DIY), losing as much as possible short of losing all (learning use-value), to then stand to gain equally from this more level playing field—such strategic self-deprivation and politicization of poverty are the bona fides and principle of today's agitator for change. Personal divestment—seeing how much you and others, as a group, can stand to lose—becomes a measure not only of excess, but of what matters most. The call to scale back desire may smack of the austerity measures it ought to be attacking. It might seem a mere taunt, but look again: in the crisis of sustainability, doing with less[44] is no longer necessarily bad, while prosperity looms ever larger as a disastrous mirage.

NO MORE ALIBIS

Twentieth-century-vintage utopianism of the spirit, even when it expressed principled political commitment, was also self-consciously politically "useless" in that it fell outside the means-ends structure of political action. In his *Procès des maîtres rêveurs* (1978), Miguel Abensour, proponent of the critical "utopian spirit," laments the *glaciation* of utopianism, the "extinction of all transcendence, theoretical and practical, passing into a flat immanence, grey and indefinite."[45] My attempt here is to theorize its *thaw*. For that, it is necessary to historicize *together* politics' rejection of utopia and utopia's withdrawal from politics. What this historical stereoscopy can do that looking at each of these parallel histories separately cannot is bring out their *shared* basis, which may not only hold at least part of the answer to the discursive disconnect between utopian and radical democratic energies, but also, by thereby bringing them closer together and establishing their mutual affinity, help stave off the bankruptcy of vision of each. A *utopian politics* would, however, require moving past critical-cognitive utopianism without returning to elaborate formulas for the future and crude instrumentality—of politics for utopia, and vice versa. Rather than maintain utopia in its status as alibi, in its self-exonerating abstractness—rather than abandon politics as a sphere devoid of ideals or invest in cyberutopias of universal connectivity, leaving the (digitally unaugmented) body out of the equation altogether—we might recognize recent political activism as the site of inchoate, undertheorized encounters that are nonetheless encounters between radicalism and utopianism. And where radical democratic politics meets the desire called utopia out in the dialogical open we will also find desiring bodies, often many of them, in public space.

The apparent opposition between politics and utopia can be resolved either in their *productive tension*, as was the case for much of the nineteenth century, or in their punctual *convergence*, as proved possible in 1789, when, the story goes, people were roused to politics, *coram publico*, by food shortages. The distance between utopianism and meaningful political action in public consciousness is great indeed: as Fredric Jameson notes, it is "only in the present age that narratives have emerged in which characters stage a revolution against utopia itself—and in which this process is felt to be more satisfying than the founding of utopia in the first place."[46] What makes nonviolent radicalism so compelling is less its utopian message—prefiguring a world without alienation and precarity—than the appeal, in part nostalgic, of physical effort and personal risk in setting oneself against the purveyors of plenty, living within one's means, cutting back unnecessary production and consumption, and reconstituting a sense of community in the process. Seen in its "new light," "we're all already communists when working on a common projects [sic], all already anarchists when we solve problems without recourse to lawyers or police, all revolutionaries when we make something genuinely new."[47] This could just be the momentum of youth, though youth increasingly stands for a generalized condition of insecurity, one method of coping with which is preempting poverty from above by bodily occupying the condition of poverty. If *youth*, then emphatically not *wasted*.

Utopia and politics, then, appear to be converging again in prefigurative practice, giving prominence (over much-maligned clicktivism) to the social-bodily dimension, its heart set on the concrete, public performance of a community to come.[48] A recent anarchist pamphlet puts forth *daydreaming* as one of three "spiritual exercises" for anarchists at the intersection of anarchy and philosophical practice.[49] Such indeterminate practices could hardly be farther from the blueprint tradition of planning a perfected future and putting it into practice (they are also at a considerable remove from the practical utopianism of intentional communities).

Of course, we cannot assume the commensurability of anarchist practice with politics; the above-named exercises, we learn, "ought, eventually, to put into question every political project—first, as project, and, again, as political."[50] Nonetheless, in a survey of the contemporary constellation of radicalism, there is much to suggest that all that is required to make good on Lucy Sargisson's thesis about the necessary *symbiosis* of politics and utopia[51] is a revalorization of bodies from oppositional sites of lack and *vis inertia* to both active agents and sites of utopia. For politics and utopia to go hand in hand, politics must first "come to terms" with "being built on utopias."[52] One could go farther and say that, for the two to join forces pragmatically, both must theorize the living body as fundamental to the much needed radical social transformation.

What possible bodily satisfactions does practical prefiguration enable, given its on-a-shoestring, go-for-broke MO? An unbroken spirit is one thing but—public-spiritedness and *esprit de corps* aside—nobody finds utopia in a damp tent in a skyscraper's shadow. The inadequacy of past figurations of the ideal society, if it doesn't leave us paralyzed, frees us to develop new civic models of living. Embracing this freedom and the way of informed improvisation accounts for much of the appeal of Occupy-anarchism. Yet if we are to give radical politics its due as an alternative to politics-as-usual and the alienated, fetishistic lifestyles of perhaps all but the wealthiest and the poorest, we must factor in the joy of physical experience and the sensual pleasure of being a vital part of the commons for all to see. For enthusiastic participants, fair-weather friends, sympathizers, and observers alike, the suspension of social hierarchy in makeshift lodging and dealing flexibly with the natural fixity of desire[53] become not merely thinkable but doable.

Above, I have foregrounded physical need as the source of utopian longings, with a possible transformation of the condition of lack into pleasure, the liberation of desire in the embrace of want, as its outcome (*not*, however, its objective). I have also suggested finding fault with utopia's migration from happiness *in corpore* to more abstract and negative conceptions of individual and collective fulfillment. A concomitant phenomenon was the abstraction of politics away from somatics (body-politics), and the abstractions of representative government and citizenship—notwithstanding the compensatory prevalence in the nineteenth century, a time of unprecedented division of labor, of the "body-politic" metaphor.

At the source of its modern resurgence, the body-politics of the sovereign *demos* was anyhow subordinated to the principle of public safety, enacted by "engaging bodies to rescue right as the condition of liberty," at the price of bodily sacrifice. In Sophie Wahnich's account,

> The sentiment of revolutionary humanity does not lead to protecting suffering bodies above everything else, regardless of who and where they might be. The object is to protect above all humanity as a group constituted politically by its respect for declared natural right, from the most local to the most cosmopolitan level. We might say that this sentiment of humanity is entirely on the side of political life, sometimes accepting the need to despise the "fine day of life" that may conceal within it the oppression of the whole human race.[54]

In the counterrevolutionary narrative "ma[king] way for a providentialism 'which made meaningless any human desire for earthly happiness,'"[55] the principles of equality, liberty, and fraternity forged in the revolutionary crucible continued to lose touch with the particulars of suffering individuals and minorities in the name of universality. The "democratizing" spirit of liberalism took care of living bodies, eliding their differences, rationalizing multiplicities in the process of administering populations. More than that, the detachment and even erasure of the body of the *demos* from the normal sphere of political transactions progressively hampered the positive thinking of politics. Comtean positivism thrived in the social sphere, and even there emphasis was laid on the spiritual and moral dimension of *travail organique*. We have no difficulty recognizing that most claims to equality and freedom come from below, from the socially inferior and needy, from the condition of discrimination or indigeneity. But the vast majority of such claims could not live up to the expectations of ascetic utopianism, which sees through the productivist ideal of prosperity and the egalitarian one of redistribution, with their mantras of material happiness.[56] In its gimlet eye, trained in the scrutiny of desire, dreaming of "lemonade seas" and "fountains of youth" (motifs from medieval body utopias, some of which resurfaced in Fourier's *phalanstère de l'avenir*) reflects the naïveté of a limited, untutored imagination.

Even if, on account of their limited aspiration to the otherwise-given (that is, the everyday luxe those better off take for granted as *their* world), such crude dreams are not self-evidently *utopian*, they are nonetheless claims to happiness, and hence what I have called *utopianizing* claims. The otherwise-given as a step up from the given delineates a relative utopia—if not in reality then at least in the minds of those who would wish it for themselves, but are kept from enjoying it. Regardless of how one judges the content of these claims and their potential to bring about equal freedom, the vision of attainable happiness acts as a concrete placeholder for the utopian absolute, and is for this reason alone an improvement over hopeless nothing. To see here only the narrowness of popular horizons is to err on the side of caution in support of good old liberal antiutopianism: "Do not aim at establishing happiness by political means.... The attainment of happiness should be left to our private endeavours."[57] To leave the making of progressive utopia to the disenfranchised is, the paternalistic story goes, to set the standard disastrously low. Effectively denied moral (if not, de facto, political) sovereignty, the disadvantaged and ever undereducated cannot be trusted to know what is best for them—or for anyone else—and suffer a "cap" on imagination, rendered incapable by their circumstances of wanting more than the elite already has.

To be sure, fanciful, imitative "overeating" represents a danger of such utopianizing: the further privatization of happiness and its confinement between "pastoral" parentheses, in the nominally private sphere which is entirely our business and which it is our business to protect from others. It is not hard to see the downside of such purported autonomy. On the other hand, one is justified in seeing, as Judith Butler does, problems with Arendt's notion of a purely *public* happiness secured through the *vita activa*: the sequestering of the living, laboring, utopianizing body, reflecting its mistrust as a guide to a new kind of polity, effaces the body as a condition of action.[58] A positive eudaemonic imagination openly motivated by individual physical need, rather than by *rationality*, seems less prone to fancying the immoderate or unreal impossible. While it does not guarantee agreement, it is less likely to be contested; it is hard to dispute that everyone knows what feels good to them. And perhaps this tendency to concretize the satisfaction of want is the main reason for the body's confinement, its dismissal from the realm of politics. Power has an interest in keeping utopia abstract and negative. Might this fact not lift at least some of the stigma from provisional utopian imagery, the legacy of the postwar *Bilderverbot*?

Most theorists bothering with utopia today would stand by the view that, for utopianism to be politically attractive, it needs to go beyond imagining a just state of *happiness for all*, one that might follow if utopia, in its concrete civic form, were ever realizable. Utopia's impossibility, as well as utopianism's consequent futility, is most evident in this *for all*, in the universal inclusiveness of social dreaming of equal freedom. Assuming it were possible to make everyone's day (creating a one-size-fits-all kind of happiness), would not a *refusal* of happiness in any existing form by even one person be a failure of utopia? Our utopian image could only pass this test by pushing the logic of individualism into overdrive and endlessly pluralizing happiness, and this would amount to all but abandoning the concrete, shared imagery of utopia and holding on to its *sense*.

This conclusion and associated doubts should not obscure the value of the ethical thrust of utopian social theory, building on the "ruthless critique of everything existing" (Marx), *docta spes*, or "educated hope" (Bloch), the "education of desire" for social transformation (Abensour), and "the coming community" (Giorgio Agamben). In this critical-cognitive utopian tradition, pleasure, the simplest sort of pleasure, should not be taken uncritically and universalized. It too needs to be dislocated, displaced—indeed, *utopianized*. As Levitas, whose work both synthesizes and falls in this tradition, describes the task:

> The central characteristic of this process is the disruption and transgression of the normative and conceptual frameworks of everyday experience, and the provision of a space within which it is possible to imagine not just the satisfaction of familiar wants unmet by existing society, but to envisage wanting something other than the satisfactions which that society endorses and simultaneously denies: above all, to desire in a different way.[59]

The critique of desire must, however, be rooted in actual desire, instead of being approached systematically, sociologically, or morally. Rather than a critique of ends—of the content of desire *as* an end—it starts with means and is thus a critique of desire as a means. This involves asking such questions as: What effects, what "ends," do our present, end-less means-to-no-end imply? That, in turn, calls for the specification of desire qua means: What form does our desiring take, how is it expressed? How, then, do we conduct ourselves toward what we believe would be a better future? Our means must already model (that is, be consistent with) what we want collectively to become, never simply what we have lost or given up.

Utopianism need not be aspirational any more than it need take the telic form of well-meant blueprints and untested recipes, bringing back protoutopian visions like "body utopias" to serve as political goals. Solving the problem of utopia's relation to political practice—manifest in both its distance from "normal," legitimate politics and its taken-for-granted coziness with radicalism—does require letting go of much of the (increasingly scientific) "headiness" of the utopian tradition, together with its comprehensive schemes for physical appearance, sexual and reproductive behavior, nourishment, rest, and manual labor, to which the body was, more than anything else, *subject*. The historical argument presented here is concerned neither with the history of utopia nor with that of radical politics simpliciter, but with the gradual disappearance of their shared element, the living body—common denominator, nucleus, spring of the pursuit of happiness in this life. But simply reinscribing the physical, the material, at the core of utopia and of politics is not enough; the relation between them must be rewritten. If we are to avoid a contradiction in terms, *political utopia* cannot be a mere political narrative let alone prepolitical values threaded through desiring bodies (even if its presence as the memory of struggles and as popular imaginary cannot be denied). Rather than this *fil rouge*, it is like the *ballon rouge*, flushing with red, out of the blue, the life of a boy from a working-class Paris suburb in Albert Lamorisse's *court métrage* from 1956. Utopia is neither the end nor the means of politics, but its *incitement*; similarly, the film's protagonist is led to confront bullies who want his red companion destroyed, a course of action we immediately see the timid boy would never have taken up on his own. In the end, the death of the balloon—of one boy's emanation of hope, of the activation of his desire for "the color of the concrete" (Adorno)—rallies a whole mass of tethered, private balloons, which gather and float above the rooftops to lift up his spirits and carry him away. And this final, public emanation of hope is a general activation of desire accompanying and animating individual corporalities—which would come together just over a decade later.⁶⁰

Reactivating a politics of "happiness," a *utopian politics*, certainly cannot be done without imagination. It demands envisaging the flesh-and-blood community as happier—the happiest it can hope to become. This is a temporary happiness by virtue of its constitution in the present (rather than in a fantasized future state). It requires rejecting equally escapist fantasies, leading desire astray, and unreflected everyday experience, while sweeping aside pressures to conform. More basically, however, its carrier is the labile body, moved to act by its desire to materially share its happiness with everyone party to the movement and wary of state-legislated and corporate-sponsored joy (material, psychological, or otherwise). Utopian politics is an ephemeral and open-ended practice attuned to the vital needs of such a body. It takes the form of concrete utopianizing claims and compellingly political acts of will, even those as dramatic and desperate as Bouazizi's.

Sacrifice of the flesh and vindication of individual corporality as the locus of worldly happiness resonate with the secular West, where the body is becoming the preeminent stake, its renewed centrality for utopia guarding against its ruthless colonization by the market.⁶¹ Is it any wonder that a revival of corporal potential not only as a "machine for pleasure that is an end to itself"⁶² but also in its radical political capacity should come as bodies are relieved of overt physical labor, unfettered from psychical contact, and technologically boosted? One day, let us hope, capitulation to a capitalism-to-come will not be the price for "bodies on the line" everywhere becoming superfluous. For now, however, they are still everywhere necessary.

NOTES

1 Peter Osborne brings out nicely the corporal dimension of the modern, political cynicism of the Occupier in Osborne, "Disguised as a Dog: Cynical Occupy?," *Radical Philosophy* 174 (2012): 15–21.

2 See especially the introduction and essay under this title in David Graeber, *Revolutions in Reverse: Essays on Politics, Violence, Art, and Imagination* (London: Minor Compositions, 2011). In the "vast bureaucratic apparatus for the creation and maintenance of

hopelessness" that is Western capitalism, "a kind of giant machine that is designed, first and foremost, to destroy any sense of possible alternative futures" (31–32), hope in fact flies off the shelves (the problem is that, if spread too thin, it will not work). The crisis of capitalism, writes Benjamin Kunkel, "has not only sharpened anxieties but introduced new hopes," finding manifold collective expression in 2011. Kunkel, *Utopia or Bust: A Guide to the Present Crisis* (New York: Verso, 2014), 3. In arguing for the need for a provisional, "minimum utopian program," Kunkel commends the crop of new postcapitalist visions of political economy (16, 15). Franco "Bifo" Berardi offers a version of hope with a twist: "Since September 11th, 2001 suicide is the decisive political act of our times. When human life is worthless, humiliation grows until it becomes intolerable and explosive. Perhaps hope can only come from suicides." Berardi, *Precarious Rhapsody: Semiocapitalism and the Pathologies of the Post-Alpha Generation*, trans. Arianna Bove et al. (London: Minor Compositions, 2009), 55, sec. "Hope."

3   See part 3, section 3, "Critical-Utopian Socialism and Communism," in Karl Marx and Friedrich Engels, *The Communist Manifesto*, trans. Samuel Moore (London: Pluto, 2008).

4   Judith Shklar, "The Political Theory of Utopia: From Melancholy to Nostalgia," *Daedalus* 94, no. 2 (1965): 374–375.

5   Lyman Tower Sargent identifies the mythic "body utopia" as the foundational and simplest form of utopianism, because it is all about sensual gratification—initially "achieved without effort," and later with rites of passage. He opposes it to "city utopia," or "utopia of human contrivance," describing the other of the two main traditions of *utopian literature* (itself representing but one of three faces of utopianism, the other two being intentional communities and utopian social theory). Sargent, "The Three Faces of Utopianism Revisited," *Utopian Studies* 5, no. 1 (1994): 10, 4; Sargent's original treatment of utopianism from 1967—"The Three Faces of Utopianism," *Minnesota Review* 7, no. 3 (1967): 222–230—does not refer to "body utopia." The bodily type peaked in the medieval period, based on the model of natural abundance and organic social organization in a village setting. In contrast to both the classical man-made utopias of Plato and More and the modern ones of Cabet and Bellamy, aiming to engineer a flawless subset of humanity, the simple "utopian visions of the Middle Ages . . . start from man as he is and seek to fulfil his present desires." F. Graus, "Social Utopias in the Middle Ages," *Past and Present* 38 (1967): 6. They range from imagined lands of luxury and idleness set at the edge of the world to the popular images of a prosperous Golden Age, whose roots lay deep in Antiquity. The former, the fabled *pays de cocagne*, seems, in fact, to have originated as parody; "there is food and drink in abundance—there is no desire 'to nourish oneself' sensibly, but only to feast and gluttonize just as one has longed to do in everyday life" (9, 6). The latter and more common visions, the stuff of legend, brought back the "classical" quasi-paradisiacal model: barely elaborated beyond having "no private property, no excess, and consequently no thieves, no wrongdoers, no judges and no laws," they approached biblical conceptions "of a kingdom of peace where nature itself would be in perfect harmony, where wolves would house with lambs, a small boy would keep watch over lions and cattle together and no poisonous creature would ever do any harm" (12). Whether representing a past (pre)his-

torical era or "precisely determined theologically, and . . . strictly separated from the history of mankind by the dogma of original sin" (10), medieval renderings of the Golden Age admitted of no further progress, a desired earthly perfection having been reached once and lost forever. It is this limitation on history that utopianism's foundational Renaissance text reacted against. Yet even from More's early-modern perspective, the later notion of collective striving for a happy society in time (or *euchronia*) that underpins nineteenth-century literary utopias would make little sense. What unifies these diverse moments into a single "utopian tradition" must surely include the periodic recurrence of naïve ancient and medieval pictures of "fool's paradise" at least as late as the industrial age (with the socialist Fourier envisioning whole roast chickens raining from the sky and other heart-warming fantasies meant to do the body good).

Despite sometimes making explicit use of the human body—drawing on its Vitruvian proportions to imagine a harmonious social organization—the "city utopias" envisioned in the early-modern to modern period are ideal city-states, many of them autarchic: a closed and self-regulated system, ingesting and excreting nothing, or very nearly. As unsubtle as this sounds, they are not natural bodies but artificial constructs, intellectual designs whose economic rationality proceeds to write desire out of existence. To the author of *Christianopolis*, "the origin of life . . . is putrid. Ultimate blessedness . . . only of the resurrected body purified and refined in heaven." Frank E. Manuel and Fritzie P. Manuel, *Utopian Thought in the Western World* (Cambridge: Harvard University Press, 1977), 305. As Jean-Michel Racault reminds us, the life cycle and bodily functions pose a threat to the city's immobility. The real body is a "potential menace" and, while released from corporal punishment, requires denaturing through socialization, discipline in nourishment, sexuality, sleep, and exercise. Racault, "Corps utopique, utopies du corps," in *Pratiques du corps*, ed. A. Bullier and J.-M. Racault (Saint-Denis: Publications de l'Université de la Réunion, 1985), 121–124, 127, 133. Twentieth-century literary utopias focus more on a body whose excesses can no longer be ignored; the midcentury utopias of Aldous Huxley and B. F. Skinner represent two starkly contrasting responses to it. Mental passion, on the other hand, rarely needs to be tamed; often, the utopia is itself the fruit of passionate sublimation. In some corners, however, body utopia retained its appeal. The surrealist André Breton's rediscovery of Fourier in the 1940s resonated with the situationist movement, finding unlikely latter-day expression in Raoul Vaneigem's novel *Voyage to Oarystis*, the City of Desire. See Joël Gayraud, "Au miroir des analogies," *Critique* 812–813 (2015): 115–130; see also Emmanuel Guigon, "L'Écart absolu: Sur quelques rapports du fouriérisme et du surréalisme," *Luvah* 16 (1989): 81–91. Finally, as the utopian imagination forgets its modern tradition, we may yet witness a return to the needs of the body in both individual fantasy and collective social simulation combining script with immersive virtual reality.

6   Judith Shklar, "What Is the Use of Utopia?," in *Political Thought and Political Thinkers* (Chicago: University of Chicago Press, 1998), 176, 190, 186, 190.

7   Relevant titles representative of the "new materialism" in political theory include Moira Gatens, *Imaginary Bodies: Ethics, Power and Corporeality* (London: Routledge, 1995); John Tambornino, *The Corporeal Turn: Passion, Necessity, Politics* (Lanham,

Md.: Rowman and Littlefield, 2002); John L. Protevi, *Political Physics: Deleuze, Derrida, and the Body Politic* (London: Athlone, 2001); Protevi, *Political Affect: Connecting the Social to the Somatic* (Minneapolis: University of Minnesota Press, 2009); Davide Panagia, *The Political Life of Sensation* (Durham: Duke University Press, 2009); Samantha Frost, *Lessons from a Materialist Thinker: Hobbesian Reflections on Ethics and Politics* (Stanford: Stanford University Press, 2008).

8   See Michel Foucault, *The History of Sexuality*, vol. 1, *An Introduction*, trans. Robert Hurley (New York: Vintage, 1978), part 5, "Right of Death and Power Over Life."

9   For how "terroristic" violence is framed by Western conceptions of morality, rationality, legitimacy, and politics, see especially Talal Asad, *On Suicide Bombing* (New York: Columbia University Press, 2007). For an account of the weaponization of the body as a political form of resistance, see Banu Bargu, *Starve and Immolate: The Politics of Human Weapons* (New York: Columbia University Press, 2014). Taking a resolutely biopolitical approach to a particular instance of such weaponization, Bargu shows how the "*biopoliticization of sovereignty* meets the *necropoliticization of resistance*" (27). Copresent with the new power regime of *biosovereignty* (as she defines it), *necroresistance* "defies instrumentality through its disruption of the means-ends relation" (335). In the repertoire of forms of resistance, it could be the unlikely counterpart of exposed *prefigurative* praxis. "While these individuals oppose the biosovereign assemblage and express a desire for nondomination and nonoppression, do they call into being another form of community founded on premises and power relations that are substantially different than those that characterize the present?" (348). Though Bargu leaves the matter undecided, I am inclined to answer in the affirmative.

10 Werner Bonefeld and John Holloway, "Commune, Movement, Negation: Notes from Tomorrow," *South Atlantic Quarterly* 113, no. 2 (2014): 214.

11 Tiqqun, "How Is It to Be Done?," in *Introduction to Civil War*, trans. Alexander R. Galloway and Jason E. Smith (2001; New York: Semiotext(e), 2010), 218–219.

12 In the concluding chapter, Guillon turns his attention to the apparent disarticulation of the body and utopia by transhumanism. To show the poverty of this vision, he digs up Fourier's most colorful idea of physical enhancement in his utopian Harmony, namely, the *archibras*, a caudal, dexterous third arm—"as redoubtable as it is industrious." Charles Fourier quoted by Guillon, *Je chante le corps critique: Les Usages politiques du corps* (Béziers: H et O, 2008), 355. Far out though it might seem, this extra member was not an especially surprising desideratum in an age inventing a million new means of the body's industrial exhaustion.

13 Florent Perrier's *Topeaugraphies de l'utopie: Esquisses sur l'art, l'utopie et le politique* (Paris: Payot, 2015) supports this thesis in taking as its point of departure the loss of the sensible and bodily in political readings of utopia. The monograph appeared in Miguel Abensour's series "Critique of the Political"; the diagnosis of a "long-standing mutilation" suffered by utopia is thus, to some extent at least, endorsed by one of the very exponents of what I take here to be utopia's twentieth-century spiritualization. Perrier devotes himself to the thought of Saint-Simon and Fourier (also giving its due to Babeuf's concrete utopianism) in an effort to evoke the once-vibrant meeting of

utopia and art on the political plane, a utopian imaginary anchored in the "skin of the real"—as it had been in the nineteenth century, while harkening back to sixteenth-century millennialist movements (14–15).

14 As Shklar pointed out, classical utopias like More's rejected the doctrine of original sin, diminishing the suspicion of the body as inherently corrupt. Shklar, "Political Theory of Utopia," 370. The repertoire of pleasure in *Utopia* includes bodily pleasures insofar as these enhance health. More's target is the generalized misery responsible for the association of physical pleasure with the mere alleviation or absence of pain, rather than with physical well-being, from which happiness derives. Thomas More, *Utopia*, trans. Robert M. Adams, ed. George M. Logan and R. M. Adams, rev. ed. (Cambridge: Cambridge University Press, 2002), 72. The discussion is worth recalling in full:

> The first [and lower, of the two classes of pleasure] is that which fills the senses with immediate delight. Sometimes this happens when bodily organs that have been weakened by natural heat are restored with food and drink; sometimes it happens when we eliminate some excess in the body, as when we move our bowels, generate children, or relieve an itch somewhere by rubbing or scratching it. Now and then pleasure arises, not from restoring a deficiency or discharging an excess, but from something that affects and excites our senses with a hidden but unmistakable force, and attracts them to itself. Such is the power of music.
>
> The second kind of bodily pleasure they describe as nothing but the calm and harmonious state of the body, its state of health when undisturbed by any disorder. Health itself, when not oppressed by pain, gives pleasure, without any external excitement at all. Even though it appeals less directly to the senses than the gross gratifications of eating and drinking, many still consider this to be the greatest pleasure of all. Most of the Utopians regard it as the foundation and basis of all the pleasures . . . Mere absence of pain, without positive health, they regard as insensibility, not pleasure.
>
> (Ibid., 72)

Sensations of "beauty, strength and agility" dissociated from pain thus constitute the higher form of physical pleasure. This naturally opens onto the condemnation of bodily abuse on spiritual grounds: "it is crazy for a man to despise beauty of form, to impair his strength, to grind his agility down to torpor, to exhaust his body with fasts, to ruin his health and to scorn all other natural delights, unless by so doing he can more zealously serve the welfare of others or the common good. Then indeed he may expect a greater reward from God. But otherwise to inflict pain on oneself without doing anyone any good—simply to gain the empty and shadowy appearance of virtue, or to be able to bear with less distress adversities that may never come" goes against Nature. Ibid., 74. Yet "While Christian asceticism and the mortification of the flesh are rejected," writes Frank E. Manuel, "the spiritual and intellectual life is nevertheless valued above any other." Manuel, "Toward a Psychological History of Utopias," *Daedalus* 94, no. 2 (1965): 300. It is not sensate delight but the "freedom and culture of the mind" that guarantees the "happiness of life" in *Utopia*. More, *Utopia*, 53. Within the utopian frame, a return to the body as the site of innocence was radical, but the political melancholy of More's fiction outweighs the real political import of an "indirect approach" to counseling rulers on the ideal commonwealth: utopia was a "moralist's artifact," "a model, an ideal pattern that invited contemplation and judgment but did not entail any other activity"—an impression, we might add, justified by More's last work, *A Dialogue of Comfort from Tribulation*, composed in the Tower of London. Shklar, "Political Theory of Utopia," 371.

My use of the term "spiritualization" differs from that of Mannheim, for whom it means the *addition*, to politics, of the utopian element (whose beginnings he traces to sixteenth-century chiliasm, in its original "robust and corporeal" form) and which, were it not for its specifically eschatological character, could describe my goal. Karl Mannheim, *Ideology and Utopia: An Introduction to the Sociology of Knowledge*, trans. Louis Wirth and Edward Shils (1929; New York: Harcourt, 1954), 191, 213. Mannheim's *spiritualization* highlights the "motor function," the "orgiastic energies and ecstatic outbursts," of spiritual striving coming to infuse the politics of the lowest, oppressed strata, combining "spiritual fermentation and physical excitement," yielding a *politically* embodied utopianism that was still rooted in physical experience, that is, when utopia's disembodiment was not yet so far along (191, 192). By contrast, my notion of the "spiritualization of utopia" is the outcome of a *subtractive* process, leaving behind the corporal element that once grounded utopia. In the larger, two-step plan just laid out, the first step is thus to put the body back into, or *resomatize*, politics while the second—the project of this chapter—is to *despiritualize* or *reembody* utopia, making the ultimate goal a reutopianized politics of reloaded, utopianized bodies. Mannheim's thesis and project to recast utopia in opposition to ideology aimed to demonstrate that utopia and politics necessarily work hand in hand, regardless of whether and what political actors think about "utopia." His contribution notwithstanding, it is entirely possible that Mannheim's conception of utopia as a *mentality* helped deliver it to an even less corporeal future.

The *spiritualization* of utopia as meant here also differs from Manuel's usage in the above-cited essay, where the term refers to the *content* of the first of two polarized styles of twentieth-century blueprint utopia, one virtually desomatized, the other thoroughly libidinized. The latter utopianism described the anti-/neo-Freudian current of German Marxism epitomized by Wilhelm Reich's *Verlag für Sexualpolitik/Der Sexuelle Kampf der Jugend* (The sexual struggle of youth, 1933), his "apotheosis of the body in all its parts," which, according to Manuel, constituted a return to the legacy of Saint-Simon and Fourier (315). Herbert Marcuse, among its followers, brought reason and happiness back together.

15   Michel Foucault, *Birth of the Clinic: An Archaeology of Medical Perception*, trans. A. M. Sheridan (London: Routledge, 1989), 36–39. On "equaliberty" as the basic value of modern insurrectional politics, see Étienne Balibar, *Equaliberty: Political Essays*, trans. James D. Ingram (Durham: Duke University Press, 2014).

16   Robert Owen, *An Address Delivered to the Inhabitants of New Lanark on the First of January, 1816*, 3rd ed. (London: Longman, Hurst, Rees, Orme, and Brown, 1817), 27.

Nonetheless, Marx acknowledged Owen's "three utopias" rolled into one as having been realized in the Factory Acts. Karl Marx, *Capital: A Critique of Political Economy*, vol. 1, trans. Ben Fowkes (New York: Penguin, 1990), 413n58.

17 See Marx, *Capital*, 1:125n2.

18 In Abensour's estimation, "Fourier succeeded in surmounting the pre-Fourierist opposition of politics and desire" and "linking them. . . . no longer to channel the movement of the passions toward the political (utopia's habitual falling back on the state), but to take the political out of its traditional orbit, to open it to desire, to connect it to other types of sociability. . . . Beyond the desire for politics, the greatness of Fourier is to have proposed, on the basis of this decentering of the political, a politics of desire." It is likewise "Thanks to Fourier [that] utopia made a leap from need (lack) to desire (the expansion of being)" (chapter 1 of this volume, 32–33). The shift has most often been expressed in spatial terms, as physical stasis versus expansion of the utopian community. Thus, Manuel credits Fourier with having "widened the dimensions of utopia beyond anything that had been dreamed of before," making him the "greatest utopian after More": "Where More insisted on continent adequacy, Fourier dreamed of progressively greater pleasurable excitements," with (especially amorous and creative) desire unrepressed to lessen the burden of work (his concept of *travail attractif*, attractive work). Manuel, "Toward a Psychological History of Utopias," 308. All this did not, however, stop Marx and Engels in 1848 from lumping him together with Saint-Simon and Owen for "inculcating universal asceticism and social levelling in its crudest form." Marx and Engels, *Communist Manifesto*, 78.

19 While the utopianizing body is elementary in *L'Humanisphère*, its particularity ultimately gives in to universalism:

> The social body, like the human body, suffers from a malady that gets worse each day. There is only one means of saving them, which is to treat them with a new system, to employ homeopathy. . . . So let us provoke a terrible crisis, a renewed outbreak of the disease, so that tomorrow, at the end of that crisis, Humanity, taking possession of its senses and entering an era of convalescence, can nourish heart and mind on the juice of fraternal and social ideas, and so that, finally rendered healthy and strong in its movements, it testifies thus to the free and generous circulation of all its nutritious fluids, of all its productive forces, by a physiognomy radiant with happiness!

Joseph Déjacque, "The Extremes: Note on *The Humanisphere*," trans. Shawn P. Wilbur, *Contr'un*, http://libertarian-labyrinth.blogspot.com/2012/11/joseph-dejacque-humanisphere-note-on.html.

20 Even in these visions, emphasizing free heterosexuality (and, in Fourier's *Le Nouveau monde amoureux* [1808–1829], generalized eroticism), sensual relations were regimented and assigned productive ends. Morris's *News from Nowhere* ends with haymaking and a harvest feast in which erotic desire is sublimated and channeled toward fellowship after the pleasures of working the land. Marx's pointed reflection in the *Grundrisse* on the importance of work to happiness, partly critical of Fourier's scheme, reads:

In the sweat of thy brow shalt thou labour! was Jehovah's curse on Adam. And this is labour for Smith, a curse. "Tranquility" appears as the adequate state, as identical with "freedom" and "happiness." It seems quite far from Smith's mind that the individual, "in his normal state of health, strength, activity, skill, facility," also needs a normal portion of work, and of the suspension of tranquility. ... But Smith has no inkling whatever that this overcoming of obstacles is in itself a liberating activity—and that, further, the external aims become stripped of the semblance of merely external natural urgencies, and become posited as aims which the individual sets himself—hence, as self-realization, objectification of the subject, hence real freedom whose action is, precisely, labor. He is right, of course, that, in its historical forms as slave-labor, serf-labor, and wage-labor, labor always appears as repulsive, always as *external forced labor*; and not working, by contrast, as "freedom, and happiness." This holds doubly: for this contradictory labor; and, relatedly, for labor that has not yet created the subjective and objective conditions for itself (or also, in contrast to the pastoral etc. state, which has lost [these conditions]), in which labor becomes attractive work [*travail attractif*], the individual's self-realization, which in no way means that it becomes mere fun, mere amusement, as Fourier, with all the naïveté of a *grisette*, conceives it. Truly free working, for example, composing, is at the same time precisely the most damned seriousness, the most intensive exertion. The work of material production can acquire this character only (1) when its social character is affirmed, (2) when it is of a scientific and at the same time general character, not merely human exertion as a specifically harnessed natural force, but exertion as subject, which appears in the production process not in a merely natural, spontaneous form, but as an activity regulating all the forces of nature.

Karl Marx, *Grundrisse: Foundations of the Critique of Political Economy*, trans. Martin Nicolaus (London: Penguin, 2005), 611–612, translation modified.

21 On the movement's political history and fate in the Third Reich, see Bernd Wedemeyer-Kolwe, *Der neue Mensch: Körperkultur im Kaiserreich und in der Weimarer Republik* (Würzburg: Königshausen und Neumann, 2004), pt. 3; Arno Klönne, "Das 'Ja zum Leibe'—mehrdeutig: Zur politischen Geschichte des Freikörperkulturbewegung," *Vorgänge* 33, no. 3 (1994): 27–32; Arno Krüger, "Zwischen Sex und Zuchtwahl: Nudismus und Naturismus in Deutschland und Amerika," in *Liberalitas: Eine Festschrift für Erich Angermann*, ed. Norbert Finzsch and Hermann Wellenreuther (Stuttgart: Steiner, 1992), 353–354; and Dietger Pforte, "Zur Freikörperkultur-Bewegung im nationalsozialistischen Deutschland," in *"Wir sind nackt und nennen uns Du": Von Lichtfreunden und Sonnenkämpfern: Eine Geschichte der Freikörperkultur*, ed. Michael Andritzky and Thomas Rautenberg (Gießen: Anabas, 1989), 136–145.

22 Aldous Huxley, *Brave New World, and Brave New World Revisited* (New York: Harper, 2005), 62. In his utopia from 1962, however, the body's addictions are forgiven, and a different drug is taken medicinally. Moksha-medicine is "the reality revealer, the truth- and beauty pill": "with four hundred milligrams of moksha-medicine in their blood-

streams, even beginners—yes, and even boys and girls who make love together—can catch a glimpse of the world as it looks to someone who has been liberated from his bondage to the ego." Huxley, *Island* (New York: Harper Perennial, 2009), 166.

23 The idea can be traced back to at least the French evangelical and romantic socialists as well as to the German activist-expressionist anarchism circa World War I. The socialist-revolutionary content of *la politique de l'esprit* is clarified in this passage from Lamennais: "What we call, for lack of a better term, the politics of the spirit is politics that believes in the spiritual laws of man, and that endeavors to connect these sovereign laws to the great phenomena of society. Material politics, on the contrary, either negates these laws or refuses to take them into account in its judgments of the present and in its previsions of the future." Hugues Félicité R. de Lamennais, "De la politique de l'esprit et de la politique matérielle," in *Politique à l'usage du peuple: Recueil des articles publiés dans* Le Monde, la Revue des Deux Mondes, *et la* Revue du Progrès, vol. 1, 4th ed. (Paris: Pagnerre, 1839), 58. (Where not otherwise credited, translations are mine.) Lamennais, no less than Auguste Comte under the spell of Saint-Simon, saw the transformation of spirit as fundamental to social-political change. For the later German use of this expression, see the left-libertarian Kurt Hiller's yearbook: Hiller, *Das Ziel: Aufrufe zu tätigem Geist* (The goal: Appeals to the active spirit, 1916–1918), published in 1919–1924 with the subtitle *Jahrbücher für geistige Politik* (Yearbook for spiritual politics) and featuring contributions by such figures as Walter Benjamin, Max Brod, Hans Blüher, Gustav Landauer, and Heinrich Mann (who already in 1900 mocked the apolitical capitalist utopia in his novel *Im Schlaraffenland: Ein Roman unter feinen Leuten* [In the land of Cockaigne]). Klaus Vondung gives an overview of this new, pacifist-socialist current—calling it "the spirit of utopia" after Ernst Bloch, one of its advocates—in Vondung, *The Apocalypse in Germany*, trans. Stephen D. Ricks (Columbia: University of Missouri Press, 2000), 184–209. He finds that its exponents' "positive understanding of Utopia bound them together and at the same time separated them not only from the conservative opponents of utopian ideology, but also from the champions of socialism and of revolution who accorded spirit no role in the historical process," most notably Marx and Marxists; they usually defined their socialism as "'anarchic' or connected to anarchism," while claiming the rule of spirit and, effectively, a spiritual elite, a kind of *Geistesaristokratie* (185, 189ff.). The impending utopian transformation was, for Bloch as for Landauer, also a *disrealization* (*Entrealisierung*)—the "elimination of the physical world" through spirit/mind, drawing inspiration from Christian millenarianism and Jewish apocalyptic messianism or Hegel's system (190, quoting Bloch's *Spirit of Utopia* (1918), part 2, "Karl Marx, Death, and the Apocalypse"). The Landauerian tendency to posit spirit before, and as the motor behind, concrete social transformation is also evident in the work of Martin Buber: see Ephraim Fischoff's introduction to the English edition of *Paths in Utopia*, trans R. F. C. Hull (1946; Boston: Beacon, 1949).

Bloch's contemporary Paul Valéry appears down to earth by comparison. He invokes the expression "politics of the spirit" (*la politique de l'esprit*) in a lecture from 1932, where the spirit/mind is the "power" and "agent" of transformation in all domains of human endeavor. At the same time, it acts as a defense against brutality, the demonism of politics: "Politics, political action, and political forms are necessarily inferior values and inferior activities of the mind [*esprit*]," he writes in "The European Spirit" (1935), in *The Collected Works of Paul Valéry*, vol. 10, *History and Politics*, trans. Denise Folliot and Jackson Mathews, ed. J. Mathews (New York: Pantheon, 1962), 327. When the mind stoops to politics, with its "always deceptive" reasoning, it raises it (328). It does so, however, not through hope, but through *prevision* ("the foundation of all politics" and "the use of the possible"). Valéry returns here to his "Crise de l'esprit" from 1919: "Hope, of course, remains. . . . But hope is only man's mistrust of the clear foresight of his mind [*esprit*]. Hope suggests that any conclusion unfavorable to us must be an error of the mind." Valéry, *La Politique de l'esprit: Notre souverain bien* (Manchester: Manchester University Press, 1941), 24. And, second, the mind's power lies in foreseeing, not prophesying. It is a "paradoxical instinct," one "that tries somehow to remake the milieu in which we live, and to give us occupations that are sometimes excessively remote from those imposed on us by the pure and simple concern for our animal existence; it creates new needs, it gives us numerous artificial needs, it introduces alongside the natural instincts, . . . alongside the several goads of vital necessity (instinct means goad), many other impulses. In particular it has created a quite remarkable need to accumulate experience, to assemble and record the various kinds, to make structures of thought from them, and even to project them beyond the present, as though trying to get hold of life where it does not yet, or can no longer, exist." Valéry, *The Outlook for Intelligence*, trans. Denise Folliot and Jackson Mathews, ed. J. Mathews (New York: Harper and Row, 1963), 96. The spirit transforms the world in the imagination, the body supplies it with raw material, grounds it without anchoring down, and stimulates it. "The mind seems to abhor and shun the very process of deep organic life which (unlike the mind) requires repetition, requires that the elemental acts on which vital exchanges depend be repeated"—satisfying needs and desires and putting the body to sleep. Yet the spirit's "initial spark" comes from sensibility, which "introduce[s] into the living system an element of imminence, of always impending change," that "trait of changeableness required to set in motion [the mind's] power of transformation" (99–100). It is "the functional properties of the mind" that have "influenced the course of invention" and pushed it to its limit (102). The body plays here the role of manual laborer, with the spirit taking all the credit for "build[ing] for itself a kind of world quite different from the world as it originally was" (104). In Valéry's conception, the mind's individuality and universality make of it a "rebel, even in the act of bringing order" (groups and political parties are abhorrent to it—here as elsewhere Valéry hews close to Nietzsche) (103). Given that the wider "struggle between yesterday and tomorrow" is a struggle raging in the mind between preservation and transformation, that is to say, a crisis of values (103, 109), *la politique de l'esprit* is the only way out of the crisis of the mind, "torn between futility and anxiety" and dulled by a general desensitization (110–111). The "politics of the spirit," then, consists in employing the mind's "constructive," transformative capacity in the political realm. It is to his credit that Valéry speculates on the consequences of, and warns against, the simple application of scientific truth to politics, leading to the political subjection of bodies to empirical experiments. Keeping them apart, however, only deepens the fracture in modern thought. From this angle, a somatization of politics—*la politique du corps*—looks much more congenial than the hypertrophy of *l'esprit*. But Valéry's conclusion leaves us in no doubt about his view on the matter—not only of political being but of utopian aspirations: "It is clearly possible to conceive an almost happy condition for humanity, or at least a stable, pacified, organized, comfortable condition (I do not say that we are anywhere near it); but in conceiving such a state, we realize that it brings with it, or would bring, a most tepid intellectual temperature: in general, happy peoples have no mind. They have no great need of it" (109–110). They are reduced to bodily existence. It is tempting to read in the political turn to the spirit a countercurrent to calls for *biocracy* and *biopolitics*, terms first employed around 1919 by the psychiatrist Édouard Toulouse, radical socialist advocate of democratic eugenics as a scientific utopian project. See Guillon, *Je chante le corps critique*, 357–359; Marc Renneville, "Le Propre de l'ordre: Hygienisme et biopolitique en republique," *Revue de synthèse* 120, no. 4 (1999): 621–635. For the origin of *biopolitics* as a liberal technology of the state, see Foucault, *History of Sexuality*, vol. 1. On the figure of the Muselmann in Nazi concentration camps as the basis for an expanded notion of biopolitics that makes the depoliticized, suffering body, *la nuda vita*, the center of political modernity, see Giorgio Agamben, *Homo Sacer: Sovereign Power and Bare Life*, trans. Daniel Heller-Roazen (Stanford: Stanford University Press, 1998).

24   An alternative way of saving utopia was to argue for it as a necessary counterweight to ideology, as Mannheim, Paul Ricœur, and Fredric Jameson did, decades apart from one another. Mannheim went even farther in his valuation, seeing utopia as a means of staving off humanity's spiritual crisis. While humanity could get by well enough with less ideology, it simply could not afford a further decline of utopia, already removed from political activity ("we approach a situation in which the utopian element, through its many divergent forms, has completely [in politics, at least] annihilated itself"); without utopias we can look forward to human unidimensionality and the decay of the will—in short, to a world not of men but *things* (Mannheim, *Ideology and Utopia*, 225, 236). And as even Shklar, for whom Mannheim's utopia-or-ideology breakdown of political thought was a "Manichean strait-jacket," herself recognized, "There may be little use for utopia now, but that is not a good reason for abusing it." Shklar, "Political Theory of Utopia," 368; Shklar, "What Is the Use of Utopia?," 190.

25   One could make a case for the widespread denial of applied utopianism as a precondition of Rawls's (benignly) normative abstractions and "realistic utopianism," distinguishing his own dynamic, liberal-democratic "primacy of Right" from a generic utopian "primacy of the Good" (to which individual freedom could be sacrificed, and which closed or insulated itself in nondemocratic forms of government). See also Corinna Mieth, "Liberalismus und Utopie—ein Widerspruch?," in *Utopie heute*, ed. Beat Sitter-Liver (Freiburg: Stuttgart, 2007), 79–110.

26   Georges Duveau, *Sociologie de l'utopie et autres essais* (Paris: Presses Universitaires de France, 1961), 192.

27 Hannah Arendt, *The Human Condition*, 2nd ed. (1958; Chicago: University of Chicago Press, 1998), 112.
28 Michel Foucault, "Le Corps utopique," in *"Le Corps utopique," suivi de "Les Hétérotopies"* (Paris: Nouvelles Éditions Lignes, 2009), 18.
29 Johann Valentin Andreae, *Christianopolis: The Ideal of the 17th Century*, trans. Felix Emil Held (New York: Cosimo, 2007), 245.
30 Foucault, "Le Corps utopique," 18.
31 Nietzsche put it well: the sick in body who despise it and "preach afterworlds"—"may they become convalescents and overcomers and create for themselves a higher body." Friedrich Nietzsche, *Thus Spoke Zarathustra*, trans. Adrian del Caro, ed. A. del Caro and Robert Pippin (Cambridge: Cambridge University Press, 2006), 22. He too—in a book addressed to modern "Hyperboraeans," the *freie Geister* ("free spirits")—traces all imaginings of the "ages of happiness" not only to "primeval times" but, more precisely, to that physical "condition in which, after violent exertion in hunting and warfare, man gives himself up to repose, stretches his limbs and hears the pinions of sleep rustling about him." Nietzsche, *Human, All Too Human: A Book for Free Spirits*, trans. R. J. Hollingdale (Cambridge: Cambridge University Press, 1996), 170, §471. The link explains the intensity of utopian desire in our current sleep-deprived age "of toil and deprivation" (Kunkel's title, a slogan from the French youth protests in 2006, frames this all-or-nothing attitude: *utopie ou rien*, "utopia or bust"). But Nietzsche's insight is framed by the striking claim that utopia—"that condition of happiness *correspondingly enhanced and protracted*"—is impossible not because we lack the means to build it or would not agree on its design, but because we do not really desire it; it is a desire that does not want fulfillment. The utopian dream is merely the "false conclusion" drawn by the experience of bodily fatigue and presumably disappears with restful sleep. There is something equally false and lazy in Nietzsche's claim, with its lingering suspicion of the body as deceiving and clouding our judgment, about the ultimate undesirability of utopia-debunking. For even if it were true that "every individual who experiences good times learns to downright pray for misery and disquietude," the cause of this "prayer" is not our natural inclinations; the desire for the return of the bad is, as he himself says, "learned" (with little indication how or why). A likelier cause is that disquiet soon puts an end to the "good times," because we have not yet learned to enjoy unabated happiness or to extend the "happy moments" indefinitely, shaking off all notions of hedonism. Out of some mixture of "slave morality" and sociocultural circumstances perhaps, we still feel more "at home"—more normal, more socially integrated—in anxiety and despair. But it need not always be so.
32 Neoliberal dream-weavers will remind us that utopia has always been an insular place, that it remains a private realm of privilege that can be bought, that its present obscurity has little to do with a ruined imagination and limits on virtual sociality, and more with an imagination that has not yet been liberated by money. The "privatization" of (bodily) utopia, bemoaned by theorists today, continues apace with the decline of *civic* hope, if its retreat from public expression and action is any indication. For a discussion of Blochian "speculative materialism" as remedy for present hopelessness, see Frances Daly's essay in *The Privatization of Hope: Ernst Bloch and the Future of*

Utopia, ed. Peter Thompson and Slavoj Žižek (Durham: Duke University Press, 2013). Bloch, a critic of (happily alienated) high-bourgeois family life, preferred "concrete utopia" to banal "abstract" utopia; it is the *docta spes*, "educated hope," that takes us to the concrete, rooted in material realities.

33 Manuel, like others, distinguishes between the mostly unrecorded, personal utopias without a history and those that have "won a measure of public acceptance (and become at least *folie à deux*), the main currents of utopian feeling, the dreams shared widely enough to be social utopias with a general history." Manuel, "Toward a Psychological History of Utopias," 293. But it is important to stress the continuum of utopian imaginings: from extreme autonomic solipsism, to atomized collectivity, shared only to the extent that the individuals in it are part of a system of their own devising that must be maintained, to the coalescing of such individual utopias into a public collectivity—by most standards the healthiest sort.

34 The solipsistic fantasy that may have preceded that of living autonomically and autarchically—namely, living autoerotically and autophagically, severed from all needs save those satisfiable locally and automatically—is nobody's idea of utopia. No more, in any case, than a world where everyone agreed, decreed, was indoctrinated or engineered to walk the same mental and physical paths in perfectly synchronized harmony to avoid conflict and ensure equality in every respect.

35 William Morris, *News from Nowhere, or, An Epoch of Rest, Being Some Chapters from a Utopian Romance*, ed. Krishnan Kumar (Cambridge: Cambridge University Press, 1995), 96, 109.

36 To informed critics of this revolutionary tradition, who see utopia and workerist Marxism as one dysfunctional, inwardly divided, paradoxical project, utopia inverts the revolutionary figure of the Legislator—a deliberative rhetorician, at best—into the figure of the Procrastinator.

37 I have in mind here principally the reception of the early Bloch of the *Geist der Utopie* (Spirit of utopia) all the way to Abensour, who sees utopianism as a spiritual antidote to the ills of the modern world. What Abensour calls the "new utopian spirit" (*nouvel esprit utopique*) dates from the mid-nineteenth century to the 1930s. It grew out of critical reflection, in light of the failure of 1848, on the modern dialectic of emancipation in which utopia participates, and involved utopianism's "critical reactivation" as "either theoretico-practical (Morris, certain tendencies within surrealism) or purely theoretical (for example, Bloch and Walter Benjamin)" (chapter 1 of this volume, 43). The post-1848 revival of utopia clearly cost it something: the body began to wither away as a basis of utopian desire. Despite engaging with the socialism of Morris and Pierre Leroux, who saw the possibility of a convergence between utopian and revolutionary democratic energies, Abensour views later attempts at their reunion disapprovingly: utopia's "joining with politics takes place only at the price of a loss of original content" (ibid.). In any such future prospect, a trade-off remains unavoidable, even if the content in this case is *negative*. For more, see, for example, Miguel Abensour, "Le Nouvel esprit utopique," *Cahiers Bernard Lazare* 128–130 (1991): 132–163, and, in English, Abensour, "To Think Utopia Otherwise," trans. Bettina Bergo, *Graduate Faculty Philosophy Journal* 20, no. 2/21, no. 1 (1998): 251–279, as well as Abensour, "Persistent Utopia," trans.

James D. Ingram, *Constellations* 15, no. 3 (2008): 406–421. "All hope lies in thought," "It is in language that the idea that all should be well can be articulated," noted, along Aristotelian lines, Max Horkheimer, who falls in the lineage of negative spiritual utopianism. Theodor W. Adorno and Max Horkheimer, "Towards a New Manifesto?," *New Left Review* 65 (2010): 42, 44. Clearly, utopia cannot be reduced to the expression of hope or to a species of hoping; it is, in Bloch's account (dismissed by Adorno), hope *as a principle (das Prinzip Hoffnung)*, built on the structure of desire, on wishfulness (recapitulated in Raymond Geuss's "projective principle," devoid of any *particular* positive content, making it universalizable). But if utopia were simply the principle of hope, even of a particular kind of hope—for example, political hope—it would still be uncontroversial, passive, politically ineffective.

38 The phrase comes from Adorno's utopianizing fragment "Sur l'eau," in Adorno, *Minima Moralia: Reflections on a Damaged Life*, trans. E. F. N. Jephcott (New York: Verso, 2005), 165. Summing up his and Horkheimer's respective attitudes toward cultural theorizing, he notes: "[Theory] negates itself. When ideas become too concrete, I protest; when they become too abstract, you protest." Adorno and Horkheimer, "Towards a New Manifesto?," 60.

39 Max Horkheimer and Theodor W. Adorno, *Dialectic of Enlightenment: Philosophical Fragments*, trans. Edmund Jephcott (Stanford: Stanford University Press, 2002), 192–193, sec. "Interest in the Body."

40 In Marcuse's reading, the category of happiness in Marxian theory displaced that of reason, long the "higher universal independent of the 'base' impulses and drives of individuals." The new category "made manifest the positive content of materialism. Historical materialism appeared at first as a denunciation of the materialism prevalent in bourgeois society, and the materialist principle was in this respect a critical instrument of exposé directed against a society that enslaved men to the blind mechanisms of material production. The idea of the free and universal realization of individual happiness, *per contra*, denoted an *affirmative* materialism, that is to say, an affirmation of the material satisfaction of man." Herbert Marcuse, *Reason and Revolution: Hegel and the Rise of Social Theory*, 2nd ed. (1941; London: Routledge and Kegan Paul, 1955), 294.

41 Herbert Marcuse, "The End of Utopia," in *Five Lectures: Psychoanalysis, Politics and Utopia*, trans. Jeremy Shapiro and Shierry M. Weber (Boston: Beacon, 1970), 62. Marcuse uses "utopia" pejoratively; what would end with the realization of radical ideas of social transformation is their dismissal as utopian.

42 Adorno, *Minima Moralia*, 185.

43 This distinction between voluntary, or cultivated, and involuntary pauperism must be understood on a religious-to-lay spectrum of attitudes. It takes us back to that protean utopian mentality, chiliasm: "The Chiliastic experience is characteristic of the lowest strata of society. Underlying it is a mental structure peculiar to oppressed peasants, journeymen, an incipient *Lumpenproletariat*, fanatically emotional preachers, etc." Mannheim, *Ideology and Utopia*, 204. This spectrum underpins Mannheim's claim about revolutionary anarchism not only as part of the chiliastic lineage, but as "preserv[ing this mentality] in its purest and most genuine form," and continuing the late-medieval revolution begun by it (202). He follows this up with a passage from En-

gels's *Peasant War in Germany* that defines chiliasm's/radical anarchism's (particularly the school of Bakunin's [196]) ahistorical revolutionary impetus in physiological terms: "It is part of the fact and the concept of revolution that, like a convalescent fever, it comes between two spells of sickness. It would not exist at all if it were not preceded by fatigue and followed by exhaustion'" (203). This intense "ecstatic" relation to temporality accounts for its modern "disappear[ance] almost entirely from the political scene, as a result of which an element of tension was eliminated from the remaining forms of the political utopia. It is, of course, true that many of the elements constituting the Chiliastic attitude were transmuted into and took refuge in syndicalism and in Bolshevism, and were assimilated and incorporated into the activity of these movements. Thus the function devolves upon them, particularly in Bolshevism, of accelerating and catalyzing rather than deifying the revolutionary deed" (223). It is, however, Mannheim stresses, a highly adaptive outlook, which "emerges even now at decisive moment" (203).

44   Doing with less blends into precariousness, which is to be taken here as a condition of felt lack and existential vulnerability, stripped of the definite political and socioeconomic factors present in precarity. Cf. Judith Butler's distinction between these terms in *Precarious Life: The Powers of Mourning and Violence* (New York: Verso, 2004) and *Frames of War: When Is Life Grievable?* (New York: Verso, 2009). In *Notes toward a Performative Theory of Assembly* (Cambridge, Mass.: Harvard University Press, 2015) she links the condition of precarity with persistence and resistance, and hence with the political power of physical popular assemblies.

45   Miguel Abensour, *"Le Procès des maîtres rêveurs,"* suivi de *"Pierre Leroux et l'utopie"* (Arles: Sulliver, 2000), 22.

46   Fredric Jameson, "Politics of Utopia," *New Left Review* 25 (January–February 2004): 42. Evidently, writing what Marx dismissed in the afterword to *Capital* from 1873 as "recipes for the cookbooks of the future" is not nearly as satisfying as having your fill in the present, and nothing lines an empty stomach like "going hungry" read backward—like the desperation of Blochian *hunger*. Habermas explains: "The ever-renewed hunger drives people about, sets the tone for self-preservation as self-expansion, and, in its enlightened figure, is transformed into an explosive force against the prisons of deprivation in general. This learned hunger, another form of the *docta spes*, develops to the point of a resolution to eliminate all relationships under which people live as forgotten beings. Hunger appears as the elemental energy of hope." Jürgen Habermas, "Ernst Bloch: A Marxist Schelling" (1960), in *Philosophical-Political Profiles*, trans. F. G. Lawrence (Cambridge: MIT Press, 1983), 61. Blochian hunger, though an emphatically corporal figure, is both hypostatized and insatiable; it registers the modern loss of embodied experience. Compared with (sexual) desire, its *social* character is less than clear. And, rather than through enlightened education, its release of a quantum of hope and transformation into a utopian force would seem to require redirection through discipline.

To be sure, volume 1 of Bloch's magnum opus—the sprawling *Principle of Hope* (1938–1947, revised 1959), a treasure trove of concrete-utopian fragments—makes of the corporal the site of striving-longing-wishing foundational to his investigation of utopianism, both theoretically and historically. The story of utopias is, in his account, thoroughly somatized, the "not yet" a dream incarnate. It is, however, language that is said to bring the body's utopian wishes, otherwise latent and vague, to light. These in turn give shape to mediated, disembodied "mental feelings," "states of mind," and, finally, hope for a better world—which is what Bloch's followers Ruth Levitas, Abensour, and Jameson overwhelmingly took from him. The Blochian "utopia of the concrete" is educated hope, predicated on awakening not instincts or drives but "the dormant consciousness of the proletariat" (Manuel and Manuel, *Utopian Thought in the Western World*, 806)—absent the concretization that, without the repressive agency of the mind to steer bodily economy not toward eudaemonia but toward eupsychia, is the upshot of a utopian carte blanche.

47 Graeber, *Revolutions in Reverse*, 38.

48 "Prefiguration" names the utopian dimension of anarchism and of other nonviolent communitarian forms of direct action (see Ruth Kinna's chapter in this volume). Andrew Boyd sums up its purpose in his (multiauthor) manual for activists: "To give a glimpse of the Utopia we're working for; to show how the world could be; to make such a world feel not just possible, but irresistible." Boyd, "Tactic: Prefigurative Intervention," in *Beautiful Trouble: A Toolbox for Revolution*, ed. A. Boyd and Dave Oswald Mitchell (New York: OR, 2012), 82. The concept of prefiguration involves, at least from his standpoint, not only the articulation of ultimate social desiderata as immediate guidelines to present praxis, which is to embody them in microcosmic "foreshadowings," but also a physical attraction to a better world in the here and now, without deferral and systematic planning for *after* the piecemeal social revolution, when the right conditions are already in place. *Pace* Carissa Honeywell, the link between anarchism and utopianism is thus greater than their "thematic convergence." Honeywell, "Utopianism and Anarchism," *Journal of Political Ideologies* 12, no. 3 (2007): 245.

49 The other two interstitial "styles," psychogeography and fieldtrips, make more demands on the body. All these "wild," an-archic forms "exemplify *in thought* that aspect of anarchist practice called *direct action*." Daydreaming, for one, stresses the value of "affirmative meditation" on, for example, the writings of Fourier, whose practical utility is doubtful: "The famous and pathetic theses of the innate goodness of humans or of a future utopia have perhaps no value other than their role as themes for meditation and affirmation in the present." Alejandro de Acosta, "Anarchist Meditations, or: Three Wild Interstices of Anarchism and Philosophy" (2010), 19.

50 Ibid.

51 Lucy Sargisson, "The Curious Relationship Between Politics and Utopia," in *Utopia Method Vision: The Use Value of Social Dreaming*, ed. Tom Moylan and Raffaelle Baccolini (Oxford: Peter Lang, 2007), 25.

52 Ibid.

53 *The German Ideology* clarifies the relationship between the (natural) fixity of desire and that of universal needs:

> A desire is already by its mere existence something "fixed," and it can occur only to Saint Max and his like not to allow his sex instinct, for instance, to become "fixed"; it is that already and will cease to be fixed only as a result of castration or impotence. Each need, which forms the basis of a "desire," is likewise something

"fixed," and try as he may Saint Max cannot abolish this "fixedness" and for example contrive to free himself from the necessity of eating within "fixed" periods of time. The communists have no intention of abolishing the fixedness of their desires and needs, an intention which Stirner, immersed in his world of fancy, ascribes to them and to all other men; they only strive to achieve an organization of production and intercourse which will make possible the normal satisfaction of all needs, i.e., a satisfaction which is limited only by the needs themselves.

Karl Marx and Friedrich Engels, *The German Ideology* (Amherst, N.Y.: Prometheus, 1976), 273, abstract of chap. 3, "Idealist Mistakes and Materialist Corrections."

One might add that such minimal, subsistence-level needs, shared with other species, do not fix a specifically *human* nature, defining rather a broader, creaturely condition; the physical, psychic, and symbolic expression of desires, meanwhile, is culturally contingent.

A negative view of this fixity—determination by nature, being pinned to desire (crucified by it, to speak floridly)—stems from the Christian dialectic of spirit and flesh. Even more to the point, the denial of satisfaction, whether by choice or by necessity, works to (unnaturally) fix desire:

Whether a desire becomes fixed or not, i.e., whether it obtains exclusive [power over us]—which, however, does [not] exclude [further progress]—depends on whether material circumstances, "bad" mundane conditions permit the normal satisfaction of this desire and, on the other hand, the development of a totality of desires. This latter depends, in turn, on whether we live in circumstances that allow all-round activity and thereby the full development of all our potentialities. On the actual conditions, and the possibility of development they give each individual, depends also whether thoughts become fixed or not.

(Ibid., 272)

Capitalism's contribution is "the discovery, creation and satisfaction of new needs arising from society itself; the cultivation of all the qualities of the social human being, production of the same in a form as rich as possible in needs, because rich in qualities and relations—production of this being as the most total and universal possible social product, for, in order to take gratification in a many-sided way, he must be capable of many pleasures [*genussfähig*], hence cultured to a high degree—is likewise a condition of production founded on capital." Marx, *Grundrisse*, 409, quoted in Abensour, chapter 1 of this volume, 29. Satisfying in new ways existing needs to producing new ones entails the expansion ("unfixing") of the sensorium, its historical development. Conversely, capital's unequal withholding of gratification serves to fix and naturalize newly minted needs, maintaining us in its thrall while stunting human historical development on Marx's terms. The question is: Can we "return" in some meaningful measure to an earlier, less elaborate "version" of our sensorium, more in keeping with our political goals and material conditions? The work of "undoing" needs brought forth by capital and then left unsatisfied would seem to be one of the greatest challenges facing complex ground-up social remodeling. Its vanguard must then lie somewhere along the eroded and replenished shores of desire, which a hurricane gave reprieve for recovery—for a "managed retreat," reining in and regaining "control" of our desire. There is nothing contradictory or defeatist in this, once grasped politically. What is being rejected is the relentless mobility of desire and thought that masks its real conditions: the exhaustion and boredom of desire targeted by images prodding it to react as long as "Don't feed the animals". does not apply to people, the stagnation of thought strapped in the media wheel on a ride that will never end. Recovering the creative act of imagination and the momentum of one's thought starts there, on the edge, on the coastline that recedes when hordes come to amuse themselves. To extend these initial "sacrifices," which in the West draw their strength not from an *ethic* of self-sacrifice (though the latter might be resorted to on an ad hoc basis) but from self-recovery and communal survival, it may become crucial to reach for the rhetoric of spiritual renewal. For the time being, however, it is about feeling good about others and comfortable in one's own skin, free of competition for scarce resources as well as the frustration and self-hatred that our addictive consumption tends to elicit in us.

54 Sophie Wahnich, *In Defence of the Terror: Liberty or Death in the French Revolution*, trans. David Fernbach (London: Verso, 2012), 23, 89–90.

55 Ibid., 93.

56 To wit, here is Bloch in 1918 (nb, rev. ed. 1923): "Hunger must not be cheated; it only knows that this [utopian surplus in existence] cannot satisfy it, nor can that, but of what will finally allay it [it] can have only a presentiment, as it is not yet here. Certainly the question how one imagines bliss is so far from forbidden that it is basically the only one permitted. Meanwhile even this question, trying to brighten the twilight, already aims frivolously at something named, accustomed, already commits us to a weak, restrictive word";

> But most work without knowing what they do, and base it only on trite, inferior goals. So our fierce collective striving is guided by nothing but the profit motive, a flimsy, barbaric content, which soon enough expires from its own sterility. It helps us little, in contrast, when other, more idealistic endeavors also appear, for as long as they are not granted enough power to decisively transform, decisively to be put to use, then the cooperative factor, the spiritual factor, remains as arbitrary as the economic factor of meaningless record-breaking. The one merely an abdominal question, the other a lie roundabout the social question, or, after hunger has been stilled and luxury liberated, a gaffe, a buffoonery, an amusement and an entertainment, a science in itself . . . in other words the spirit becomes a baseless and basically odious cliché.

Ernst Bloch, *The Spirit of Utopia*, trans. Anthony A. Nassar (Stanford: Stanford University Press, 2000), 196, 267.

57 Karl R. Popper, "Utopia and Violence" (1948), in *Conjectures and Refutations: The Growth of Scientific Knowledge* (New York: Routledge, 2002), 361.

58 Judith Butler, "Bodies in Alliance and the Politics of the Street," *Transversal*, September 2011. As in the later *Notes Toward a Performative Theory of Assembly*, Butler here muses on the unacknowledged role of bodily, nonverbal communication in the cre-

ation of political community, challenging Arendt's Aristotelian definition of politics through the use of language. The theoretical evacuation of the body from politics, its relegation to the private realm of silence, smacks of ideology and impedes, to Butler's mind, the redefinition of revolutionary politics for our time.

59   Ruth Levitas, "For Utopia: The (Limits of the) Utopian Function in Late Capitalist Society," in *The Philosophy of Utopia*, ed. Barbara Goodwin (London: Routledge, 2001), 39. Levitas is here echoing Abensour's maxim (in an old translation by E. P. Thompson), "desire better ... more, and ... above all ... *otherwise*." Miguel Abensour, "William Morris: The Politics of Romance," trans. Max Blechman, in *Revolutionary Romanticism: A Drunken Boat Anthology*, ed. M. Blechman (San Francisco: City Lights, 1999), 146, italics mine. (In Morris's utopia, the same river of desire, the Thames, runs through both Victorian and deindustrialized England.) Levitas also adopts Abensour's expression "the education of desire." But, as Christine Nadir demonstrates in her rectifying account of this filiation, Levitas oversimplifies matters in treating desire as liberatory and immanently (as opposed to, for Abensour, imperatively) educable. Nadir, "Utopian Studies, Environmental Literature, and the Legacy of an Idea: Educating Desire in Miguel Abensour and Ursula K. Le Guin," *Utopian Studies* 21, no. 1 (2010): 24–56, esp. 25–32. Once again, Marx and Engels's clarification of what "desiring otherwise" might entail comes in handy:

> Since they attack the material basis on which the hitherto inevitable fixedness of desires and ideas depended, the Communists are the only people through whose historical activity the liquefaction of the fixed desires and ideas is in fact brought about and ceases to be an impotent moral injunction. . . . Communist organization has a twofold effect on the desires produced in the individual by present-day relations; some of these desires—namely desires which exist under all relations, and only change their form and direction under different social relations—are merely altered by the Communist social system, for they are given the opportunity to develop normally; but others—namely those originating solely in a particular society, under particular conditions of [production] and intercourse—are totally deprived of their conditions of existence. Which [of the desires] will be merely changed and [which eliminated] in a Communist [society] can [only occur in a practical] way, by [changing the real], actual [conditions of production and intercourse]. (Marx and Engels, *German Ideology*, 273)

60   This is also the tenor of Levitas's conclusion to her *Concept of Utopia*, where she turns to "the political question" and begins to clarify the relation between *desire* (wish/dream and vision), *hope*, and *agency/will*: "If utopia arises from desire [in her definition, utopia is "the desire for a better way of being"], the transformation of reality and the realization of utopia depend on hope, upon not only wishful thinking but will-full action. The presence of hope affects the nature of utopian expression," which, however, is not its source, does not entail it. "The dream becomes vision only when hope is invested in an agency capable of transformation," or at least seeing transformation as its task. "The political problem remains the search for that agency and the possibility of hope." Ruth Levitas, *The Concept of Utopia* (1990: Oxford: Peter Lang, 2011), 230–231. Hope, in

other words, inflects utopia, directs and often focuses it. But things cannot be as unidirectional as Levitas makes them sound. It is also plausible that, to have real, transformative effects, utopian desire or dreaming must fuel hope (which is then "invested" in action), rather than the other way around. Thus inflected, utopia supplies the stimulus for political action, the *wish* (now hopeful "vision") inciting the *will*. While utopia does not generate hope, it can be channeled through and rub off on hope, politicizing it. It seems to me that hope cannot become political without utopia—an intuition confirmed by another slogan of the protests in 2006, "UTOPISTE DEBOUT: RÊVE GÉNÉRALE," Utopian, awake: the general dream—playing on *grève générale*, general strike (this May '68 pun was taken up yet again in 2012 in Quebec's Maple Spring). Sorel can turn over in his grave all he likes; utopia, let's remember, was to him anathema to the "will to act": "Whilst contemporary myths lead men to prepare themselves for a combat which will destroy the existing state of things, the effect of utopias has always been to direct men's minds towards reforms which can be brought about by patching up the system." Georges Sorel, "Introduction: Letter to Daniel Halévy," in *Reflections on Violence*, trans. and ed. Jeremy Jennings (Cambridge: Cambridge University Press, 1999), 28–29. Despite the use of myths (expressions of the active will) in utopian constructs ("intellectual products" that describe things and can be refuted), there can be no greater strike against utopia than that it lures the people away from the revolutionary vanguard (ibid.). Secession from consumer culture—a form of cultivated poverty—is embraced for its power to activate the imagination, giving today's creative activists an opportunity "to point up the poverty of imagination of the world we actually do live in" by "liv[ing] out values, test[ing] out ideas and experiment[ing] with the future in real time" (Boyd, "Tactic," 82). The real test lies in directing the active imagination to new horizons. Its touchstone is still hope, but this can only be *exercised* by "playing with utopian visions": "If hope truly is a muscle that we build by exercising, then interventions that prefigure the world we want to live in—whether by prophetic acts of civil disobedience, the formation of alternative communities or the staging of prankish provocations—are one of the best ways to work that muscle" (83). More concretely still, Berardi's constructive proposal for our age of depression, urging the "psycho-affective reactivation" of the now-desolidarized social body ("frail" in both work and sensibility), trains social imagination on poetry as the interfacing language for reattracting bodies to one another: "Only the conscious mobilization of the erotic body of the general intellect, only the poetic revitalization of language, will open the way to the emergence of a new form of social autonomy." "The uprising is not a form of judgment, but a form of healing," therapy for "the disempathetic pathologies crossing the social skin and social *soul*," rebuilding empathy and solidarity through temporal continuity and "the territorial proximity of social bodies," which—as he says elsewhere—have "lost contact with their soul and hence no longer know anything about their corporeality." Berardi, *The Uprising: On Poetry and Finance* (New York: Semiotext(e), 2012), 55, 8, 133, 132, 55; Berardi, *Precarious Rhapsody*, 86.

61 Perry Anderson, "The World Made Flesh," review of Hervé Juvin, *L'Avènement du corps* (Paris: Gallimard, 2006), *New Left Review* 39 (2006): 133.

62 Ibid.

CONTRIBUTORS

MIGUEL ABENSOUR is Emeritus Professor of Political Philosophy at the Université Paris VII, Paris-Diderot, and a former president of the Collège International de Philosophie. His books include the four-volume *Utopiques* (Sens et Tonka, 2013–2016), with vol. 3, *Utopia from Thomas More to Walter Benjamin*, forthcoming in English from Univocal Publishing.

ÉTIENNE BALIBAR is Emeritus Professor of Moral and Political Philosophy at the Université Paris-Ouest-Nanterre-La Défense (Paris X) and Visiting Professor in the Department of French and Romance Philology at Columbia University. His recent books include *Saeculum: Culture, religion, idéologie* (Galilée, 2012) and *Europe, crise et fin?* (Le Bord de l'eau, 2016).

S. D. CHROSTOWSKA is Associate Professor of Humanities and Social and Political Thought at York University, Toronto, and the author of, most recently, *Matches* (Punctum, 2015).

FRANCISCO FERNÁNDEZ BUEY (1943–2012) was Professor of Political Philosophy at the Universidad Pompeu Fabra de Barcelona, where he coordinated the UNESCO Chair in Intercultural Studies. His books include *Poliética* (Losada, 2003), *Guía para una globalización alternativa* (Ediciones B, 2004), and *Leyendo a Gramsci* (El Viejo Topo, 2001)/*Reading Gramsci* (Brill, 2014).

FRANCK FISCHBACH is Professor of Modern and Contemporary German Philosophy at the Université de Strasbourg, and the author of, most recently,

Philosophies de Marx (Vrin, 2015) and *Le Sens du social: Les Puissances de la coopération* (Lux Éditeur, 2015).

RAYMOND GEUSS is Emeritus Professor in the Faculty of Philosophy at the University of Cambridge. His most recent books are *A World Without Why* (Princeton University Press, 2014) and *Reality and Its Dreams* (Harvard University Press, 2016).

JOHN GRANT is Assistant Professor of Political Science at King's University College, Western University, and the author of *Dialectics and Contemporary Politics: Critique and Transformation from Hegel Through Post-Marxism* (Routledge, 2011).

PETER HALLWARD is Professor of Modern European Philosophy at the School of Humanities, Kingston University London, and the author of, most recently, *Damning the Flood: Haiti, Aristide, and the Politics of Containment* (Verso, 2007).

JAMES D. INGRAM is Associate Professor of Political Science at McMaster University, and the author of *Radical Cosmopolitics: The Ethics and Politics of Democratic Universalism* (Columbia University Press, 2013).

RUTH KINNA is Professor of Political Theory in the Department of Politics, History, and International Relations at Loughborough University, and the author of, most recently, *Kropotkin: Reviewing the Classical Anarchist Tradition* (Edinburgh University Press, 2016).

MICHAEL LÖWY is Emeritus Research Director in Sociology at the Centre National de la Recherche Scientifique in Paris. His recent books include *On Changing the World: Essays in Marxist Political Philosophy, from Karl Marx to Walter Benjamin* (Haymarket, 2013) and *Ecosocialism: A Radical Alternative to Capitalist Catastrophe* (Haymarket, 2015).

JACQUES RANCIÈRE is Professor of Philosophy at European Graduate School in Saas-Fee and Emeritus Professor of Philosophy at the Université Paris VIII, Vincennes à Saint-Denis. His most recent book is *Le Sillon du poème: En lisant Philippe Beck* (Nous, 2016).

MICHÈLE RIOT-SARCEY is Emeritus Professor of Contemporary History and of the History of Gender at the Université Paris VIII, Vincennes à Saint-

Denis, and the author of, most recently, *Le Procès de la liberté* (La Découverte, 2016).

RICHARD SAAGE is Emeritus Professor of Political Theory and the History of Ideas at the Martin-Luther-Universität Halle-Wittenberg. His books include the four-volume *Utopische Profile* (LIT, 2001–2004).

ÉTIENNE TASSIN is Professor of Political Philosophy at the Université Paris VII, Paris-Diderot (Sorbonne Paris Cité), and the author of, most recently, *Le Maléfice de la vie à plusieurs: La Politique est-elle vouée à l'échec?* (Bayard, 2012).

INDEX

Abbey of Thélème (Rabelais), 74, 89, 281
Abensour, Miguel, xiii, xviii, 105–6, 199, 212, 263, 289, 294n19, 297n18, 303n37, 306n46, 309n59; on Marx, 179, 263; utopia defined by, 205–06, 257–59; utopianism revived by, xxiv; on utopian spirit, xxiv–xxvi, 284
Abstract utopia, xx, 126, 132, 203, 209; Bloch on, 102, 153n1, 302–03n32; versus concrete utopia, 102, 132, 153n1, 302–3n32
Académie Française, 27
Action utopia (Gordon), 198
"Act of association" (Rousseau), 136
Adorno, Theodor W., 52n28, 98, 106, 172, 234, 246, 280, 282, 304n3738
Against the Robbing and Murdering Hordes of Peasants (Luther), 88
Age of Absolutism, 70, 74
Amaurot (More), 81, 84–86, 88
America, 75–76, 80–81, 89–90, 231; idea of, 82–84
Amerindians, 89, 91–94
Anarchism, xxiv, xxv, 119, 180, 286; chiliasm and, 299n23, 305n43; commitment to, 199; historical, 206, 209; political uses of utopia and, 209–13; practice of, 200–205; prefiguration relating to, 198–202, 306n48; revolutionary, 304n43; systems of, 200–207; utopian element of, 207–8; Weber on, 200
Anarchism and Its Aspirations (Milstein), 203
Anarchistic model of utopian thinking (Voigt), 65–68
Anarchy, decade of, 273
Ancients, 66, 251, 254
Anders, Günther, 98, 109, 113n31
Anticapitalist/ism, xiv, 123, 201, 211
Anticommunism, 126
Antiessentialists, 234
Antipolitical, utopia as, ix, xxxin1
Antiquity, 65, 67, 71, 84, 89, 237, 292n5
Antitotalitaranianism, 68
Antiutopia, 97
Antiutopianism, xi, xii–xiii, xviii, xxi, xxxvin6, xxxiiin30, 5, 52n29, 65, 117, 127, 206, 261; anarchist, 205; liberal, xiii, 204, 214n23, 288; Marxist, 107, 117; postwar, xii–xiii, xviii, xxiii, xxxiiin30; utopian, 199, 206, 210

Antiutopian utopia, 223
Antliff, Mark, 204
Applied ethics, 235–36, 246
Applied normative theory, xviii–xx
Archaeologies of the Future (Jameson), 169, 170, 172, 173, 174
Archistic model of utopian thinking (Voigt), 65–68
Arendt, Hannah, xiii, xxiii, 127, 129, 155*n*12, 252, 257, 279, 288, 308–9*n*58
Aron, Raymond, xiii, xxxi*n*6, xxxiii*n*30
Arts and Crafts movement, 276
Ascetic utopianism, 106, 145–46, 287, 295*n*14, 297*n*18
Attac, 194
Australian utopia, 74
Autarchy, 40, 293*n*5, 303*n*34
Autonomous development (Déjacques, Cœurderoy), 39–43, 46
Autonomous will, 133, 135
"Autopia" (Foucault), 280

Bacon, Francis, ix, 67, 71, 84, 111*n*5
Bakunin, Michael, 54*n*47, 204, 207, 212, 305*n*43
Balibar, Étienne, 296*n*15
Ballanche, Pierre-Simon, 183
Balzac, Honoré de, 220–23, 224, 227, 229
Barbarians, 18, 34
Bargu, Banu, 294*n*9
Barrault, Émile, 220
Barthes, Roland, 32, 42
Bataille, Georges, 34
Bell, Daniel, xxxi*n*6, xxxiii*n*30, 39
Bellamy, Richard, ix, 39, 70, 74, 259, 292*n*5
Belvedere (Gauny), 230–31
Benhabib, Seyla, xix, xxxiii*n*27
Benjamin, Walter, 25, 32, 45–48, 53*n*43, 98, 107, 109, 130, 263, 299*n*23, 303*n*37
Berlin, Isaiah, xiii, 127
Bernstein, Eduard, 5
Bible, 101, 231, 232*n*3
Biopolitics (Toulouse), 301*n*23

Bilderverbot, 289
Bildung, 10
Blanqui, Jérôme-Adolphe, 18, 19
Blanqui, Louis-Auguste, 15, 16, 19, 20, 23, 31, 55*n*61, 130, 147, 148, 150, 206
Bloch, Ernst, xiii, xv, xx, 43, 45, 59, 60–61, 98, 105, 107, 123, 263, 299*n*23, 302–03*n*32, 303–4*n*37, 305–6*n*46, 308*n*56; on "concrete utopia" and hope, 101–4, 130, 255; ideas of, xix, xxx, xxxiii*n*27, 302*n*32, 305*n*46; legacy of, 109
Blueprint, xxiii, xxiv, 68, 77, 78, 132, 280, 285, 290; utopianism, xviii–xix, 199, 203–6, 209, 296*n*14
Body, 222–23, 227–28; confinement of, 289; grounding in, 275, 294*n*13; happiness of, 282; of hope, 273–84; as sovereign utopia, 280, 302*n*31
Body-centered utopia, 276–78
Body-politics, 272–74, 286–87
"Body utopia," 271, 287–88, 290, 292–93*n*5
Bogdanov, Alexander Alexandrovitsch, 71, 77
Bolshevism, 305*n*43
Book of Acts, The, 227
Book of life, 227, 231
Bookchin, Murray, 99, 201
Bouazizi, Mohamed, 273–74, 291
Brave New World (Huxley), 74, 278
Brecht, Bertolt, 107, 109, 237
Breton, André, 53*n*43, 293*n*5
Buber, Martin, 259, 261, 299*n*23
Butler, Judith, 288, 305*n*44, 308–9*n*58

Cabet, Étienne, 55, 70, 74, 108, 259, 292*n*5; Icaria relating to, 12, 46, 75–76, 231, 248–49, 261–62, 263, 265*n*30; on utopian socialism, 249
Callenbach, Ernest, xiv, 71
Campanella, Tommaso, ix, 69, 70, 73, 76
Capital, 14, 21, 121, 123, 148, 193, 194, 195, 211, 28–31, 193, 195, 278, 283, 307–8*n*53
Capital (Marx), 123, 147–48, 158*n*110, 205*n*46

Capitalism, 123, 162, 169, 172, 193, 210, 242, 276, 282, 283, 291, 307n53; global, xxiii, 167; late, xxxii, 172, 175, 283; neoliberal, xvi, 97; scientific, 162; utopian, 162, 299n23; Western, 292n2

Capitalist globalization, 191, 192

Capitalists, 238–39

Capitalist society, 120, 123

Castoriadis, Cornelius, xxix, 99, 107

Castro, Fidel, 144, 151, 152, 159n125, 160n134

Cave allegory (Plato), 251, 254, 265n15; philosopher, 255; prisoners, 255–56; truth relating to, 255–56

Changes: impossibility of, 169; institutional, 161–62; to society, xiii

Chiapas, 191

Chiliasm, 35, 41, 66–67, 68, 69, 196n14, 295n13, 299n23, 304–05n43; Anabaptist, 59, 60, 61

"Christian utopia," 69

Christians, 87, 109, 196, 237

Citizenship, 161, 188, 286

City of the Sun (Campanella), 76

City, ix, 23, 66, 86, 144, 223, 229; future, 103; garden (Morris), 76; ideal, 68, 251, 256, 257; unsociable, 77; utopian, 76, 229–31, 277, 292–93n5. *See also* Paradox of perfect city

Classical thesis, 15, 24–25, 48

Classical utopia, 65–67, 72–74, 76–77, 79; approach of, 61; Bloch and, 60; closed society, 61; criteria for, 64; from destruction to construction, 58; Landauer's concept of, 58–60; Mannheim's concept of, 59–60; Popper and, 61–62; scientific technological progress integrated in, 62, 75; in social sciences, 57, 61; sociopolitical context of, 71; solutions of, 78; as spatial, 59, 68; totalitarianism and, 63; tradition of, xvi–xvi; virtues of, 63–64

Cockaigne, Land of, 222, 281, 292n5, 299n23

Cœurderoy, Ernest, 39–40, 43, 54n48

Cold War, xi, xiii, xv, xxiv, 126, 209

Collective action, 170, 207, 275

Collective capacity, 129, 133, 137, 146, 151

Columbus, Christopher, 34, 82–83

Committee for the Abolition of Third World Debt, 194

Committee of 100, 209

Common good, ix, 91, 127, 133, 152, 196, 295n15

Common will, 137–38

Communes, xxiv, 75–76, 277, 283. *See also* Paris Commune

Communism, xii, xv–xvi, xxi, 12, 37, 54n45, 99; affirmation of, 21; critical, 3, 4, 7, 9, 14, 20, 48, 49, 50n6, 51n17; critico-utopian, 14, 14, 51n17; Engels and, 118; estate-based, 61; of Marx, 3, 8, 31, 45, 49, 117–18, 133; projection of, 46; socialism and, 23, 106–7; utopia and, 18, 21, 77

Communist Manifesto, The (Marx and Engels), xxvii, 6, 7–8, 14, 38, 49n4, 50–51n15, 101, 118, 119, 277

Communitarian: body, 225–26; experiments, 261; face of utopia (Sargent), x, xxiv; law, 225

Communitarianism, 65, 181

Communities, 224–25, 226; constitution of, 227–28; creation of, 248; new, 229; religious, 237; sense of, 231; of women and children, 251

Comte, Auguste, 14, 19, 182, 299n23

Concepts of utopia, 122; ambiguities of, 16, 18; broad, 17–19; classical, 58–60; definition of, 17; narrow, 17–19; totalitarianism, 57, 61, 108

Conceptual analysis, 233, 234

Concrete utopia: Babeuf's, 294n13; Bloch on, 98, 101–4, 130, 184, 302–3n32, 305–6n46; versus abstract utopia. *See* Abstract utopia

Considerant, Victor, 28, 33, 38, 41, 262, 265n33

Constant, Benjamin, 127

Constitution, of community, 135, 164, 227–28
Construction: from destruction, 58; of political theory, 234; of utopia, xi, 70, 72, 121
Constructivism, 77
Consumerism, xxii, 71, 310
"Contribution to a Critique of Hegel's Philosophy of Right" (Marx), 8, 21
Convention, French Revolutionary, 28
Conversations (Lukács), 100
Cooke, Maeve, xix
Counterglobalization, 104–6
Counterutopia, 97
Critical communism, 3–4, 7, 14, 20, 48, 49; Marx relating to, 9, 14, 50*n*6, 51*n*17
Critical Marxists, 106–7, 109
Critical spirit, 282, 303*n*37
Critique of desire, 289–90
Critique of utopia: bourgeois and radical, 16–22; conservative, 16, 18, 21; by Engels, 5, 6–15, 50*n*12; of ideal theory, xxix; of ideology, 238, 243; left and right, 15; liberal, 17, 18, 26, 204; by Marx, 5–16, 148; revolutionary, 19, 45; texts on, 8–9
Critique, Norm, and Utopia (Benhabib), xix
Cuban Revolution, 149, 190
Cultural history, xiv, xv
Cultural studies, xv

"Dark utopia," 70, 72
"Dawn of Socialism" (Leroux), 26
Daydreaming, 60, 102, 110, 252, 285, 306*n*49
Debellandis indis, De (Quiroga), 90, 93, 94, 112*n*16
Debord, Guy, 14, 51*n*16, 99
Déjacque Joseph, 23, 31, 39–43, 51–52*n*22, 54*n*48, 55*n*56, 188, 259, 276, 297*n*19
De la Franc-Maçonnerie et de ses propriétés encore inconnues (Fourier), 33
de Lahontan, Louis Armand, Baron, 70, 74
Democracy, 148, 163–64, 183, 223, 224, 243; Greek, 61; liberal, 282; representative, 153*n*3, 186–87; participatory, 195–96, 201; revolutionary, 127; socialist, 196
Démocratie pacifique (journal), 36
Demos, 223, 224, 287
Derrida, Jacques, 127, 192, 260, 265*n*29
Desire, 205, 208, 248; actualization of, 250; critique of, 289–90; despotism, 254–56; dimensions of, 249; education of, xx, xxvii–xxvii, 276, 289, 309*n*59; fixity of, 286, 306*n*53; for happiness, 287; new, 28, 32–33, 35, 48; paradox of unrealizable city, 250–54; for perfection, 258; realization of, 254–56, 257, 258, 260, 261; shipwrecks, or real politics, 260–64; for social transformation, xxii, 289; for society, 250; straight path and oblique faces, 257–60; for stuff, 283; surplus of, 257; utopian, xxii, xxix, 209, 211–12, 250, 256, 263, 280, 302*n*31, 303*n*37, 310*n*60
Despair, 109, 210–12; 302*n*31
Despotism, 127, 254–56, 259
Destruction, 7, 24, 30, 43, 58, 117, 202, 207, 212; of environment, 78, 192
Dialectic, 49, 109, 281, 303*n*37, 307*n*53; Jameson and, xxviii, 165–66, 170–72, 175
Dictatorship, 195, 202, 278; educational, 77; of financial markets, 193, 195; neocolonial, 151; of planning, 261; of the proletariat, 117, 237
Dictionnaire critique du marxisme (Bensussan and Labica), 119
Diderot, Denis, 70, 74
Discourse, 202; of domination, 186; political, 186–87; realist, 260–61. *See also* Utopian discourse
Dispossessed, The (Le Guin), 75
Diversity, 40, 54*n*48, 196, 210
Divine punishment, 67
Division: of "is" and "ought," 235, 238; of powers, 236
DIY, do-it-yourself, 201, 284
Doctrinaire science, 13, 40

Domination, 37, 39, 41, 68, 71, 124, 134, 175, 181, 184, 193, 206, 223, 248, 278; discourse of, 186; fascist, 62; of nature, 28, 44; order of, 227–28; real politics and, 261; structures of, 57–58, 260; technologies of, 254; totalitarian, 74
Dystopia, 63, 69–71, 74, 96–98, 211–13, 278

Ecotopia (Callenbach), xiv
"Educated hope" (Bloch), 289, 303*n*32, 306*n*46
Education, 50, 90, 124, 156*n*28, 185, 194, 252; dictatorship of, 77; moral, 33; political, xxi, 152; of desire, xx, xxvii–xxviii, 276, 286, 289, 309*n*59
Egalitarian ideals, 126, 128, 199, 287
1844 Manuscripts (Marx), 8, 29, 50*n*6, 158*n*110, 193
Elective Affinities (Goethe), 103
Elements of the Philosophy of Right (Hegel). See *Philosophy of Right*
Emancipation, xxii, xxix, 51*n*17, 58, 99, 126, 133, 137, 256, 273; bourgeois, 12, 50*n*6; proletarian, 13, 40
Embodied utopia, 280, 296*n*14
Émile (Rousseau), 134, 140, 156*n*28
Empowerment, collective, 133, 141
"Endangered Socialism" (Nieuwenhaus), 46
End of utopia, xxxi*n*6, 20, 22, 77, 96–101, 103, 107–08; Marxism as, 25, 43, 49
"End of Utopia, The" (Marcuse essay), xxvii, xxxii*n*13, 96, 100–1, 283
Enfantin, Barthélemy Prosper, 32, 221, 225, 226, 229, 232*n*3
Engels, Friedrich, xiii, xxvii, 149; on communism, 118; critiques by, 5, 6–15, 50*n*12; Marx, utopia question, and, 5, 6–15, 50*n*12; on neoutopianism, 36–38; on new utopian spirit, 43, 44, 45; utopianism criticized by, 15–22, 51*n*22; on utopian socialism, 26, 34, 119, 271, 277, 281; writings of, xxvii, 6, 11, 12, 14, 36, 117, 118, 233

Environmentalism, 191, 194–96, 201
Epigones, xviii, 9, 26, 36, 38–39, 43–44, 45
Equality, 127, 194, 195, 207, 224, 229, 248, 254, 262, 263, 287, 303*n*34
Erasmus, 80, 81, 82, 84, 85, 86, 89
Estates: as basis for communism, 61; collapse of order of, 63; three, 228
Ethos, 222, 225, 282–83
Ethics, 204, 234, 246, 278; applied, 235–36; of conviction, 161, 200; of responsibility, 161, 200; virtue, 199
Eugenics, 277, 301*n*23
Euthanasia, 277
Eutopia (More), 80, 84, 257
Experimental science, political philosophy as, 237
"Exposition of the Doctrine of Saint-Simon" (Barrault, Enfantin), 183

Fascism, xii, xxi, 62, 108, 129, 195
Fatherland in Danger, The (Blanqui), 23
Feminism, 191, 194, 196, 201
Feudal order, 70, 278; collapse of, 63
Florentines, 83–84
Focus on Global South, 194
Foigny, Gabriel de, 69, 70, 74
Force, 136, 139–40, 143–44
Foucault, Michel, 18, 28, 99, 162, 173, 242–43, 246, 280, 301*n*23
Fourier, Charles, 12, 26, 27–29, 31, 32–40, 44, 47, 48, 53*n*30, 54*n*48, 70, 74, 75, 77, 108, 110, 184, 208, 215*n*38, 260, 293*n*5, 294*n*12, 296*n*14, 297*n*18, 306*n*49; influence of, 23, 98, 262, 265*n*33; Marx's relation to, 19, 44, 51–52*n*22, 266*n*35, 271, 276, 298*n*20; *phalanstères* of, xxvi, 23, 27, 38, 237, 287–88;
Frankfurt School, xix–xx
Franks, Benjamin, 199–200, 202–9
Fraternity, 195, 196, 262, 287
Freedom, 65, 108, 138, 139, 195, 273, 282; aspiration to, 206, 207, 254, 256, 263, 295; beauty and, 32, 54*n*48; Christian, 87, 88;

Freedom (*continued*)
  of community, 88; collective, 145; equal (Balibar), 288, 289, 296*n*15; as ideology, 242; individual, 74, 76, 133–35, 243, 301*n*25; Marx on, 148–49, 298*n*30; of movement, 73, 76, 278; realm/reign of, xxii, 45, 46, 148–49; Rousseau on, 127, 133–37, 145–46, 156*n*33; sexual, 275–78, 280–81, 297*n*20, 302*n*32; sovereignty and, 129, 137–38, 188
"Free men," 182, 184
Free University of Berlin, 96
Free will, 120–21, 130, 133–36, 137, 145, 156*n*38
"Free woman," 180
Freikörperkultur. See Naturism
French Peasants' Confederation, 191
French Revolution, xii, 153*n*3, 261, 273
Freud, Sigmund, 250–51
Frugality, 72, 277
Fukuyama, Francis, 96, 113*n*21
Furet, François, xxxiii*n*30, 127

G8 Summit, 190, 192, 201
Galeano, Eduardo, 104, 105
Gargantua (Rabelais), 88–89
Genealogy, 173, 243
"General will" (Rousseau), 127, 129, 133, 137–40, 142–46
German Idealism, xxvii, 243
German Ideology, The (Marx and Engels), 8, 12, 14, 36, 117, 233, 306–7*n*53, 309*n*59
German philosophy, 37, 54*n*45. *See also* German Idealism
Glaciation of utopianism, 284
Globalization, 163; capitalist, 191, 193; of globe, 161; neoliberal, 104, 110, 192
Global justice movement, xxix; adversaries of, 191; Via Campesina, 191, 194, 196; concrete proposals, 192; democracy, 195; diversity, 196; fraternity, 196; French Peasants' Confederation, 191; G8, 190; for humanity, 191; Iraq War, 190; Landless Workers Movement of Brazil, 191; movement of movements, 190; negativity of resistance, 192; plurality of, 190; proposals of, 193–94; protest demonstrations, 190; solidarity of, 190–91, 196, 197; utopian dimension, 194–95; utopia of another world, 192, 195; values of, 195; Women's World March, 191; WTO, 190, 191, 192; Zapatistas, 191, 192, 196

Godfather, The (Coppola), 166, 167, 170
Goethe, Johann Wolfgang von, 54*n*47, 76, 103
Golden Age, 17, 64, 68, 84, 281, 292–93*n*5
Goodman, Paul, 98, 211
Gordon, Uri, 198, 205
Governmentality, 261
Graeber, David, 198, 202, 291–92*n*2
Gramsci, Antonio, 106, 129–31, 146, 147, 149
"Great Refusal" (Marcuse), 98, 105
Greeks, 251, 253
Growing Up Absurd (Goodman), 98
Grundrisse (Marx), 29, 297–98*n*20, 307*n*53
Guattari, Félix, 4–5
Guerrilla warfare, 143, 150, 151
Guevara, Che, 98, 107, 110, 127, 130, 131, 144, 147; Cuban revolution and, 149; education and, 152; guerrilla warfare and, 150; moral compulsion, 152; political ideals of, 150–53, 159*n*128, 160*n*134; socialist revolution and, 151
Guillon, Claude, 274, 294*n*12
Guise Familistère, 39
Guizot, François, 127, 155*n*12, 157*n*62, 183, 186

Habermas, Jürgen, xix, 98–99, 246, 305*n*46
Happiness, xix, 51*n*22, 53*n*37, 140, 215*n*42, 275, 288–89; of body, 282, 286; desire for, 287; material, 276, 287–89, 308*n*56; Marcuse and, 304*n*40; More and, 295*n*14; politics of, 291; will to, 27, 32
Hebertism, 23
Hedonism, 32, 276, 302*n*31; hedonistic mass consumption, 72

Hegel, Georg Wilhelm Friedrich, xxvii, 4, 10–11, 14, 34, 37, 50n4, 61, 101, 117, 124n1, 147, 246, 299n23; Hegelianism, 99; right-Hegelianism, 59;
Hermeneutics, 64, 98, 165, 172–73, 226
Heroism of spirit, 106
Heterotopia, 162, 231, 232, 280
"Heuristic utopia," xviii, 65, 70
Hiller, Kurt, 299n23
Historicity, of politics, 162, 173; of utopia, 181–85, 259–60
Historiography, 179
History, 3–4, 23–25; bourgeois critique and radical critique, 15–22; continuity of, 179; economic, 180; margins of, 180; Marx, Engels, and utopia question, 5, 6–15, 50n12; meaning of, 180; neoutopianism, xvii, xix, 35–39; new utopian spirit, 39–49; political, 187; of political philosophy, 234; real, 233; of science, 234; of technology, 180; utopian socialism, 26–35
"History of Civilization in Europe" (Guizot), 183
Holism or entity thinking (Popper), 61
Holy Family, The (Marx and Engels), 8, 11, 123–24
Holy Spirit, 87, 92
Hombre nuevo, El (Guevara). *See* "New Man"
Homogeneity, 19, 21, 34, 39, 73, 77
Hope, 101–4, 109, 111, 130, 210, 240, 255, 269, 290–91, 292n2, 300n33, 304n37, 305–6n46, 309–10n60; body of, 273–84; educated (Bloch), 289, 303n32; political, 271–72, 304n37; politics of, 269–76
Human beings, 32, 69; cultivation of, 29 (Marx); nature of, 134; "new." *See* "New Man"; production of (Déjacque), 40; rights of, 239; self-image of, 240; survival of, 72, 78; utopian classic concept values of, 63; value of, 195
Human nature, 104, 134, 136, 141, 307n53; changing of, 129, 147

Humanism, 12, 124, 183; Christian, 85; Renaissance, 89
Humanisphere, The (Déjacque), 31, 40–42, 52–52n22, 52n25, 297n19
Humanitas, 258
Huxley, Aldous, 68, 70, 71, 74–75, 278, 293n5, 298–99n22
Hythloday, Rafael (More), xviii, 74, 81, 82–83, 85, 86, 93

Icaria (Cabet), 12, 40, 231, 248–50, 259, 261–62, 263, 265n30
Idealism, 244; German, xxvii, 243; pragmatism as, 159n28; utopian, 35, 53n43
"Ideal theory," xvii–xviii, xix, 235
Ideal-typical approach to utopian thinking, 64, 65–68, 70
Ideology, xxiii, 59, 220, 226, 242; critique of, 148, 238–39, 241, 243, 309n58; dominant, 110; end of, xxxin6; of Jameson on, 165–67, 170, 172–73, 174; Mannheim on, xiii, 17, 59–60, 124, 296n14, 301n24, 304n43; neoliberal, 97, 98; liberalism as, 246; progress as, 270, 275; socialism as, 44, 99, 101; utopian, 299n23; and wishful thinking, 241–42, 245
Ideology and Utopia (Mannheim), xiii, 124
Illusion: failure of, 107; of good regime, 258; of governmentality, 261; of justified omnipotence, 256; natural, 110, 111; paradox of, 254–55; of realizing desire, 258; in real politics, 261; of sovereignty, 261
Imagination, xxx, 89, 123, 161, 163–64, 173, 181, 202, 280, 288, 291, 302n32, 308n53, 310n60; utopian, 48, 65, 168–71, 175, 219, 254, 277, 293n5
Indefiniteness, 241
Indians. *See* Amerindians
Indies, Quiroga and, 93–94
Indignation, 123, 192, 211, 212

Individual: freedom of, 133–35; free will of, 120–21, 130; social, 121, 125n12; society and, 182
Individualism, 61, 181–82, 289
Industrialization, 71
Industrial Revolution, 66, 71
Información en derecho (Quiroga), 90, 91, 94, 112n12
In Praise of Folly (Erasmus), 80, 86
Institutional change, 161–62
Instrumental reason, 49, 76
Instrumentalism, 200
International, Communist: Second, 44; Third, 44
International relations (IR) theory, 244
IR. *See* International relations theory
Iraq War, 190
Irony, utopia and, xviii, xx, xxiv, 23, 84–86, 93, 106, 283
Island, of utopia, 84–86
Island (Huxley), 298–99n22

Jacobins, 127, 128, 129, 139, 143, 146, 153n3, 259; neo-, 129, 147, 151
Jameson, Fredric, xv–xvi, xviii, xx, xxviii, xxiin14 105, 106, 122, 165–75, 285, 301n24, 306n46; dialectical approach of, 165–66; on genealogy, 173; on *The Godfather*, 166, 167, 170; on ideology, 166, 170, 172–73; on *Jaws*, 166; mass culture, 166–67; on money, 171, 174; on politics, 165–76; positive and negative theories of, 166, 170, 172; transcendence, 166–67; utopia, critique, and politics, 167–71; utopia, ideology, and mass culture, 166–67; utopia and dialectics, 171–75; on utopian thought, 165–76, 176n4
Jaws (Spielberg), 166
Je chante le corps critique (Guillon), 274
Jesus of Nazareth, 87, 89
Jewish diaspora, 143
Jouffroy, Théodore Simon, 183
Just city. *See* Perfect city

Justice, 206, 207, 248; criminal, 65; desire for, 249–51, 253–56, 262; dream of, 252, 263; global, 191; Marx on, 124; perfect city requirements for, 252–53; racial, 201; Rousseau on, 136, 141; social, 151; system, 70; utopia beyond, xix. *See also* Global justice movement

Kautsky, Karl, 25, 55n61, 119
Klossowski, Pierre, 47, 48, 53n43
Korsch, Karl, 37, 49n4, 98, 106
Kropotkin, Peter, 108, 200, 205, 207–8, 210

Laissez-faire proletarian, 239
Landauer, Gustav, 57–60, 208, 299n23
Landless Workers Movement of Brazil, 191
Las Casas, Bartolomé de, 82, 91, 93, 95, 108, 111n5, 112n16
Law of Peoples, The (Rawls), xiv
Laws (Plato), 224, 225
Left Hand of Darkness, The (Le Guin), xiv, 69
Legitimacy, 155n12, 225, 237–38, 294n9
Le Guin, Ursula K., xiv, 69, 71, 75
Lenin, Vladimir, 5, 44, 49, 55n61, 127, 129, 147, 149, 153, 200, 237, 246
Leninism, 4, 205, 207, 255
Leroux, Pierre, 26, 28, 29, 31, 32, 39, 52n29, 53n37
Lettera della isole nuovamente trovate (Vespucci), 82
"Letter to Arnold Ruge" (Marx), 3, 8, 248–50, 261, 263
"Letter to Doctor Deville" (Leroux), 39
Levitas, Ruth, xv–xvi, xix–xx, 271, 289, 306n46, 309–10nn59–60
Liberalism, xiii, 108, 195, 243, 272, 287; as utopia, 60; Cold War, xiii, xxiv
Libertarian (emancipatory), 42, 98, 113n23, 196, 299n23; Marxism, 102; utopia, 42, 103
Liberty, equality, fraternity, 195–96, 287
Literary studies, xv, xvi

Logos, 224–25, 251, 253
Looking Backward (Bellamy), 39
Ludditism, 24
Lukács, Georg, 100–1, 106
Luther, Martin, 86–88
Luxemburg, Rosa, 106, 147

Machiavelli, Niccolò, 84, 105, 144
Machiavellianism, 200, 258
"Machiavellian moment" (Pocock), 83
Maeckelbergh, Marianne, 201
Malevich, Kazimir, 77
Manifesto of the Communist Party. See Communist Manifesto
Mannheim, Karl, xiii, xx, 16–17, 34–35, 61, 124, 271, 296n14, 301n24, 304–5n43; social-epistemological approach of, 59–60; *topias* and, 59
Mao Zedong, 129, 147, 149
Maple Spring, 264, 266n40, 310n60
Marazzi, Christian, 205
Marcuse, Herbert, xiv, xxvii, xxxii$n$13, 17, 32, 37, 96, 98, 169, 283, 296n14, 304n40; on end of utopia, 99–101
Marin, Louis, 180–81
Mars utopia, 77
Marx, Karl: Abensour on, 179, 263; on anarchy, 206; on capital, 29–31; on capitalism, 123; communism of, 3, 8, 31, 45, 49, 117–18, 133; critical communism and, 9, 14, 50n6, 51n17; critique of utopia, 5–16, 148; Engels, utopia question, and, 5, 6–15, 50n12; on materialism, 120–21; messianism of, 122; Morris on, 45, 46, 48; on neoutopianism, 36, 37–38; on new utopia spirit, 40, 43–46, 49; on real history, 233; Rousseau and, 146–47; Ruge and, 248–50, 261, 263; scientificly and, 13; as target, 126–27; themes of, 146–49; utopia and, 117–25; utopianism criticized by, xiii, xx, xxv, xxvii, 5, 15–22, 25, 43, 51n22, 179; on utopian socialism, 26, 29–30, 31, 34, 119–20, 162, 263–64, 271, 277, 281; as voluntarist, 146–49; Weitling and, 4–5, 9, 50n6; writings of, xxvii, 3, 5, 6–7, 11, 12, 13–14, 29, 36, 38, 49n4, 101, 117, 118, 123, 147, 158n110, 193, 233, 277
Marxism, xxiii–xxvi, xxxiii$n$31, 43–44, 119, 175; libertarian, 102; neo-, 44, 107; orthodox, 107; western, 98
Mass culture, 166–67, 172
Materialism, 12, 33, 55n61, 119–21, 153n3, 282–83, 293n7, 302n32, 304n40; historical, xvii, 60, 101, 120, 281, 304n40; new, 293–94n7
Maturity, 24–25, 52n26
May '68, xxi; slogans, 261, 310n60l; utopianism after, xiv–xv, xxiv, xxxii$n$12
Means-ends relationship, 137, 149, 199–200, 203–4, 207–9, 212–13, 281, 284, 290, 294n9
Messianism 127, 163; Christian, 87, 299n23; Jewish, 299n23; Marxian, xxix, 122
Mexico, Quiroga in, 93–95
Michoacán, 89–90, 92
Middle Ages, 71
Migration, of utopia, 89–90, 286
Mill, John Stuart, 200
Millenarianism. *See* Chiliasm
Milstein, Cindy, 200, 203–5
Modern utopia, 89–90, 97, 225, 257–60
Money, abolition of, 171, 174, 212
Montesquieu, Baron de, 135
More, Thomas, 34, 73, 88, 107–8, 279; America and, 89–90; Erasmus and, 80–81; Quiroga and, 90–95; *Utopia* written by, x, xviii, 58, 62, 63, 65, 66, 74, 80, 82–84, 86, 92, 93–95, 111n5, 112n13, 257
Morris, William, ix, xiv, 39, 43, 48, 54n48 55n59, 70, 74, 76, 105, 210, 259–60, 276, 281; and Marx, 45, 46
Moses, 89, 143
Movement of movements, 104, 113n26, 190
Mundus Novus (Vespucci), 82
Müntzer, Thomas, 86–88

324 INDEX

Nationalism, xii
National Socialism, 277
Nature, 17, 31, 65, 66, 68, 75, 76, 100, 121, 144, 149, 205, 277, 292n5, 298n20, 307n53; domination of, 28, 44, 45; law of, 74, 119; mastery of, 71–72; protection of, 195; revolt of (Marcuse), 34; state of, 63, 134, 136, 163
Naturism, 277, 298n21
Nazism, xii, 108, 301n23
Necropolitics, 294n9
Need for Roots, The (Weil), 108
Needs, 12, 29, 32–33, 36, 41, 71–72, 73–74, 77, 92, 93, 109, 124, 195, 297n18, 303n34, 306–8n53; bodily, 134, 275–76, 278, 282, 286, 288, 291; new, 28, 100, 102, 300n23
Negation, 41, 122–23, 147, 282; double, 220; of philosophy, 37; of negation, 227; of present, 219; of reality, 219; of utopia, 107, 223
Negative ontology, 123
Negative utopia, 98
Negativity, 109, 192, 212; of resistance, 192; radical, 192
Negri, Antonio, 99, 123
Neoliberal: capitalism, xvi, 97, 127, 279; globalization, 104, 110, 192; policies, 169, 192–94
Neoliberalism, 96, 98, 107, 169–70, 191, 270, 302n31; fundamentalist, 103
Neoutopianism, 25, 31; description of, 36; Engels on, 36–38; history of, xvii, xix, 35–39; influence of, 36; manifestations of, 38; Marx on, 36, 37–38; new utopian spirit and, 43–44
Nettlau, Max, 54n48
New Atlantis (Bacon), 67, 84, 111n5
New Book, The (Enfantin), 225–26, 229
New Harmony (Owen), 275
New Lanark, xxiv, 275
New Left, xiv, 283
Newman, Saul, 205, 206
"New Man," 67, 100, 277

New materialism, 293–94n7
News from Nowhere (Morris), 45, 281, 297n20
"New utopian spirit" (Abensour), xxiv, 5, 25, 31, 51n22, 54n48, 55n61, 107–8, 284, 303n37; of autonomous development, 39–43; constellation of utopian phenomena related to Marx's theory, 43–44; Engels on, 43, 44, 45; functions of, 41; fundamental tension of, 42; history of, 39–49; inspiration for, 44–45; manifestations of, 45–46; Marx on, 40, 43–46, 49; neoutopianism and, 43–44; partisans of, 41, 43, 44, 46, 49; self-criticism, 39; simulacrum, 47–48
New World, 81–84, 248–49
NGOs, 190, 193
Nieuwenhaus, Domela, 46
Nihilism, 96, 102, 103, 164
1984 (Orwell), 74, 75
Nonplace, 89, 92, 181, 184, 187, 219, 258; democratic, 224; of language, 220; of nonplace, 220, 232; of place, 220, 230–31
Nonsignification, 226
Nonutopianism, 171
Nonviolence, 207, 274, 285, 306n48
No-where versus now-here, 261
Nudity. See Naturism

Occupy, xxiv, 201, 270–71, 291n1; anarchism, 286; Wall Street, 198–99, 201
Old utopia, 106, 107–8
Oligarchs/oligarchy, 126, 132, 150, 223
"On the Concept of History" a.k.a. "theses on the Philosophy of History" (Benjamin), 109, 130
Origins of Totalitarianism, The (Arendt), 257
Orwell, George, 68, 70, 71, 74, 75
Otherness, xxiv, 93–95
Outlines of a Critique of National Economy (Engels), 11
Owen, Robert, ix, 25, 26–27, 31–32, 34–35, 40, 44, 53n30, 53n37, 70, 75, 77, 108, 275;

influence of, 8, 275; Marx's relation to, 12, 19, 51–52n22, 118, 266n35, 271, 297n16; New Lanark of, xxiv, 275

Pannekoek, Antonie, 46, 106
Pantagruel (Rabelais), 88
Paradox, 24, 42, 89, 99, 223, 300n23, 303n36; of illusion, 254–55; of perfect city, 250–54, 259; of unrealizable city, 250–54
Paris Commune, 22–24, 52n25 119, 120, 148, 188
Partisans, of new utopian spirit, 41, 43, 44, 46, 49, 55n61
Pasolini, Pier Paolo, 99, 107
"Passional movement" (Fourier), 30
Passionate Attraction, 31, 33, 35, 53n43
Peasants' War, 60, 61, 87–88, 102
Pecqueur, Constantin, 26, 52–53n30
Perfect city: education with, 252; good with, 254; justice relating to, 252, 253; paradox of, 250–54, 259; Socrates on, 251–53; status of, 253; violence relating to, 252
Perfectability, 69, 214n29
Perfection, desire for, 258, 393n5
Peterloo Massacre, 183
Phalanstère. See Phalanstery
Phalanstery (Fourier), xxiv, 23, 27, 38, 208, 237, 287–88
Philosophers: bourgeois, 50n6; and prince, 85; in cave allegory, 251, 255, 265n15; city affairs and, 252, 279; plebeian, 32
Philosophy, 33, 37, 85, 130, 250, 255; analytical, 235, 243, 245; continental, xxv; critique of, 19; enlightenment, 206; of history, 73, 109; liberation, 102; of life, 28; Marxism as end of, 25; natural, 15; and politics, 279; positivist, 19; of progress, 180, 184; Rawlsian, 246; of reason, 32, 124; social, 53n37; space, 69; task of, 249. *See also* Political philosophy
Philosophy and Real Politics (Geuss), xxix, 233, 234, 243, 245–46

Philosophy of Right (Hegel), 117, 122, 124n1; Marx's critique of, 8, 21, 119, 124n1
Plato, ix, xvi, 66, 81,84, 111n5, 223–25, 233, 252, 255, 256, 257, 273, 292n5; *Republic* of, xviii, 61, 68, 84, 132, 224, 225, 251–56; totalitarianism and, 257; Platonic, 85, 230, 234, 279
Pleasure, 29, 30, 32, 33, 106, 260, 271, 279, 281, 286, 289, 291, 295n14, 297n20, 307n53
Plurality, x, xxiii–xxiv, 190, 196
Political apathy, 269–70
Political economy, 11, 20, 50n12, 292n2; Marx's critique of, 119, 148
Political Liberalism (Rawls), xvi
"Political life," 234
Political philosophy, 233; academic, 108; applied ethics, 235–36; conditions of, 234–35; as experimental science, 237; English-language, xix, xx; history of, 234; Marx and, 117; normative, xvii; power relating to, 237; questions relating to, 235, 237; recognition, 237; tasks of, 238, 242–43
Political possibility and collective capacity, 126–29; *hasta la victoria*, 149–53; political virtue and, 138–46, 142; Rousseau and voluntary self-determination, 130, 131–38, 148
Political science, 233, 235
Political theory, 233; construction of, 234; English-language, xi–xii, xvii, xix, xxv–xxvi; new materialism in, 293–94n7; prefiguration and, 199. *See also* Utopia, political theory and
Political utopia, ix, 12, 34, 62, 63, 64, 290, 305n43
Political virtue, 138–46
Political will, 129, 139, 147, 149, 152
Politics, 162, 281, 303n36; Enlightened, 275; of happiness, 291; of hope, 269–76; Jameson on, 165–76; left-radical, 269; legitimate and illegitimate, 273; mass, 273; physicalization of, 273; prefigurative,

Politics (*continued*)
  202, 211; radical, 166, 169, 170, 171, 175;
  reinvention of, 164; social-political
  transformation, xxi; somatization of,
  273; of spirit, 278, 299*n*23;
  transformative, xxi, 272; utopian, 172,
  203, 284, 291. *See also* Real politics
"Politics of Utopia, The" (Jameson essay),
  165, 168
Popper, Karl, xiii, xxii, 61–62, 153*n*4
Popular sovereignty, 137, 150, 182, 186
Porto Alegre, 104, 195,
Positivism, 15, 27, 39, 44, 49*n*4, 131, 181, 235;
  Comtean, 19, 287
Positive utopia, 98, 109
Postmaterial utopia, 71, 72, 75
Postwar antiutopians, xii–xiii, xviii, xxiii,
  xxxiii*n*30
Pouvoir, 133
Poverty, 28, 100, 124, 183, 283–84, 285,
  304*nn*43–44, 310*n*60
Poverty of Philosophy, The (Marx), 7, 8, 13
Power, 245; of division, 236; figure of, 259;
  political philosophy and, 237; will-
  power, 139. *See also* Empowerment
Precarity, 148, 270, 285, 305*n*44
Prefiguration, 213*n*10, 285–86, 306*n*48;
  abstract ideal utopia, 203; actions of,
  198–203; anarchism relating to, 198–202;
  blueprint utopianism, 199, 203–5, 208,
  209; centrality of, 199; concept of, 210;
  description of, 202, 214*nn*17–18; Franks,
  on, 199–200, 202–9; instrumentalism,
  200; means-ends relationship, 203–4,
  207, 212–13, 281, 290; Milstein on, 200,
  203–5; utopianism and, 203–9
Prefigurative politics, xxix, 202, 211
Prisoners, in cave allegory, 255–56
Private property, 11, 17, 77, 85–86, 207, 292*n*5
"Private utopias," 276
Procès des maîtres rêveurs (Abensour), xiii,
  284
Productivity, 71, 239

Progress, xiii, xxi–ii, 24, 44, 51*n*22, 59, 62,
  96, 98, 109, 163, 179, 185, 270, 278, 293*n*5,
  307*n*53; ideology of, 275; philosophy of,
  180, 184; scientific-technical, xxxi*n*6, 62,
  69; teleological, 66, 73
"Progress Versus Utopia; or, Can We
  Imagine the Future?" (Jameson essay),
  169
Proletarianization, 27–28, 276
Proletariat, 11, 13, 14, 27, 28–29, 40, 50*n*6,
  51*n*17, 118, 122, 146–47, 238–39, 242,
  247*n*11, 306*n*46; dictatorship of, 117, 237
Propaganda, 7, 187, 274; utopian, 187
Protests, 190, 192, 212, 270–71, 302*n*31,
  310*n*60
Proudhon, Pierre-Joseph, 7–8, 11–12, 13–14,
  23, 50*n*6, 51*n*17, 180, 188, 205, 210;
  influence of, 98
Public opinion, 182, 194
Punishment, 144, 207; corporal, 293*n*5;
  divine, 67,
Purpose, 129, 137, 138, 147

Quiroga, Vasco de, 89; background of, 90; as
  bishop of Michoacán, 90, 92; Indies and,
  93–94; in Mexico, 93–95; as More
  follower, 90–95; war protests of, 91;
  writings of, 90, 91, 93–94; 112*n*16
"Quixote Today: Utopia and Politics"
  (World Social Forum), 104

Rabelais, François, 74, 86, 88–89
Radical critique. *See* Bourgeois critique,
  radical critique and
Radicalism, 43; nonviolent, 285; political,
  269–70; utopia and, 271–73, 285–86, 290
Radical negativity, 192
Radical politics, xxix, xxxii, 166, 169–71,
  174–75, 269, 271, 272, 286, 290
Radical transformation, xix, xxiii,
  xxxiii*n*32, 184, 286, 304*n*41
Rancière, Jacques, 261
Rationalism, xxiv, 35, 73, 76, 130, 174, 275

Rawls, John, xiii, xvi–xvii, xviii, xxxiii*n*24, 245, 246, 301*n*25; followers of, xvii, xviii, 246
Realism, 128, 161, 179, 185; in political theory, xxix, xxxii, 246, 249, 260, 269; different meanings of, 243–45; versus utopianism, 245–46, 249, 256; utopian, 261; wishful thinking, utopia, and, 233–47
"Realistic utopia" (Rawls), xvi–xvii
Reality, 241; heterogeneous, 34, 39; of negation, 219; of utopia, 184–86
Realization, of desire, 254–56, 257, 258, 260, 261
Realized ideal, wished-for ideal and, 250
Real politics, 260–64; domination, 261; formula for, 261; illusion in, 261; social relations managed with, 261
Real(ly existing) socialism, 101, 106
"Real utopias" (Wright), xvii
Reformation, 65, 70, 71, 73, 87, 88
Reformism, xvii, 23, 87, 168, 180, 184–87, 205, 277
Reich, Wilhelm, 98, 296*n*14
"Reification and Utopia in Mass Culture" (Jameson essay), 165, 166
"Reign of freedom," 32, 45, 46
Reinvention of politics, 164
Relative utopia, 59, 288
Renaissance, 65, 70, 71, 73, 76–77, 81, 89, 235
Republic (Plato), xviii, 61, 68, 84, 132, 224, 225, 251–56
Revolt, xxiii, 26, 34, 40, 74, 87, 192, 195
Revolution: Cuban, 149; of 1848, 18, 22–23, 25; 1848, xii, 6, 22, 23, 25, 39, 122, 148, 180, 186, 188, 266*n*33, 275, 303*n*37; French, xii, 261, 273; Industrial, 66, 71; object of, 281; partial, 5; radical, 12; social, 44; socialist, 151; state, 259
Revolution (Landauer), 57, 58
Revolutionary Question, The (Déjacque), 23
Revolutionary Romanticism, 46
Revolutionary science, 40
Revolutionary theory, 19–20, 22, 274
Revolutionary transformation, 206
Ricœur, Paul, 301*n*24
Riesman, David, 39
Rights: of human beings, 239; to liberty, 134
Robespierre, 132, 147, 153*n*3
Robinson Crusoe (Defoe), 231
Romanticism, 46, 52*n*29, 226
Root-of-all-evil utopia, 168
Rousseau, Jean-Jacques, xxv, xviii, 127–29, 275; critics of, 133; on force, 143–44; Marx and, 146–47; as political visionary, 132; on self-mastery, 141; Stalinism and, 257; on unity, 142; on virtue, 138–46; writings of, xviii, 128, 132, 135–36, 141, 144
Rousseau, voluntary self-determination and, 130–32, 137–39, 148, 156*n*28, 156*n*33, 157*n*48; empowerment and, 133, 136, 141; free will, 133–36, 156*n*38; human nature, 134; individual freedom, 133–35; *pouvoir*, 133; right to liberty, 134; social development reconstructed by, 135; *vouloir*, 133
Rubel, Maximilien, 107, 263, 266*n*35

Saint-Simon, 26, 27, 32, 34, 35, 44, 52*n*22, 53*n*30, 70, 182, 183, 189*n*5, 294*n*13, 296*n*14, 299*n*23; Marx's relation to, 19, 50*n*12, 51*n*22, 118, 266*n*35, 271, 297*n*18
Saint-Simonians, 14, 31, 35, 180, 182, 184, 189*n*5, 220, 224–26, 229, 230, 276
Salve-mentality, 270
Samasota, Luciano de, 81
Saramago, José, 104, 105
Sargent, Lyman Tower, x, xxiv, 292*n*5
Sargisson, Lucy, 214*n*23, 286
Schnabel, Johann Gottfried, 69, 70
Science, 71–72; doctrinaire, 40; experimental, 237; of history, 234; political, 235; revolutionary, 40; techno-science, 97, 98; and utopia, 99
Science fiction, 67–68, 69–70
"Science of revolt," 40

Scientific socialism, 8, 15, 25–26, 107, 162, 208; radical separation from utopian socialism, 4, 5, 22
"Scientific utopia," 46
Second Audiencia, 91
Self-abnegation, 240
Self-criticism, 151, 283; anarchist, 205; of utopia, xx, xxiv, xxvi, 39, 64, 74, 75, 77,
Self-determination, 130, 138, 148, 200. *See* Rousseau, voluntary self-determination and
Self-interest, 132, 146
Self-mastery, 141
Self-sufficiency, 281. *See also* Autarchy
Sexual freedom, 275–78, 280–81, 297n20, 302n32
Shaw, George Bernard, 55n59, 104
Shklar, Judith, xiii, xxii, 127–28, 271–72, 275, 295n14, 301n24
Simulacrum, 47–48
Situationists, 98, 293n5
Skinner, B. F., 71, 293n5
Sloterdijk, Peter, 105–6
Social Contract, The (Rousseau), xvi, xviii, xxxiii, 128, 132, 135–36, 141, 144
Social democracy, 171
Social development, 57, 135, 185
"Social economy" (Pecqueur), 26
Social-epistemological approach, of Mannheim, 59–60
"Social individual" (Marx), 121, 125n12
Socialism, 37, 49, 196, 197n4; African, 126; authoritarian, 206–7; communism and, 23, 106–7; end of utopia relating to, 97–101; female part of, 180; genesis of, 181, 189n5; historical, 208; National, 277; real, 101; scientific, 4, 8, 15, 25, 26, 107, 162, 208. *See also* Utopian socialism
Socialism: Utopian and Scientific (Engels), xxvii, 6, 50n4, 118
Socialist-communist utopia, 3, 23, 27–31, 32, 37, 53n37, 118
Socialist democracy, 196

Socialist revolution, 151
Socialist utopia, 118, 131, 206
Social nudity. *See* Naturism
Social organization, 32, 51n16, 72, 149, 179, 262, 292–93n5
"Social palingenesis" (Ballanche), 28
Social relations, 59, 73, 149, 181, 181–83, 189n5, 210, 259, 261; depraved, 76; of production, 120, 125n12; new or different, 26, 33, 201, 207, 211, 214n18, 283, 309n59; transformation of, 184–85, 205, 210
Social revolution, 9, 12, 60, 198, 306n48; theory of, 37, 44
Social science: nineteenth-century, 13, 15, 40, 50–51n15, 51–52n22; modern, 57, 59, 61, 234
Social thought, 97, 182, 183
Social transformation, 17, 99, 102–3, 187, 202, 274; desire for, xxii, 289; framing of, 208; models of, 282; radical, xxi, 286
Social utopia, 15, 24, 52n29, 99, 276, 281, 303n33; experiments, 275; new desire, 28, 32–33, 35, 48; statist, 74; as will to happiness, 27, 32
Social wealth, 71, 72
Society: capitalist, 120, 123; closed, 61; desire for, 250; fundamental changes to, xiii; individual and, 182; new, 282; oligarchic, 126; utopian, 259
Sociology: positivist, 27; of utopia, 17–18
Socrates, xviii, 225, 250; on desirability, 252; on perfect city, 251–53
Solidarity, x, 63, 70, 136, 196, 197, 270, 310n60; in struggle, 142–43, 152; with the oppressed, 190–91, 284
Somatics. *See* Body-politics
Somatization, of politics, 273
Sorel, Georges, 5, 204, 209, 310n60
Sovereignty, 137–38, 140, 144, 147, 150, 188, 236; criticism of 127, 129, 288, 294n9; illusion of, 261; of law, 182; popular, 137, 150, 182, 186

Sovereign utopia, body as, 280
Space-utopia, 67, 72–73
Spatial utopia, 59, 68
Specters of Marx (Derrida), 192
Spirit, 226, 301n25; critical, 282, 303n37; heroism of, 106; of politics, 278, 299n23; utopian, xxiv–xxvi, 284. *See also* "New utopian spirit"
Stalinism, 100, 257
State: concept of, 243; modern, 34, 119, 235, 236; Welfare, 171
Strauss, Leo, 251, 252, 253
Suicide, 274, 292n2
"Surplus consciousness" (Marcuse), 100
Surrealism, 43, 293n5, 303n37
Survival: communal, 308n53; of human beings, 72, 78, 240; of utopia, 163, 277–79, 301n24
Survivors of the "Jonathan," The (Verne), 262, 266n34

Talmon, Jacob, xiii, 127
Technology, 71–73, 98, 230; history of, 180; science and, 66; science fiction and, 67; social, 61, 108, 301n23; utopia and, 72
"Technology and Science as Ideology" (Habermas essay), 99
Techno-science, 96–97
Techow, Gustav Adolf, 7–9
Terror, 61; Jacobin, 127; totalitarian, 62; virtue and, 144
Thales, 269
Theoreticism, 165, 174, 271
Theory of Justice (Rawls), xvi
Thompson, E. P., xiv, xxvi, 52n26, 209n59
Thoreau, Henry David, 269
Thought experiment, xxiii, 62, 203
Time-utopia, 66, 68, 72–73
Tiqqun (journal), 274
Topia: elements of, 58; Landauer and, 57–58; level of, 58; Mannheim and, 59; structures of domination, 57–58
Topia-utopia model (Landauer), 59

Totalitarianism, xi, 64, 71, 75, 108, 193, 257, 277; and utopia, xii, xix, 61–63, 74–75, 77, 108, 153n3, 257, 258; Popper and, 61–62;
Toulouse, Édouard, 301n23
Transcendence, 18, 19, 103, 166–67, 284
Transhumanism, 277, 294n12
Transformative politics, xxi, 272
Tratado comprobatorio (las Casas), 95
Trotsky, Leon, 55n61, 76, 130, 147, 153, 155
Truth, xvii, 10, 35, 39, 41–42, 48, 77, 109, 111, 174; absolute, 29; becoming flesh, 225; discourse of, 182, 185; eternal, 15; Marx on, 250; Plato on, 254–56; pursuit of, 10, 41; scientific, 300n23

Unionism, 191, 194
Unity, xii, 40, 58, 59, 146, 243; of human race, 163; of linguistic formations, 186; Rousseau on, 136, 141–42
Unrealizable city paradox, 250–54
Utopia: after, 161–64; after 1945, xii–xvi; abandoning of, xxii, xxxiiin30; Abensour on, 205, 257–59; anarchism and, 209–13; of another world, 192, 195; as antipolitical, ix, xxxin1; changing status of, 251; communism and, 18, 21, 77; concepts of, 16–19, 122; construction of, xi, 70, 72, 121; critical function of, 257; criticism of, ix, xiii, 24, 48; critique, politics, and, 167–71; decline of, 96; definition of, 17, 119; detachment of, 22; dialectics and, 171–75; discourse on, 15–16, 73–75, 76, 181, 184–86; documentation of, xv; end of, 96–101, 107; in era of suspicion, 48; estrangement of, 275; *eutopia* (More), 80, 84, 257; exile of, xxi; form of, 103, 108; foundation of, 66; of future, 229; genre of, 258; historicity of, 181–85, 259–60; identification of, xix–xx; ideology, mass culture, and, 166–67; ideology and, 17; island of, 84–86; Marx on, 117–25; negation of, 107–8; new look for, xi, xii;

Utopia (*continued*)
  of "new man," 67; overview of, xxv–xxxi; Plato on, xxvi, 66, 81, 223–25, 233, 252, 256, 257, 273, 279; as political, ix, 12, 34, 62, 63, 64; political solutions of, ix; political specificity of, xii; political theory and, x–xii, xiv, xvi–xx, xxi, 205,; prominence of, xiii; radicalism and, 271–73, 285–86, 290; realism, wishful thinking, and, 233–47; reality of, 179–89; recovery of, 98; resurgence of, 24; scholarly works on, 180; to science, 99; specificity of, xii, 20, 60; survival of, 163, 277–79, 301*n*24; three faces of, x; totalitarian concept of, 61; transitional periods within, 170; two types of, 258; value of, 27; violated structure of, 38; weaknesses of, 20, 40. *See also specific utopias* (Abstract, Action, Australian, Body, Christian, Concrete, Embodied, Mars, Modern, Old, Positive, Postmaterial, Private, Relative, Root-of-all-evil, Scientific, Social, Socialist, Socialist-communism, Sovereign, Space-, Spatial, Time-)
Utopia (More), x, xviii, 58, 62, 63, 65, 66, 74, 80, 82–84, 86, 92, 93–95, 111*n*5, 112*n*13, 257
Utopia, political theory and: classical utopian tradition, xvi–xvii; education of desire relating to, xx, xxvii–xxviii; form relating to, xviii, xx; normative ideals, xx–xxi; political insights into, xviii; uses of, xx
Utopian: Fourier as, 26, 27–29, 32–40, 44, 47, 70, 74, 75, 108, 110, 208, 294*n*18; Morris as, ix, xiv, 55*n*59, 70, 74, 76, 105, 210, 259–60, 276, 281; Owen as, ix, 25–27, 31–32, 34–35, 40, 44, 70, 75, 77, 108
Utopian concept: classical, 59–60, 61–62, 63–64; of totalitarianism, 57, 61, 108
Utopian dimension, 259; of anarchism, 306*n*48; of collective action, 274; of counterglobalization movement, 194–95; of left-radical politics, 269; of Marx's project, 263; of popular culture, 166; of utopia, 256, 261
Utopian discourse, xiv, 15–16, 73–77, 181, 184; of Bolsheviks, 76; classical 73, 75–77; postmaterialist, 75; in social sciences, 61
"Utopian energies" of 1960s, xiv
Utopian Essays and Practical Proposals (Goodman), 98
"Utopian function" (Bloch), xv, xx
Utopian goals, 62, 73, 213
Utopian imagination, 48, 65, 168–71, 175, 181, 254, 277, 293*n*5
Utopian impulse, xxix, 168, 171–72, 175, 203
Utopianism, xxviii, 290; anarchist, 58, 203, 204, 209–10; antiutopian, 199, 210, 223; ascetic, 106, 145–46, 287, 295*n*14, 297*n*18; blueprint, xviii–xix, 199, 203–5, 208, 209, 296*n*14; conception of, 204–5; critical-cognitive, 284, 289; as dangerous, xii, xvi; deep connection to, xxv; dismissal of, x; Engels' criticism of, 15–22, 51*n*22; faces of (Sargent), x, 292*n*5; glaciation of, 284; history of, xxv; ignorance of, x; introduction to, x; literary face of, x, 292*n*5; Marx's criticism of, xiii, xx, xxv, xxvii, 5, 15–22, 25, 43, 51*n*22, 179; nadir of, x, xii; of 1960s, xiv; political distance of, x–xi, xii; post-'68 tendencies of, xiv–xv; prefiguration and, 203–9; prefigurative, xxix; primitive, 273; rethinking of, xi–xii; surveys of, xv; Western, xxiv. *See also* Antiutopianism; Neoutopianism; Nonutopianism
"Utopianization," 45
Utopianizing claims, to happiness, 273, 288
"Utopian moments," xvi
Utopian pedagogue, 34
Utopian politics, 284, 291; and prefigurative action, 199, 203, 213; and utopian impulse, 171
Utopian socialism, xiv, 4, 8, 15, 25, 41, 76–77; Cabet on, 249; Engels on, 26, 34, 119, 271,

277, 281; history, 26–35; Marx on, 26, 29–30, 31, 34, 119–20, 162, 263–64, 271, 277, 281

Utopian society, 171, 259, 263

Utopian spirit, xx, 81, 98, 109, 284. *See also* "New utopian spirit"

Utopian studies, ix, xi, xv–xvi, xix, xxi, xxv–xxi, xxx, 10, 205–6, 209; conferences, xv; renaissance of, xiv

"Utopian surplus" (Bloch), 255, 256, 263, 308*n*56

Utopian thinking: anarchistic model, 65–68; ancient models, 66; archistic model, 65–68; contribution to politics, xii, xxvi; effectivity of, 76; ideal-typical approach to, 65–68; Jameson on, 165–76, 176*n*4; learning impairment of, 77; mixed models, 68, 69

"Utopophobia" (Estlund), xvii

Valences of the Dialectic (Jameson), 172, 173

Valéry, Paul, 299–300*n*23

Valladolid, 90, 93, 112*n*15

Vaneigem, Raoul, 293*n*5

Verne, Jules, 262, 266*n*34

Vespucci, Amerigo, 81, 82–84, 85, 89

Via Campesina, 191, 194, 196

Village Priest, The (Balzac), 229; characters in, 220–23; configurations of place, 222; democracy relating to, 223; plot of, 220–23

Violence, 34, 148, 153*n*3, 252–53, 273, 281, 295*n*14; Sorel's myth of, 204; "terroristic," 294*n*9

Virtue, 91, 135; political, 138–46, 142; revolutionary, 151; Rousseau on, 138–46; terror and, 144; of utopian classic concept, 63–64

Virtue ethics, 199

Vis utopica, 250, 258, 260

Voigt, Andreas, 65

Volkswille, 129

Vormärz, 122

Vouloir, 133

Voyage to Icaria (Cabet), 46–47, 248, 265–66*n*30

Waldseemüller, Martin, 82

We (Zamyatin), 73, 74

Weber, Max, 64–65, 200, 237, 246, 273

Weil, Simone, 107, 108–9

Weitling, Wilhelm, 4–5, 9, 50*n*6, 266*n*35

Welfare State, 171

Wells, H. G., 68, 70, 74

Western utopianism, xxiv, xxxiii*n*34

What Is Property? (Proudhon), 11; as scientific manifesto, 11

What We Are Fighting For (Marazzi), 205

Wickedness, 145

Will: autonomous, 135; common, 137; free, 120–21, 130, 133–36, 156*n*38; general, 129, 137, 144, 146; to happiness, xxviii, 27, 32; law-giving, 137; 129, 139, 147, 149, 152, 139; wish and, 130

Williams, Raymond, xiv, xxvi

Will-power, 129, 139

Winstanley, Gerrard, xvi, 70

Wish, self-referential, 242

Wished-for ideal, realized ideal versus, 250

Wish-fulfillment, 168, 251

Wishful thinking, 239–42, 246, 247*n*16

Women equal to men, 251

Woman on the Edge of Time (Piercy), xiv

Women's World March, 191, 195

World Social Forum, 104, 113*n*26, 190; "Charter of Principles," 193; International Council, 193–94, 196

Wright, Erik Olin, xvii

Writing, 224–25

Writings from London (Weil), 108

WTO (World Trade Organization), 190, 191, 192, 201

Youth, 17, 285; eternal, 17; movement, 98

Zamyatin, Yevgeny, 68, 70, 71, 73, 74, 75

Zapatistas, 191, 192, 196

Narrating Evil: A Postmetaphysical Theory of Reflective Judgment, María Pía Lara

The Politics of Our Selves: Power, Autonomy, and Gender in Contemporary Critical Theory, Amy Allen

Democracy and the Political Unconscious, Noëlle McAfee

The Force of the Example: Explorations in the Paradigm of Judgment, Alessandro Ferrara

Horrorism: Naming Contemporary Violence, Adriana Cavarero

Scales of Justice: Reimagining Political Space in a Globalizing World, Nancy Fraser

Pathologies of Reason: On the Legacy of Critical Theory, Axel Honneth

States Without Nations: Citizenship for Mortals, Jacqueline Stevens

The Racial Discourses of Life Philosophy: Négritude, Vitalism, and Modernity, Donna V. Jones

Democracy in What State?, Giorgio Agamben, Alain Badiou, Daniel Bensaïd, Wendy Brown, Jean-Luc Nancy, Jacques Rancière, Kristin Ross, Slavoj Žižek

Politics of Culture and the Spirit of Critique: Dialogues, edited by Gabriel Rockhill and Alfredo Gomez-Muller

Mute Speech: Literature, Critical Theory, and Politics, Jacques Rancière

The Right to Justification: Elements of Constructivist Theory of Justice, Rainer Forst

The Scandal of Reason: A Critical Theory of Political Judgment, Albena Azmanova

The Wrath of Capital: Neoliberalism and Climate Change Politics, Adrian Parr

Media of Reason: A Theory of Rationality, Matthias Vogel

Social Acceleration: The Transformation of Time in Modernity, Hartmut Rosa

The Disclosure of Politics: Struggles Over the Semantics of Secularization, María Pía Lara

Radical Cosmopolitics: The Ethics and Politics of Democratic Universalism, James Ingram

Freedom's Right: The Social Foundations of Democratic Life, Axel Honneth

Imaginal Politics: Images Beyond Imagination and the Imaginary, Chiara Bottici

Alienation, Rahel Jaeggi

The Power of Tolerance: A Debate, Wendy Brown and Rainer Forst, edited by Luca Di Blasi and Christoph F. E. Holzhey

Radical History and the Politics of Art, Gabriel Rockhill

The Highway of Despair: Critical Theory After Hegel, Robyn Marasco

A Political Economy of the Senses: Neoliberalism, Reification, Critique, Anita Chari

The End of Progress: Decolonizing the Normative Foundations of Critical Theory, Amy Allen

Recognition or Disagreement: A Critical Encounter on the Politics of Freedom, Equality, and Identity, Axel Honneth and Jacques Rancière, edited by Katia Genel and Jean-Philippe Deranty

What Is a People?, Alain Badiou, Pierre Bourdieu, Judith Butler, Georges Didi-Huberman, Sadri Khiari, and Jacques Rancière

Death and Mastery: Psychoanalytic Drive Theory and the Subject of Late Capitalism, Benjamin Y. Fong

Left-wing Melancholia: Marxism, History, and Memory, Enzo Traverso

Foucault/Derrida Fifty Years Later: The Futures of Genealogy, Deconstruction, and Politics, edited by Olivia Custer, Penelope Deutscher, and Samir Haddad

GPSR Authorized Representative: Easy Access System Europe, Mustamäe tee 50, 10621 Tallinn, Estonia, gpsr.requests@easproject.com